English Composition and Grammar
BENCHMARK EDITION

Introductory Course

English Composition and Grammar

BENCHMARK EDITION

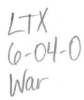

LTX
6-04-0
War

John E. Warriner

Introductory Course

HBJ **Harcourt Brace Jovanovich, Publishers**

Orlando   San Diego   Chicago   Dallas

THE SERIES:

English Composition and Grammar: Introductory Course
English Composition and Grammar: First Course
English Composition and Grammar: Second Course
English Composition and Grammar: Third Course
English Composition and Grammar: Fourth Course
English Composition and Grammar: Fifth Course
English Composition and Grammar: Complete Course

Annotated Teacher's Edition and Teacher's Resource Book

CORRELATED SERIES:

English Workshop: Introductory Course
English Workshop: First Course
English Workshop: Second Course
English Workshop: Third Course
English Workshop: Fourth Course
English Workshop: Fifth Course
English Workshop: Review Course

Composition: Models and Exercises, First Course
Composition: Models and Exercises, Second Course
Composition: Models and Exercises, Third Course
Composition: Models and Exercises, Fourth Course
Composition: Models and Exercises, Fifth Course
Advanced Composition: A Book of Models for Writing, Complete Course

Vocabulary Workshop: Introductory Course
Vocabulary Workshop: First Course
Vocabulary Workshop: Second Course
Vocabulary Workshop: Third Course
Vocabulary Workshop: Fourth Course
Vocabulary Workshop: Fifth Course
Vocabulary Workshop: Complete Course

John E. Warriner taught English for thirty-two years in junior and senior high schools and in college. He is chief author of the *English Composition and Grammar* series, coauthor of the *English Workshop* series, general editor of the *Composition: Models and Exercises* series, and editor of *Short Stories: Characters in Conflict.* His coauthors have all been active in English education.

Printed in the United States of America
ISBN 0-15-311675-7

CONTENTS

2. Writing Stories 30

USING NARRATION AND DESCRIPTION

3. Writing Paragraphs 51
STRUCTURE AND DEVELOPMENT
OF PARAGRAPHS

6. Writing Exposition   113
REPORTS AND COMPOSITIONS OF OPINION

Part Two: COMPOSITION: Writing and Revising Sentences

Part Three: Tools for Writing and Revising

GRAMMAR

USAGE

MECHANICS

Part Four: RESOURCES FOR WRITING AND STUDYING

23. Using the Library 409
A GUIDE TO RESOURCES IN A LIBRARY

24. Using the Dictionary 428
A GUIDE TO INFORMATION IN A DICTIONARY

25. Vocabulary 443
LEARNING AND USING NEW WORDS

Part Five: SPEAKING AND LISTENING

PART ONE

COMPOSITION:
The Writing Process

CHAPTER 1

Writing and Thinking

THE WRITING PROCESS

When you write, you take out a pencil and a piece of paper and try to get comfortable. Then you move the pencil along the paper, making marks that stand for letters. That is the process, or series of steps, you go through with your body.

With your mind, you go through another series of steps, using in each step certain thinking skills. Together, these steps are known as the *writing process*. In this chapter you will learn about and practice the thinking skills of the writing process. You will learn that you can use these skills for any kind of writing you do, not just in your English class.

THE WRITING PROCESS

Six basic stages make up the writing process. Each stage is broken down into separate steps.

PREWRITING

1. Deciding on a purpose, or reason, for writing
2. Thinking about your audience, or readers

3. Searching for possible subjects to write about
4. Choosing one subject to write about
5. Narrowing the subject to fit the length of your paper
6. Gathering information about your topic
7. Organizing this information

WRITING A FIRST DRAFT

8. Putting your ideas into sentences and paragraphs

EVALUATING

9. Reading your writing to look for ways to improve it

REVISING

10. Changing words and sentences to improve your writing

PROOFREADING

11. Reading your paper closely to check your spelling, punctuation marks, capital letters, and word use
12. Correcting mistakes

MAKING A FINAL COPY

13. Copying your paper into its final form
14. Correcting any copying mistakes

You will not always follow these steps straight through from beginning to end. Instead, you may move back and forth among the stages. For example, you may think of a new idea to add while you are revising, or you may find that you need additional information. When this happens, you are moving from the revising stage *back* to the prewriting stage. You may correct the spelling of a word while you are writing. When this happens, you are moving *ahead* from the writing stage to the proofreading stage. You should be thinking about your audience during all the stages of the writing process.

PREWRITING

The steps of the prewriting stage make up the thinking and planning you do *before* you put your ideas into complete sentences. During this stage, you are preparing to write.

DECIDING ON A PURPOSE

1a. Decide on a purpose for writing.

You write for any of several different purposes, or reasons. Knowing why you are writing will help you decide what ideas to include and what style of language to use.

In a letter, you may *tell a story* about a camping trip. In a geography paper, you may *describe* a tropical island. In a science paper, you may *explain* why Halley's comet returns every seventy-six years. In a newspaper article, you may try to *persuade* parents to support your school's book fair.

These reasons—to tell a story, to describe, to explain or give information, and to persuade—are the four main reasons for writing. Each reason lends itself to a different kind of writing.

1. Writing to tell a story is *narrative* writing.

EXAMPLE   The first night at camp, we had a campfire. We sang songs and listened to ghost stories. The counselors and the older campers told the most frightening stories. At the end of the evening, we all joined hands and sang "On Top of Old Smoky" as the fire died down.

2. Writing to describe is *descriptive* writing.

EXAMPLE   The bubble gum stuck to my fingers, my face, my hair. Each time I touched my face, I left a dark, sticky mark. Pink strings hung from my hair. A pink ring lined my mouth. All this for one bubble!

3. Writing that explains or informs is *expository* writing.

EXAMPLE   In 1985, scientists used a robot to find the *Titanic*, which sank in 1912. The robot explored the bottom of the sea. It sent back pictures of the sunken ship.

4. Writing to persuade is *persuasive* writing.

EXAMPLE   People who care about our soccer team will bring their cars to the Saturday car wash. The money we raise will buy new soccer uniforms. Don't you want our players to look their best?

A piece of writing may have more than one purpose. For example, when you *tell a story* about camping, you may also *describe* the sounds you hear at night. Your most important reason for writing, however, is to tell a story. That is your main purpose.

Before You Write.   Decide on your main purpose. Is it

● to tell a story?   ● to explain or give information?
● to describe?   ● to persuade?

EXERCISE 1. Finding Examples of Purposes for Writing.
Choose two of the following five activities. Copy the sentences you find and bring them to class. Your teacher may want you to bring the newspaper, magazine, or book to class instead.

1. In a story, find several sentences that *describe* a person, animal, place, or thing.
2. In a newspaper, find several sentences that *tell a story* about an event.
3. In a newspaper or magazine advertisement, find several sentences that try to *persuade* you.
4. In a cookbook or repair manual, find several sentences that *explain* how to do something.
5. In an encyclopedia, find several sentences that *give information* about a person, place, object, or animal.

EXERCISE 2. **Identifying Purposes for Writing.** After the proper number, tell what your reason would be for writing about the topic. Use the terms *narrative, descriptive, expository,* and *persuasive.*

1. Why you should join the book club
2. The night our rowboat sank
3. My pet pigeon
4. Why I like to sleep late
5. How we found the buried treasure
6. Geronimo as a young man
7. How to make a candle
8. Why the sky looks blue
9. The time I was lost in the desert
10. Why you should eat Brand X bread

THINKING ABOUT YOUR AUDIENCE

1b. Think about the interests of your readers.

When you write, you try to make your ideas clear to the people who will read your writing. These readers are your *audience.*

Thinking about your audience will help you plan your writing. Suppose you are writing about a recent field trip for your classmates. Now suppose you are writing about the same field trip for your parents.

What you would write about the field trip would be different for each of these two groups of readers. You would use different ideas and language to make your writing clear and interesting. For your classmates, you might emphasize how enjoyable the field trip was. For your parents, you might emphasize the educational value of the field trip.

Before You Write.   Consider your audience by asking:

- How old are my readers?
- How well do I know them?
- What subjects might they be interested in knowing about?
- What subjects might they already know about?

EXERCISE 3. Thinking About an Audience. Each numbered item in this exercise names an audience, and the lettered items name topics for writing. Number your paper 1–5. After each number, write the letter of the topic that that group of readers would be most interested in.

EXAMPLE 1. Second-graders
> a. How to enter the Olympics
> b. Crossing a street safely
> c. Choosing a college
> 1. *b*

1. Sixth-graders
   a. My new pencil case
   b. After-school programs for preteens
   c. Why you should plan for retirement
2. Senior citizens
   a. How to tie your shoes
   b. How I won the bicycle race
   c. Trips to Canada for people over sixty-five
3. Members of a craft club
   a. Making Halloween costumes
   b. Why sports practice should be held after school
   c. Mr. Brown's chowder recipe
4. Members of the Chicago Symphony
   a. The best audience I've ever played for
   b. Taking music lessons
   c. How to get to the football field
5. Computer engineers
   a. New computer designs
   b. My friend's new computer
   c. Why you should buy a computer

EXERCISE 4. Thinking About Your Audience. On a sheet of paper, write the three items listed here. Then, with this purpose, audience, and topic in mind, write your answers to the questions about readers (page 7).

Purpose: To describe
Audience: My classmates
Topic: My favorite room at home

SEARCHING FOR SUBJECTS

1c. Search for subjects from your everyday life.

You can find many possible subjects to write about by looking closely at your everyday life. The things you know about and like to do are possible subjects, as are the things you notice in the world around you. Family experiences or stories told to you by family and friends can give you ideas.

There are many ways of looking for possible subjects to write about. Two that are interesting and easy to use are keeping a writer's notebook and brainstorming.

Keeping a Writer's Notebook

A *writer's notebook* is a collection of ideas, feelings, and happenings you may want to share with other people. It can be any kind of notebook or even just a folder of papers.

You decide what to write in this notebook. Then, when you need a subject for writing, you can search your notes for possible subjects.

Here is part of a page from one student's notebook. What possible subjects does it include?

> Last night Grandma told me about when she was growing up in Austria. One very cold night she and her sisters and brothers were lying in their beds when they heard a wolf howling. They thought the wolf was right outside the door. All the children were afraid the wolf would get into the house.

These notes gave the student several possible subjects for writing: Grandma's childhood, Austria, wolves, and being afraid. You can use the notes you write in your notebook to find possible subjects for your writing, too.

EXERCISE 5. Keeping a Writer's Notebook. Keep a writer's notebook for three days. In it, write the ideas, feelings, and happenings that you want to share with other people. After three days, read your notes. List at least three possible subjects to write about. Save your list.

Brainstorming

Brainstorming is another way to find possible subjects. To brainstorm, list ideas as fast as you can think of them. Write down whatever comes into your mind. Do not stop to judge whether the ideas are good ones. You can decide that later.

An easy way to begin brainstorming is to ask yourself questions and list your answers. One student asked the question "What am I interested in?" The list of answers looked like this:

collecting shells
playing the drums
doing gymnastics
reading about robots
drawing with colored chalk
playing games on the computer
camping

Before You Write. To brainstorm, answer one of these questions:

● What am I interested in?
● What do I know how to do?
● What have I done this week?
● What have I recently noticed for the first time?
● What have I read about or seen on television lately?

EXERCISE 6. Brainstorming for Subjects. Choose one of the four reasons for writing: *to tell a story, to describe, to explain or give information,* or *to persuade.* Then brainstorm to find at least five possible subjects for this kind of writing. Begin with any of the questions above. Save your list.

EXAMPLE   *Purpose:* To explain
          Question: What do I know how to do?
          Subjects: ride a horse
                   collect coins
                   make pancakes
                   find nearby ski areas
                   make a long-distance telephone call

CHOOSING A SUBJECT

1d. Choose one subject to write about.

Once you have found several possible subjects, your next step is to choose one subject to write about. The best subjects for writing are the ones you know the most about and are most interested in. Knowing your subject well will help you write about it in a way that is clear and interesting to your readers.

Before You Write.   Choose a subject by asking yourself:

- Which subject do I know the most about?
- Which subject am I most interested in?
- Which subject will my readers find most interesting?

REVIEW EXERCISE A. Using Your Knowledge of Prewriting. Begin planning to write a short paper. Think about your purpose for writing and your audience. Develop a list of possible subjects; then choose one. Use the following list of steps as a guide. Save your work.

1. Decide what your main purpose will be (to explain, describe, persuade, or tell a story).
2. Think about your readers: How old are they? How well do you know them?
3. List possible subjects for writing, from your writer's notebook or from the brainstorming list you made for Exercise 6. (Brainstorm again with another of the five questions if you want to.)

4. From your list of subjects, choose one to write about. (Answer the three questions that come just before this exercise.)

LIMITING A BROAD SUBJECT

1e. Limit your subject to a narrow topic.

A *subject* is a broad area, one that has many different parts. For example, the subject "camping" has many different parts, such as these:

how to prepare for a camping trip
clothes for camping
buying a tent
safety tips for campers
good camping areas in our country
easy meals for campers
rainy day activities for campers

A paper that covered all of these different parts in a clear and interesting way would be as long as a book. For a short paper, you need to narrow your subject to a *topic*—a narrow, or limited, part of the subject. For example, each part of the subject "camping" listed above is a topic and could be covered in a short paper.

To limit your subject, begin by thinking about the length of your paper. For a paper only four or five sentences long (usually a paragraph), you need a very narrow topic. Otherwise, your sentences will be too general. They will not have enough details to make the topic clear and interesting. For a longer paper, such as a report, you can use a topic that is not so narrow. You have more space in which to give details.

☞ NOTE Keep this general rule in mind: The shorter the paper, the more limited, or narrow, the topic should be.

EXERCISE 7. Recognizing Subjects and Topics. Number your paper 1–10. After each number, write *S* if the item is a broad subject. Write *T* if it is a topic narrow enough for a paper four or five sentences long. Be ready to explain your answers.

EXAMPLE   1. Lightning
           1. *S*

1. Pete Rose's hitting record
2. How to select ripe peaches
3. Jonathan's favorite movie
4. Comets and your telescope
5. How I spent Saturday

6. Summer camp
7. Television shows
8. Vacations in Canada
9. Women scientists
10. Why we should do a play

CRITICAL THINKING:
Analyzing a Broad Subject

When you write, you use special thinking skills. One of these is *analysis.* You use this thinking skill when you limit a subject to find a narrow topic.

To analyze something, you divide it into its smaller parts. When you narrow a subject to find a topic, you divide the subject into its parts.

Several questions can help you divide a broad subject to find narrow topics. Suppose you want to write a short paper about robots. You could divide this broad subject into topics by asking yourself, "How are robots used?"

EXAMPLE   *Subject:* Robots
           Uses: as kitchen helpers
                   to aid blind persons
                   to walk dogs
                   in making cars

Any of these uses could be a narrow topic for a short paper. Your paper could be about "robots as kitchen helpers," "robots as aids to blind persons," and so on.

Before You Write. Limit your subject by asking one or more of these questions:

- What are *uses* for the subject?
- What *people, places, things,* or *happenings* does the subject include?
- What are *examples* of the subject?

EXERCISE 8. Limiting Subjects to Find Topics. Five broad subjects follow. Select one subject. Then divide it into smaller parts to find at least three topics narrow enough for a short paper. Use at least one of the questions above.

1. Collecting things
2. Selecting games
3. Homework
4. Scary stories
5. Strange animals

EXERCISE 9. Limiting Your Subject to Find Topics. Using any or all of the questions above, limit the subject you chose for Review Exercise A. Then decide which topic you will write about. Think about what will interest your readers and keep in mind your reasons for writing. Save your paper.

GATHERING INFORMATION

1f. Gather details about your topic.

Now you are ready to gather information, or details, about your topic. These details will help you make your topic clear and interesting to your readers.

Use the following ideas to gather information. You will learn about using the library to gather information in Chapter 23.

Listing Details

One way to gather information is by listing details. Two forms of listing are brainstorming and clustering.

As you learned on page 10, *brainstorming* is listing as many details as you can think of in a short time. One student used brainstorming to make this list:

Topic: Last night's snowstorm
Details: five-foot drifts of snow
          wind howling at the windows
          cold air coming in under the door
          tree branches smashing against the windows
          talking to Grandma about her childhood
          making cocoa

In *clustering,* you make a diagram. You start by writing your topic in the middle of a sheet of paper and circling it. Then you write down details as you think of them. Circle each detail and connect it to the idea that made you think of it.

One student used clustering to gather information on the topic "our canoe trip." His paper looked like this:

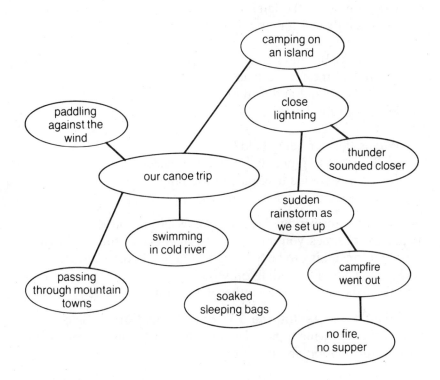

EXERCISE 10. **Listing Details.** For each of the following activities, gather enough information for a short paper.

1. Use brainstorming to gather information on the topic "the hallways before school."
2. Use clustering to gather information about the topic "my favorite television show." Begin with the name of the show.

Asking the 5 *W-How?* Questions

Newspaper writers often use six questions to gather information. These questions, which are called the *5 W-How?* questions, are *Who? What? Where? When? Why?* and *How?* Asking these questions will help you gather details about your topic.

Suppose you want to write a paragraph that gives information about your school's science fair. You might decide to use the *5 W-How?* questions in this way:

Who is holding the fair?
    Students at Elmhurst School
What is a science fair?
    Display of interesting science projects
Where will the fair be held?
    In the school auditorium
When will the fair be held?
    May 23–28
Why is the fair being held?
    To get young people interested in science
How can students take part in the fair?
    By entering a science project

Notice how answering these questions gives you details for a paper. Sometimes you can also find answers to the *5 W-How?* questions by talking to people and by reading books, newspapers, and magazines. Depending on your topic, you may not need to ask all of the questions to gather details for your paper.

EXERCISE 11. **Asking the 5 *W-How?* Questions.** Select any one of the following topics. Then use the *5 W-How?* questions to gather information about the topic.

1. The mystery of my missing math homework
2. Collecting books for the school library
3. Making sandwiches for lunch
4. My surprise Thanksgiving trip
5. My best friend

ORGANIZING INFORMATION

1g. Organize the details you have gathered.

You are almost ready to write your paper. Before you begin writing, however, you need to organize your information. To do this, you remove details that do not fit and arrange the remaining ones in a clear order.

Suppose you gathered information on the topic "how to make a papier-mâché piñata." Your list of details might look like this:

blow up a large balloon and hang it on a string
my parents hate big messes
fill piñata with surprises and hang it up
cut newspaper into one-inch strips
coat newspaper strips with paste
paste tastes horrible
decorate with colored paper and paints
break balloon and pull it out
make paste of flour and water
pat coated strips around balloon
allow paste to dry
put on another layer of strips

Notice that two details do not really fit: "my parents hate big messes" and "paste tastes horrible." These ideas do not help explain how to make a piñata. They should be removed.

Next you would arrange the remaining details in a clear order. The way you arrange details depends on your reason for writing. To explain how to make a papier-mâché piñata, you would arrange the details in the order in which the steps should be done, like this:

cut newspaper into one-inch strips
make paste of flour and water
blow up a large balloon and hang it on a string
coat newspaper strips with paste
pat coated strips around balloon
put on another layer of strips
allow paste to dry
break balloon and pull it out
decorate with colored paper and paints
fill piñata with surprises and hang it up

This list is arranged in *time order.* It shows the order in which the steps take place in time. You also use time order to arrange the actions of a story in the order in which they happen.

Two other ways to arrange information are according to space and according to importance. To describe something, you arrange the details in the order in which you see or picture them. This order may be from right to left, front to back, top to bottom, and so on. To persuade, you may arrange details from the least important to the most important, or just the opposite. This order is also useful for giving information.

By removing details that do not fit and arranging the remaining ones in a clear order, you make a *writing plan.* You can follow this plan when you write your paper. It will remind you which ideas you want to use and in what order to present them. In Chapter 5 you will learn about another kind of writing plan called an *outline.*

Before You Write. To organize your details,

● *remove* details that do not fit.
● *arrange* the remaining details in a clear order.

EXERCISE 12. Organizing Information. Read the following list of details carefully. First, decide which details should be removed. Then copy the remaining ones on a sheet of paper in a clear order. Be prepared to explain why you used this order for arranging the details.

Topic: Making orange juice
Details: Cut the oranges in half carefully.
　　　　　Put the oranges on the squeezer and squeeze.
　　　　　I like orange juice better than apple juice.
　　　　　Wash the oranges.
　　　　　Pour the orange juice into a glass.
　　　　　Remove the seeds.
　　　　　Select several large juice oranges.
　　　　　Cranberry juice is also good.
　　　　　Orange juice has vitamin C.
　　　　　Fresh orange juice is much better than packaged juice.

REVIEW EXERCISE B. Using Your Knowledge of Prewriting.
In Exercise 9, you limited your subject and chose a topic to write about. Keeping in mind your purpose and the interests of your readers, use this topic to complete the following steps. Save your paper.

1. Gather information on your topic by brainstorming, clustering, or asking the *5 W-How?* questions.
2. Make a writing plan. First, remove any details that do not fit. Then arrange the remaining ones in a clear order. Check to see whether you need to add any details.

WRITING

A *draft* is a rough form of your paper. When you write your first draft, you put your ideas into sentences and paragraphs for the first time. You review your writing plan and use it as a guide. You think again about your readers and your purpose as you try to make your ideas clear and interesting.

WRITING A FIRST DRAFT

1h. Write a first draft of your paper.

As you write your first draft, let your thoughts flow freely. Try to make your ideas clear, but do not worry about making mistakes. You will have time to improve your writing later.

Use your writing plan as a guide. It will remind you of the ideas you want to use. It will also remind you of the order in which you want to present each idea.

If you think of ideas that are closely connected to your topic but are not in your plan, include them, too. Putting your ideas into sentences helps you discover what you really want to say. As you write, one idea makes you think of another idea, often when you least expect it.

When You Write. Remember to

- write freely—you can improve and correct your writing later.
- keep in mind your reason for writing.
- keep your readers in mind.

EXERCISE 13. Writing a First Draft. Using the writing plan you made for Review Exercise B, write your first draft. Save your paper.

EVALUATING

Once you have put your ideas down on paper, you think about ways to improve your writing. You look for spots where you can make the writing clearer and more interesting. When you do this, you are judging your writing, or *evaluating* it.

EVALUATING A DRAFT

1i. Evaluate your draft to decide where to improve it.

If you can, put your draft aside for a while after you write it. Then when you evaluate your paper, you will more easily notice parts that need changing.

Imagine you are a reader seeing the work for the first time and read your draft aloud. If something does not sound right to you, you may want to change it. You can also ask someone else to read your draft. This person may notice parts of your draft that you could improve.

CRITICAL THINKING:
Evaluating a Draft

Evaluating is another special thinking skill. To *evaluate* something, you judge it. When you evaluate your draft, you judge, or decide, where the writing needs to be clearer or more interesting.

Certain *standards* can help you make these decisions. The standards give you something by which to judge. When evaluating any draft, you can use the following questions as standards to check your writing.

GUIDELINES FOR EVALUATING A DRAFT

Details   1. Are enough details given to explain the topic?
Unity   2. Does every sentence keep to the topic?
Order of Ideas 3. Does the order of the details make sense? Does the order suit your purpose for writing?
Language   4. Are all the ideas expressed clearly? Are the words exact enough?
Audience   5. Do the words and kinds of sentences suit the readers? Are they neither too difficult nor too easy?

EXERCISE 14. Evaluating Your Draft. Using the evaluation guidelines, evaluate the draft you wrote for Exercise 13. You may want to exchange drafts with a classmate to help each other decide what to improve. Save your paper.

REVISING

After evaluating your draft, you are ready to *revise,* or make changes. Like evaluating, revising involves thinking about your draft. You must think about your audience and purpose again.

When you revise, you are mainly changing words, sentences, and paragraphs, not looking for errors (that will come when you are proofreading). Of course, if you notice an error, go ahead and correct it. You may sometimes rewrite a paper totally, and you may revise a paper more than once.

REVISING YOUR DRAFT

1j. Revise your draft to improve it.

You can make four kinds of changes to improve your writing:

1. *adding* words and sentences
2. *cutting* words and sentences
3. *replacing* words and sentences
4. *reordering* words and sentences

The following chart gives examples of problems you might have found in evaluating your draft. It then shows how to use the four kinds of changes to improve your writing. These problems are ones that might turn up in any kind of writing.

If, while revising, you find that the ideas seem too general, you may need to retrace your steps and narrow down your topic.

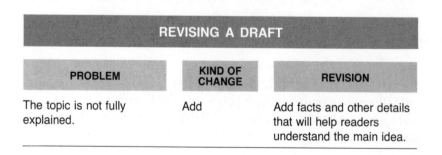

REVISING A DRAFT

PROBLEM	KIND OF CHANGE	REVISION
The topic is not fully explained.	Add	Add facts and other details that will help readers understand the main idea.

PROBLEM	KIND OF CHANGE	REVISION
Some ideas do not "belong" to the main idea.	Cut	Cut sentences or words that do not keep to the topic or to the main reason for writing.
It is hard to follow the ideas.	Reorder	Move details to fit what a reader needs to know first, second, and so on. Make sure the order of ideas fits your purpose.
Some ideas are not clear in meaning.	Replace	Replace a whole sentence, if needed, to give more exact meaning to an idea. More often, replace one or two words in a sentence to express ideas more clearly.
Some words are unnecessary.	Cut	Cut any words that repeat or that otherwise are not needed.
Some words are not clear, are too general, or are used too much.	Replace	Use more exact words to replace words that stand for a group of things. Use exact verbs that show action. Use exact and lively adjectives and adverbs.
Some important words are too hard for the readers.	Add	Explain difficult or new terms. Make sure all words fit the age and knowledge of the audience.
The writing is not interesting.	Add/ Replace	Add details that show rather than tell about something. Replace statements that are too obvious or don't say what you really want to say.

Many writers find certain symbols, or marks, useful for revising their writing. These marks are a quick way to show the four different kinds of changes. Learn the symbols in the chart that follows.

REVISING SYMBOLS

Symbol	Example	Meaning of Symbol
℘	in the the yard	cut
∧	*the* in yard	add
∧‾	*his* in the yard	replace
⤺◯	over in the yard by the tree	reorder

Notice how the marks are used here to show changes:

1. The *Hindenburg* was the world's biggest lighter-than-air balloon in the world.   **2.** It *mysteriously* exploded in New Jersey in 1937.   **3.** Some people believe that it was *sabotaged* tricked.   **4.** Others just think it was a terrible accident.

In the first sentence, a word that was not needed was *cut*. In the second sentence, a word that would make the writer's idea clearer was *added*. In the third sentence, a general word was *replaced* by a more exact word. In the fourth sentence, a word was *reordered* to make the meaning more exact. These changes help make the sentences clearer and more interesting. Another writer might make different changes to improve the sentences.

EXERCISE 15. Studying a Writer's Revisions.   Number your paper 1–5. Each of the following sentences contains one change. After each number, write *add, cut, replace,* or *reorder* to show the kind of change. Be ready to explain how the change improves the sentence.

pounced

EXAMPLE   1. The sleek cheetah ~~jumped~~ on her prey.
          1. *replace; using a more exact word*

1. The chef *skillfully* ʌtossed the pizza dough into the air.

2. Our class completed the ~~whole~~ entire workbook in two months.

3. A galaxy is a large *group* ~~bunch~~ of stars, as well as the planets and gases around those stars.

4. Swahili is an important *African* ʌlanguage.

5. The rescue squad (immediately) needs help.

EXERCISE 16. Revising Your Draft.   Look again at the paper you evaluated for Exercise 14. Make changes where you decided they were needed. Use the symbols on page 24 to mark the changes on your paper. Save your paper.

PROOFREADING

Proofreading is reading your paper carefully to make sure that everything is correct. You check your spelling, capital letters, and paragraphing. You make sure each sentence is complete and has the correct punctuation mark at the end. You also read to see whether you have used words correctly.

PROOFREADING YOUR DRAFT

1k. Proofread your paper.

Read your paper carefully, line by line. Cover with blank paper the lines below the one you are reading. This will help you pay close attention to each word and punctuation mark.

Use the following symbols when you proofread. These marks show the different kinds of changes you want to make when you copy your paper over.

PROOFREADING SYMBOLS

Symbol	Example	Meaning of Symbol
≡	uncle George	Use a capital letter.
/	his Uncle	Use a small letter.
∧	plan_a_t	Change a letter.
∼	recieve	Switch letters around.
⊙	He is my uncle	Add a period.
⌃	Dear Tim	Add a comma.
¶	¶ The day dawned	Begin a new paragraph.

Notice how the marks are used here to show changes:

People who live near the ocean have special kinds of weather problems. The feirce winds of an unnamed Hurricane that struck the florida Keys in 1935 destroyed homes, boats, and beeches.

Corrected, the sentences look like this:

People who live near the ocean have special kinds of weather problems. The fierce winds of an unnamed hurricane that struck the Florida Keys in 1935 destroyed homes, boats, and beaches.

Use the following questions to check your writing.

GUIDELINES FOR PROOFREADING

1. Does every sentence begin with a capital letter? Are other capital letters correct? (pages 337–52)
2. Are all words spelled correctly? Have I checked unfamiliar spellings in a dictionary? (pages 338–405)
3. Does every sentence end with the correct punctuation mark—period, question mark, or exclamation point? Are other punctuation marks, such as commas, correct? (pages 353–87)
4. Is every sentence a complete sentence, not a fragment or a run-on? (pages 151–60)
5. Is the first line of each paragraph indented (set in from the left margin)? (page 51)

EXERCISE 17. Proofreading Sentences.   Each of the following sentences contains one mistake. Copy the sentence as it is. Then use the symbols above to correct each mistake. Finally, rewrite each sentence correctly.

EXAMPLE   1. My uncle visited mt. Kilimanjaro.
        1.

1. My brother prepared hard-boiled eggs celery sticks, and bananas for our lunch today.
2. Did you go to Camp with Coach Jacobs and the basketball team this summer?
3. Yesterday I recieved a telegram from the judges of the contest.
4. My classmates and I are learning how to revise our writing on a microcomputer
5. Dick fosbury, an Olympic high jumper, invented the Fosbury Flop.

EXERCISE 18. Proofreading Your Paper.   Read the paper that you revised for Exercise 16. Check for correctness, using the proofreading guidelines and symbols. Save your paper.

MAKING A FINAL COPY

After you proofread your rough draft, you are ready to make a final copy. It should be prepared carefully, to show the time you have spent thinking and writing about your topic.

MAKING A FINAL COPY

1I. Make a final copy of your paper.

The *final copy* of your paper is the clean copy that you give to your readers. When you make this copy, follow your teacher's directions. Your teacher may want you to use the following rules for manuscript form. (A *manuscript* is any paper that is written by hand or typed.)

RULES FOR MANUSCRIPT FORM

1. Use lined composition paper for papers written by hand. Use $8\frac{1}{2}$ X 11-inch white paper for typed ones.
2. Leave about one inch blank at the top, at each side, and at the bottom of each page.
3. Indent (move in) the first line of each paragraph about one-half inch from the left margin (blank space).
4. Follow your teacher's directions for placing your name, the class, and the date on the paper.
5. Write clearly and neatly. Form your letters carefully. If you have to erase, do so neatly.

After you make your final copy, proofread it. Make sure that you did not misspell a word or leave out a punctuation mark as you copied. Also check any words you had to divide at the end of a line (see page 385). If your teacher allows, you may ask someone else to double-check your writing.

EXERCISE 19. Making the Final Copy. Make a final copy of your paper, following your teacher's directions. Be sure to proofread this copy, too. Then, give your paper to the audience for whom you wrote the paper.

CHAPTER 1 WRITING REVIEW

Using the Writing Process. Use the writing process to write a short paper on a topic of your own. Use the following steps as a guide as you plan, write, and improve your paper:

1. Decide on a purpose for writing.
2. Think about your readers.
3. Search for possible subjects to write about.
4. Choose one subject, and limit it to a narrow topic.
5. Gather details about your topic and organize them.
6. Write a first draft.
7. Evaluate and revise your paper.
8. Proofread your paper, and make a final copy.

CHAPTER 2

Writing Stories

USING NARRATION
AND DESCRIPTION

Suppose someone were telling you an exciting story and stopped in the middle. You would probably be upset and would want to find out what happened.

Most people enjoy a good story. In this chapter you will learn how to plan and write your own story. You will learn how to tell your readers what happened.

PREWRITING

CHOOSING A SUBJECT

2a. Choose a subject for your story.

Identifying Subjects for Stories

A suitable subject for any short story begins with someone's problem. The actions in the story show what happens and how the problem is worked out. For example, look at the following well-known children's story.

PROBLEM A wolf is roaming around the countryside hunting for pigs to eat. The pigs must find a way to protect themselves.

WHAT HAPPENED One pig built a house of straw, but the wolf blew it down. Another pig built a house of sticks, but the wolf blew it down. The third pig built a house of brick. The wolf could not blow it down, so he climbed up on the roof to go down the chimney.

OUTCOME The pig removed the lid from a pot of boiling soup in the fireplace, and the wolf fell in. The pigs lived happily ever after.

EXERCISE 1. Identifying a Problem and an Outcome. Choose a story from the following list, or choose another story that you know well. On your paper, write the problem, list what happened, and write the outcome. Follow the example above.

Little Red Riding Hood
Rumpelstiltskin
Cinderella
Hansel and Gretel

Finding Subjects in Your Own Experience

The best place to begin looking for a subject for a short story is among your own experiences. Many things have happened to you that other people would find interesting. You might, for example, choose the time you went swimming in a lake. Using that subject, you could tell the story as it actually happened. Perhaps you got into trouble for going swimming in a lake not guarded by a lifeguard. Another way to use that subject would be to imagine what might have happened. You might make up a story about stumbling upon a cousin of the Loch Ness monster.

Before You Write.   To find a subject for your story,

- use your writer's notebook or brainstorm (see pages 9–11).
- ask yourself questions like, "What experience have I had that was special? Exciting? Funny? Sad? Helpful?"
- list all the possible experiences that you can recall.
- choose the most interesting experience for your story.
- make sure you would not mind sharing this experience.

EXERCISE 2. Choosing a Subject for Your Story.   Use the suggestions above to think of personal experiences. Write at least ten subjects that would make a good story. Circle the one subject that would make the *best* story. Save your list.

THINKING ABOUT YOUR READERS

2b. Think about your readers.

You would not want to tell a story if no one wanted to listen. You also would not want to write a story no one wanted to read.

Different people are interested in different subjects. Your five-year-old sister might enjoy reading a story about a talking cat. Your sixteen-year-old neighbor might prefer a story about a high-school football player. When you choose your subject and plan your story, you need to think about your readers and their interests.

Before You Write.   When you think about your readers, ask yourself these questions:

- Who are my readers?
- How old are they?
- What are they interested in?
- Will they find my story subject interesting?

EXERCISE 3. Thinking About the Interests of Readers. The following story subjects would be more interesting to some readers than to others. Number your paper 1–5. Match each story subject with the group of readers that would be most interested in it. Be prepared to explain your answers.

EXAMPLE   1. A fox shows a pig how   a. five-year-olds
               to tie his shoes   b. sixth-grade students
          1. *a*   c. high-school students
                               d. adults

      Story Subjects   *Readers*
1. A senator discovers a spy   a. five-year-olds
   in her own office.   b. sixth-grade students
2. A stuffed bear rescues a   c. high-school students
   doll from an angry mouse.   d. adults
3. A timid boy becomes president
   of the senior class.
4. A rescue team finds two boys
   who were lost in a cave.
5. A young girl saves money from
   her paper route to buy a horse.

EXERCISE 4. Thinking About Your Readers. Use the subject you chose for Exercise 2. On a sheet of paper, write the answers to the four questions in the *Before You Write* on page 32. If you decide that your readers may not find your subject interesting, go back to your list from Exercise 2 and select another subject. Save your work.

GATHERING DETAILS FOR YOUR STORY

2c. Gather details to make your story interesting.

Read the following sentences and decide whether they make an interesting story.

My friend and I were on our way home from school when a tornado hit. We found a place to hide until it went by. We were not hurt.

Although these sentences tell about a problem and an outcome, they do not make an interesting story. The readers will want to know more. How did the two people know it was a tornado? What did they do? Were they frightened? Were they in danger? Adding those details would help readers share the experience and would make the story more interesting.

One way to gather details for your story is to ask yourself the *5 W-How?* questions—*Who? What? Where? When? Why?* and *How?* For example, the girl who wrote about the tornado listed the following details:

Who? my friend Carla and I (two eleven-year-old girls)

What? a tornado—a huge dark cloud with a swirling funnel dropping out of it
roaring sound
loud crash

Where? between my house and school
on a street with huge oak trees
in a deep ditch at side of street

When? on the way home from school
a hot spring day

Why? didn't notice dark clouds in sky

How? heard roar and saw funnel hanging down from cloud
grabbed Carla's arm and dragged her to ditch
hid in deep ditch

Before You Write. To gather details for your story,

● talk to other people.
● review your writer's notebook.
● brainstorm.
● ask yourself the *5 W-How?* questions.

EXERCISE 5. Gathering Details for Your Story. Use the subject you chose in Exercise 2 or choose a new subject for a story. Gather details for your story by asking the *5 W-How?* questions. Write your answers to these questions. Save your list of details for later use.

DEVELOPING A PLAN FOR YOUR STORY

2d. Develop a plan for your story.

You will find it easier to write a story if you have a plan for it. You will not always follow your plan exactly. Instead, use it like a map to guide you.

Your story plan should contain the following information:

SETTING	the **time** and **place** of the story
CHARACTERS	the **people** in the story
PLOT	the **problem;** the **actions** that happened as a result of the problem in the order they happened; and the **outcome**

Read the following plan for the story about the tornado.

SETTING	on a hot spring day after school on a wooded street near our house
CHARACTERS	my adventurous friend Carla and me
PLOT	*Problem:* My friend and I were out in the open when a tornado struck.
	What happened: walked home from school didn't notice clouds suddenly saw flash of lightning started to run, called to Carla grabbed Carla's arm dragged her to ditch

Outcome:
   lay flat in ditch
   heard loud roar and crash
   crawled out of ditch
   saw tree on sidewalk
   learned lesson about clouds

Compare this story plan with the details gathered with the *5 W-How?* questions (page 34). Notice that the answer to the question *Who?* gives the details about the characters. The answers to the questions *Where?* and *When?* give the details about the setting. The answers to the questions *What? Why?* and *How?* give the details for the plot.

EXERCISE 6. Identifying a Story Plan. Choose a story from your literature or reading textbook, or use a story that your teacher suggests. Read the story carefully. Then write a plan that might have been used to develop the story. Use the plan for the tornado story as a guide.

EXERCISE 7. Developing Your Own Story Plan. Using the details you gathered for Exercise 5, develop a story plan. Use the plan for the story about the tornado as a guide. Save your work for later use.

WRITING

DESCRIBING SETTING

2e. Use description to create a clear picture of the setting.

In some stories, setting plays an important part. It may directly affect the characters and what happens to them. Notice that the girl writing about the tornado includes the time, the weather, and the place.

> On a hot spring afternoon, my friend Carla and I learned the importance of watching clouds. As we walked home from school that day, we barely noticed the dark clouds overhead. Suddenly we saw a bright flash of lightning.

To write about setting, you must be a good observer. As you observe, you can gather details to help your reader see the setting clearly and understand why it is important in your story. For example, is it a bright, sunny day or are there dark overhanging clouds? Is it midday or is it late at night? When you have gathered these kinds of details, you can help your reader see *when* and *where* your story takes place.

When You Write. When you observe, ask yourself these questions:

- Where is the place? What does the place look like? What are the sounds? The smells?
- What is the weather like? Is it cloudy? Sunny? Does the air feel cold? Damp?
- When does the reader see the place? Is it during the day or during the night? Is it in the past or in the future?

EXERCISE 8. Observing Details. Choose a place you know that would make a good setting for a mystery story. Go to the place and observe it again, or picture the place in your mind. Write answers to the three questions above. Exchange papers with a classmate and discuss whether your details would create a good setting for a mystery.

EXERCISE 9. Writing a Description of Setting. Use the setting you identified in your story plan for Exercise 7 or another setting you might like to write about. Go to the place and observe it again, or picture the place in your mind. Write answers to the three questions above and then write three sentences describing your setting. Save your answers.

DESCRIBING CHARACTERS

2f. Use description to make your characters seem real and interesting to your readers.

You cannot have a story without characters. When readers ask "What happened?" they really want to know "What happened to the characters?" Did the character survive the storm? Or, in other stories, did she learn to get along with other people? Did he overcome his fear of high places?

People enjoy reading about characters who are like real human beings instead of stick figures. To make these characters seem real, you must know about them yourself. Observe real people closely and think carefully about imaginary characters. Then use these details to make your characters seem real and interesting.

When You Write. Ask these questions about your characters:

- *Appearance:* What does this person look like? How does he or she walk and talk? Is the way this person looks important to what happens in the story?
- *Personality:* How does this person think or feel? How does he or she behave? Is the way this person thinks or feels important to what happens in the story?

EXERCISE 10. Asking Questions About Characters. Choose a character from your favorite television program. Watch the program and carefully observe the character. As you observe the character, write the answers to the questions in *When You Write*. Then ask a classmate to read your answers and identify the character.

EXERCISE 11. **Writing a Description of a Character.** Use a character you identified in your story plan for Exercise 7, or another character you might like to write about. Observe the character or picture him or her in your mind. Write answers to the questions in *When You Write* (page 38), and then write a one-paragraph description of your character using these specific details. Save your work.

USING DIALOGUE

2g. Use dialogue to make your story more interesting.

In a story, the conversation between characters is called *dialogue*. By adding dialogue to your story, you can do two things:

1. Make your characters seem real and interesting.
2. Show the action in the story.

Making Characters Seem Real and Interesting

In the following paragraph, the girl writing about the tornado *describes* what she and her friend say to each other. The result is a paragraph that is not very interesting. The characters do not seem real.

> Carla pointed at the sky. She asked why that cloud looked like a funnel. I told her it was a tornado and we should run for cover. I started to run. Then I looked over my shoulder and told her to come on.

The same conversation is written in dialogue below. Notice how the characters come alive.

> Carla pointed at the sky. "Why does that cloud look like a funnel? It's strange."
> "It's a tornado!" I screamed. "Run for cover!"
> I started to run. Then I looked back over my shoulder. Carla wasn't running. "Come on, Carla!" I shouted.

Showing Action in the Story

Dialogue can show action, too. The dialogue above tells us several things that happened in the story.

What problem do the girls have?
What does Carla do?
What does the girl who is telling the story do?

The answers to these questions tell *what happened*. They show some of the action in the story.

> *When You Write.* In writing dialogue,
> - use quotation marks around the exact words of each speaker.
> - make a new paragraph to show when the speaker changes.
> - punctuate carefully. (See page 378.)
> - have the dialogue tell something about the characters or about the action of the story.
> - make the dialogue sound like the words that real people would use.

EXERCISE 12. Writing Dialogue. The following paragraph describes a conversation between two characters. Rewrite the conversation in dialogue. Use the above suggestions in *When You Write*.

Yoshi pointed across the lake. He told Jim they should go explore the island. Jim said that there might be wild animals there. Yoshi said that he had been there before and had only seen birds. Jim said it might be fun to go.

EXERCISE 13. Writing Dialogue for Your Own Story. Write a short dialogue between two characters. Use two characters from your story plan in Exercise 7. Use the suggestions in *When You Write*. Save your work.

WRITING A FIRST DRAFT OF YOUR STORY

2h. Write a first draft with a beginning, a middle, and an ending.

Every story has three parts: the *beginning,* the *middle,* and the *ending.* You can use your story plan to write a first draft of each part.

Read the following first draft of the story about the tornado. The beginning, the middle, and the ending of the story are clearly marked in the margin.

On a hot spring afternoon, my friend Carla and I learned the importance of watching clouds. As we walked home from school that day, we barely noticed the dark clouds overhead. Suddenly we saw a bright flash of lightning.

beginning

Carla pointed at the sky. "Why does that cloud look like a funnel? It's strange."

"It's a tornado!" I screamed. "Run for cover!"

I started to run. Then I looked back over my shoulder. Carla wasn't running. "Come on!" I shouted.

Carla is usually the brave one, but now she looked scared. She opened her mouth. A squeaky sound came out. "I can't," she said. She stood rooted to the spot.

I ran back and said, "We've got to hurry!" Then I grabbed her arm. I dragged her to a ditch beside the street.

We flattened ourselves out on our stomachs in the ditch. The tornado roared like a train over our heads. We heard a loud crash. Then the roaring went away.

middle

We crawled out of the ditch and stood up. ⎤ ending
A giant oak tree was lying across the street,
right where we had been walking. We were
safe, but we had learned a lesson. Don't
ignore the clouds. ⎦

Writing the Beginning

The beginning of your story should make your readers curious or
interested. If your first paragraph is dull, they may not go on
reading.

> *When You Write.* The beginning of your story should
>
> ● introduce the setting (the time and the place).
> ● introduce the characters.
> ● interest the readers by hinting what will happen.

In the story on pages 41–42, how long is the beginning? Where
does the story take place? When does the story happen? Who are
the characters? What does the writer do to try to get the reader
interested?

EXERCISE 14. Identifying the Beginning of a Story. Select a
story; one you would like to read or one your teacher suggests.
Write down the name of the book and the page numbers of the
story. (You will use the story again.) Read the story and decide
what part is the beginning. On a sheet of paper or in a class
discussion, tell what the setting is, who the characters are, and
what hints or clues in the beginning give you an idea about what is
going to happen.

EXERCISE 15. Writing the Beginning of Your Story. Write a
beginning for your story. Use your story plan from Exercise 7, or
make a new plan. You may also want to use the papers you saved
from Exercises 9, 11, and 13. Use the suggestions in *When You
Write,* above.

Writing the Middle

The middle of a story tells the plot. The plot includes the important actions and what happened to the characters. Writers sometimes use dialogue and description to tell what happened in the middle of the story.

When You Write. The middle of your story should

- show the problem your characters face.
- tell the actions in the order they happen.
- include dialogue and description if they would make the story more interesting.

Review the story on pages 41–42. Where does the middle start and where does it end? What important actions does it include? Does it have dialogue? Does it include any description?

EXERCISE 16. **Identifying the Middle of a Story.** Use the same story you used in Exercise 14. Decide which part of the story is the middle. On a sheet of paper, list the actions that the writer includes in the middle. Be prepared to discuss your list.

EXERCISE 17. **Writing the Middle of Your Story.** Write a first draft of the middle of your story. Use the story plan you used for Exercise 15. You may also want to use your character description from Exercise 11 and your dialogue from Exercise 13.

Do not worry about getting everything just right in this draft. You will have time to revise later. Use the suggestions in *When You Write,* above.

Writing the Ending

The ending of the story should answer all the readers' remaining questions about what happened. It should tell how the characters' problem was solved.

Look again at the story about the tornado (pages 41–42). What part is the ending? What is the outcome of the story? What happens to the characters?

Many good stories also include how the storyteller felt about the problem. Perhaps he or she learned a special lesson. What does the writer tell you that she learned from her experience with the tornado (page 42)? Would the story seem complete without this part of the ending?

When You Write. The ending of your story should

- answer your readers' remaining questions about what happened.
- tell how your characters' problem was worked out.
- tell how you felt about the experience or what you learned from it (if you think this will be meaningful to your readers).

EXERCISE 18. Identifying the Ending of a Story. Use the story you used for Exercises 14 and 16. Identify the ending. On a sheet of paper or in a group discussion, tell how the characters' problem was solved.

EXERCISE 19. Writing the Ending of Your Story. Write the ending for the story you began for Exercises 15 and 17. Use the suggestions in *When You Write,* above. Remember that this is only a first draft. You will have time to improve it later.

EVALUATING

EVALUATING YOUR STORY

2i. Evaluate the first draft of your story.

CRITICAL THINKING:
Evaluating a First Draft

Evaluation is a thinking skill you use often. When you evaluate, you judge something according to standards, or guidelines. You use this skill when you decide which shirt to buy, what to have for lunch, or which color to paint your bike. You use it to judge whether you made a good or bad decision. You also use it when you decide how to improve your story.

Once you finish your first draft, you need to go back over your writing. You need to look for ways to improve your story. Deciding where to make these improvements is *evaluating*. When you evaluate your story, look carefully at *content, arrangement,* and *language.*

> *Content:* What you say
> *Arrangement:* The order in which you say it
> *Language:* The words and kinds of sentences you use

The questions in the Guidelines for Evaluating Stories will help you improve the first draft.

GUIDELINES FOR EVALUATING STORIES

Subject	1. Is the subject of the story a specific experience that presents a problem?
Beginning	2. Does the beginning catch the readers' attention? Does it introduce the setting and the characters?
Middle	3. Does the middle of the story tell the important actions of the plot? Is enough information given so the readers can understand the plot?
Order	4. Are all of the actions arranged in time order?
Dialogue	5. Does the dialogue tell something about the people or the actions in the story?
Ending	6. Does the ending of the story tell how the problem was worked out?
Language	7. Do the words and sentences suit the readers? Are they too hard or too easy? Have you used specific words to describe the setting, characters, and action?

EXERCISE 20. Evaluating Your Story. Allow some time to pass between writing and evaluating your story. Use the Guidelines for Evaluating Stories. On your paper, mark the places that need improvement. Save your work. You may also want to exchange papers with a classmate to evaluate each other's work. Make comments on both the strengths and the weaknesses of your classmate's paper.

REVISING

REVISING YOUR STORY

2j. Revise the first draft of your story.

When you evaluated the draft of your story, you marked places where it should be improved. *Revising* is making those improvements. To revise, you can *add* or *cut* words or details. You can also *reorder,* or change the order of actions to make the plot clearer. You can *replace* some words with other words. The chart below will help you revise your story. For each problem, the chart suggests which kind of change you can use. If you have trouble deciding whether a certain change improves your paper, it is probably better to go ahead and try it. Then you can get some response from your reader.

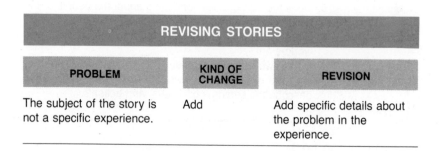

REVISING STORIES		
PROBLEM	**KIND OF CHANGE**	**REVISION**
The subject of the story is not a specific experience.	Add	Add specific details about the problem in the experience.

PROBLEM	KIND OF CHANGE	REVISION
The beginning does not catch the reader's attention.	Replace	Replace the beginning with details that will make the reader wonder what is going to happen. Do not give away the ending.
The beginning does not introduce the setting and the characters.	Add	Add *where* and *when* the story took place. Then find a good place to introduce the characters.
The middle does not tell all the important actions of the plot.	Add	Review your story plan to make sure that every step is included. Then compare your story with the plan and add any missing details.
The order of the actions is confusing.	Reorder	Read your story out loud to figure out where the action becomes confused. Change the order of the actions until the plot is clear.
The dialogue does not do anything.	Cut/Add	Cut dialogue that does not tell about the characters or the action of the plot. Add dialogue about the characters and actions.
The ending does not tell how the problem was worked out.	Add	Add details that make the outcome clear. If you desire, add a statement about the meaning of the story.
The words in the story are too general or vague.	Replace	Replace general, vague words with specific ones that describe clearly.
The words and sentences do not suit the readers.	Replace	Think about your readers. Then, replace words and sentences that are too easy or too hard for these readers.

EXERCISE 21. Analyzing a Writer's Revisions. Read the following first draft of the story on pages 41–42. Study the writer's changes. Then write answers to the questions that follow the story.

My friend Carla and I learned an important lesson about clouds.

^As we walked home from school one day,   add
we barely noticed the dark clouds overhead.
Suddenly we saw a bright flash of lightning.

Carla pointed at the sky. "Why does that
cloud look like a funnel? It's strange."

"It's a tornado!" I screamed. "Run for
cover!" I started to run. Then I looked back
over my shoulder. Carla wasn't running.
"Come on!" I shouted.

Now Carla looked scared. She opened her
mouth. A squeaky sound came out. "I can't,"
she said. She stood rooted to the spot.

I ran back and said, "We've got to hurry!"
I dragged her to a ditch beside the street.
Then I ^grabbed her arm.   ^   add

^The tornado roared like a train over our
heads. We heard a loud crash. |We flattened| reorder
(ourselves out on our stomachs in the ditch.)
Then the roaring went away.

crawled
We ~~got~~ out of the ditch and stood up. A   replace
giant oak tree was lying across the street, right
where we had been walking.^ *We were safe, and never*   add
again would
we ignore the clouds.

1. Why did the writer add the sentence to the beginning?
2. Why did the writer add the sentence about dragging her friend to the ditch?
3. Why did the writer move one sentence?
4. Why did the writer change *got* to *crawled*?
5. Why did the writer add the last sentence to the story?

EXERCISE 22. Revising Your First Draft.   Using the evaluation of your story from Exercise 20, revise your first draft. Use the Revising Stories chart to help you.

PROOFREADING

PROOFREADING YOUR STORY AND MAKING A FINAL COPY

2k. Proofread your story and make a final copy.

When you proofread, you look for problems with *spelling, punctuation, capitalization*, and *sentences*. Use the Guidelines for Proofreading on page 27.

If you have included dialogue in your story, check to see whether you have used quotation marks for each speaker's words. Check also to see whether you have started a new paragraph each time the speaker changes.

Remember that readers may have trouble reading a messy paper. Recopy your story neatly after you have made all changes and corrections. Follow the standards for manuscript form (page 28) or your teacher's directions. Proofread again to catch any mistakes.

EXERCISE 23. Proofreading Your Story.   Proofread the story you revised in Exercise 22. Use the proofreading guidelines on page 27. Make a neat final copy. Then proofread your story one more time and make any needed changes.

CHAPTER 2 WRITING REVIEW

Writing a Story About a Personal Experience. Write a story about a personal experience in which you faced a problem and finally worked it out. The experience should be one you do not mind sharing with others. Use the process you practiced in this chapter.

CHAPTER 3

Writing Paragraphs

STRUCTURE AND DEVELOPMENT

When you read, you look at the words and think about what they mean. If you look at the page itself, however, you will notice that it is divided into groups of sentences. You will also notice that the first line of each group is indented (set in from the edge). These groups of sentences are called *paragraphs*.

In this chapter you will learn how paragraphs are put together. You will also learn to use the writing process to write your own paragraphs.

THE STRUCTURE OF A PARAGRAPH

Well-written paragraphs are centered around one main idea, and they give enough details to make that idea clear.

THE MAIN IDEA

3a. A *paragraph* is a group of sentences that states and makes clear one main idea about a topic.

A well-written paragraph states only one main idea about one topic. All of its sentences are directly connected to that main idea. They help make the idea clear.

In the following paragraph, the first sentence tells what the topic is: space cities. It also states the main idea: *Space cities will be very different from cities on Earth.* The other sentences help make that idea clear.

> Space cities will be very different from cities on Earth. They will look like a number of giant bicycle tires tied together. Over all of the "tires" will be a roof made of glass and metal. Within each ring will be a large open space with trees and fountains. As many as ten thousand people will live in the rings of a single space city.

To be a paragraph, a group of sentences must meet these three tests: (1) It must be about only one topic. (2) It must state only one main idea about the topic. (3) All of its sentences must be directly connected to that main idea.

As you read the following group of sentences, check to see whether it meets these three tests.

> My friend Tamara has a Great Dane. The best kind of guard dog is a Doberman. My brother had a cat named Boots that used to hiss at strangers. You can get a dog at the animal shelter. I hope my parents will let me get a dog.

This group of sentences looks like a paragraph, but it is not one. It does not state only one main idea about one topic. Also, its sentences are not directly connected to any one main idea.

EXERCISE 1. Identifying Paragraphs. Number your paper 1–3. Read the following groups of sentences. If a group of sentences meets the three tests for a paragraph, write *P* after its number. If it does not, write *NP*. Your teacher may ask you to explain your answers.

1.   Saturday is my favorite day of the week. I can sleep late, and then I can watch the cartoons on television. Once I have

cleaned my room, I am free to play with my friends. Sometimes on Saturdays my parents take me to a movie. Staying up late Saturday night is the perfect ending to the week.

2.   Blue jeans have become very popular. Many people enjoy wearing jeans because they are so comfortable. I like to wear skirts and blouses. My mother likes to wear dresses and suits. Blue jeans will be around for many years.

3.   Holly is planning to be a writer. She began writing stories when she was five years old. Her first stories were about birds and squirrels. Now she writes in her journal every day. She also enters every writing contest she can find out about. Last year she won a prize for one of her stories.

THE TOPIC SENTENCE

3b. The *topic sentence* states the one main idea of a paragraph.

The topic sentence tells what the topic is. It also gives the writer's main idea.

Most often, the topic sentence is the first sentence in the paragraph. In that position, it tells the reader what the paragraph will be about. It also helps the writer remember to keep to the main idea.

In the following paragraph, the first sentence gives the main idea. The other sentences help make that idea clear.

> **A fennec is an unusual member of the fox family.** It is the smallest kind of fox in the world. When it is full grown, it is no bigger than a very small dog. Fennecs are sometimes called desert foxes because they live in the deserts of North Africa. Like many desert animals, they can live for a long time without water.

Sometimes, as in the next paragraph, the topic sentence is the last sentence. The other sentences lead up to the topic sentence.

Dentists use drills with diamond tips. Similar drills are used in industry to cut very hard materials. Many record-player needles have diamond tips. In addition, diamonds are used in the windows on spacecraft because they can stand up under high pressure and very hot or very cold temperatures. **The hardness of the diamond makes it one of the world's most useful minerals.**

EXERCISE 2. Identifying Topic Sentences. Tell which sentence in each of the following paragraphs is the topic sentence.

1. Some animals use color to hide from their enemies. The green color of a grasshopper, for example, blends into the color of the grass in which it lives. In the winter, the brown fur of the snowshoe hare turns white to match the snow. The skin of the chameleon, a kind of lizard, changes color to look like the area around it.

2. It snowed almost every day, and the wind howled day and night. Snowdrifts higher than the fences blocked the road to our farm. Father got up early each morning to light a fire in the fireplace, our only source of heat. The winter of 1928 is the coldest winter I can remember.

3. Mandy had thought that her first day at the new school would be frightening and lonely, but it turned out to be a good day after all. Her new teacher, Mrs. Thompson, already knew Mandy's name and seemed happy to have her join the class. In science, the class was studying the four basic food groups, which Mandy had also been learning about at her old school. Mandy's last fear left her at lunchtime, when two friendly girls asked her to eat with them.

4. Crocodiles and alligators are both reptiles, but they are very different in certain ways. A crocodile has a longer, narrower head than an alligator does. In addition, one of its teeth can be seen even when its mouth is closed. Most importantly, a crocodile is more likely to attack a human being without any cause.

SUPPORTING SENTENCES

3c. The other sentences in the paragraph help make the main idea clear.

These other sentences are called *supporting sentences*. They give details (specific information) such as facts, examples, and reasons. The details help make the main idea clear. (You will learn more about the different kinds of details in Chapter 4.) To make the main idea clear, a paragraph should have at least three supporting sentences. Read the following two paragraphs. Notice that both use the same topic sentence, but that the other sentences are different.

WEAK   **Running has become a popular American sport.** Many people run every day. Some people enter races all over the country.

IMPROVED   **Running has become a popular American sport.** Every day of the year runners can be seen in almost any park and along many streets and roads. The number of Americans who run two or more times a week has more than doubled in the last five years. Big cities such as New York and Boston hold races each year for runners from all over the world. Even small towns often hold races to raise money for good causes.

In the second paragraph, each supporting sentence gives details that help the reader understand the main idea in the topic sentence.

EXERCISE 3. Improving a Weak Paragraph. The following paragraph is weak because it does not contain enough supporting details. Read the paragraph and then make up answers to the questions that follow it. Rewrite the paragraph on another sheet of paper, using your list of answers to write supporting sentences.

The circus parade began at 10:00 Saturday morning. People arrived early to find places where they would be able to see the parade. The parade began with the clowns, who made the children laugh.

1. What was the weather like?
2. How many people watched the parade? Where did they sit or stand? Did they bring anything with them?
3. What sounds could be heard?
4. What did the clowns look like?
5. How did they make the children laugh?

EXERCISE 4. Writing Supporting Sentences. After each number, a topic sentence is given. It is followed by several details. For each number, write a paragraph. Use the topic sentence as it is and use the details to write supporting sentences. You will need to add some words.

1. *Topic sentence:* Steven likes skiing more than anyone else I know.
   Possible details:
   gets out skis as soon as first snow falls
   skis every Saturday and Sunday
   reads a skiing magazine every month
2. *Topic sentence:* Our class play was a big success.
   Possible details:
   sold all tickets
   actors remembered their lines
   audience laughed at lines meant to be funny
   they stood up and cheered at end

REVIEW EXERCISE. Analyzing and Evaluating Paragraphs. Read each of the following groups of sentences. On your paper, write its number. If the group of sentences is a paragraph, write its topic sentence and list the details that help make the main idea clear. If it is not, rewrite it so that it meets the three tests for a paragraph on page 52.

1. One day I saw our new puppy chasing a bright blue butterfly. Then I saw our neighbor's cat creep into our yard.

2.   Robert earns money by doing chores for his neighbors. During the summer, he mows the lawn every week for the Woods and the Thomases. When Mrs. Ruiz goes on a business trip, Robert feeds her cat and waters her plants. When it snows during the winter, he shovels the sidewalk for his next-door neighbors, the Washingtons, before school.

THE DEVELOPMENT OF A PARAGRAPH

You have learned how paragraphs are put together. Now you will learn how to write your own paragraphs.

PREWRITING

CHOOSING A SUBJECT

3d. Choose a subject to write about.

Planning a paragraph begins with choosing a subject. A *subject* is a broad area. It includes many different parts. For example, the subject "animals" includes all of the different *kinds* of animals.

The best subjects are ones you know well. If you know your subject, you will be able to make it clear to your readers.

Reading your writer's notebook (see page 9) can help you find subjects that you know well. Making an *interest inventory* is another way to find possible subjects. This is a list of the subjects that you are interested in.

EXERCISE 5. **Making an Interest Inventory.**   Write down any of the following subjects that you know something about or that you are interested in. Then think of at least five more subjects

Keep this list. You can look at it whenever you need to choose a subject for writing.

Art	Heroes	Pets
Cars	Insects	Plants
Clothes	Movies	Science
Computers	Music	Sports

LIMITING THE SUBJECT

3e. Limit the subject to find a topic that is narrow enough for a paragraph.

A paragraph has only a few sentences. To write a clear paragraph, you need to find a topic—one narrow part of your subject.

The topic for a paragraph should be narrow enough to cover in a few sentences. For example, "cartooning" is one *kind* of art. This topic is still too broad for a paragraph, however. To narrow it even more, you might think of *examples* of cartoons, such as "Peanuts," "Cathy," and "Garfield." You could cover any one of these topics in a single paragraph.

Three of the ways to limit a subject to find a topic for a paragraph are brainstorming, clustering, and asking the *5 W-How?* questions.

Brainstorming

To *brainstorm,* you write a subject at the top of a piece of paper. Under it, you write down any connected ideas that come to mind. You work quickly, without stopping to judge your ideas.

One girl made this list from the subject "television."

commercials	new shows
sports	old shows
news	TV in the classroom
comedies	stars
game shows	my favorite show

Clustering

In *clustering,* you make a diagram instead of a list. First you write a word or phrase in the center of a sheet of paper and circle it. Then you add as many ideas as you can think of. Each time you add an idea, you circle it and connect it to the idea that made you think of it.

Here is the diagram one boy made:

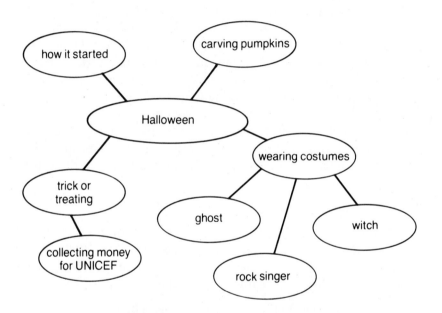

Asking the 5 W-How? Questions

The *5 W-How?* questions are *Who? What? When? Where? Why?* and *How?* Here is a sample list of questions for the subject "dogs."

EXAMPLE   *Subject:* Dogs
          Questions:
                Who first trained dogs to lead blind persons?
                What are the three most popular kinds of dogs?

When did dogs first become pets?
Where should you keep a dog when you go away?
Why should a dog have a checkup each year?
How should a person choose a dog?

CRITICAL THINKING:
Analyzing a Subject

When you divide a subject into its smaller parts, you *analyze* it. You do this often, both in school and out. Suppose you want to arrange all of your books in order, for example. You might first divide them into smaller groups such as animal stories, space stories, and true stories about real people. Doing this would make it easier for you to decide how to arrange the books.

Depending on your subject, you may limit (divide) it by using one or more of these divisions: kinds, examples, time periods, or uses. Suppose you want to write about the subject "dancing." To limit this subject for a paragraph, you might divide it in the ways listed here:

Subject: Dancing

Kinds	Uses	Time Periods
break-dancing	exercise	dances of the 1980's
ballet	hobby	dances of the 1960's
square dancing	career	dances of the 1920's

Sometimes the first division of your subject will give you a topic that is narrow enough for a paragraph. At other times, you will need to subdivide the topics you list, to find still smaller parts. For example, all of the topics listed under *Time Periods* are still too broad for a paragraph. Subdividing these topics would help you find narrower topics. For example, subdividing "dances of the 1960's" into examples would give you several different dances to choose from: the twist, the stroll, and so on. One specific dance would be narrow enough for a paragraph.

EXERCISE 6. Limiting a Subject. Choose one of the subjects you listed for Exercise 5, or choose another subject. Use brainstorming, clustering, or the *5 W-How?* questions to divide the subject. Keep dividing the subject into smaller parts until you have three topics that are limited enough for a paragraph. Save your paper.

DECIDING ON YOUR PURPOSE

3f. Choose a purpose for writing.

All writing has a purpose, a reason for being written. Three of the most important reasons for writing are to tell a story, to describe, and to explain or give information.

Writing to tell a story is *narrative* writing.
Writing to describe is *descriptive* writing.
Writing to explain or give information is *expository* writing.

Often, a piece of writing has more than one purpose. When you *explain* how to decorate a birthday cake, for example, you might also *describe* how it will look. Your most important reason for writing, however, is to *explain*. Deciding on your purpose before you write helps you choose details to include.

Before You Write.   Decide which of the following is your most important reason for writing:

- to tell a story
- to describe
- to explain or give information

EXERCISE 7. Choosing a Purpose for Writing.   Number your paper 1–5. Decide what your most important reason would be for writing a paragraph on each of the following topics. Use these choices: *narrative, descriptive, expository*. Your teacher may ask you to explain your answers.

1. My coin collection
2. Sights to see at the lake
3. Our day at Sea World
4. Making a clay bowl
5. A morning to remember

EXERCISE 8. Deciding on a Purpose for Writing. Look again at the list of topics you made for Exercise 6. For each topic, decide whether you would tell a story, describe, explain, or give information. Put your answers in writing, and check them with your teacher.

THINKING ABOUT YOUR AUDIENCE

3g. Think about the people who will read your writing.

The people who read your writing are your audience. You want your readers to be interested in what you write. You also want them to be able to understand the words and kinds of sentences you use.

Suppose you are writing a paragraph about bicycle racing. For members of your town's bicycle club, you might explain how to enter a race in a nearby city. For people who have never seen a bicycle race, you might instead describe one.

Before You Write. Ask yourself these questions:

- How old are my readers?
- What do they already know about my topic?
- What might they like to know about it?

EXERCISE 9. Thinking About Your Audience. Choose an audience for your paragraph, or use the one your teacher gives you. Then look again at your topics from Exercise 6 and your answers for Exercise 8. Choose one topic and one purpose for your paragraph. Save your paper.

GATHERING INFORMATION

3h. Gather information about your topic.

Once you have chosen a topic, your next step is to gather information about it. You will use this information (facts and other kinds of details) to write your paragraph.

If you know your topic well, you can find information by thinking carefully about it. You may want to use brainstorming, clustering, and the *5 W-How?* questions (see pages 58–60). Write down the details as you think of them, and be sure to save your notes.

EXERCISE 10. Gathering Information. Gather information on the topic you chose for Exercise 9. Use brainstorming, clustering, or the *5 W-How?* questions. Save your paper.

MAKING A PARAGRAPH PLAN

3i. Make a plan for your paragraph.

A *paragraph plan* is made up of the topic sentence and a list of supporting details arranged in order. You will find it easier to write your paragraph if you make a plan first. You need not follow it exactly, but you can use it as a guide.

Writing a Good Topic Sentence

To write a topic sentence, first read your list of details carefully. You may find that some of them are too broad to explain clearly in one or two sentences. Others may not be closely connected to the other details on your list. Cross out these details and use the ones that are left.

EXAMPLE *Topic:* Skiing safety
        Details: checking equipment
                many different kinds of ski bindings
                [*not closely connected to other details*]

skiing only on open hills
watching out for other skiers

Next, look again at the details that are left on your list. Ask yourself how they are alike. For example, the three details that are left on the list above are all important things skiers can do to keep from getting hurt. This general idea covers all three details.

Change the general idea that covers all of your details into a sentence. This will be your topic sentence. (You will change your details into sentences when you write your first draft.)

Try to write your topic sentence in a way that will catch the attention of your readers. You may want to write it several different ways. Choose the one you like best. Then check to make sure that it covers all of your details. Also make sure that it does not cover any ideas that are not on your list.

Arranging Details in Order

Finally, arrange your details in order. To do this, think about your readers. Will they need to understand certain ideas before they can understand others?

For example, for a paragraph on how to wash windows, you would arrange the steps in the order in which they should be done. (You will learn about the kinds of order later in the chapter on pages 67–68.)

Here is a plan for the paragraph about skiing safety:

EXAMPLE *Topic sentence:* Snow-skiers can do three important things to keep from getting hurt.
Details: a. checking equipment
b. watching out for other skiers
c. skiing only on open hills

Before You Write. Make a paragraph plan:

● Write a topic sentence.
● List your details in order.

EXERCISE 11. Making a Paragraph Plan. Read the following paragraph. On a piece of paper, write a plan that might have been used for the paragraph. Use the plan on page 64 as a model.

The first license plates for cars were made by hand by car owners. Some drivers attached metal numbers to pieces of leather or wood. Others pounded tin cans flat and painted numbers on them. Some people even painted the numbers right on their cars.

EXERCISE 12. Making Your Own Paragraph Plan. Using the details you gathered for Exercise 10, make a paragraph plan. Use the plan on page 64 as a model, and save your paper.

WRITING

UNITY

3j. Every sentence in a paragraph should help make the main idea in the topic sentence clear.

A paragraph in which all of the sentences keep to the main idea has *unity*. All of its sentences work together. Sentences that do not keep to the main idea confuse the reader. Such sentences should be removed.

The underlined sentence in the following paragraph does not keep to the main idea in the topic sentence (the first sentence). It breaks the unity of the paragraph.

Gerbils make good pets. For food, they need only seed, grain, and water. A glass tank with wood chips on the bottom makes a fine home for these frisky little animals. A snake can also live in such a tank. They quickly become tame if they are handled gently. They will even take food from their owner's hand.

When You Write. Check your paragraph for unity:

- Test supporting sentences against the topic sentence.
- Remove any sentences that do not help make the main idea clear.

EXERCISE 13. **Identifying Sentences That Break Unity.** Read each of the following paragraphs carefully. On your paper, write the number of the paragraph. If all of the sentences keep to the main idea, write *U* after the number. If the paragraph has a sentence that does not keep to the main idea, write the sentence that should be removed.

1. A healthful diet is one that includes foods from each of the four food groups. The first group is made up of fruits and vegetables. Foods in the second group are breads and cereals. In the third group are milk and other dairy products such as cheese. Swiss cheese tastes good in a salad. The fourth group is called the meat group. It includes not only meats such as beef, chicken, and fish but also certain food pairs such as dried beans and rice. When they are served together, these food pairs have the same food value as meat.

2. Many license plates give information about history and geography. For example, on Minnesota's plates are the words "10,000 Lakes." Even someone who has never visited that state learns about its many lakes. The Colorado plate shows an outline of the Rocky Mountains which are in that state. The words "Land of Lincoln" on the Illinois plates remind people that Abraham Lincoln was living in that state when elected President.

3. A jet stream is a narrow current of air that circles the earth. It flows east around the world about 7 to 8 miles (11.3 to 12.9 kilometers) above the ground. Its average speed is 35 miles (56 kilometers) per hour in the summer and 75 miles (120 kilometers) in the winter. Have you ever taken a trip in a

plane? Planes that go east fly with the jet stream. It helps them gain speed and save fuel. Planes that go west stay away from it because it would slow them down.

COHERENCE

3k. The ideas in a paragraph should be arranged in a clear order and smoothly connected.

A paragraph in which the ideas are arranged in a clear order and smoothly connected has *coherence.* It is easy to follow. Two ways to arrange ideas are by time and by space. For both time and space order, it is natural to use certain connective words to make the paragraph flow smoothly.

Time Order

When you tell a story, you tell what happened first, what happened next, and so on. This order is called *time order.* Time order is also used to explain how to make or do something.

The following paragraph explains how to make rice. Each step is given in the order in which it should be done. The words in heavy type help the reader follow the steps.

> Rice is easy to make. To make rice for four people, **first** put two cups of water into a large pan. Bring the water to a boil over high heat. **Then** add one cup of long-grain rice. **When** the water returns to a boil, cover the pan tightly and turn the heat to "low." Let the rice cook slowly for seventeen minutes, and **then** remove the pan from the heat. **After** two minutes, take off the cover, fluff the rice up with a fork, and put it into a serving bowl.

You can use certain words to connect the ideas in a time-order paragraph. These words are called **transitions.** They help the reader follow the ideas. Here are some transitions that show time order.

after	finally	next
before	first, second, etc.	now
during	later	then

EXERCISE 14. Arranging Ideas in Time Order. Use the following ideas to write a paragraph using time order. First decide on the order of the details. Then write the paragraph, adding words from the list above to connect the ideas.

Topic Sentence: Making a terrarium is an easy way to cheer up a dull Saturday.

Details:

Wash and dry a glass jar.
Add soil on top of the gravel.
Plant small plants in the soil.
Put gravel on the bottom of the jar.
Water the plants.
Put your terrarium in a well-lighted place.
Cover the top of the jar with plastic wrap.

Space Order

When you describe something, you first picture it in your mind. Then you tell where its parts are in relation to one another. This order is called *space order.* It helps your readers picture the topic in their own minds.

To describe your room, for example, you might first picture it as you would see it from the door. Then you might tell what you see as your eyes move around the room in order from left to right.

Other orders for describing something are from top to bottom, from front to back, and from near to far. You can also use the opposite of any of these orders. In any case, it is important to keep to one order so that you do not confuse your readers.

Read the following paragraph. The words in heavy type help the reader picture where the parts of the school are.

Crestview's oldest high school sits grandly **in the center** of town. **In front of** the three-story red brick building is a large grassy area with a water fountain. A brass sign bearing the words "Crestview High School—1925" stretches **above** the wide front doors. Crowning the building is a gold-toned tower with curved windows.

These are some of the transitions that help readers follow ideas in a space-order paragraph.

above	below	in the distance
across	beyond	near
ahead	in back of	next to
around	in front of	outside
behind	inside	to the left, right

EXERCISE 15. Arranging Ideas in Space Order. Use the following ideas to write a paragraph using space order. You may add other details if you want to. Use words from the list above to connect your sentences, and be sure to keep to one order.

Topic Sentence: My Uncle Karl's kitchen is cozy.
Details:
    white stove and refrigerator
    white counters over dark brown cabinets
    round table covered with yellow tablecloth
    flowers in a vase on the table
    four chairs around the table
    square window with yellow curtains above the sink
    bowl of fresh fruit on one counter
    back door with yellow curtains over door windows
    baskets of different colors on top of the cabinets

WRITING A FIRST DRAFT

3l. Write your first draft.

You are now ready to write the first draft of your paragraph. Write quickly to get all of your ideas down on paper. You will have time later to improve your writing.

    Use your paragraph plan as a guide. As you write, you may change the plan. You may decide to add ideas or change the order in which you present them. You may even decide to leave out a detail that was in your plan.

EXERCISE 16. Writing a First Draft. Using the plan you made for Exercise 12, write the first draft of your paragraph.

EVALUATING

EVALUATING YOUR PARAGRAPH

3m. Evaluate your first draft.

To *evaluate* means to judge. When you judge your writing, you read it carefully with your audience and purpose in mind. You look for places in your writing that can be made clearer and more interesting.

If you can, put your first draft away for at least a few hours before you judge it. When you return to it, you will more easily see ways to improve it. If your teacher agrees, you may also ask a classmate to judge your writing. She or he may notice places that could be improved.

The following guidelines will help you judge any paragraph you write. In Chapter 4 you will find specific guidelines for judging three types of paragraphs: narrative, descriptive, and expository.

GUIDELINES FOR EVALUATING PARAGRAPHS

Topic Sentence	1. Does the topic sentence tell what the topic is and clearly state one main idea?
Completeness	2. Are enough details given to make the main idea clear?
Unity	3. Does every sentence keep to the main idea?
Order of Ideas	4. Are the ideas arranged in a clear order?
Connections Between Ideas	5. Are the ideas smoothly connected?

| Word Choice | 6. Are the words lively and colorful? Are they all words that the readers will understand? Are they all needed? |
| Sentence Variety | 7. Are different kinds and lengths of sentences used? |

EXERCISE 17. Evaluating a Paragraph. Number your paper 1–7. Read the following first draft of a paragraph. Use the guidelines on pages 70–71 to judge it. Write *yes* or *no* after the number of each guideline. Be prepared to explain your answers.

Snow skiers can keep from getting hurt. They can ski on hills that are open. Officials close a hill when the snow is dangerous to ski on and people could get hurt. They can check their equipment. They can make sure that their bindings and safety straps work. They can watch out for others. They can look to see whether anyone else is already coming. Last weekend some guy ran right into me and knocked me down.

EXERCISE 18. Evaluating Your Own Paragraph. Use the guidelines on pages 70–71 to judge the paragraph you wrote for Exercise 16. Mark the places in your paragraph where improvement is needed. Save your paper.

REVISING

REVISING YOUR PARAGRAPH

3n. Revise your first draft.

Revising means making changes to improve your writing. Four kinds of changes you can make to improve your writing are *adding, cutting, reordering,* and *replacing*. The following chart shows how you can use these four kinds of changes to improve a paragraph.

REVISING PARAGRAPHS

PROBLEM	KIND OF CHANGE	REVISION
The paragraph does not have a topic sentence.	Add	Add a sentence that tells what the topic is and clearly states one main idea.
The topic sentence covers more than one main idea.	Cut/Replace	Remove information from topic sentence that does not keep to one main idea. Rewrite the topic sentence to cover only the main idea in the paragraph.
The topic sentence does not cover all of the details in the paragraph.	Add	Add words, a phrase, or a clause that will make the sentence cover all the details.
The topic sentence is dull.	Add/Replace	Add colorful details to make the topic sentence more interesting. Replace general words with specific ones.
One or more sentences do not keep to the main idea.	Cut	Remove the sentence(s).
The ideas are not easy to follow.	Reorder	Rearrange the sentences in a clear order.
The ideas are not smoothly connected.	Add/Replace	Add transitions. Use clearer transitions.
The language is dull.	Add/Replace	Replace general words with specific ones. For example, change *dog* to *border collie, nice* to *polite, run* to *scurry.*
The language is too hard for the readers.	Add/Replace	Tell what the hard words mean. Use easier words.
The sentences all sound the same.	Replace	Combine sentences. Use different kinds of sentences. Use sentences of different lengths.

EXERCISE 19. Analyzing a Writer's Revisions. Study the following revised paragraph. (The notes in red show the kinds of changes the writer made.) Then answer the questions that follow the paragraph.

Snow-skiers can *do three important things to* keep from getting hurt.　　add

Finally, skiers They can ski *only* on hills that are open. *Ski* Officials　　add; reorder; replace

close a hill when the snow is dangerous to ski

on and people could get hurt. *First,* They can check　　cut; add

their equipment. *before they start* They can make sure that *(For example,)*　　add

their bindings and safety straps work. *Second,* They

can watch out for others. *skiers* They can look to see *before entering a hill*　　add

whether anyone else is already coming. *down it* Last　　add; cut

weekend some guy ran right into me and　　cut

knocked me down.　　cut

1. Why did the writer add *do three important things to* to the topic sentence (the first sentence)?
2. Why did the writer add the words *First, Second,* and *Finally?*
3. Why did the writer move sentences 2 and 3 to the end?
4. Why did the writer add the phrases *before they start* and *before entering a hill?*
5. Why did the writer cut the last sentence?

EXERCISE 20. Evaluating and Revising a Paragraph. Use the guidelines on page 70–71 to judge the following paragraph. Then revise the paragraph, using the chart on page 72. Write your paragraph on a separate sheet of paper.

Scrambled eggs are my favorite breakfast, and they are easy to make. Break two fresh eggs into a bowl. Beat them with a fork until they are smooth. Add one tablespoon of water. Mix the water with the eggs. Last week my cousin Jason showed me how to make stuffed eggs. Melt one tablespoon of butter in a frying pan over medium heat. You can use margarine instead. Pour the mixture into the frying pan. As they are cooking, stir them gently with a wooden spoon. When they are firm, they are done.

EXERCISE 21. **Revising Your Own Paragraph.** Use your answers for Exercise 18 and the chart on page 72 to revise your own paragraph. Save your paper.

PROOFREADING AND MAKING A FINAL COPY

PROOFREADING YOUR PARAGRAPH AND MAKING A FINAL COPY

3o. Proofread your paragraph, make a final copy, and proofread again.

To proofread your paragraph, read it carefully. Look at your spelling, use of capital letters, and punctuation separately. Correct any mistakes you find. After you make a final copy, proofread again.

Use the following guidelines to proofread your paragraph.

GUIDELINES FOR PROOFREADING PARAGRAPHS

1. Does every sentence begin with a capital letter?
2. Are all words spelled correctly?
3. Does every sentence end with the correct punctuation mark?
4. Is every sentence a complete sentence?
5. Is the first line of the paragraph indented?

EXERCISE 22. **Proofreading Sentences.** Each of the following sentences contains one mistake. After the number of the sentence, write the sentence correctly.

1. Every july, my cousins visit us.
2. Ryan and Kelly played checkers Kelly won.
3. Mr. Lieu rased money for the Heart Association.
4. Heather's team won the baseball game
5. Ben moved to Los Angeles California.
6. We bought too tickets to the game.
7. We tired to finish on time.
8. Bob and Jane came on on the train.
9. French, Spanish, and latin are taught at our school.
10. Gold has many usages.

EXERCISE 23. Proofreading Your Own Paragraph.
Proofread your own paragraph, using the guidelines on page 74.
Then make a clean copy to give to your readers. Use the rules on
page 28, or follow your teacher's directions. Remember to
proofread your paper again after you copy it.

CHAPTER 3 WRITING REVIEW

Writing a Paragraph.   Narrow one of the following subjects to
find a topic, or use a topic of your own.

Contests	School
Fairy tales	Secrets
Heroes	Video games
Reading	Winter
Roller-skating	

PREWRITING   Limit your subject to a topic that you can cover
in one paragraph. After you have decided on your purpose and
thought about your audience, list details for your paragraph.

   To make a paragraph plan, first cross out any details that do
not fit. Then write a topic sentence, and list the details in the
order in which you will write about them.

WRITING   As you write your first draft, use your plan as a
guide. Keep your purpose and audience in mind as you write.

EVALUATING AND REVISING Use the guidelines on page 70 to judge your writing. Then use the chart on page 72 to improve it.

PROOFREADING AND MAKING A FINAL COPY Proofread your paragraph, using the guidelines on page 74. Then make a final copy to give to your readers, and proofread it.

CHAPTER 4

Writing Paragraphs

KINDS OF PARAGRAPHS

All well-written paragraphs follow certain rules. Not all paragraphs are alike, however. The kind of paragraph you write will depend on your purpose, or reason for writing.

In this chapter you will learn how to write three kinds of paragraphs:

KIND OF PARAGRAPH	PURPOSE	EXAMPLE
Narrative	To tell a story	A paragraph telling what happened when you entered your dog in a dog show
Descriptive	To describe	A paragraph describing your dog
Expository	To explain or give information	A paragraph explaining how to groom a dog

THE NARRATIVE PARAGRAPH

A narrative paragraph tells a story. The story may be true, or it may be made-up. It may have happened to the writer or to someone else.

The details (small pieces of information) in a narrative paragraph show the actions that took place, in the order in which they happened. They answer the question *What happened?*

Developing Narrative Paragraphs

4a. Develop a narrative paragraph with the details of an incident.

An *incident* is something that happens in a short time. Narrowing the amount of time to no more than a few hours makes it possible to tell a clear and interesting story in just one paragraph.

Read the following paragraph. The first sentence tells how the incident came about. The other sentences give details that help the reader picture the incident. Notice that the actions are arranged in the order in which they happened.

> On my birthday last year, my friend Rosa and I decided to go roller-skating in front of my house after school. When I got home from school, I put my skates on the front porch and went back inside to drink a glass of milk. A few minutes later I heard Rosa call my name, and I grabbed my skate key and rushed outside. Forgetting that my skates were on the porch, I tripped over them and went flying headfirst onto the sidewalk. Instead of spending the rest of the afternoon skating, I spent it having a cast put on my broken wrist.

Writing a Beginning, a Middle, and an Ending

A narrative paragraph should have three parts: a *beginning,* a *middle,* and an *ending.*

The *beginning* is the first sentence. Usually, it gives the time and place of the incident or tells how it came about. It should also catch the attention of the readers and make them want to keep reading.

Look at the narrative paragraph above. The first sentence tells how the incident came about: the writer and her friend decided to go skating. Notice too that this sentence tells the *setting* (the time and place) and the *characters* (the people). In just one sentence, the writer prepares her readers for her story.

The *middle* of the paragraph should give details that help the readers picture the important actions. It should make clear how each action leads to the next one, and it should show how a problem arises.

In the narrative paragraph above, the girl leaves her skates on the porch and goes back inside the house. This action leads to the problem: she forgets that she left her skates on the porch, trips over them, and breaks her wrist.

The *ending* should show how the problem is worked out. It should not go on to tell about other problems. For example, the problem of the broken wrist is worked out by a trip to the hospital. The writer does not tell about other problems such as having to wear a cast on her wrist. Those would be separate incidents.

Before You Write. Plan these three parts of your narrative paragraph:

- A beginning that catches the attention of the reader
- A middle that shows how a problem arises
- An ending that shows how the problem is worked out

Using Narrative Details

Narrative details are ones that help the reader picture the action of a story. They may be specific nouns, lively verbs, or precise adjectives and adverbs.

Read the following two paragraphs. The first one does not have enough details to help the reader picture the action. Notice how the narrative details in the second one make the story clearer and more lively.

WEAK   It was the last race. Jerry, Ralph, and I ran. Jerry led at first, but I won.

BETTER   The last race of Lincoln School's spring track meet pitted Jerry, Ralph, and me against one another. Jerry took the lead early, while Ralph and I paced ourselves, saving our strength for the final stretch. Just as we rounded the final curve, I passed Jerry, who had begun to slow down. I sensed, rather than saw, that Ralph was right behind me. As he passed me, he turned his head to look at me and broke his stride. With my eyes firmly on the flag at the finish line, I put on an extra burst of speed and won the race.

EXERCISE 1. Adding Narrative Details. Revise each of the following sentences. Add specific nouns, lively verbs, and precise modifiers. You may make up any details you want to add.

EXAMPLE   1. The dog went over the fence.
             1. *The excited Irish setter leaped over the chainlink fence.*

1. The girl kicked the can.
2. The cat walked along the fence.
3. The horse ran from the barn.
4. The waves moved toward the beach.
5. The car stopped.

Before You Write.   To plan a narrative paragraph,

- choose an incident that takes place in no more than a few hours.
- use the *5 W-How?* questions to gather details.
- arrange the events in time order.
- write an opening sentence that sums up the incident or tells how it came about.

EXERCISE 2. Writing a Narrative Paragraph. Choose one of the following subjects, or search your memory for an incident that your teacher and classmates will find interesting. Write a narrative paragraph; include narrative details that will help your readers picture the action of the story.

1. A surprise party
2. Your first airplane ride
3. Winning a prize
4. Taking care of a pet
5. A trip to the beach

PREWRITING   First decide who your readers will be. Then arrange the actions in time order, and write an opening sentence that sums up the incident, tells how it came about, or introduces the setting and characters.

WRITING   As you write, add narrative details to make the actions come to life. Remember to keep your readers in mind, and be sure to tell how the problem was worked out.

EVALUATING AND REVISING   Ask yourself: Have I included enough details so that my readers will be able to picture the actions? Have I arranged the actions in time order? Then use the questions in the chart below to judge your writing and the chart on page 72 to improve it.

PROOFREADING AND MAKING A FINAL COPY   Use the guidelines on page 27 to proofread your writing. Proofread again after you make a clean copy for your readers.

Evaluating and Revising Narrative Paragraphs

The following questions will help you evaluate, or judge, the narrative paragraphs you write. The chart on page 72 will help you improve your writing.

GUIDELINES FOR EVALUATING NARRATIVE PARAGRAPHS

Opening Sentence	1. Does the first sentence sum up the incident or tell how it came about?
Completeness	2. Are enough details given so that the reader can picture the actions?
Unity	3. Does every sentence help the reader understand what happened?
Order of Ideas	4. Are the actions arranged in time order?

Connections
Between Ideas

5. Do the ideas flow smoothly? Are they connected with transitions (first, next, later, etc.)?

Word Choice

6. Is the language colorful and lively? Is it neither too difficult nor too easy for the readers?

EXERCISE 3. Evaluating and Revising a Narrative Paragraph. Number your paper 1–6. Use the guidelines above to judge the following paragraph. Answer each question in writing. Then, on a separate piece of paper, revise the paragraph. Use the chart on page 72 for help. You may make up any details you want to add.

On the Fourth of July, my family and I went to the park after dinner. We found a place to sit. When it finally became dark, we watched the fireworks. One of the firecrackers landed on our blanket. My sister Dana put it out.

REVIEW EXERCISE A. Writing a Narrative Paragraph. Write a narrative paragraph. Use the following plan, or make a plan for a paragraph of your own. If you use this one, you may make up any details you want to add.

Opening sentence: Our drive home from Boise during a blizzard last February was the most frightening experience I have ever had.

Possible details:
 a. according to forecast, snow flurries expected
 b. couldn't see more than a few feet ahead
 c. roads covered with ice
 d. cars in ditches along road
 e. wind blowing, snow falling thickly
 f. could only drive ten miles per hour
 g. no one talking at all
 h. car sliding
 i. night coming
 j. four hours for a one-hour drive

THE DESCRIPTIVE PARAGRAPH

A descriptive paragraph creates a word picture of a person, an animal, a place, or a thing. The details are arranged in space order to help the readers picture the topic in their minds.

Developing Descriptive Paragraphs

4b. Develop a descriptive paragraph with concrete details and sense details.

Concrete details are things you can see or touch—persons, places, and things. Most often, they are specific nouns. For example, *rowboat* is a specific noun because it names one kind of boat. If you use the general word *boat* instead, some readers may picture a motorboat, others a canoe, and still others a sailboat.

Sense details are ones that appeal to the senses: sight, hearing, smell, touch, and taste. Read the following paragraph. Notice how the author uses concrete details and sense details to create a clear picture of the place.

> The sky was a ragged blaze of red and pink and orange, and its double trembled on the surface of the pond like color spilled from a paintbox. The sun was dropping fast now, a soft red sliding egg yolk, and already to the east there was a darkening to purple. Winnie, newly brave with her thoughts of being rescued, climbed boldly into the rowboat. The hard heels of her buttoned boots made a hollow banging sound against its wet boards, loud in the warm and breathless quiet. Across the pond a bullfrog spoke a deep note of warning.
>
> NATALIE BABBITT

EXERCISE 4. Gathering Concrete and Sense Details. Choose one of the following places or things, or choose one of your own. Spend several minutes studying the place or thing. (If you cannot see it from where you are, close your eyes and picture it in your mind.) Then list as many concrete and sense details about it as you can.

A bumblebee
A sunflower
A park
A spider web
A fish tank

Creating a Main Impression

The topic sentence of a descriptive paragraph tells who or what will be described. It also tells what stands out about the topic. This is the *main impression* that the writer wants to create. The other sentences give details that help the reader understand that idea.

In the following paragraph, the author wants the reader to see how sorry-looking the dog is. That is the main impression that she wants to create. Notice that all of the details help make that idea clear. Other details have been left out.

> It was about the sorriest-looking hound Matt had ever seen, with a coat of coarse brown hair, a mangy tail, and white patches on its face that gave it a clownish look. Its long pointed nose was misshapen with bumps and bristles. By the look of its ears, it had survived many battles. The instant it spied Matt, a ridge of hair went straight up on its back and it let out a mean growl.
>
> ELIZABETH GEORGE SPEARE

EXERCISE 5. Gathering Concrete and Sense Details. Think of a person or an animal you know well. Watch or think about this person or animal carefully. Then use the *5 W-How?* questions to make a list of concrete and sense details you could use to describe the person or animal.

EXAMPLE   *What* color is the person's hair?
           What is the person wearing?
           Where do I see (or picture) this person?
           What do I see (or picture) this person doing?
           What stands out about this person?
           How does this person move?

Before You Write. To plan a descriptive paragraph,

- study the topic carefully, or picture it in your mind.
- take notes on what you see, hear, taste, touch, and smell.
- decide what main impression you want to create. Remove any details that do not help make that idea clear.
- arrange the remaining details in space order or in the order that your senses noticed them.
- write a topic sentence that states your main impression.

EXERCISE 6. Writing a Descriptive Paragraph. Choose one of the lists of details you made for Exercises 4 and 5. Use the list to write a descriptive paragraph.

PREWRITING First decide what main impression you want to give. Then review your list and remove any details that do not help make that idea clear. Arrange the remaining ones in space order or in the order in which your senses noticed them, and write a topic sentence that states your main idea.

WRITING Keep your readers in mind as you write. Remember to use specific nouns and words that appeal to the senses and help the reader picture what is being described.

EVALUATING AND REVISING Ask yourself: Have I included enough details to make my main idea clear? Are the details arranged in space order? Then use the questions on page 86 and the chart on page 72 to judge and improve your writing.

PROOFREADING AND MAKING A FINAL COPY Use the guidelines on page 27 to correct your paragraph. Then make a final copy and proofread it.

Evaluating and Revising Descriptive Paragraphs

The following guidelines will help you judge the descriptive paragraphs you write. The chart on page 72 will help you improve your writing.

GUIDELINES FOR EVALUATING DESCRIPTIVE PARAGRAPHS

Topic Sentence	1. Does the topic sentence give a main impression of the topic?
Completeness	2. Are enough concrete and sense details given for the readers to picture the topic clearly?
Unity	3. Does every sentence help make the main idea clear?
Order of Ideas	4. Are the details arranged in space order?
Connections Between Ideas	5. Do the ideas flow smoothly? Are they connected with transitions (*above, to the left*, etc.)?
Word Choice	6. Are the words specific rather than general? Are they neither too difficult nor too easy for the readers?

REVIEW EXERCISE B. Writing a Descriptive Paragraph.
Choose one of the following situations. List as many concrete and sense details as you can think of to describe what you see, hear, taste, touch, or smell. Using these details and any others that occur to you, write a descriptive paragraph. Evaluate and revise your paragraph. Then proofread it and make a final copy.

1. You are watching fireworks from a blanket on the ground.
2. You are looking out a top-floor window of a tall building.
3. You are swimming in a crowded swimming pool.
4. You are standing on the stage at a school assembly.
5. You are eating lunch in the lunchroom.
6. You are riding your bike and get caught in a sudden storm.
7. You are studying in your room.
8. You are trying on some new clothes.
9. You are watching your pet play or sleep.
10. You are decorating a Christmas tree.

THE EXPOSITORY PARAGRAPH

An expository paragraph gives information or explains how to make or do something. This kind of paragraph often uses examples or step-by-step directions to make the main idea clear.

Before You Write.   To plan an expository paragraph

- use brainstorming, clustering, or the *5 W-How?* questions to gather details if you know your topic well. If not, use library sources.
- arrange the details in time order or in another order that will be easy for your readers to follow.
- write a topic sentence that states your main idea and catches the attention of your readers.

Developing with Details of a Process

4c. Develop an expository paragraph with details of a process.

A paragraph that explains how to make or do something is called a *process paragraph.* In this kind of paragraph, the details are the supplies and tools needed and the steps to be followed. The steps are arranged in time order so that the readers can learn how to do the process.

Read the following paragraph. Notice how the transitions (the underlined words) help the reader follow the order of the steps.

Finding a book of fiction in the library is easy. Suppose you want to find *The Witch of Blackbird Pond* by Elizabeth George Speare. First, find the part of the library where the books of fiction are kept. Those books are arranged in alphabetical order by the last name of the author. Next, find the books by authors whose last names begin with *S*. After you find the books by Elizabeth George Speare, look at their titles. All of the books by one author are arranged in alphabetical order by the first important word in the title. Before coming to *The Witch of Blackbird Pond,* you may find *The Bronze Bow,* which is arranged under *B,* not *T,* and *Sign of the Beaver.*

EXERCISE 7. Writing a Process Paragraph.   Write a paragraph explaining how to make or do something. You may choose one of the following topics or one of your own.

1. How to make popcorn (fruit salad, hard-boiled eggs)
2. How to do a magic trick
3. How to enter a contest
4. How to wash windows (bathe a dog, clean a fish tank)
5. How to get to your house from school

PREWRITING   Take notes as you carry out the process you have chosen. Be sure to include all of the supplies, tools, and steps needed. Arrange the steps in time order. Then write a topic sentence that will catch the attention of your readers.

WRITING   Keep in mind that your readers should be able to carry out the process by following your directions. Give the meanings of any words that your readers may not know.

EVALUATING AND REVISING   Ask yourself: Have I included all of the details needed? Have I arranged the steps in time order? Then use the questions on page 90 and the chart on page 72 to judge and improve your writing.

PROOFREADING AND MAKING A FINAL COPY   Use the guidelines on page 27 as you correct your writing. Proofread again after you make your final copy.

Developing with Examples

4d. Develop an expository paragraph with examples.

An *example* is one item that stands for many other items of the same kind. In the following paragraph, the writer gives examples of the kinds of information that can be found in a dictionary.

A dictionary contains much more than just meanings and spellings of words. It tells what part of speech a word is, how it is pronounced, and how it is used. It may also tell where a word came from. The word *potato,* for example, came into English from the Spanish language; the Spanish had borrowed it, with a slight change, from the Taino Indians of the West Indies. A dictionary may also give information about people and places. Under *Marshall, Thurgood,* for example, a reader can learn that this Supreme Court justice was born in 1908 and joined the court in 1967.

EXERCISE 8. Writing a Paragraph Using Examples. Write an expository paragraph using at least two examples. You may use the following topic sentence or choose a topic of your own. Use the library to find the information you need.

Topic Sentence: People have recorded many surprising world records.

PREWRITING   If you know your topic well, you may be able to use brainstorming or clustering to find examples to use. If not, use library resources (see Chapter 23). Think about your readers as you decide which examples to use. Then arrange the information in an order that will be easy for your readers to follow. If you do not use the sentence given above, write a topic sentence that states your main idea.

WRITING   Write freely, keeping your readers in mind. Try to use words that are neither too difficult nor too easy for your readers. Use connective words such as *for example, also,* and *another.*

EVALUATING AND REVISING   Ask yourself: Have I used enough examples to make my main idea clear? Will my readers find them interesting? Then use the questions on page 90 and the chart on page 72 to judge and improve your writing.

PROOFREADING AND MAKING A FINAL COPY   Use the guidelines on page 27 to correct your writing. Remember to proofread again after you make your final copy.

Evaluating and Revising Expository Paragraphs

Use the following questions to judge the expository paragraphs you write. The chart on page 72 will help you improve your writing.

GUIDELINES FOR EVALUATING EXPOSITORY PARAGRAPHS

Topic Sentence	1. Does the topic sentence clearly state one main idea? Does it catch the attention of the readers?
Completeness	2. Are enough details given to make the main idea clear? Are the details correct?
Unity	3. Does every sentence help make the main idea clear?
Order of Ideas	4. Are the ideas arranged in an order that will be easy for the readers to follow?
Connections Between Ideas	5. Do the ideas flow smoothly? Are they connected with transitions (*first, for example,* etc.)?
Word Choice	6. Are the words specific rather than general? Are they neither too difficult nor too easy for the readers?

EXERCISE 9. Studying a Writer's Revisions. The writer of the paragraph on page 88 made the following changes in his first draft. Study the changes carefully. Be prepared to tell whether each change (1) adds, (2) cuts, (3) replaces, or (4) rearranges information. Your teacher may also ask you to tell why you think the writer decided to make each change.

1 A dictionary ~~is a very valuable book.~~ It contains much

2 more than just meanings and spellings. It tells what part *of words* a *of speech*

3 word is, how it is pronounced, and *how it is* used. It may also tell

4 where a word came from. The word *potato,* for example,

5 came from the Spanish language *into English* the Spanish had borrowed it

6 *with a slight change* from the Taino Indians *of the West Indies* A dictionary may also give informa-

7 tion about people and places. Under *Thurgood,* *Marshall,* for

8 example, a reader can learn that *this Supreme Court Justice* he was born in 1908 and

9 joined the court in 1967.

REVIEW EXERCISE C. Writing an Expository Paragraph. For this review, your teacher may tell you to write a paragraph that explains a process or one that uses examples. You may instead be allowed to decide for yourself. First, choose a subject that is suited to an expository paragraph. Then plan and write an expository paragraph, keeping in mind your purpose for writing and your audience. Using the guidelines on page 90, evaluate and revise your paragraph.

CHAPTER 4 WRITING REVIEW

Writing Three Kinds of Paragraphs. Write each of the following three kinds of paragraphs. Use the steps in the writing process for prewriting, writing, evaluating, revising, and proofreading.

1. Write a *narrative paragraph* about something that happened to you at school this year.
2. Write a *descriptive paragraph* about a person, animal, place, or thing in your life.
3. Write an *expository paragraph* in which you teach a new classmate how to make or do something.

CHAPTER 5

Writing Exposition

COMPOSITIONS THAT INFORM OR EXPLAIN

The purpose of exposition is to explain or to give information. For example, you may give information about the Statue of Liberty. You may explain how to make a leather belt. You may explain why you like to sing in the chorus.

A *composition* is a group of closely connected paragraphs. Together, the paragraphs present and make clear one main idea about a topic.

Most of the writing you do for school gives information or explains. In this chapter you will use the steps of the writing process to write expository compositions.

PREWRITING

SEARCHING FOR SUBJECTS

5a. Search for subjects from your everyday life.

Sometimes your teacher will give you a subject to write about. At other times, you will be allowed to choose your own subject. To find a subject for an expository composition, begin by taking a close look at your everyday life.

(1) Think about what you know and what you like to do.

You may know how to build a model airplane or make a box kite or carve animals from wood. You may like to ride a horse, or paddle a canoe. All of these are possible subjects for an expository composition.

EXERCISE 1. Thinking About What You Know and What You Like to Do. For each of the following questions, write two possible composition subjects. Save your paper for use later in this chapter.

1. What do you know how to do well?
2. What do you like to do when you are not in school?
3. What do you like to read about or see on television or at the movies?
4. What have you always wondered about?

(2) Use your senses to observe the world around you.

Observing means paying close attention to what you see, hear, taste, touch, or smell.

You may see a television show about lizards. You may hear the whistle of a faraway train. You may feel the sand on the ocean floor slip from beneath your feet as the tide goes out. Just by observing, you have found three possible subjects: lizards, trains, and tides.

EXERCISE 2. Observing to Search for Subjects. Use your senses to observe the world around you. Then write at least two possible subjects for each of the following assignments. Save your answers.

EXAMPLE 1. Explain how to do something.
  1. *Packing for a move*
  Riding a bicycle safely

1. Give information about a place.
2. Explain how to make something.
3. Explain how to repair something.
4. Give information about an event.
5. Explain how to put something together.

(3) Use a writer's notebook.

Some writers keep a separate notebook in which they write the ideas they want to share with other people. You may want to keep a writer's notebook of your own.

Here is a page from one writer's notebook.

> Today Dad took Janell and me to the Farm Day Festival. Many different people showed how foods were prepared in 1900. One man was making syrup from sugar cane. He boiled the sugar cane in water in an eighty-gallon cast-iron kettle. As he stirred the sugar water, he had to keep skimming the pulp from the top to keep it clear. He also had to keep putting wood on the fire to keep the sugar water bubbling. At the end of the day we went back to where he was and tasted the syrup. It was good, but it didn't taste like the kind we buy in the store.

If these were your notes, you could use them to help explain how homemade syrup is made from sugar cane. They might also remind you of other foods you saw people making that day. That idea might make you think about why people still enjoy making homemade foods.

EXERCISE 3. Using a Writer's Notebook to Search for Subjects. Keep a writer's notebook for at least three days. Then read your notes. List one or two possible subjects for a composition. Save your answers.

(4) Use brainstorming to search for subjects.

Brainstorming helps you think of many subjects in a short time. When you brainstorm, you do not stop to judge your ideas. You simply list all the ideas that come to mind.

Suppose your teacher asks you to write about an event. Your brainstorming list might look like this:

the Olympics	the county fair
our last field trip	space shuttle landings
the school play	summer vacation
school elections	movies
Halloween	parents' night at school

EXERCISE 4. Using Brainstorming to Search for Subjects.
Brainstorm for subjects for a composition about an animal. List at least five subjects. Keep your list.

(5) Use clustering to search for subjects.

In clustering, write a word or phrase in the middle of a sheet of paper and circle it. Then write down as many ideas as you can. As you add each idea, circle it and connect it to the idea that made you think of it. Do not stop to judge your ideas.

Suppose, for example, that you are searching for subjects for a composition that explains how to do something. Your clustering diagram might look like this:

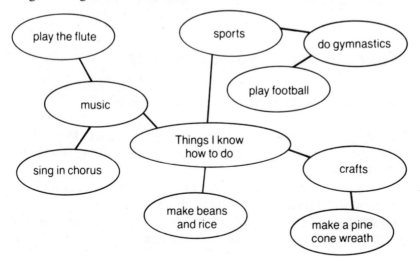

EXERCISE 5. Using Clustering to Search for Subjects.
Write *Things I know how to do* in the middle of a sheet of paper and circle it. Then write down as many ideas as you can, circling them and connecting them with lines. Save your paper.

CHOOSING A SUBJECT

5b. Choose one subject to write about.

The subject you write about should be one you know well. Your knowledge will help you make the subject clear to your readers.

> *Before You Write.* To choose a subject, ask yourself these questions:
> - Which subject am I most interested in?
> - Which subject do I know the most about?

EXERCISE 6. Choosing a Subject. Look over the lists of subjects you made for Exercises 2–5. Choose one subject for a composition that explains how to make or do something.

THINKING ABOUT YOUR AUDIENCE

5c. Think about the audience for your composition.

The people who read your writing are your audience. Most often, your classmates and your teacher will read the writing you do for school.

You want to make your writing clear and interesting for your readers. To do this, you must think about what your readers know and what they will find interesting. For example, suppose you are writing about telescopes. For your classmates, you might explain how to make a simple telescope. For adults, you might explain the study programs that the local planetarium offers.

> **Before You Write.** To think about your audience, ask yourself these questions:
>
> - How old are my readers?
> - What do they probably already know about my subject?
> - What might they be interested in learning about it?

EXERCISE 7. Thinking About Your Audience. Think about the subject you selected in Exercise 6 on page 96. Choose an audience for your composition, or use an audience that your teacher assigns. Think carefully about these readers. Then write your answers to the above questions about audience.

LIMITING THE SUBJECT

5d. Limit your subject to a topic.

A *subject* is a broad area; it has many different parts. Suppose you chose the subject "house plants." You could write a book about all the different parts of this subject.

For a short composition, a subject should be limited to one of its smaller parts. This smaller part is called a *topic*. You can explain a topic in several paragraphs. For example, you could explain the topic "how to grow an avocado plant from a seed" in a short composition.

CRITICAL THINKING:
Analyzing a Broad Subject

When you analyze something, you divide it into its smaller parts. Several questions can help you limit a subject by analyzing it.

What are *types* of the subject?
What are *examples* of the subject?
What are *uses* for the subject?
What *activities* can you do with the subject?
What *time periods* does the subject cover?

The subject "house plants," for example, can be divided in these ways:

Subject: House plants
Types: With flowers, without flowers
Examples: Spider plants, African violets, crocuses, avocados
Activities: Growing, watering, transplanting

Notice that to find a topic you do not have to list all the parts of a subject. The parts you know the most about will give you many different topics.

EXERCISE 8. Recognizing Subjects and Topics. Number your paper 1–10. After each number, write *S* if the item is a broad subject. Write *T* if it is limited enough to be a topic for a short composition. Save your paper.

EXAMPLE   1. Electricity
          1. *S*

1. How to make tacos
2. Sports
3. Why I enjoy camping
4. South Africa
5. Band instruments
6. Outer space
7. Making applesauce
8. Chipmunks
9. How to play checkers
10. Medicine

EXERCISE 9. Finding Limited Topics. Choose two of the subjects for which you wrote *S* in Exercise 8. Limit each subject to find three topics for a short composition. Use any or all of the questions at the top of this page.

EXERCISE 10. Finding Your Own Limited Topics. Limit the subject you chose in Exercise 6 on page 96. Use any or all of the questions on page 98. Then decide which limited topic you will explain or give information about.

GATHERING INFORMATION

5e. Gather information on your topic.

The way you gather information will depend on how much you already know about your topic. For some topics, you will need to use books and magazines to find information. For others, you can use your own knowledge. Use the following ways of gathering information if you know your topic well.

(1) List ideas and details about your topic.

Listing details is like brainstorming (page 94). You just list as many details as you can think of.

Suppose your topic is "how to grow an avocado plant from a seed." Your list might look like this:

avocados taste good	resting toothpicks on edge of jar
seed	potting soil
removing seed	clay pot and saucer
adding water to jar	placing in soil
small glass jar	watering soil
rinsing seed	I grew one for Uncle Fred
placing seed in warm, sunny spot	stem breaking through
adding water as it evaporates	placing plant in warm, sunny spot
pushing toothpicks into seed	watering once a week
	pinching off top

EXERCISE 11. Listing Details.   Choose one of the following topics. List as many details about it as you can.

1. Taking care of a cat (or dog)
2. How to reach the library from school

3. Moving to a new town
4. How to make a cassette tape from the radio
5. Studying for a test

(2) Use your writer's notebook to gather information on your topic.

On page 94 you learned about keeping a separate notebook for writing ideas. This kind of notebook can also be a good place to look for details about your topic.

EXERCISE 12. Using a Writer's Notebook. Read the writer's notes on page 94 again. List three details about the topic "making syrup from sugar cane."

EXERCISE 13. Using a Writer's Notebook. If you keep a writer's notebook, read it to look for details about your own topic. List all the details you find.

(3) Ask the *5 W-How?* questions about your topic.

Newspaper writers ask questions to find information. These questions are called the *5 W-How?* questions. They are *Who? What? When? Where? Why?* and *How?*

You can use these questions too. Suppose your topic is a field trip your class took. You could use the *5 W-How?* questions in this way:

> *Who* went on the field trip? Mr. Morales' sixth-grade class
> *What* place did the class visit? The Museum of Science and Industry
> *When* did the field trip take place? After lunch on October 24, 1988
> *Where* is the museum? At Lake Shore Drive and Fifty-third Street in Chicago
> *Why* did the class go there? To see the new exhibit on the space shuttle
> *How* did the class get there? On a school bus

EXERCISE 14. Using the *5 W-How?* Questions. Think of a field trip your class could or did take. Write a specific question about the trip for each of the *5 W-How?* questions. Then write your answer to each question.

EXERCISE 15. Gathering Information on Your Topic. Gather information on the topic you chose in Exercise 10 on page 98. Use any or all of these ways: listing details, reading your writer's notebook, asking the *5 W-How?* questions. Save your notes.

GROUPING INFORMATION

5f. Group the information you have gathered.

To *classify,* or group, information, you look for items that are alike in some way. Then you list them under a heading that explains how they are alike.

Look again at the list on page 99. These items are alike: seed, small glass jar, water, toothpicks, clay pot and saucer, potting soil. They are all materials needed for growing an avocado plant from a seed. They can be grouped under the heading "Materials."

The other items can be grouped under the headings that are shown here:

Sprouting the seed	*Planting the seed*
adding water to jar	stem breaking through
removing seed	placing in soil
rinsing seed	watering soil
placing seed in warm, sunny spot	pinching off top
pushing toothpicks into seed	placing plant in warm, sunny spot
adding water as it evaporates	watering once a week
resting toothpicks on edge of jar	

Notice that the writer removed two items: "avocados taste good" and "I grew one for Uncle Fred." These items would not help the writer explain the topic.

> *Before You Write.* To group your information, use these questions:
>
> ● Which items are alike?
> ● What heading explains how each group of items is alike?
> ● Should any items be removed because they will not help me give information about or explain my topic?

EXERCISE 16. **Grouping Information.** Group the following details about the topic "hurricane tips." Use these three headings: *Before the storm, During the storm, After the storm.* (*Hint:* A hurricane may cut off the power and water.)

Fill clean jars and bottles with water
Throw away spoiled food from refrigerator
Stay calm
Stock up on canned and dried foods, candles, batteries
Open a window on the side of the house away from the wind
Stay away from fallen power lines
Go to a room without windows
Listen for "all clear" on a battery radio
Stay home so repair workers can do their jobs

EXERCISE 17. **Grouping Your Own Information.** Group the information you listed for Exercise 15. Use the questions above. Save your paper.

ARRANGING IDEAS IN ORDER

5g. Arrange your ideas in order.

You want your readers to be able to follow your ideas. For the topic "how to make banana bread," for example, you would arrange your ideas in time order. That order would help your readers learn the order in which to do the steps. For the topic "my favorite movie," on the other hand, you might arrange your ideas from least important to most important. The last reason is usually the one the reader remembers best.

> **Before You Write.** To arrange your ideas in order, ask yourself these questions:
>
> ● Will my readers need to learn the steps in time order to be able to do them?
> ● Will my readers need to know certain information before they can understand other information?
> ● What is the most important idea that I want my readers to remember?

EXERCISE 18. Arranging Your Ideas in Order. Arrange the ideas for your composition in order. Use the above questions. Save your paper.

MAKING AN OUTLINE

5h. Make an outline for your composition.

An *outline* is a writing plan. It shows the order in which you plan to use your information. It also shows which items are main ideas and which ones are smaller parts of the main ideas.

Here is a sample outline. Notice how the items are labeled and how they are worded in a similar form.

GROWING AN AVOCADO PLANT FROM A SEED	title
I. Gathering materials	main heading (main idea)
A. Materials for sprouting	subheading (smaller part of the main idea)
B. Materials for planting	

II. Sprouting the seed   main heading
    A. Preparing the seed   subheading
    B. Taking care of the seed
III. Growing the plant   main heading
    A. Planting the seed   subheading
    B. Taking care of the plant

Notice that each main heading has two subheadings. A sheet of paper cannot be divided into fewer than two pieces. In the same way, a main heading cannot be divided into fewer than two subheadings.

Before You Write. When you make an outline, use these guidelines:

- Write a title that tells what your topic is.
- Use at least two main headings, though usually you will have three or more. Place a Roman numeral and a period before each one.
- Use at least two subheadings for each main heading. Place a capital letter and a period before each one.
- Begin each main heading and subheading with a capital letter.
- Indent the subheadings under the main headings.

EXERCISE 19. Using Outline Form. Copy the following outline. Fill in each of the six blanks with an item from the column on the right.

MAKING MACARONI AND CHEESE

I. Ingredients   Heating oven to 350°
    A. ——   4 ounces grated cheese
    B. ——   3 cups water
    C. 1 tablespoon butter   Baking for 45 minutes
    D. ——   4 ounces macaroni
    E. 1 cup milk   Steps to follow

II. ⸺
    A. Cooking macaroni
    B. ⸺
    C. Mixing ingredients
    D. ⸺

EXERCISE 20. Making Your Own Outline. Using the ideas you arranged in Exercise 18, make an outline for your composition. Use the guidelines in *Before You Write.*

WRITING

WRITING YOUR COMPOSITION

5i. **Write your composition. Include an introduction, a body, and a conclusion.**

When writing your composition, use your outline as a guide. As you write, you may think of ideas that do not appear on your outline. Include these ideas, too. You will be able to decide which ideas to keep later.

    A story has a beginning, a middle, and an ending. In the same way, a composition has three main parts: an introduction, a body, and a conclusion.

Writing the Introduction

Look at the sample composition on pages 107–108. The first paragraph is the *introduction.* Notice how the first sentence catches the reader's attention. The reader is curious to find out how to add a touch of the tropics to a room. Next, the introduction tells what the topic is (*Growing a houseplant from an avocado seed*). It also gives the main idea (*is an easy, interesting project*).

When You Write. In your introduction,

- catch the attention of your readers.
- tell what your topic is.
- give your main idea about the topic.

EXERCISE 21. Writing an Introduction. Write an introduction for the composition you outlined in Exercise 20.

Writing the Body

The body explains the main idea stated in the introduction. Look at the sample composition on pages 107–108. The body explains the steps to be taken in growing a houseplant from an avocado seed.

The red labels on pages 107–108 tell where the body begins and show each main heading and each subheading. Each paragraph in the body covers one main heading in the outline and has a topic sentence supported by details about the subheadings in the outline.

When You Write. As you write the body of your composition, keep these points in mind:

- Include enough information to make your main idea clear.
- Connect your ideas with transitions (*first, next, finally*) where they are needed. (See pages 67–69.)
- Make sure the information you give is correct.
- Use words and sentences that your readers will understand.

EXERCISE 22. Writing the Body. Write one paragraph for each main heading in your outline. Use a topic sentence for each paragraph, and support it with details about the subheadings.

Writing the Conclusion

Look at the sample composition on pages 107–108. The conclusion once again calls attention to the main idea about the topic. It does this by using the phrase *With very little work or money.* At other times a conclusion may, instead, sum up the main points in the body. You will study this kind of conclusion in Chapter 6.

EXERCISE 23. Writing the Conclusion. Write your conclusion. Call attention again to your main idea.

GROWING A HOUSE PLANT
FROM AN AVOCADO SEED

You can add a touch of the tropics to your room with something most people just throw away. Growing a house plant from an avocado seed is an easy, interesting project.

You will need two sets of materials. To get the seed to <u>germinate</u>, or sprout, you will need a small glass jar, three toothpicks, and water. To plant the seed once it has sprouted, you will need a large clay pot with a saucer. You will also need potting soil made of equal amounts of soil, sand, and peat moss.

Sprouting the seed is the first step. Remove the seed from the fruit and rinse it in water. <u>Next</u>, push the toothpicks into the seed around the middle. Rest the toothpicks on the edge of the glass jar with the pointed end of the seed up. <u>Then</u> put enough water into the jar to cover the bottom of the seed. Place the jar in a sunny spot, and check the seed daily. Roots grow from the bottom of the seed. Add water as it evaporates, to keep the bottom of the seed wet.

introduction

topic

main idea

body begins

Outline I. A.

term explained

Outline I. B.

Outline II. A.

Transitional words show order of steps

Outline II. B.

When the stem breaks through the top of
the seed, the seed is ready to plant. Fill the
clay pot with potting soil to within two inches
of the rim. Scoop a shallow hole in the soil,
and gently place the seed into the hole. Be
sure that the roots are below the surface of the
soil and the stem is above it. Pat the soil down
so that the seed stands up straight. Then place
the pot on the saucer and water the soil well.
To keep the plant green and shiny, place it in a
warm, sunny spot, and water it once a week.
When the stem is seven inches high, pinch off
two inches from the top. Continue to pinch off
the new top growth every week. This will
shape the avocado into a house plant.

Outline III. A.

Outline III. B.

The next time you spot an avocado in your
kitchen, ask for the seed. With very little work
or money, you can bring a bright spot of
greenery to even the coldest climate.

conclusion

EVALUATING

EVALUATING YOUR COMPOSITION

5j. **Evaluate your composition.**

When you evaluate your composition, you judge what is right
about it and what is wrong about it. The questions below will help
you take this next step in the writing process.

Read each guideline question and answer it honestly. When
you answer no, something needs to be changed.

GUIDELINES FOR EVALUATING EXPOSITORY COMPOSITIONS

Introduction	1. Does the first paragraph catch the attention of my audience?
	2. Does it (a) tell what my topic is and (b) give my main idea about the topic?
Body	3. Do the paragraphs in the body explain my main idea fully and accurately?
	4. Is each main heading and subheading in my outline covered?
	5. Does each paragraph include a topic sentence that is supported by details?
	6. Have I arranged my ideas in an order that will be easy to follow?
	7. Have I used words and sentences that will help my audience understand my topic?
Conclusion	8. Does the conclusion call attention to my main idea by stating it in a different way or by summing up main points?

EXERCISE 24. Evaluating Your Composition. Using the above guidelines, evaluate the composition you wrote for Exercises 21, 22, and 23. Mark the places where you think changes should be made.

REVISING

REVISING YOUR COMPOSITION

5k. Revise your composition, making any changes needed to improve it.

Now that you have evaluated your composition, you are ready to revise it. The chart below shows how you can make improvements by adding to, cutting, or reordering (rearranging) your composition.

REVISING EXPOSITORY COMPOSITIONS

PROBLEM	KIND OF CHANGE	REVISION
The introduction does not give the main idea.	Add	Add a sentence that gives the main idea.
The main idea is not explained fully.	Add	Add ideas and details that will make the explanation more complete.
An idea or a detail does not support the topic sentence of a paragraph.	Cut	Remove any ideas or details that do not help make the main idea clear.
The order of ideas is not easy to follow.	Reorder	Move a sentence or a phrase that interrupts the order of ideas.
The steps in an explanation are difficult to follow.	Add	Add words like *first, next, finally.*

EXERCISE 25. Studying a Writer's Revisions. The person who wrote the sample composition on pages 107–108 made these changes in one paragraph of the first draft. Tell whether each change (1) adds, (2) cuts, or (3) reorders information. Also tell why you think the writer made each change.

1   *Remove the seed from the fruit and*   *it*
     Sprouting the seed is the first step. ˄Rinse ~~the seed~~ in water⊙

2   *Next* ˄ *push*   *the seed*
     ~~and then put~~ the toothpicks into ˄it. ~~They go~~ around the

3   middle.˄ Then put enough water into the jar to cover the

4   *of the seed*   *glass jar with the pointed side of the seed up.*
     bottom.˄ ~~Rest the toothpicks on the edge of the jar.~~ Place the

5   *the seed daily*
     jar in a warm, sunny spot, and check ˄it ~~every day~~. Add water

6   *to keep the bottom of the seed wet* ⊙
     as it evaporates˄

EXERCISE 26. Revising Your Own Composition. Using the Guidelines for Revising Expository Compositions, improve the composition you evaluated in Exercise 24. You may also want to ask a classmate to read your writing.

PROOFREADING

PROOFREADING YOUR COMPOSITION

5l. Proofread your composition.

When you proofread, you read your writing several times to make sure that it is correct. Each time, you check for a different kind of error: spelling, capital letters, punctuation marks, grammar, or usage.

EXERCISE 27. Proofreading Your Composition. After you have finished revising your composition, read it several times. Check it carefully for correctness. Use the Guidelines for Proofreading on page 27 and the Revising and Proofreading Symbols on pages 24 and 26.

MAKING A FINAL COPY

MAKING A FINAL COPY

5m. Make a final copy of your composition.

Your final copy is the clean copy you give to your audience. Follow your teacher's directions for preparing this copy. Then proofread it carefully to make sure that you have copied it correctly.

EXERCISE 28. **Making Your Final Copy.** Following your teacher's directions, make your final copy. Proofread this copy carefully before you give it to your audience.

CHAPTER 5 WRITING REVIEW

Writing an Expository Composition. Use the steps of the writing process to write an expository composition. Use the information in this chapter as you plan, write, evaluate, revise, proofread, and make a final copy of your expository composition.

CHAPTER 6

Writing Exposition

REPORTS AND
COMPOSITIONS OF OPINION

For school, you often write about subjects that you have learned about in the library, books that you have read, and ideas that seem true to you. In this chapter you will use the writing process to write these three kinds of compositions.

WRITING LIBRARY REPORTS

A library report brings together facts about a topic. A *fact* is information that can be proved to be true. For example, it is a fact that Helen Keller was born in 1880. The facts in a library report come from sources such as books and magazines.

PREWRITING FOR LIBRARY REPORTS

6a. Choose and limit the subject of your report.

You begin prewriting for a library report as you do for all your writing. You first choose a subject and narrow it.

Personal subjects such as a trip you took are not suitable for a library report. You would not be able to find facts about your trip in the library. However, you may have seen unusual plants on your trip. "Unusual plants" is a possible subject for a report. You could find facts about this subject in the library.

Most often, your classmates and teacher will read your reports. Ask yourself: What do my readers already know about? What might they like to know about?

A general subject covers too many ideas for a short report. For example, books could be written on the different kinds of unusual plants. You could divide this subject into examples. You might think of redwood trees, bamboo plants, and Spanish moss. Any of these plants could be a topic, or a smaller part of the subject, for a report. (For more help on limiting a subject to a topic, see pages 12–14.)

Check your school library. Make sure that you can find at least three books or magazines with facts about your topic. If not, you will need to choose another topic. (See Chapter 23 for help in using the library.)

Before You Write. To choose and limit a subject for your report, follow these hints:

- Choose a subject that interests you and about which you can find facts.
- Choose a subject that will interest your audience.
- Limit your subject by dividing it into smaller parts.
- Choose a topic about which your library has sources.

EXERCISE 1. **Choosing a Subject.** Number your paper 1–10. After each number, write *yes* if the subject would suit a short report. Write *no* if it would not. Be prepared to explain your answers.

EXAMPLE 1. Our move to a new town
           1. *No—too personal*

1. My life as an only child
2. Astronauts
3. China
4. Our trip to Florida
5. Gold mining
6. Planets
7. Why I enjoy swimming
8. Bridges
9. Our last field trip
10. The best dog I ever owned

EXERCISE 2. Limiting Subjects.   The following subjects cover too many ideas for a short report. Write at least three topics for each subject. Use the hints on pages 97–98.

EXAMPLE   1. *Subject:* The Middle Ages in Europe
        1. *Topics: Knights, Cathedrals, Guilds*

1. Minerals
2. Egypt
3. Famous scientists
4. American Indians
5. Mountains
6. South America
7. Birds
8. Storms
9. Sea mammals
10. Inventions

EXERCISE 3. Choosing a Topic.   Choose one of the following topics for a report, or limit a subject of your own to find a topic. Your teacher may want to check your choice.

1. Why the sea is salty
2. Redwood trees
3. Harriet Tubman
4. The invention of radio
5. The bald eagle
6. The first modern Olympics
7. Giant pandas
8. The pyramids of Egypt
9. How the Eskimos live
10. Cesar Chávez

6b. Search for information about your topic.

To find information for a library report, you search for facts. In this search, you will use several methods.

One method is the *5 W-How?* questions: *Who? What? When? Where? Why?* and *How?*. The ones you use will depend on your topic. For example, for a report on bamboo, one student, Mai, asked these three questions: *What* is bamboo? *How* is it used? *Where* does it grow? Then she looked for facts to answer those questions.

An encyclopedia will give you some facts for your report. It may also list other books in which you can find more facts. (See pages 420–21 for help in using an encyclopedia.)

The subject cards in the card catalog (see pages 413–15) may list books in which you can find facts. The *Readers' Guide to Periodical Literature* (see pages 423–24) may list magazine articles in which you can find facts.

Before You Write. To search for facts, follow these suggestions:

● Ask the *5 W-How?* questions about your topic.
● Read an encyclopedia article about your topic.
● Use the card catalog and the *Readers' Guide*.

EXERCISE 4. Asking Questions About Your Topic. Using the *5 W-How?* questions, write at least three questions about your topic. Save your list.

6c. Take notes on your sources of information.

List each source in which you find facts. Make a separate 3- by 5-inch note card or sheet of paper for each source. List the following information, using the form and punctuation shown in the sample cards.

For books:
1. Name of author (last name first)
2. Title of book (underlined)
3. Place of publication
4. Name of publisher and year of publication

For encyclopedias:
1. Name of author of article, if given (last name first)
2. Title of article (in quotation marks)
3. Title of encyclopedia (underlined)
4. Year of edition

For magazine and newspaper articles:

1. Name of author, if given (last name first)
2. Title of article (in quotation marks)
3. Title of magazine or newspaper (underlined)
4. Date of magazine or newspaper
5. Page number(s) of article

magazine —

> Bruno, Mary. "A New
> Guide to Patient Power."
> *Newsweek* 25 Nov. 1985:
> 78.

encyclopedia —

> Pohl, Richard W.
> "Bamboo." *World Book
> Encyclopedia*. 1985 ed.

book —

> Thompson, Vivian L.
> *Hawaiian Tales of
> Heroes and Champions*.
> New York: Holiday
> House, 1971.

Sample Source Cards

EXERCISE 5. Making Source Cards. Make source cards for the following sources. Study the sample cards to be sure you are using the correct form.

1. An article titled "Baltimore Oriole" by Albert Wolfson. It is in the 1985 edition of the *World Book Encyclopedia*.
2. A book titled *Good Manners for Girls and Boys* by Martha Whitmore Hickman. It was published in 1985 in New York by Crown.
3. An article titled "The Great Lakes of Oklahoma" by Cyndi Maddox. It is in the *Southern Living* magazine of May 1985 on pages 128–33.

EXERCISE 6. Making Source Cards for Your Own Sources.
In your library, find at least three books or magazines with facts that will answer your questions from Exercise 4. Using the form shown on page 117, list these three books or magazines.

6d. Take notes about the information you read.

Note the key facts you find. Key facts are ones that answer your questions about the topic. Use a separate index card or sheet of paper for *each* key fact.

Do not copy the author's sentences. Use your own words. You need not use complete sentences. Use your own abbreviations. Just be sure your notes are clear to you.

Mai read this paragraph for her report.

> BAMBOO is a giant grass noted for the usefulness of its hollow woody stem. Bamboos are distantly related to wheat, oats, and barley. But unlike these crop grasses, most bamboos are of giant size. Some may stand as much as 120 feet (37 meters) high and have stems 1 foot (30 centimeters) in diameter. Bamboo stems are used as fishing poles and in ornamental screens, cooking utensils, tools, baskets, and building materials.
>
> THE WORLD BOOK ENCYCLOPEDIA

These are the notes she took:
1. giant grass
2. stems hollow and woody
3. related to wheat, oats, barley

4. size—up to 120 ft. (37 m) tall, 1 ft. (30 cm) thick
5. uses—fishing, building, screens, pots, tools, baskets

Mai made a card for each of the five facts. At the top of the card she wrote the question that the fact answered. At the bottom she wrote the title and author of the source. Here is one of her cards:

> *What is bamboo?*
>
> *— — giant grass*
>
>
> *Pohl, World Book*

EXERCISE 7. Taking Notes.   Take notes for your report. Use the sources you found for Exercise 6. Make at least five note cards, putting only one fact on each card.

6e. Arrange your notes and make an outline.

After you have completed your reading and note taking, you are ready to plan your report.

First, put all the cards that answer one of your questions into a separate pile. For example, Mai made three piles of cards. All the cards in one pile had the question *What is bamboo?* on them. The second pile had all the cards with the question *Where does it grow?* In the third pile were all the cards with *How is it used?*

Next, take out any cards that repeat a fact. Then group the cards in each pile. (See pages 101–102 for help with grouping.)

Third, think about your readers. Which facts will they need to know in order to understand the other facts? Mai decided her readers would first need to know what bamboo is and where it grows. These facts would help readers understand how it is used.

Finally, make an outline. To do this, change each question into a main heading. Then give each group of facts a title that explains how the facts are alike. These titles will be your subtopics. Also, give your outline a title. (See pages 103–104 for help with making an outline.)

Here is a sample outline:

BAMBOO

I. What bamboo is
   A. Size
   B. Strength
II. Where it grows
   A. Most in Asia
   B. Most acres in India
   C. Greatest number of different kinds in China
III. How it is used
   A. Household items
   B. Buildings
   C. Clothing
   D. Food

Before You Write. To arrange the notes for your report,

- sort your note cards into piles.
- read the cards in each pile again.
- arrange your cards in order.
- make an outline for your report.

EXERCISE 8. Arranging Your Notes and Making an Outline.
Arrange the note cards you made for Exercise 7, using the hints above. Then make an outline for your report.

WRITING A FIRST DRAFT

6f. Using your outline, write your first draft.

Read the following sample library report. The red labels mark the introduction, the body, and the conclusion. (See pages 105–107 for help in writing these parts in your report.) Notice the *bibliography,* the works cited, at the end of the report. In your report, this list should be on a separate page.

BAMBOO

The only bamboo most Americans ever see is a fishing pole. For half of the people in the world, however, this plant is an important natural resource.   *introduction*

Although it looks like a tree, bamboo is actually a grass. It is related to grasses such as wheat and oats. Most bamboo plants are very large; some kinds grow up to 120 feet (37 meters) tall and up to 1 foot (30 centimeters) thick. Joints along the hollow woody stems make the plant almost as strong as steel.   *body*

Bamboo is native to every continent except Europe and Antarctica. Most of the 10 million tons grown each year come from Asia. India grows 25 million acres each year, more than any other country. China grows more different kinds than any other country—more than 300, in fact.

Bamboo has more uses than any other plant on earth. It is used to make household items such as beds, cups, chopsticks, tools, and baskets. In buildings, it is used to make concrete stronger or to take the place of wood. Many Asians wear shoes and hats made of bamboo. Some kinds of bamboo are even used as food. People cook the young shoots and eat them as a vegetable. The shoots are also the main food of the giant pandas of China.

Bamboo is one of the world's most valu-　conclusion
able plants. Without it, life would be very
different for millions of people.

Works Cited

"Battling a Bamboo Crisis." *Time* 28 Nov. 1983: 94.
"Kosuge Shochikudo: The Language of Bamboo." *American Craft* June/July 1982: 10–11.
Pohl, Richard W. "Bamboo." *World Book Encyclopedia*. 1985 ed.
Simmons, James C. "The Most Useful Plant in the World." *Audubon* Jan. 1986: 58–69.

EXERCISE 9. Writing Your First Draft. Write the first draft of your report in your own words. Follow your outline, and try to make your ideas clear to your readers. List your sources in alphabetical order at the end of the report.

EVALUATING AND REVISING LIBRARY REPORTS

6g. Evaluate and revise your report.

As you evaluate your report, look for places where it could be improved. The guidelines below will help you evaluate your report. After you evaluate your report, revise it by making changes where they are needed. You may also want to exchange papers with a classmate to get another opinion.

GUIDELINES FOR EVALUATING LIBRARY REPORTS

Topic	1. Is the topic narrow enough for a short report?
Facts	2. Is the report based on facts from library sources? Are enough facts included to make the main idea clear?
Order	3. Are the ideas arranged in an order that is easy to follow?
Language	4. Is the report written in the writer's own words? Are the words and kinds of sentences suitable for the readers?

Introduction	5. Does the introduction catch the readers' interest? Does it tell what the topic is and give the writer's main idea?
Body	6. Does each paragraph in the body have a topic sentence? Do the facts given help make that sentence clear?
Conclusion	7. Does the conclusion either call attention again to the main idea or sum up the main points?
Sources	8. Are the sources listed correctly at the end of the report? Are they in alphabetical order?

When You Revise. To revise your report, ask yourself:

- If there is not enough information about the topic, what should be *added?*
- If information is not clear, which sentences or details should be *cut* or *reordered?*
- If information is not exact, which general words should be *replaced* with more specific ones?

EXERCISE 10. Evaluating and Revising Your Report.   Using the Guidelines for Evaluating Library Reports, evaluate your report. Then revise it, using the chart on page 110 and the *When You Revise* suggestions above.

PROOFREADING LIBRARY REPORTS

6h. Proofread your report and make a final copy.

After you revise your report, proofread it carefully. Make sure you have correctly copied facts such as numbers and dates. Then make a final copy for your readers. Proofread this copy, too.

EXERCISE 11. Proofreading and Making a Final Copy. Using the guidelines on page 27, proofread your report. Make a final copy for your readers, and proofread it again.

WRITING BOOK REPORTS

A book report tells what a book is about. It also tells why the writer of the report did or did not like the book.

PREWRITING HINTS FOR BOOK REPORTS

1. *Choose a book that will interest your audience.* Most often, your classmates and teacher will read your book reports. Choose a book they will enjoy reading about.

2. *Read the book carefully.* Pay close attention as you read. You not only want to enjoy the book, you also want to be able to tell your readers about it.

3. *Take notes on the content of the book.* First write down what you remember about the book. Then look back through the book and note important details you may have forgotten.

For a *novel,* a made-up story, note the setting (time and place). Also note the names of the most important characters. Tell about some of the most important events, but do not give away the ending. For a *biography,* the true story of a person's life, give the important dates of the person's life. Explain why he or she is important. Tell about some of the most important events in the person's life. For other *nonfiction* (true) books, explain why the subject is important. Give some of the writer's most important ideas about the subject.

4. *Take notes on what you thought about the book.* You want to help your readers decide whether they would like to read the book. Do not just tell whether you liked the book; give your reasons, too.

5. *Arrange your ideas in order.* Your teacher may give you a format to use. If not, first write down the title and author of the book. Next, plan to tell what the book is about, using the same order the author uses. Then plan to tell what you thought of the book and why.

EXERCISE 12. Planning a Book Report. Choose a book to report on and read it carefully. Then make notes on its content and on what you thought of it. Arrange your ideas in order.

WRITING A FIRST DRAFT

Read the following sample book report. As you read, ask yourself these questions:

1. What is the book about?
2. What important events does the writer tell about?
3. What does the writer think of the book?
4. How does the writer explain what he thinks about it?

A Report on *The Lion, the Witch,*
and the Wardrobe

The Lion, the Witch, and the Wardrobe is a novel by C. S. Lewis. The events happen during World War II, partly in England and partly in the magic land of Narnia. It follows the adventures of four children who are brothers and sisters: Peter, Susan, Edmund, and Lucy. The children have been sent to live with a wise professor who owns a huge old house in the country.

Lucy, the youngest child, finds the land of Narnia when she explores a kind of closet. No human beings live in Narnia, only animals and strange creatures such as fauns. From one faun, Lucy learns that the land is under the spell of the evil White Witch. As long as the witch rules, it will always be winter in Narnia, but Christmas will never come. The witch also has the power to change herself into anything she chooses and to turn living things into statues.

At first, the older children do not believe Lucy's stories about Narnia. One day, however, they find themselves there with her. The beaver family warns them that the witch will try to kill them. Only Aslan the lion, who is on his way to Narnia, can break the witch's spell.

Hoping that the witch will reward him, Edmund, the younger boy, tells her that Aslan is coming. Instead of rewarding

Edmund, however, the witch plans to kill him. When Aslan offers himself to the witch in place of Edmund, Peter must fight the witch alone.

I liked this book very much. The children act and talk the way real brothers and sisters do. The story is full of action and adventure, and the suspense builds to an exciting high point. I was glad to learn that this is just the first of seven books about Narnia. I plan to read every one of them.

EXERCISE 13. Writing Your First Draft. Write the first draft of the book report you planned for Exercise 12.

EVALUATING AND REVISING BOOK REPORTS

Read your first draft, keeping in mind the two purposes of a book report. A report should tell what the book is about. This includes the important events and ideas that the author wrote about. A report should also tell what you (the writer of the report) thought about the book. Why did you like or dislike it? Use the following guidelines to evaluate your book report. Then revise it, making changes where they are needed.

GUIDELINES FOR EVALUATING BOOK REPORTS

Title and Author	1. Are the title of the book and the name of the author given early in the report?
Characters	2. Are the names of the most important characters given?
Content	3. Does the information given suit the kind of book? (See page 124.)
	4. Are only the most important events or ideas given?
Reasons	5. Does the writer tell why she or he liked or disliked the book?

EXERCISE 14. Evaluating and Revising Your Book Report. Using the Guidelines for Evaluating Book Reports, evaluate the book report you wrote for Exercise 13. Then revise it by referring to the chart on page 110 and to the *When You Revise* suggestions on page 123.

PROOFREADING AND MAKING A FINAL COPY

Proofread your book report carefully. Then make a final copy for your readers, and proofread it.

EXERCISE 15. Proofreading and Making a Final Copy. Using the Guidelines for Proofreading on page 27, check your writing. Then, following your teacher's directions, make a final copy. Proofread this copy as well.

WRITING COMPOSITIONS OF OPINION

An *opinion* is an idea that seems true to the person who believes it. For example, you may believe that dogs make better pets than cats do. Unlike a fact, an opinion cannot be proved to be true. It can, however, be explained by a reason or reasons. For example, you could point out that dogs can protect their owners. That reason would help explain your opinion.

PREWRITING HINTS FOR COMPOSITIONS OF OPINION

1. *Choose an opinion that will interest your audience.* Most often, your readers will be your teacher and classmates. Choose an opinion they will want to read about. For example, your readers may already think that a cat can be a good pet. Instead, you might write about why you believe that owning two cats is better than owning just one.

2. *List at least three reasons that explain your opinion.* Think about what you have seen, heard, or read that makes you think that your opinion is true. For example, you may enjoy seeing your two cats play together. That may be one of your reasons.

3. *Use the 5 W-How? questions to find details about each reason.* For example, you might ask, *When* do the cats play together? *How* do they play together? *Where* do they play together? Your answers would help make your reason clear to your readers.

4. *List your reasons in order.* Most often, the last reason is the one a reader remembers best. Think about which reason you want your readers to remember. Then list your reasons in order, from least important to most important.

EXERCISE 16. Planning a Composition of Opinion. Choose an opinion that you think will interest your readers. List at least three reasons that explain why it seems true to you. Next, use the *5 W-How?* questions to find details about each reason. Then list your reasons in order, from least important to most important.

WRITING A FIRST DRAFT

In your introduction, state your opinion. Use one of your reasons as the topic sentence for each paragraph of the body. Build each paragraph with details that will make the reason clear to your readers. In the conclusion, sum up your main points. To do this, remind your readers of your reasons, using different words and leaving out the details.

Read the following sample composition of opinion. Note the three main parts: the introduction, the body, and the conclusion.

TWO CATS ARE BETTER THAN ONE

When I hear the saying "Two heads are better than one," I picture two cats, not two people. I think owning two cats is better than owning just one for several reasons. *introduction*

First, two cats are good company for each other. During the week, my mother works and I go to school. My two cats, Muffin and Stormy, are left alone each day, but they do not get lonely. They always have each other. They even share a cage at the vet's when my mother and I go away on a trip. *body* *first reason*

Second, two cats are more company for their owner. When one wants to be left alone, *second reason* the other is willing to stay with me. Muffin likes to jump into my lap right after dinner, while Stormy checks to see if any food is left. Stormy likes to curl up on my desk when I do my homework later in the evening. Meanwhile, Muffin takes a long bath in private.

Finally, two cats are much more fun to watch than one. At least once a day Stormy and Muffin race through the house, leaping over the furniture, each other, and me. It's especially funny to see both of them turning in circles at the same time when I am giving them their evening snack. — third reason

By itself, a cat might get lonely. It would not be as much company for its owner or as much fun to watch. For both the animals and the owner, therefore, two cats are better than one. — conclusion

EXERCISE 17. Writing Your First Draft. Write your first draft. Give at least three reasons for your opinion. Make each reason clear by using details.

EVALUATING AND REVISING COMPOSITIONS OF OPINION

Use the following guidelines to evaluate your writing. Then revise your composition to correct any problems you find.

GUIDELINES FOR EVALUATING COMPOSITIONS OF OPINION

Introduction   1. Does the introduction catch the readers' interest? Does it include the writer's opinion?

Body	2. Does each paragraph in the body begin with a topic sentence that states a reason? Are at least three reasons given? Are details given to make each reason clear?
Order	3. Are the reasons arranged in order from least important to most important?
Conclusion	4. Does the conclusion sum up the writer's main points?
Language	5. Do the words and kinds of sentences used fit the readers?

EXERCISE 18. Evaluating and Revising Your Composition. Using the Guidelines for Evaluating Compositions of Opinion, evaluate your composition. Revise it, using the chart on page 110 and the suggestions on page 123.

PROOFREADING AND MAKING A FINAL COPY

Proofread your revised composition carefully. Then make a final copy for your readers, and proofread it.

EXERCISE 19. Proofreading and Making a Final Copy. Using the guidelines on page 27, check your writing. Then, following your teacher's directions, make a final copy. Proofread this copy as well.

CHAPTER 6 WRITING REVIEW

Applying What You Know About Reports and Compositions of Opinion. Use the steps of the writing process to do any of the following activities:

1. Write a library report on a new topic.
2. Write a book report. Use a book different from the one you wrote about in this chapter. For example, if you reported on a novel, choose a biography.
3. Write a composition of opinion on a new topic.

CHAPTER 7

Writing Letters

SOCIAL LETTERS, BUSINESS LETTERS, AND FORMS

Do you look forward to getting mail? Isn't it fun to read magazines, look through catalogs, or, even better, get a letter from a friend or relative?

There are many situations in your life that require letter-writing skills. You might write personal news to distant family and friends. You might order something through the mail. You might want to write to your local newspaper about an important topic. This chapter will help you learn to write proper social and business letters and to complete forms.

THE SOCIAL LETTER

Have you ever put off writing a friendly letter because you felt you had nothing to say? Almost everyone has. Sometimes you want to write just because you are thinking of a friend, not because you have exciting news to tell. Don't postpone writing. When you begin writing, you will find things to say. You can always share one or two experiences that might interest your friend. You may also have thoughts you would like to share.

PREWRITING

DECIDING WHAT TO SAY

7a. In a friendly letter, write about things that interest you and the person to whom you are writing.

3415 Tangerine Street
Largo, FL 33540
September 12, 1988

Dear Pat,

Do you remember how much I admired your ten-speed bicycle when you got it last year? For my birthday last month, my parents gave me a silver 26-inch ten-speed bike. I really love it!

My Dad and I are talking about joining a bicycle tour group that goes riding in the country for about fifteen miles each Saturday. I'll let you know if we join and where we tour.

Are you enjoying your new school? Write and tell me all about it.

Your friend,
Lee

Model Friendly Letter

As a first step, think about what you and the receiver of the letter have in common. If you are writing to someone your age, you could write about school, your friends, and after-school activities and hobbies. If you are writing to a neighborhood friend who has moved, you could write about neighborhood activities. When writing to a relative, you could share family news as well as news about yourself. Including your own thoughts and feelings about any of these subjects can give you plenty to say.

You will also find topics in the letter you are answering. Look back at what your friend has said. Comment on parts of the letter and answer all your friend's questions.

EXERCISE 1.Finding Topics to Write About. Read the letter on page 132, and list the items of news that you could comment on if you answered the letter.

WRITING

WRITING A FRIENDLY LETTER

7b. Write friendly letters neatly on appropriate stationery.

You may use either white or colored paper of good quality and blue or black ink. Typing a friendly letter is all right if you can type well.

If you write, be neat. A letter that is blotched with inky fingerprints or filled with crossed-out words and erasures may be hard to read or give your reader the impression you do not really care about writing to him or her.

A short note should be centered on the page. Keep equal margins on the sides and on the top and bottom of a long letter.

7c. Follow generally accepted rules for the form of a friendly letter.

The model form shows you where to place the five parts of a friendly letter and how to punctuate them. Study the form and the instructions which follow.

709 *Folsom Street*
1 *Huntsville, AL 35802*
November 23, 1988

2 *Dear James,*

3

4 *Sincerely,*

5 *Tamara*

Model Form of a Friendly Letter

1. Heading

In the upper right corner, write your street address on one line; your city, state, and ZIP code number on the second line; and the date on the third. Do not use any punctuation between the state and the ZIP code number. No punctuation is needed at the end of each line. Notice that only the name of the state is abbreviated.

2. Salutation (Greeting)

Write the salutation, or greeting, a short space below the heading, even with the left margin. In a friendly letter, the salutation begins with *Dear* ____. Put a comma after the salutation.

3. Body

Indent the first line of the body of the letter, and use the same indentation for the first line of each following paragraph. Other lines should begin at the left margin.

4. Closing

Begin the closing a little to the right of center, even with the heading. Capitalize the first word of the closing, and put a comma at the end. The closing of a friendly letter is most often *Your friend, Love, Sincerely,* or something similar.

5. Signature

Sign your first name directly beneath the closing. Do not put any punctuation after your name.

EXERCISE 2. Writing a Friendly Letter. Think of someone who would like to get a letter from you. Write a short letter that would interest that person. Write about real experiences, such as family celebrations, school projects, sports activities, vacation plans, and so on.

ADDRESSING AN ENVELOPE

Address the envelope for your letter with care. Use ink, not pencil or marker pen, which can smear. Double-check the address and ZIP code number. Always put your return address on the envelope in case the letter has to be returned to you.

When you address an envelope, place the name and address of the receiver just below the middle and to the left of the center of the envelope. Place your name and address in the upper left-hand corner. Study the example that follows.

Nancy Aumiller
1701 Pine Tree Lane
Kirkland, WA 98033

Mr. Greg Kaneshige
2130 Jordon Drive
Sylman, CA 91342

A Model Envelope

Every word in the address begins with a capital letter. Remember to put a comma between the city and the state. Notice that the ZIP code number is written after the state and that there is no comma between the state and the ZIP code.

EXERCISE 3. **Addressing an Envelope.** Address an envelope for the letter you wrote in Exercise 2.

WRITING A SOCIAL NOTE

7d. Social notes are short letters, such as thank-you notes, written on certain social occasions.

Social notes are not just for adults. When you receive a gift or a favor, you should write a note. The social note has the same form as a friendly letter.

The Thank-You Note

A thank-you note should be written on personal stationery. The main purpose of the note is to express thanks for a gift or favor, but the note may also include a paragraph on another subject. Try to write the note as soon as possible after you receive the gift or favor.

1113 South Carr Avenue
Crested Butte, CO 81224
December 3, 1988

Dear Aunt Nell,

Thank you so much for the beautiful ski cap and scarf you knitted for my birthday. They will certainly keep me warm when I'm out skiing.

Dad must have told you he had registered me for ski lessons starting next week. I can't wait! I already have great ambitions to enter a ski competition someday.

I'll have Dad send a picture of me on the slopes in my new cap and scarf. I hope to be skiing, not falling, down the mountain!

Love,
Emily

A Thank-You Note

EXERCISE 4. Writing a Thank-You Note.   Think of a gift or favor that you have received (for example, a new bike or a trip to Sea World). Write a letter of thanks to the person who gave you this gift or favor.

The Bread-and-Butter Note

If you have spent some time visiting a friend or relatives, you should write a note of thanks as soon as you return. This kind of note is called a "bread-and-butter" note.

7315 Sunset Blvd.
Temple, AZ 85281
June 25, 1988

Dear Mr. and Mrs. Simpson,

Early American history seems so much more real to me after having visited you in Boston. Thank you so much for showing me the historical monuments, the bay, the museums, and so many other interesting things. I especially liked eating the fresh seafood.

We are looking forward to Andrew's visit next month, so we can show him this part of the country.

Sincerely,
Doug

A Bread-and-Butter Note

EXERCISE 5. Writing a Bread-and-Butter Note.   If you have visited someone recently, write a bread-and-butter note expressing your thanks. Or, you may write a bread-and-butter note for one of the following situations:

1. Your grandparents who live near the ocean let you and your friend stay at their house for a weekend.
2. You just returned from a three-week visit to your aunt's farm.

EVALUATING AND REVISING

EVALUATING AND REVISING

Use the following guidelines to evaluate your friendly letters and social notes. Then revise your letters using the chart on page 145. Proofread your letters by referring to the guidelines on page 27. Make final copies and proofread them again.

GUIDELINES FOR EVALUATING SOCIAL LETTERS

Content	1. In a friendly letter, is news included that would interest the reader? Are questions from the friend's last letter answered?
Order	2. Is the letter easy to follow?
Thank-You Note	3. In a thank-you note, is the gift or favor specifically mentioned?
Form	4. Is each part of the letter correctly placed?
Heading	5. Does the heading contain the writer's address and the date?
Salutation	6. Is the salutation followed by a comma?
Body	7. Is each paragraph of the body indented?
Closing	8. Does the closing fit a social letter? Is the first word capitalized? Does a comma follow the closing?
Envelope	9. Are the addresses on the envelope complete and correctly placed?

REVIEW EXERCISE. Writing a Social Letter. Choose one of the following situations or make up your own. Write a social letter, following correct friendly letter form. Address an envelope for your letter, too. Evaluate your letter with the guidelines on page 139. Then revise it, using the chart on page 145, and proofread it.

1. Your soccer team has just won its first game. Write a thank-you note to your grandparents, thanking them for coming to the game.
2. You have just spent a week at your friend's mountain cabin. Write a bread-and-butter note thanking your friend's family for the visit.
3. You have just seen a movie that you think your friend will like. Describe it enthusiastically, so that your friend will be sure not to miss it.

THE BUSINESS LETTER

Sometimes you write letters to request information or to order merchandise. In this section, you will practice writing business letters.

PREWRITING

PLANNING A BUSINESS LETTER

The hints that follow will help you plan your business letters.

1. *Decide on your purpose.* Think about why you are writing the letter. Are you ordering or returning merchandise? Are you asking for information?

2. *Think about your audience.* Keep your readers in mind. What does the audience already know? What does the audience need to know? What response do you want from your audience?

3. *Think about your choice of words.* In a business letter, you want to be clear, polite, and reasonable.

4. *Gather your ideas.* Make notes of what you want to say. Include all the necessary information to explain the situation. Be as exact as possible.

5. *Be brief.* Do not include unnecessary information. However, do not leave out important details; just be sure to state your business in a few words.

WRITING

WRITING A BUSINESS LETTER

7e. Use the correct form for a business letter.

Use unlined white paper. Type the letter, or write it in blue or black ink. Center the letter on the page so that the margins are even all around; to do this you have to plan ahead. The appearance of a business letter is important, so be neat. If the letter is too long for one page, do not write on the back; use a second sheet of paper.

The form of a business letter is somewhat different from the form of a social letter. Study the following explanations and the model.

1. Heading

The heading of a business letter is the same as the heading for a friendly letter. However, many businesses use the two-letter state codes (page 148) for both the heading and the inside address.

2. Inside Address

The inside address is placed a short space below the heading, in line with the left margin. The form of the address is the same as that used for addressing an envelope.

```
                              ┌ 126 Holmes Avenue
                         1    │ Leonardville, KS   66449
                              └ March 30, 1988


                    ┌ Customer Service Department
                    │ Hardy Backpacking Company
                 2  │ 431 W. Jackson Street
                    └ Imperial, NE   69033

              3  ┌ Gentlemen:

                 ┌    I am returning sleeping bag #1569 that
                 │ was delivered yesterday.  It was received
                 │ with a broken zipper.
              4  │    Please replace the bag or refund my pur-
                 │ chase price of $94.95 plus $5.15 postage and
                 └ handling.


                         5  ┌ Yours truly,

                         6  ┌ Jacob Walsh
                            └ Jacob Walsh
```

A Model Business Letter

3. Salutation

The salutation is placed two lines below the inside address and is followed by a colon. *Gentlemen,* which people understand to include both men and women, is a standard greeting when you are not writing to a particular person. You may instead use *Dear Sir, Dear Madam,* or a department's name. If you are writing to a person whose name you know, use *Dear Mr., Miss, Mrs.,* or *Ms.* before the name.

4. Body

Begin the body of the letter two lines below the salutation. Indent the first line of the body of the letter and the first line of each paragraph. If typing, use five spaces for each paragraph indentation.

5. Closing

Yours truly, Sincerely yours, and *Very truly yours,* followed by a comma, are standard closings for business letters. The closing is placed in line with the heading. Only the first word of the closing is capitalized.

6. Signature

Sign your first and last name in ink, directly below the closing. If you type the letter, type your name four lines below the closing and sign your name in the space between the two typed lines.

As the following diagrams will illustrate, there are two main ways to fold a business letter. The way you choose depends on the size of the paper and the envelope.

If the sheet of paper is the same width as the envelope, fold it up from the bottom and down from the top.

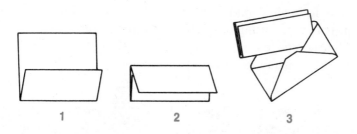

If the sheet is wider than the envelope, fold the paper up from the bottom almost to the top of the sheet. Then fold the right side over a third of the way; fold the left side over that. Put the folded edge of the letter into the envelope first.

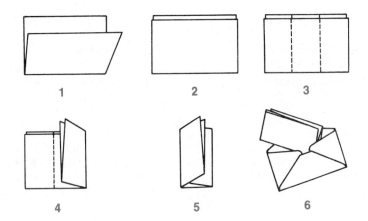

Address the envelope for a business letter the same way you address the envelope for a friendly letter.

EVALUATING AND REVISING

EVALUATING AND REVISING A BUSINESS LETTER

Use the following guidelines to evaluate your business letter. Then revise it, using the chart on page 145. Refer to the guidelines on page 27 to proofread your letter. Make a final copy, proofreading again to catch mistakes.

GUIDELINES FOR EVALUATING BUSINESS LETTERS

Content	1. Does the letter include all information necessary for its purpose? Is the letter brief and to the point? Is the letter polite?
Form	2. Is the form correct, with each part properly placed? Is the letter neat and its spacing attractive?

Heading	3. Does the heading include the writer's complete address and the date, correctly punctuated?
Inside Address	4. Is the inside address complete, accurate, and properly spaced?
Salutation	5. Is the salutation appropriate and followed by a colon?
Body	6. Is each paragraph of the body indented?
Closing	7. Is the closing appropriate? Is it correctly capitalized and punctuated?
Envelope	8. Is the address on the envelope identical to the inside address? Is it correctly placed? Is the return address on the envelope? Is the letter folded to fit the envelope?

Revising is important primarily for business letters and social notes, which need to be formal and exact. You can revise your letters by adding, cutting, replacing, and reordering. The following chart shows the kinds of changes you can make to improve your letters.

REVISING SOCIAL AND BUSINESS LETTERS

PROBLEM	KIND OF CHANGE	REVISION
Not enough information, news, or details are included.	Add	Add news, details, and information so your reason for writing is clear.
The ideas are hard to follow.	Reorder	Put sentences or paragraphs in a different order to make your ideas clear.
The parts of the letter are in the wrong places.	Reorder	Put the parts of the letter in the right places (see pages 141–43).
The letter includes too many details or unnecessary ones.	Cut	Cut extra details that may confuse your reader.

PROBLEM	KIND OF CHANGE	REVISION
The parts of the letter are not correctly punctuated and capitalized.	Replace	Replace the wrong punctuation marks (see pages 134–35). Capitalize correctly.
Information is missing from the heading or inside address.	Add	Be sure the heading includes the writer's complete address and the date. Be sure the inside address includes the receiver's or the company's name and complete address.
The envelope is not addressed correctly.	Add/Reorder	Add missing details to the addresses. Put the addresses in the right places on the envelope.

EXERCISE 6. Writing a Business Letter. Write a business letter to a nearby museum, asking for a schedule of exhibits. Tell why you are interested in this information. Evaluate your letter, using the guidelines on page 144. Revise your letter (see the chart above) and proofread it. Make a final copy and proofread again.

COMPLETING FORMS

7f. Fill out forms completely, correctly, and neatly.

As you go through school, you will fill out forms about yourself. Forms usually ask for your name, address, age, and phone number. When you complete a form, give all the information it asks for. Also be sure that you supply correct information. Always write the information neatly. Notice how one student completed the following form.

Public Library Card Application

Name _Jonathan Marshall_

Address _8016 Old Orchard Lane_

City _Erie_ State _Pennsylvania_ ZIP _16508_

Phone _814-989-4445_ Age _12_ Date of Birth _January 15, 1976_

Parent's or Guardian's Name _Elizabeth M. Marshall_

School _West Hills Middle School_

A Model Form

EXERCISE 7. Completing Forms. Complete a form your teacher gives you. Give complete and accurate information, and fill out the form neatly.

CHAPTER 7 WRITING REVIEW

Writing a Letter. Write one of the letters suggested below. Address an envelope for the letter. Evaluate, revise, and proofread your letter before you make a final copy.

1. You won a contest (baking, art, etc.). Write to a relative, describing your winning entry and the prize.
2. You would like historical information about a city. Write to its Chamber of Commerce, requesting information.

☞ **NOTE** The United States Postal Service recommends using two-letter codes for states, the District of Columbia, and Puerto Rico. The Service also recommends using nine-digit ZIP code numbers.

EXAMPLE   Mr. Joseph Ferree
               2152 Harbor Lane
               Orlando, FL 32806-2545

The two-letter code is never followed by a period. Following is a list of two-letter codes for states, the District of Columbia, and Puerto Rico. Refer to this list whenever you address envelopes.

Alabama AL	Montana MT
Alaska AK	Nebraska NE
Arizona AZ	Nevada NV
Arkansas AR	New Hampshire NH
California CA	New Jersey NJ
Colorado CO	New Mexico NM
Connecticut CT	New York NY
Delaware DE	North Carolina NC
District of Columbia DC	North Dakota ND
Florida FL	Ohio OH
Georgia GA	Oklahoma OK
Hawaii HI	Oregon OR
Idaho ID	Pennsylvania PA
Illinois IL	Puerto Rico PR
Indiana IN	Rhode Island RI
Iowa IA	South Carolina SC
Kansas KS	South Dakota SD
Kentucky KY	Tennessee TN
Louisiana LA	Texas TX
Maine ME	Utah UT
Maryland MD	Vermont VT
Massachusetts MA	Virginia VA
Michigan MI	Washington WA
Minnesota MN	West Virginia WV
Mississippi MS	Wisconsin WI
Missouri MO	Wyoming WY

PICTURE THE POSSIBILITIES:

IDEAS FOR WRITING

Pictures can bring back memories, awaken strong feelings, and make you wonder, "What if...?" In these pages you will learn how to use pictures to discover ideas for writing.

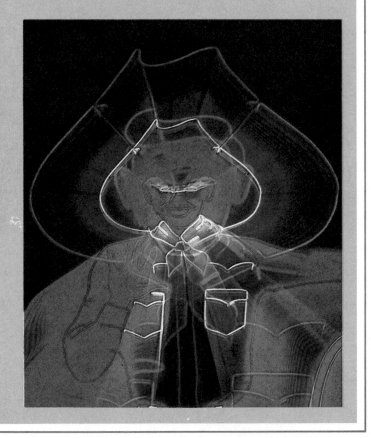

Probing the Picture

One way to use this picture would be to write a **descriptive** paragraph. To gather concrete and sense details, you could imagine yourself jumping off the diving board and ask, *What colors and shapes do I see? Do I notice any smells? How do the sun and the air feel on my body as I bounce on the board? What sounds do I hear as I bounce? As I hit the water? What do I taste when I accidentally swallow some water?* Then you could review your notes and decide what main impression to use in your topic sentence.

Another way to use the picture would be to write a composition of **opinion.** To find possible opinions, you could brainstorm on the subject "swimming." For example, you might ask, *Is swimming in a lake more fun than swimming in a pool? Is swimming in the ocean more exciting than swimming in either a lake or a pool? Is swimming my favorite sport? Is it my least-favorite sport? Do I enjoy* (or *dislike*) *taking swimming lessons?* Using the *5 W-How?* questions *(Who? What? When? Where? Why? and How?)* would help you find details to make clear your reasons for your opinion.

Writing Activities

Use the steps of the writing process to write one of these papers.

- Use the picture to write a descriptive paragraph.
- Write a composition of opinion on the subject "swimming." You may use one of the ideas listed above or one of your own.

Probing the Picture

You could use this picture of a water wheel to write a true **story.** To find possible subjects, you could brainstorm to remember experiences you have had in or near old, deserted buildings. Then you could choose one experience and use the *5 W-How?* questions to plan your story. For example, *when* and *where* did the actions take place? *Who* was with you? *What* problem did you face? *What* happened? *How* was the problem worked out? *What* did you learn from the experience?

Another idea would be to write a **report** on the subject "water power." First, you would need to limit the subject to a topic you could cover in a report. To do this, you could divide the subject into its parts by asking, *How is water power used?* Then you could choose one topic and use the *5 W-How?* questions to gather information. For the topic "how water power is used to produce electricity," for example, you might ask, *Where* does the water come from? *How* is it brought to the power plant? *What* are the steps in changing the energy from moving water into electric energy? Using library sources would help you find answers to questions such as these. You might also want to draw a diagram of a power plant to include in your report.

Writing Activities

Use the steps of the writing process to write one of these papers.

- Use the picture to write a story about a personal experience.
- Write a report on the subject "water power."

Probing the Picture

You could use this picture to write an **expository** paragraph about road signs that use pictures instead of words. To find examples of such signs, you could brainstorm or use observation. For example, you might ask, *What road signs with pictures instead of words do I see near where I live? Near my school? In or near my neighborhood park? On the way to the grocery store? In other parts of town?* If you know people from other countries, you could ask them whether they remember any such signs in their native lands. After you have collected several examples, you could choose the most interesting ones and write a topic sentence that gives your main idea.

Another way to use the picture would be to make up a **story.** You could imagine that you took the picture and ask, *What happened just before* (or *just after*) *I took the picture?* Then you could use the *5 W-How?* questions to find details to use in your story. For example, *What* country was I in? *What* month, day, and time of day was it? *What* was the weather like? *Who* was with me? *What* problem did I (*or* we) face? *How* was the problem worked out? Your answers to these questions would help you prepare a story plan.

Writing Activities

Use the steps of the writing process to write one of these papers.
- Write an expository paragraph using examples.
- Use the picture to write a made-up story.

Probing Pictures to Discover Writing Ideas

These questions will help you use any picture to discover ideas for writing.

1. What is the first thing I think of when I see this picture? What idea does the picture give me?
2. For what writing purpose could I use this idea?
3. What are the most interesting parts of the picture? How could I use those parts for my writing purpose?
4. Would using the 5 *W-How?* questions help me gather information?
5. What might have happened just before or just after the picture was taken? What might the person(s) have said?
6. What stands out most about the picture?
7. What concrete and sense details do I observe when I study the picture? What details do I imagine when I pretend I am the person in the picture?
8. Could I explain how to make or do what the picture shows?
9. Could I give information about what the picture shows by telling about its history? By telling how it is used? By giving examples?
10. What is my opinion about the subject of the picture?

On Your Own

Write a paper for your classmates on any of the pictures you have not already used. You may write a paragraph, a story, a report, or a composition of opinion. Also, you may choose your purpose: to tell a story, to describe, to give information, or to explain. Follow the steps of the writing process as you prepare your paper.

PART TWO

COMPOSITION:
Writing and Revising
Sentences

CHAPTER 8

Writing Complete Sentences

SENTENCE FRAGMENTS AND RUN-ON SENTENCES

Readers can become very confused if you do not use punctuation correctly in your writing. If you use an ending punctuation mark (period, question mark, or exclamation point) before your sentence expresses a complete thought, you have written a *sentence fragment*. If you write two sentences without an ending punctuation mark between them, you have written a *run-on sentence*.

To avoid sentence fragments and run-on sentences, you should learn to recognize them by practicing your "sentence sense." This is the ability to "hear" complete sentences as you read and write. This chapter will help you to practice your sentence sense and to write clear, complete sentences.

THE SENTENCE FRAGMENT

A sentence is a group of words expressing a complete thought. A sentence begins with a capital letter and ends with a punctuation mark.

EXAMPLES   Jan has a red bicycle.
               What is his name?
               That's a great idea!

Sometimes a group of words that does not express a complete thought is incorrectly punctuated as a sentence. The result is a *sentence fragment.* It begins with a capital letter and ends with a period, question mark, or exclamation point. The fragment looks like a complete sentence, but it is only part of a sentence.

8a. A *fragment* is a separated part of a sentence that does not express a complete thought.

Read the following examples. In each one a part of a sentence looks like a complete sentence. These fragments are printed in boldfaced type. If you read them aloud, you will hear that the thoughts are incomplete.

FRAGMENTS   1. Satellites can help relay radio waves. **As well as phone messages.**
            2. **When Pete Rose made his hit number 4,192.** He broke Ty Cobb's record.

Recognizing Fragments

As you write, if you are "listening" to your sentences and think you may have written a fragment, ask yourself two questions:

   1. Does the group of words have a verb and its subject?
   2. Does the group of words express a complete thought?

FRAGMENTS   1. **As well as phone messages.** [This group of words does not have a verb and its subject.]
            2. **When Pete Rose made hit number 4,192.** [This group of words does contain a subject, *Pete Rose*, and a verb, *made.* It does not, however, express a complete thought.]

Use the subject and verb test first. If you do not find both, you have a fragment. If you find both a subject and verb, use the second test. Often, reading the group of words out loud helps you decide whether the thought is complete. For example, if you read, "When Pete Rose made hit number 4,192," you want to know, "What *happened* when he did that?"

EXERCISE 1. Identifying Fragments. Number your paper 1–10. If the group of words is a sentence, write *S* after the number. If the group of words is a fragment, write *F*. Read aloud if possible.

EXAMPLES   1. Looking for a small, healthy pet.
　　　　　　1. *F*
　　　　　　2. We decided to raise hamsters.
　　　　　　2. *S*

1. We visited the pet shop in the mall.
2. Two bright-eyed hamsters chewing on pieces of carrot.
3. Named them two silly names, Mustard and Custard.
4. Pouches inside each fat cheek.
5. The pouches are for carrying food.
6. Making their cages quite comfortable.
7. Newspaper in lots of little shreds.
8. Both are plump, with thick tan fur.
9. A diet of mostly fruit, vegetables, and grain.
10. When you decide to raise hamsters.

EXERCISE 2. Finding Fragments in a Paragraph. The following paragraph contains six sentence fragments. Number your paper 1–10. If the group of words is a fragment, write *F* after the number. If the group of words is a sentence, write *S*.

EXAMPLES   **1.** A surveyor measures things.   **2.** Such as boundaries, highway routes, and heights of land.
　　　　　　1. *S*
　　　　　　2. *F*

1. Many people like sea pictures.   **2.** Winslow Homer, born in Boston, Massachusetts.   **3.** Painted wonderful sea pictures. **4.** The waves seem real.   **5.** Of many scenes of the rocky coast of Maine.   **6.** My favorite picture is *Breezing Up.*   **7.** In the National Gallery in Washington, D.C.   **8.** The four young people in the sailboat.   **9.** Must be having a good time.   **10.** The waves and wind seem to push the boat quickly.

Correcting Fragments

A good way to correct a sentence fragment is to connect it to the sentence with which it belongs. Notice how the following fragments are corrected by being rejoined to the proper sentences. The corrected sentences sound much smoother. The fragments are printed in boldfaced type.

FRAGMENT   I hope to improve my grades this year. **By working out a study schedule at home.**

CORRECTED   I hope to improve my grades this year by working out a study schedule at home.

FRAGMENT   **If I practice.** My serve will improve.

CORRECTED   If I practice, my serve will improve.

EXERCISE 3. Correcting Fragments.   Some of the following items contain fragments. Number your paper 1–10. If an item contains only complete sentences, write *S* after the number. If an item contains a fragment, join the fragment to the sentence.

EXAMPLES   1. Our club is having a car wash. We want to raise some money for a Halloween party.
　　　　　　1. *S*
　　　　　　2. Donald has been practicing every day. To improve his hook shot.
　　　　　　2. *Donald has been practicing every day to improve his hook shot.*

1. During our field trip to the capital. We stopped for a picnic at an old fort.
2. Felix is looking through cookbooks. He needs a taco recipe.
3. I can come over. After homework and piano practice.
4. We are going shopping. If Mom isn't too tired after work.
5. Gloria is having pizza for her birthday supper. Which is also my favorite food.
6. Before you dive into the water. You should make sure it is deep enough.

7. Because of the tryouts for the all-state chorus. I have to stay after school.
8. Tomorrow is the final spelling test. I plan to use my tape recorder to practice spelling the words.
9. Teeth are covered with enamel. The hardest substance in our bodies.
10. I looked in an almanac. Because I needed the names of our state's United States senators.

Two Common Fragments

Two kinds of fragments are common in students' writing. One of these is the fragment containing a word ending in -*ing*.

FRAGMENT   I just saw Marty. *Riding her bike at full speed.*

CORRECTED   I just saw Marty riding her bike at full speed.

In the example, the word *riding* may look like a verb, but it is not. An -*ing* word must have a helping verb with it in order to stand as the verb in a sentence (*is riding, has been riding*). When you use a group of words containing an -*ing* word without a helping verb, connect the group to a sentence.

FRAGMENT   *While waiting to perform.* The gymnast tried to forget her nervousness.

CORRECTED   While waiting to perform, the gymnast tried to forget her nervousness.

CORRECTED   The gymnast tried to forget her nervousness while waiting to perform. [Note that this fragment can be put at the beginning or the end of the sentence. Either placement makes sense.]

Another common fragment is the group of words beginning with a word such as *after, although, because, if, since, unless, when,* and *while.* This fragment depends on a sentence for its meaning. Always connect it to a complete sentence.

FRAGMENT   My sister will work at a summer camp. *If she passes the lifesaving course.*

CORRECTED   My sister will work at a summer camp if she passes the lifesaving course.

CORRECTED   If she passes the lifesaving course, my sister will work at a summer camp.

EXERCISE 4. Correcting Fragments. Number your paper 1–5. The following groups of words are all fragments. Add words at the beginning or end of each to make a complete sentence. Begin each sentence with a capital letter and end with a period, question mark, or exclamation point.

EXAMPLES   1. after the artist drew the cartoon
            1. *We applauded after the artist drew the cartoon.*
            2. because it was so hot
            2. *Because it was so hot, we went swimming.*

1. when she looked for her science homework
2. although I felt tired
3. if he had planned ahead
4. looking across the lake
5. crawling up the tree trunk

EXERCISE 5. Identifying and Correcting Fragments. Number your paper 1–10. Some of the following groups of words are fragments and some are complete sentences. If a group of words is a sentence, write an *S* after the number. If it is a fragment, add words to make it a complete sentence.

EXAMPLES   1. When we arrived at midnight, I was tired.
            1. *S*
            2. Since I had never been to a fort.
            2. *Since I had never been to a fort, Dad took me.*

1. Since I had a flashlight, we could follow the path easily.
2. Hurrying to get to the circus on time.
3. Because I like to read.
4. When I fixed supper for my family.
5. Studying for the test, I stayed up late.

6. Unless you have a better idea for the weekend.
7. When it's my birthday.
8. As I was packing the tent, I remembered the pegs.
9. While you and your mom are at the mall Saturday.
10. Cleaning my room this morning.

THE RUN-ON SENTENCE

Run-on sentences occur because the writer does not know when to stop. One sentence runs right into another. The writer either leaves out the correct ending punctuation (period, question mark, or exclamation point) or uses a comma.

8b. A *run-on sentence* **consists of two or more sentences separated only by a comma or by no mark of punctuation.**

RUN-ON	The fire spread quickly, a woman yelled from a third-floor window.
CORRECTED	The fire spread quickly. A woman yelled from a third-floor window.
RUN-ON	The rescue squad arrived they used their ladder to get her down.
CORRECTED	The rescue squad arrived. They used their ladder to get her down.

EXERCISE 6. Correcting Run-on Sentences.   The following items are run-on sentences. Number your paper 1–10. Decide where each sentence should end. Then write each complete sentence separately. Remember to use a capital letter and a period.

EXAMPLE   1. Someday you may not live on earth, you may live in a space colony.

      1. *Someday you may not live on earth. You may live in a space colony.*

1. Space colonies will be important, they will be sources of raw materials and energy.
2. A space colony might look like a big erector set each new section will be added as needed.
3. Space colonies will be enclosed otherwise people could not live in the alien climate.
4. Materials for the colony may come from the moon and asteroids, construction will be difficult.
5. Electricity will come from solar cells they collect the sun's rays.
6. The space station's orbiting platform could be covered with solar cells perhaps millions will be needed.
7. The energy collected can be beamed to earth, then it can be used here for electricity.
8. Some people will build platforms, some will grow food.
9. Some kinds of materials may be manufactured in a space station computer chips, it has been been suggested, could be made there.
10. A space colony is exciting to think about, it is fun to imagine the future.

EXERCISE 7. Identifying and Correcting Run-on Sentences.
Some of the following items are correctly punctuated sentences. Others are run-on sentences. Number your paper 1–10. If an item is correct, write *S* after the number. If it is a run-on sentence, rewrite it as two or more complete sentences.

1. Some myths are interesting but sad, one is about Daedalus and his son Icarus.
2. Daedalus was an architect he worked for King Minos of Crete.
3. King Minos was ungrateful, he put Daedalus and his son in a prison.
4. Daedalus made large wings, using wax to hold the feathers together, they would help him and his son escape.
5. Daedalus gave his son a stern warning not to fly too high.
6. If Icarus flew too high, the wax might melt, without the wings he would fall into the sea.

7. The two easily escaped from Crete, the wings worked perfectly.
8. Icarus did not listen to his father's warning, unfortunately, he flew up high toward the sun.
9. When the wax melted, Icarus fell into the sea and drowned.
10. The sad Daedalus flew on safely to Sicily, where the king welcomed him.

EXERCISE 8. Finding and Correcting Run-on Sentences in a Paragraph. The following paragraph contains many run-on sentences. Rewrite the paragraph, correcting the run-on sentences. Use capital letters and periods where they are needed.

EXAMPLE   Sally Ride was the first American woman in space, she was a member of a shuttle crew. Her mission began June 18, 1983 it left from Cape Canaveral, Florida.

Sally Ride was the first American woman in space. She was a member of a shuttle crew. Her mission began June 18, 1983. It left from Cape Canaveral, Florida.

Pioneer schools were very different from schools today. The teachers often had little training, they spent much of their time keeping order. When students had to be punished, some teachers whipped them. The books that the schools owned, which students shared, had small print their subject was often good behavior. Students had to read loudly, soft reading was considered bad manners. The buildings were not very comfortable, the heat came from an iron stove or fireplace. The seats, made from split logs, were hard students probably did not like to sit very long. The rooms must not have looked very cheerful either, with few pictures. How would you have liked going to school in pioneer days?

REVIEW EXERCISE. Identifying and Correcting Sentence Fragments and Run-on Sentences. Some of the following items contain sentence fragments or run-on sentences. Number your paper 1–10. If an item is a correct sentence, write *S* after the number. If an item contains a fragment or run-on sentence, rewrite the item correctly. You will have to add words to make the fragments into complete sentences.

1. An ordinary person goes into a dressing room, a clown comes out.
2. Creating a special face. Each clown is different.
3. Clown makeup starts with white greasepaint. Which looks like a mask.
4. After painting bright colors above the eyes, the clown adds eyebrows high on the forehead.
5. A lot of red is used around the mouth. Since a broad smile is important.
6. Some clowns have a large red nose, this is fitted over the person's own nose.
7. A tight-fitting cap can make a clown look bald on each side the cap sometimes has funny, wild-looking hair.
8. Since some clowns want something else on their heads. They add a wig or a funny hat.
9. Baggy pants and a big shirt with a ruffled collar come next.
10. Sliding on floppy shoes. The clown completes the outfit.

CHAPTER 9

Writing Effective Sentences

SENTENCE COMBINING AND REVISING

When you write a first draft, you give your first attention to the content. Then, to improve the writing, you read over the draft and make changes. One important change is improving sentence structure. Two kinds of problems often occur: the short, choppy sentence and the long, rambling sentence. This chapter will help you recognize both choppy and rambling sentences and will show you several ways to revise them.

COMBINING SENTENCES

Good writers usually use some short sentences, but they do not use them all the time. An essay or a paragraph of short sentences is monotonous. Read the following paragraphs. Notice the choppiness of the first. How is this corrected in the second?

CHOPPY STYLE   An animal lives there. It is a huge animal. It lives in that river. It has a funny shape. It looks like a big pig. It looks like a bulky pig. The hippopotamus has a big mouth. Its mouth is red.

It contains long teeth. The ears are tiny. The eyes are perfectly round. You can't get near a baby hippo. The mother will be very angry. The mother will roar at you.

CORRECTED   A hippopotamus lives in that river. It is a huge animal and has a funny shape like a big, bulky pig. The hippopotamus has a big red mouth with huge teeth. The ears are tiny, and the eyes are perfectly round. You can't get near a baby hippo because the mother will roar angrily at you.

The short sentences were revised by (1) adding adjectives, adverbs, and prepositional phrases, (2) combining two sentences into one compound sentence, and (3) using a connecting word (the word *because*) to join related sentences. The result is a smoother paragraph with much more variety.

9a. Combine short, related sentences by using adjectives, adverbs, or prepositional phrases.

CHOPPY   1. The chef made pizza.
          2. It was delicious.
          3. The chef was new.

REVISED   The **new** chef made **delicious** pizza. [The sentences are combined by putting the adjectives *new* and *delicious* into sentence 1. An adjective modifies a noun or a pronoun.]

CHOPPY   1. She practiced the piano.
          2. She practiced daily.

REVISED   She practiced the piano **daily.** [The sentences are combined by putting *daily* into sentence 1. *Daily* is an adverb. An adverb modifies a verb, an adjective, or another adverb.]

CHOPPY   1. I went with Dad.
          2. We went to the boat show.

REVISED   I went with Dad **to the boat show.** [The sentences are combined by putting the prepositional phrase *to the boat show* into sentence 1.]

EXERCISE 1. Combining Sentences by Using Adjectives.
Number your paper 1–10. Combine the three sentences in each group into one sentence, using the words in *italics* as adjectives.

EXAMPLE   1. The trainer calmed the horse.
            The trainer was *kind*.
            The horse was *nervous*.

            1. *The kind trainer calmed the nervous horse.*

1. The child pasted the sticker in the book.
   The sticker was *funny*.
   The child was *young*.
2. The campers looked down into the canyon.
   The campers were *fearful*.
   The canyon was *dark*.
3. The attendant noticed the giraffe's eyes.
   The giraffe's eyes were *swollen*.
   The attendant was *observant*.
4. The explorers approached the mountain peak.
   The explorers were *eager*.
   It was *cloud-covered*.
5. The prince chased the dragon.
   The prince was *brave*.
   The dragon was *evil*.
6. The beaver's teeth can cut down trees.
   The teeth are *powerful*.
   The trees are *thick*.
7. The truck is filled with fruit.
   The fruit is *tropical*.
   The truck is *abandoned*.
8. The Egyptians used indigo for dye.
   The Egyptians were *ancient*.
   The dye was *blue*.

9. The tourists rode in a gondola.
   The gondola was *graceful*.
   The tourists were *excited*.
10. The craftsman carved figures.
    The craftsman was *skilled*.
    The figures were *wooden*.

EXERCISE 2. Combining Sentences by Using Adverbs.
Number your paper 1–10. Combine the sentences in each group
into one sentence, using the words in *italics* as adverbs.

EXAMPLE   1. I walked to the door and closed it.
                  I walked *slowly*.
                  I closed it *quietly*.
            1. *I walked slowly to the door and quietly closed it.*

1. Our puppy ran to the door and barked.
   It ran *swiftly*.
2. The winner bowed and left the stage.
   He left *quickly*.
3. He rewrote and proofread his paper.
   He *neatly* rewrote the paper.
   He proofread it *carefully*.
4. The water's smooth surface hid a dangerous undertow.
   The surface hid it *completely*.
   The undertow was *very* dangerous.
5. The red caboose came into view.
   It was a *bright* red.
   Finally it came into view.
6. She said good night and went to bed.
   She spoke *softly*.
   She went to bed *immediately*.
7. The athletes marched into the stadium.
   They marched in *afterward*.
   The athletes marched *proudly*.
8. She aimed the camera and snapped the picture.
   She aimed the camera *accurately*.
   She *quickly* snapped the picture.

9. The koala came close to us.
   It came *yesterday*.
   It came *quite* close.
10. I finished the gloomy mystery.
    I *finally* finished it.
    It was *terribly* gloomy.

EXERCISE 3. Combining Sentences by Using Prepositional Phrases. Number your paper 1–10. Use the prepositional phrases in *italics* to combine the three sentences into one sentence. Some of the prepositional phrases may be put in more than one place in a sentence. You may choose the placement.

EXAMPLE   1. We caught fish.
                 We caught fish *at camp*.
                 We were fishing *from the dock*.
              1. *At camp we caught fish from the dock.*
                              or
                 We caught fish from the dock at camp.

1. The sailboats raced.
   They raced *in the bay*.
2. The whale swam around.
   It swam *in the Sacramento River*.
   It swam there *for three and one-half weeks*.
3. They went fishing.
   They were *on Lake Louise*.
   The lake is *in western Canada*.
4. We went out.
   We went *for a walk*.
   The walk was *after dinner*.
5. We enjoyed the music.
   Music was played *by the orchestra*.
   The music was played *before the play*.
6. Everyone gave reports.
   The reports were *about current events*.
   Everyone *but me* gave reports.

7. We arranged snapshots.
They were *of our family.*
We put them *in one picture frame.*
8. They played a game.
They played the game *on the beach.*
It was a game *of volleyball.*
9. In science class we saw a movie.
The movie was *about three astronauts.*
They were *in their space capsule.*
10. We went to the museum.
We went *on Saturday afternoon.*
We went *by subway.*

9b. Combine short, related sentences by using a compound subject.

A compound subject is made up of two or more subjects that have the same verb. The parts of the subject are joined by a conjunction (or connecting word) such as *and* or *or.* In the examples, the compound subjects are printed in boldfaced type.

EXAMPLES   Your **books** and **lunchbox** are in the car.
Peanuts, pecans, and **cashews** are delicious.

You can combine choppy sentences into one sentence with a compound subject if the sentences are closely related in meaning. Join the subjects by using conjunctions (or connecting words) such as *and, or, both—and, either—or,* or *neither—nor.* Choose the conjunction that is best for the meaning of the sentence. In the examples, the compound subject is in boldfaced type, and the connecting words are in *italics.*

EXAMPLES   Apples are good at a Halloween party.
Popcorn balls are also good.
Both **apples** *and* **popcorn balls** are good at a Halloween party.

Soccer may be our fall sport.
Hockey may also be our fall sport.
Either **soccer** *or* **hockey** may be our fall sport.

Heavy rain is not forecast.
A tornado is not forecast either.
Neither heavy **rain** *nor* a **tornado** is forecast.

EXERCISE 4. Combining Sentences by Using Compound Subjects. Write each pair of sentences as one sentence with a compound subject.

EXAMPLE 1. Beans are grown on that farm.
Tomatoes are also grown on that farm.
1. *Both beans and tomatoes are grown on that farm.*

1. Plants cannot live in that polluted water.
Fish cannot live in it either.
2. Antelopes gallop like racehorses.
Zebras run like racehorses too.
3. Hot dogs would be good at the picnic.
On the other hand, hamburgers would be good too.
4. A telescope would be a great present.
A calculator would be just as good.
5. The buses are usually on time.
The subways are usually on time too.

9c. Combine short, related sentences by using a compound verb.

A compound verb is made up of two or more verbs that have the same subject. The parts of the compound verb are joined by a conjunction such as *and* or *or.* The compound verbs below are in boldface.

EXAMPLES The wild birds **warbled** and **chirped.**
I **have** either **misplaced** or **lost** my book.

Two or more short sentences that have the same subject may be combined into one sentence with a compound verb. The connecting words are usually *and, but, or, either—or, neither—nor,* and *both—and.* In the examples, the compound verb is in boldfaced type. The conjunctions are in *italics.*

EXAMPLES   Monkeys chattered to each other.
They also called to each other.
Monkeys **chattered** *and* **called** to each other.

Derek has not written since he moved.
He has not called either.
Derek **has** *neither* **written** *nor* **called** since he moved.

EXERCISE 5. Combining Sentences by Using Compound Verbs.
Number your paper 1–5. Combine each pair of sentences into one sentence with a compound verb.

EXAMPLE   1. She could not swim until last summer.
She could not dive either.
1. *She could not swim or dive until last summer.*

or

She could neither swim nor dive until last summer.

1. France's flag is red, white, and blue.
France's flag has no stars.
2. Mom was upset about my report card.
Mom gave me a lecture.
3. I cannot come over this afternoon.
I cannot talk on the telephone either.
4. Wild turkeys live in open forests.
Wild turkeys roost in trees at night.
5. Tuna are found in nearly all oceans.
They prefer warm water.

REVIEW EXERCISE A. Combining Sentences.
Number your paper 1–5. Combine each group of sentences into one smooth sentence. Remember all the methods you have learned in this chapter: using adjectives, adverbs, prepositional phrases, compound subjects, and compound verbs.

EXAMPLE   1. My brother had cooked breakfast.
It was delicious.
He had also set the table.
It was set for the whole family.

1. *My brother had cooked a delicious breakfast and had set the table for the whole family.*

1. The Pacific Ocean is the largest ocean. *and*
   It is also the deepest ocean.
2. The Pacific covers one third of the earth. *and*
   It contains more than one half of the earth's water.
3. We studied the ocean's islands. *on a map yes*
   We studied them yesterday.
   The islands were on a map.
4. We found the Aleutian Islands. *We found the*
   We saw that they reach out from Alaska.
   They reach southwest.
5. Australia is a large island. *very*
   It is in the Pacific Ocean. *Australia is a large or... is*
   It is very large. *in the*
   It is called a continent.

9d. Combine short, related sentences into one compound sentence.

A compound sentence consists of two or more simple sentences. The sentences are usually joined by the connecting words *and, but,* or *or.* A compound sentence always has two or more subjects and two or more verbs.

SIMPLE SENTENCES   The fish jumped.
                    The pelican dived.

COMPOUND SENTENCE   The fish jumped, and the pelican dived.

(S V) The fish jumped, (S V) and the pelican dived.

When you write a compound sentence, you are putting two ideas together, so the ideas must be closely related and equal in importance.

RELATED IDEAS   We reached the end of the chapter, and we went back to review.

UNRELATED IDEAS   We reached the end of the chapter, and I needed to straighten up my locker.

EQUAL IDEAS   Matt brought a checkerboard, but I forgot to bring the checkers.

UNEQUAL IDEAS   Matt brought a checkerboard, and I was fixing a cheese sandwich.

EXERCISE 6. Combining Sentences into Compound Sentences.

Most of the following pairs of sentences can be combined into compound sentences. If the ideas are related and equal, write the compound sentence. If they are not, write *U*.

EXAMPLES   1. Dad's favorite dog is a cocker spaniel.
                 Mom's favorite dog is a collie.
             1. *Dad's favorite dog is a cocker spaniel, but Mom's favorite is a collie.*
             2. The party is at 4:30 P.M.
                 I had a birthday party last year.
             2. *U*

1. A planet moves.   *but*
   The stars stay in their places.
2. The earth is one of the planets.
   It circles the sun.   *and*
3. Planets do not give off light of their own.
   Stars do give off light.   *but*
4. The sun is a boiling fire of gases.
   It gives off light.   *and*
5. Each star consists of billions of atoms.
   We often go to the planetarium.   *U*
6. I enjoy learning about the stars.
   The Big Dipper is a constellation.   *U*
7. Some stars are fainter than our sun.
   Some are many times brighter.   *and*
8. Stars are arranged in large groups.
   Our flag has stars.   *U*
9. Our sun will change.
   It will change very slowly.   *but*
10. Stars are interesting and beautiful.
    I would like my own telescope to look at them.   *and*

9e. Combine short, related sentences into one sentence by using such words as *after, although, as, because, if, since, so that, when, whether,* and *while.*

Sometimes two sentences are related in a special way. One sentence helps explain the other sentence by telling *how, where, why,* or *when.* A good way to combine these sentences is to add a word that shows the special relationship. In the examples, the connecting words are in boldfaced type. Think about how they relate one sentence to another.

EXAMPLES   The drawbridge was pulled up.
The enemy knights could not get into the castle.
The drawbridge was pulled up **so that** the enemy knights could not get into the castle.

The Panama Canal was built.
Ships no longer had to sail around Cape Horn.
After the Panama Canal was built, ships no longer had to sail around Cape Horn.

The choice of a connecting word depends on the meaning you want to give. Study the following connecting words so that you can use them in your writing.

after	before	until
although	if	when
as	since	whether
because	so that	while

EXERCISE 7. Combining Sentences by Using *As, Because, Although,* and *After.* Combine the sentences in each of the following groups by using one of the words in the list below. Choose the word that will best connect the ideas.

as   because   although   after

EXAMPLE   1. We visited Baltimore.
My dad has relatives there.
1. *We visited Baltimore because my dad has relatives there.*

1. The library opens at 8:00 on Saturday morning.
   I won't be going until 10:30.   *Although*
2. We arrived at my grandparents' house.
   I started to climb their old oak tree.   *After*
3. I rewrote my paragraph.
   I handed it in.   *After*
4. I was opening the door.
   My dog darted outside.   *as*
5. My brother put a tall, bright red flag on his bicycle.
   The traffic is heavy on our street.   *because*

EXERCISE 8. Combining Sentences by Using *Before, If, Since,* and *So That.* Combine the sentences in each of the following groups by using one of the words listed below:

> before   if   since   so that

1. Baboons cannot be trained as pets.
   They are bad-tempered.   *if*
2. I plan to lay out all of my clothes and books.
   I will not be late for the bus.   *so that*
3. We can go to Mexico.   *before*
   We must have permission from the principal.
4. Lonnie got a skateboard.
   He practices all the time.   *Since*
5. Benita has vacation next week.
   She will come to our concert.   *if*

EXERCISE 9. Combining Sentences by Using *When, While, Until,* and *Whether.* Combine the sentences in each of the following groups by using one of the words listed below:

> when   while   until   whether

1. We do not eat dessert.
   We finish all of our dinner.   *until*
2. Jenny is not sure.   *whether*
   Her dad will attend the PTA meeting or another meeting.
3. Some cheese is aged.
   The taste improves.   *while*

4. Before TV, radio, and movies, people sang and told stories.
   They wanted entertainment.
5. I am learning the music.
   I am also learning the words to the song.

REVIEW EXERCISE B. Combining Sentences by Using Connecting Words.
Combine the sentences in each group into one sentence by using connecting words from the following list:

after	because	since	when	and
although	before	so that	whether	but
as	if	until	while	or

1. We went bowling.
   My brother beat me.
   He had bowled before.
2. The batteries are old.
   The experiment may not work.
3. She is not certain.
   She will read her poem or ask Eli to read it.
4. I really like popcorn.
   I'd prefer not to have it buttered.
5. We went out in the boat.
   We checked the weather forecast.
   We put on our flotation vests.
6. The air was clear.
   We could see for miles.
   We knew we were almost home.
7. She had lost her sight and hearing.
   Helen Keller had a busy and useful life.
8. I read "Fog" by Carl Sandburg.
   I have been writing poetry.
   No one has read it.
9. Eleanor Roosevelt was a President's wife.
   She was also a humanitarian and a diplomat.
10. You are going on a long hike.
    Take along a canteen filled with water.

REVIEW EXERCISE C. Revising a Paragraph by Combining Sentences. The following paragraph is written in choppy sentences. Revise the paragraph by combining sentences.

Peter and the Wolf is a fairy tale. It is music. It is by Sergei Prokofiev. Prokofiev was a composer. He was Russian. In *Peter and the Wolf,* each character is a musical instrument. Each has a special sound. You hear the instruments. You imagine the characters in the story. You imagine easily. Peter is confident. He is the string section of the orchestra. The bird is smart. He is a flute. The cat is sly. He is a clarinet. The grandfather is clumsy. He is also bad-tempered. He is a bassoon. The bassoon is deep. The duck is sad. He is an oboe. The wolf is macho. He is the brass section. Most characters are instruments. Some are given a certain kind of music. You hear a march. You know the soldiers are near. The soldiers are cheerful. This music does not sound old. Its birthday is in the spring. In 1986 the music had its fiftieth birthday.

CORRECTING A RAMBLING STYLE

Some writers run many sentences together, punctuating them as one sentence. They tie the sentences together by using *and, so, but,* and *and then* between them. You should avoid this rambling style.

9f. Correct a rambling style by combining ideas and avoiding the overuse of *and, but,* **and** *so.*

You can follow two steps to correct a rambling style. First, break the passage into separate, complete sentences. Second, combine some of the short sentences into better sentences. These two steps were used to revise the rambling passage in the example.

We went to the Fourth of July celebration and we had a wonderful time and it rained for a little while so the fireworks were postponed but we saw them an hour later and we bought hot dogs and lemonade for supper and listened to the band play while we ate and then we went to all the crafts booths finally we were worn out and then we went home.

Step 1. Break the passage into shorter sentences.

We went to the Fourth of July celebration. We had a wonderful time. It rained for a little while. The fireworks were postponed. We saw them an hour later. We bought hot dogs and lemonade for supper. We listened to the band play while we ate. We went to all the crafts booths. Finally we were worn out. We went home.

Step 2. Use the sentence-combining skills you have learned to combine the short sentences into longer ones. Remember the connecting words that can join related sentences.

We went to the Fourth of July celebration and had a wonderful time. Because it rained for a little while, the fireworks were postponed. We saw them an hour later. We bought hot dogs and lemonade for supper and listened to the band play while we ate. Then we went to all the crafts booths. Finally we were worn out and went home.

All people do not revise the same way. Some people revise mainly in their minds. Others like to write out their revisions several times. You will learn the best method for your revisions.

EXERCISE 10. Revising a Rambling Paragraph. Correct the following rambling paragraph by using the two steps described in the example. First break the paragraph into shorter sentences, and then combine some of the sentences into better ones. You may do Step 1 in your mind if you want. Do not change the meaning of the original paragraph as you revise.

The Island of the Blue Dolphins is a story by Scott O'Dell and it is full of adventure and also unusual and it is about a girl named Karana. She was an Indian and she lived alone for years on the Island of the Blue Dolphins but she kept waiting year after year for a ship to rescue her so she built a shelter, made weapons, found food, and fought enemies and it is an exciting book and so you should read it if you like adventure stories or stories about people who survive unusual hardships.

CORRECTING A MONOTONOUS STYLE

If all the sentences in a passage begin the same way, the writing will sound dull. This dullness, or monotony, can be corrected by beginning some sentences in a different way.

9g. Correct a monotonous style by beginning sentences in different ways.

When small children are learning to write, they usually start all sentences with the subject. Read the example.

EXAMPLE   Mother took me to a park. The park is near our house. I went down the slide. I saw some of my friends. I ran to the lake quickly. I threw some bread to the ducks. The ducks came with loud quacks to eat the bread.

All of the sentences in the example begin with the subject. Although this style is common in the writing of younger children, it should be corrected in your writing.

(1) To vary sentences, begin with an adverb.

EXAMPLES   A fruit fly suddenly escaped from its container.
Suddenly, a fruit fly escaped from its container.

Our science teacher immediately caught the fly.
Immediately, our science teacher caught the fly.

EXERCISE 11. Correcting a Monotonous Style by Beginning Sentences with Adverbs.   Number your paper 1–5. Revise the following sentences by beginning each one with an adverb. Write the complete sentence.

EXAMPLE   1. I read the newspaper occasionally.
        1. *Occasionally, I read the newspaper.*

1. I will soon be old enough to deliver newspapers.
2. Dad usually scans the entire paper at breakfast.
3. My older brother wrote a letter to the editor once.

4. Each student must bring a clipping from the newspaper to class tomorrow.
5. Ms. Tufts reminded us of that assignment yesterday.

(2) To vary sentences, begin with a prepositional phrase.

EXAMPLES   Daffodils and tulips bloom in the early spring.
            In the early spring, daffodils and tulips bloom.

            The band played at half time.
            At half time, the band played.

EXERCISE 12. Correcting a Monotonous Style by Beginning Sentences with Prepositional Phrases. Number your paper 1–5. Revise the following sentences by beginning each one with a prepositional phrase. Write the complete sentence.

EXAMPLE   1. We went to Fort Knox on our class trip last year.
           1. *On our class trip last year, we went to Fort Knox.*

1. We have a homework assignment in language arts.
2. She will join us at the parade.
3. I wrote in my journal for fifteen minutes.
4. We slept in cabins at the state park.
5. I'll have a party for my birthday.

REVIEW EXERCISE D. Revising a Rambling Paragraph. Correct the following paragraph. Change the long, rambling sentence into several clear, well-written sentences. Read the whole paragraph carefully before you begin.

Robert and Dwayne wanted to go to the game and they saved their money to buy tickets but they almost missed the game, though, because Robert thought Dwayne had both tickets and Dwayne thought Robert had them so they got to the stadium and they discovered the tickets were still at Dwayne's house and then Robert's dad drove them back to get the tickets and they finally got to their seats and the game started.

REVIEW EXERCISE E. Revising a Choppy or Monotonous Paragraph. Correct the following paragraph by combining sentences and beginning sentences in different ways. You may not need to change every sentence. Read the whole paragraph carefully before you begin.

We went to Boston. We walked on the Freedom Trail. It is three miles long. It covers many historical sites. The sites are connected. They are connected by red lines. The red lines are in the sidewalk. We began at the State House. It is on State Street. We went next to Paul Revere's house. It was built in 1680. It is the oldest building in Boston. We went then to the Old North Church. Two lanterns were hung there. They were used to signal Paul Revere. We went last to the Navy Yard. We saw *Old Ironsides*. It is a frigate. It is a frigate with forty-four guns. It was in forty-two battles. *Old Ironsides* was never defeated. I enjoyed our walk. I enjoyed walking along the Freedom Trail. I hope to go back to see more of Boston someday.

GUIDELINES FOR SENTENCE COMBINING

1. Combine short, related sentences by using adjectives, adverbs, or prepositional phrases.
2. Combine short, related sentences by using compound subjects or verbs.
3. Combine short, related sentences by making them into a compound sentence.
4. Combine short, related sentences into one sentence by using such connecting words as *after, although, as, because, before, if, since, so that, when, whether,* and *while.*
5. Correct a rambling style by combining ideas and avoiding the overuse of *and, but,* and *so.*
6. Correct a monotonous style by beginning some sentences with adverbs and prepositional phrases.

PART THREE

TOOLS FOR WRITING AND REVISING

Grammar ▪ Usage ▪ Mechanics

CHAPTER 10

The Sentence

SUBJECT AND PREDICATE, KINDS OF SENTENCES

When you talk or write, you communicate with words and sentences. You do not always need to use complete sentences when you talk because you can use facial expressions and gestures to help make your meaning clear. When you write, however, you rely entirely on words and sentences, so you must know how to write complete sentences and how to punctuate them properly.

DIAGNOSTIC TEST

A. Identifying Sentences. Number your paper 1–5. Some of the following groups of words are sentences; others are not. If a group of words is a sentence, write it after its number. Begin with a capital letter, and end with an appropriate punctuation mark. If a group of words is not a sentence, write *NS*.

EXAMPLE 1. after the storm yesterday
          1. *NS*

1. leaves all over the front lawn and path
2. what is a black hole

3. every day this week I made my bed
4. our best score in a basketball game this year
5. mail this letter on your way to school

B. Identifying Simple Subjects and Simple Predicates.

Number your paper 6–10. Write each sentence. Underline the simple subject once and simple predicate (verb) twice. Be sure to underline both parts of a compound subject or compound predicate.

EXAMPLE   1. He removed the tire and patched it.
            1. *He removed the tire and patched it.*

6. The walk in space will be televised tonight.
7. On the piano was a bowl of fresh flowers.
8. After a test I check my answers carefully.
9. At the beach my brother and cousins built a castle.
10. Lucky ran to the door and barked loudly.

C. Identifying Simple Sentences and Compound Sentences.

Number your paper 11–15. If a sentence is simple, write *S* after its number. If a sentence is compound, write *C*.

EXAMPLE   1. The ship sank, but the crew was saved.
            1. *C*

11. Lucia hunted carefully and found a rare fossil.
12. I rang the doorbell, but nobody was home.
13. The plane landed, and the passengers stood up.
14. The storm slowed cars and halted trains.
15. She won the first two games, but I won the match.

D. Classifying and Punctuating Sentences by Purpose.

Number your paper 16–20. Write the following sentences and add the appropriate mark of punctuation. Then label each sentence *declarative, interrogative, imperative,* or *exclamatory.*

EXAMPLE   1. Are you ready
            1. *ready?—interrogative*

16. Look at the sky
17. What a beautiful display of fireworks this is
18. Who is setting them off
19. I always enjoy Independence Day
20. What is your favorite holiday

SENTENCE SENSE

When you talk, you do not always express your ideas as complete thoughts. For example, read this conversation:

"Ready?"
"In a minute."
"No, now!"
"OK, OK!"

In speech, your tone of voice and facial expressions help carry your meaning. In writing you do not have these aids. Your words express your ideas completely and clearly.

10a. A *sentence* is a group of words expressing a complete thought.

Each of the sentences below expresses a complete thought. Notice that each one begins with a capital letter and ends with a punctuation mark.

EXAMPLES   The book is my favorite.
            Walk in single file.
            Do you collect coins?
            Imagine me on an elephant!

Now read the following groups of words. Each leaves out something you need to know in order to understand what the writer means. The word groups are therefore not sentences.

EXAMPLES   visited the reservation [Who visited it?]
            the bell for lunch [What about it?]
            on the way to school today [What happened?]

EXERCISE 1. Identifying Sentences. Number your paper 1–10. Some of the following groups of words are sentences; some are not. Write each group of words that is a sentence. Begin with a capital letter and end with a mark of punctuation. Write *NS* for each group of words that is not a sentence.

EXAMPLES 1. a friend of mine from Canada
1. *NS*
2. we found four different kinds of leaves
2. *We found four different kinds of leaves.*

1. a scary Halloween party last Friday
2. needed some costumes and decorations
3. we hung sheets up in the doorway
4. a person in a witch costume
5. made a jack-o'-lantern with a mean face
6. my brother rattled chains
7. strange music and colorful lights
8. a funny but scary skeleton costume
9. guests reached into a bag for treats
10. the best party this year

SUBJECT AND PREDICATE

Every sentence has two main parts: a *subject* and a *predicate*.

The Subject

10b. The *subject* of a sentence is the part about which something is being said.

Read the following sentences. The subjects are in boldfaced (heavy) type.

EXAMPLES **The tooth with a point** is a canine.
Lois Lenski wrote *Strawberry Girl*.

To find the subject, ask yourself *who* or *what* is doing something or *about whom or what* something is being said.

EXAMPLES My best friend sits next to me in science. [*Who or what* is doing something? *My best friend.*]

Science is very interesting this year. [*About whom or what* is something being said? *Science.*]

The Position of the Subject

The subject does not always come at the beginning of a sentence. It may be in the middle or even at the end.

EXAMPLES Are **you** going to the picnic?
After school, **Theresa** went to band practice.
Under our house was **a tiny kitten**.

EXERCISE 2. Identifying Subjects.   Number your paper 1–10. After the proper number, write the subject of the sentence.

EXAMPLE   1. The final score was tied.
1. *The final score*

1. Many games use rackets or paddles.
2. Tennis can be a lively game.
3. The badminton racket is a lightweight one.
4. Ping-Pong paddles are covered with rubber.
5. Racquetball uses special rackets.
6. In Florida, citrus fruit is an important crop.
7. After three to five years, fruit grows on the new trees.
8. Does Florida grow all of the country's citrus fruit?
9. California also grows oranges and other citrus fruit.
10. From Texas comes the Star Ruby grapefruit.

Complete Subject and Simple Subject

You have been identifying the *complete subject*. The main word in the complete subject is called the *simple subject*.

10c. The *simple subject* is the main word in the complete subject.

EXAMPLE   A bright-red cardinal sat on the window sill.

Complete subject   A bright-red cardinal
   Simple subject   cardinal

EXAMPLE   The first prize is a gold medal.

Complete subject   The first prize
   Simple subject   prize

Sometimes the same word or words make up both the simple subject and the complete subject.

EXAMPLES   **Hawks** circled the canyon. [*Hawks* is both the complete subject and the simple subject.]

   Little Rascal is the story of a boy and his pet raccoon. [The title *Little Rascal* is both the complete subject and the simple subject.]

EXERCISE 3. Identifying Complete Subjects and Simple Subjects.   Number your paper 1–10. Write the complete subject of each sentence. Underline the simple subject.

EXAMPLE   1. From the chimney came a thick cloud of smoke.
   1. *a thick cloud of smoke*

1. Tents were set up in the park.
2. A small brown dog ran across the grass.
3. News travels fast in our town.
4. Above the fort, the flag was still flying.
5. Beyond those mountains lies an ancient village.
6. Those reporters have been interviewing the mayor.
7. On the ledge was a strange bird.
8. According to folklore, Johnny Kaw invented the catfish.
9. The blue candles burned all night long.
10. In the cabinet were several boxes of cereal.

From now on in this book, the term *subject* will mean "simple subject" unless the directions tell you otherwise.

GRAMMAR

WRITING APPLICATION A:
Varying the Position of the Subject

You can help make your writing interesting by experimenting with where you put the subject. Note the position of the subjects in the following examples.

EXAMPLES A **puppy** was in the basket. [subject at beginning]
In the basket was a **puppy.** [subject at end]
In the basket a **puppy** slept peacefully. [subject in the middle]

Writing Assignment

Write a description of your pet or of one you would like to have. Use details to help the reader picture your pet. In at least two sentences, place the subject either in the middle of the sentence or at the end.

The Predicate

The subject is only part of a sentence. The rest of the sentence is called the *predicate*.

10d. The *predicate* of a sentence is the part that says something about the subject.

In the following sentences, the predicates are in boldfaced type.

EXAMPLES The best program **was about snakes.**
The students **took turns on the new computer.**

The predicate *was about snakes* says something about the subject *The best program*. The predicate *took turns on the new computer* tells what the subject *students* did.

EXERCISE 4. Identifying Predicates. Number your paper 1–10. After each number, write the predicate of the sentence.

EXAMPLES 1. Many people would like to have a robot.
           1. *would like to have a robot*
           2. Robots can be very useful.
           2. *can be very useful*

1. Robots are machines with brains.
2. The robot's brain is a computer.
3. A robot does not always look like a person.
4. Pacemakers are little robots.
5. Pacemakers help control a faulty heartbeat.
6. Many companies use robots.
7. Some household jobs can be done by robots.
8. A robot could clean your room.
9. Cars of the future may be guided by robots.
10. Your parents might like to have a helpful robot.

The Position of the Predicate

The predicate usually comes after the subject. Sometimes, however, part or all of the predicate comes before the subject. In the following sentences, the predicates are in boldfaced type.

EXAMPLES **Quickly** we **learned the layout of the zoo.** [Part of the predicate comes before the subject.]

           At the entrance were maps of the exhibits. [All of the predicate comes before the subject.]

EXERCISE 5. Identifying Predicates. Number your paper 1–10. After each number, write the predicate of the sentence. If part of the predicate comes before the subject, write a dash between the parts.

EXAMPLE 1. At noon we went to a Mexican restaurant.
         1. *At noon—went to a Mexican restaurant.*

1. My parents like different kinds of food.
2. Last Saturday Dad prepared spaghetti for supper.
3. Sometimes Mom makes chow mein.

4. With chow mein she serves egg rolls.
5. At the Greek bakery we buy delicious bread.
6. A favorite at picnics is German potato salad.
7. At first, tacos seem messy.
8. Carefully, I spoon the meat sauce into the shell.
9. After that come the other ingredients.
10. In the United States we enjoy a wide variety of foods.

EXERCISE 6. Writing Predicates. Number your paper 1–5. Make a sentence out of each of the following groups of words by adding predicates to fill the blank or blanks. Write each complete sentence on your paper after its number.

EXAMPLES 1. My aunt and uncle —— .
          1. *My aunt and uncle visited us last weekend.*
          2. —— we —— .
          2. *Yesterday we cleaned out the garage.*

1. —— the cat —— .
2. The Egyptian exhibit —— .
3. The birthday party —— .
4. —— the goldfish —— .
5. Mr. Simmons' wheelchair —— .

Complete Predicate and Simple Predicate

Like the complete subject, the complete predicate has a main word or words. This main word is called the *simple predicate*. Another name for the simple predicate is the *verb*.

10e. The *simple predicate,* or *verb,* is the main word or group of words in the complete predicate.

EXAMPLE The nurse lifted the patient carefully.
    Complete predicate lifted the patient carefully
Simple predicate (verb) lifted

Read the following sentences. The complete predicates are underlined. The simple predicates (verbs) are boldfaced.

I **saw** a picture of a Siberian tiger.
My boxer puppy **chewed** on the old glove.
Meteorites **are** lumps of rock and iron.

The simple predicate is always a verb. In this book the simple predicate is usually called the *verb*.

EXERCISE 7. Identifying Complete Predicates and Verbs. Number your paper 1–10. Write the complete predicate. Then underline the verb.

EXAMPLE   1. Space travel fascinates me.
　　　　　　 1. *fascinates me*

1. My class traveled by train to Houston.
2. We visited the Lyndon B. Johnson Space Center.
3. The center displays moon rocks.
4. At the center the astronauts train for their flights.
5. In one room we saw several unusual computers.
6. On the way home we stopped at the Astrodome for a tour.
7. This stadium has the largest scoreboard in the world.
8. Several teams play there.
9. The Astrodome attracts many tourists.
10. Actually, I had more fun at the space center.

The Verb Phrase

A simple predicate (verb) that is made up of more than one word is called a *verb phrase*.

EXAMPLES   We **will go** to an amusement park.
　　　　　　 The park **is located** near a lake.
　　　　　　 We **are** not **planning** a picnic.

☞ **NOTE**   The words *not* and *never* are frequently used with verbs. However, they are not verbs themselves. They are never part of a verb or of a verb phrase.

EXERCISE 8. Identifying Predicates, Verbs and Verb Phrases. Number your paper 1–10. After each number, write the complete predicate of the sentence. Then underline the verb or verb phrase.

EXAMPLE   1. The Liberty Bell was cast in London.
   1. *was cast* in London

1. I am writing a report on the Liberty Bell.
2. The Liberty Bell was ordered by the Philadelphia Assembly.
3. It was made by Thomas Lester in London.
4. This bell was cracked by its own clapper in 1752.
5. American patriots hid the bell from the British Army.
6. It was not brought back to Philadelphia until 1778.
7. It cracked again in 1835.
8. The Liberty Bell has rung out on a number of historic occasions.
9. The bell is exhibited in the Liberty Bell Pavilion.
10. We will be seeing the Liberty Bell on our class trip.

WRITING APPLICATION B:
Using Colorful Verbs

"How was your school day?" asks your mother after school. You might answer, "It was OK." This answer is vague. *Vague* means "not very precise." Choose your verbs carefully so that they say exactly what you mean.

EXAMPLES   The dog walked.   The dog **limped.**
       She closed the door.   She **slammed** the door.
       I went to the gym.   I **raced** to the gym.
       They were **talking.**   They were **arguing.**

Writing Assignment

If you could do anything you wanted to for an entire weekend, what would you do? Describe this special weekend. Underline at least five precise verbs.

Finding the Subject

When the subject doesn't come first in a sentence, it may be difficult to find. Sometimes it is helpful to find the verb first. Then, using the verb in place of the blanks, ask yourself, "Who —— ?" or "What —— ?"

EXAMPLE   Next semester, you may take art or music.

In this sentence the verb is *may take.* Ask yourself, "Who may take?" The answer is *you. You* is the subject of the sentence.
    Now read the following sentence:

EXAMPLE   Can your sister drive us to the park?

The verb is *can drive.* Ask yourself, "Who can drive?" The answer is *sister. Sister* is the subject.

Diagraming the Simple Subject and the Verb

A diagram shows how the parts of a sentence work together. With one horizontal line and one vertical line, you can diagram the simple subject and the verb or verb phrase.

PATTERN

simple subject	verb or verb phrase

Write the simple subject to the left of the vertical line. Write the verb or verb phrase to the right of that line.

EXAMPLES   Dogs bark.   Children were singing.

Dogs	bark

Children	were singing

Now look at a longer sentence.

EXAMPLE   Before winter the highways were repaired.

To diagram the simple subject and verb of this sentence, follow these three steps:

1. Separate the complete subject from the complete predicate.

Complete subject   *Complete predicate*
the highways   Before winter—were repaired

2. Find the simple subject and the verb or verb phrase.

Simple subject   *Verb phrase*
highways   were repaired

3. Diagram the simple subject and the verb phrase.

highways	were repaired

In some sentences, the simple subject comes after the verb or verb phrase.

EXAMPLE   Across the meadow ran a quiet stream.

To diagram this sentence, identify the verb: *ran.* Then ask yourself, "What ran?" The answer is *stream,* the simple subject.

EXAMPLE

stream	ran

EXERCISE 9. Diagraming Simple Subjects and Verbs.
Diagram the simple subject and the verb in the following sentences. Use your ruler. Allow plenty of space between diagrams.

EXAMPLE   1. The temperature in Fort Worth was 105 degrees.

1.

1. In class we are reading a story about the Vikings.
2. These people from the North were brave in battle.

3. They were also fine shipbuilders and sailors.
4. Viking chiefs were buried in their ships.
5. On one voyage, Vikings may have discovered America.

COMPOUND SUBJECTS AND COMPOUND VERBS

In some sentences two or more subjects perform one action. In other sentences, one subject performs two or more actions. The subjects or the verbs in such sentences are connected by words such as *and* or *or*. Subjects or verbs that are connected in this way are called *compound subjects* or *compound verbs*.

Compound Subjects

10f. A *compound subject* **is two or more subjects that have the same verb. The parts of the compound subject are most often connected by** *and* **or** *or*.

EXAMPLES **Minneapolis** and **St. Paul** are called the "Twin Cities." [The two parts of the compound subject have the same verb, *are called*.]

Flutes, clarinets, and **oboes** are woodwinds. [The three parts of the compound subject have the same verb, *are*.]

Mrs. Jones or **Mrs. Lopez** will chaperone our field trip. [The two parts of the compound subject have the same verb, *will chaperone*.]

EXERCISE 10. Identifying Compound Subjects. Number your paper 1–10. Write the compound subjects in the following sentences.

EXAMPLE 1. October and June are my favorite months.
1. *October, June*

1. Wild ducks and geese migrate each year.
2. Stars and planets form a galaxy.

3. In the Tower of London are famous jewels and crowns.
4. Baseball and soccer are popular sports.
5. Eggs and flour are necessary ingredients for pancakes.
6. Every year bugs and rabbits raid our garden.
7. Pizza or hamburgers will be served.
8. At a party, balloons or horns are the best noisemakers.
9. Chihuahuas and Pekingese are small dogs.
10. Someday dolphins and people may talk to one another.

Compound Verbs

Sometimes a sentence has two or more verbs or verb phrases that are connected by *and, or, nor,* or *but.* These connected verbs or verb phrases are called a *compound verb.*

10g. A *compound verb* is made up of two or more connected verbs that have the same subject.

EXAMPLES   Barbara **sings** or **hums** all day long.
Ben **overslept** but **caught** his bus anyway.
We **will go** to the zoo and **see** the panther cub.

EXERCISE 11. Identifying Compound Verbs.   Number your paper 1–10. Write the verbs and verb phrases in these sentences.

EXAMPLE   1. I proofread my paper and made a final copy.
1. *proofread, made*

1. Our teacher wrote a poem and read it to us.
2. The restaurant has closed but will reopen soon.
3. Every week we wash and wax the kitchen floor.
4. Before supper I set the table or peel the vegetables.
5. My brother asked for a watch but received a bike instead.
6. We gathered firewood and headed back to camp.
7. Last week everyone gave a speech or recited a poem.
8. We will walk or take the bus.

9. I remembered the bread but forgot the milk.
10. I received good grades and made the honor roll.

EXERCISE 12. Writing Compound Subjects and Compound Verbs. Number your paper 1–10. Make sentences by adding compound subjects or verbs to fill in the blanks.

EXAMPLE   1. —— are coming to the party.
             1. *Fran and Terry are coming to the party.*
             2. At the mall, we —— .
             2. *At the mall, we ate lunch and went to a movie.*

1. —— are beginning a stamp collection.
2. —— were my favorite teachers last year.
3. The creature from outer space —— .
4. At the end of the play, the cast —— .
5. Last week —— were interviewed on a television talk show.
6. After school, my friends —— .
7. During the storm, we —— .
8. At the front door were —— .
9. In the garage are —— .
10. Before the birthday party, he —— .

EXERCISE 13. Identifying Subjects and Verbs. Make two columns on your paper. Label one *Subject* and the other *Verb*. After the number of each sentence, write its subject and verb in the proper columns. Some of the subjects and verbs are compound.

EXAMPLE   1. Jeff hit the ball and ran to first base.
             Subject   *Verb*
          1. *Jeff*   *hit, ran*

1. Some pets have psychologists.
2. Dogs and cats need help for their problems, too.
3. The pet psychologist studies the pet and makes suggestions to the pet owner.
4. My aunt and uncle owned two pets with back problems.

5. Their puppy growled and bit people.
6. Their kitten did not like cars and would not ride in them.
7. My aunt and uncle called the psychologist.
8. Dr. Lu came to their house and met both patients.
9. She calmed the puppy and examined him carefully and gently.
10. Eventually the pet psychologist helped the pets and made their owners happy.

A sentence may have both a *compound subject* and a *compound verb*.

EXAMPLES   **She** and **I brought** corn and **fed** the ducks.
            Carrots and **celery are** nourishing and **taste** good.

In the first example, *she* and *I* is the compound subject of *brought* and *fed*. In the second example, *carrots* and *celery* is the compound subject of *are* and *taste*.

EXERCISE 14. Identifying Compound Subjects and Compound Verbs.

Number your paper 1–5. Write the compound subject and underline it once. Write the compound verb and underline it twice.

EXAMPLE   1. Tena and Julia washed and dried the dog.
            1. *Tena, Julia—washed, dried*

1. Alice and Sally sang and played the piano.
2. Either Dwayne or I will feed the cat and put it out.
3. Patrick and she read the same book and reported on it in English class.
4. Roses and lilacs look pretty and smell good.
5. The dentist or his assistant cleans and polishes my teeth every six months.

Diagraming Compound Subjects and Compound Verbs

To diagram a compound subject, you write the subjects on parallel lines.

EXAMPLE   Asia and Europe are called Eurasia.

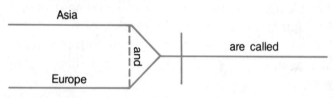

The connecting word, *and*, is put on a dotted line joining the two subjects. A compound verb is diagramed in much the same way:

EXAMPLE   Giraffes look skinny but may weigh five tons.

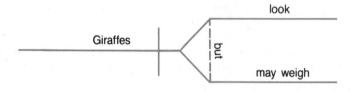

A sentence with both a compound subject and a compound verb is diagramed as follows:

EXAMPLE   The cat and her kittens ate and then slept.

EXERCISE 15. Diagraming Compound Subjects and Verbs.
Diagram the subjects and verbs in the following sentences. Use your ruler, and leave plenty of space between diagrams.

1. My mother and father took us to a state park.
2. We bought groceries and packed the car.
3. My sister and I carried the gear and studied the map.
4. Dad and I put up the tent and started the fire.
5. We ate a good dinner and slept well.

REVIEW EXERCISE A. Writing Complete Sentences.
Number your paper 1–10. Some of the following groups of words
are sentences. Write these sentences. Add capital letters and
punctuation. If a group of words is not a sentence, add a subject
or a verb to make it a sentence. Write that sentence.

EXAMPLES   1. we brought costumes from home
            1. *We brought costumes from home.*
            2. wrote a play
            2. *Our language arts class wrote a play.*

1. blew out all the candles
2. it was cold on the rink
3. helped me with my science project
4. shares a locker with me
5. how hungry I am at lunchtime
6. it is too late for a game of *Scrabble*
7. is that Niagara Falls or Horseshoe Falls
8. every single day for two weeks our class
9. what time is your mom picking us up
10. the governor of my state

SIMPLE SENTENCES AND COMPOUND SENTENCES

The sentences you have been studying so far are *simple sentences*.
Each has one subject and one verb. Although a compound
subject has two or more parts, it is still one subject. In the same
way, a compound verb or verb phrase is one verb.

10h. A *simple sentence* has one subject and one verb.

EXAMPLES   My **mother** | **belongs** to the Friends of the Library.
            Argentina and **Chile** | **are** in South America.
            Jeannette | **read** *Stuart Little* and **reported** on it.
            The **seals** and **porpoises** | **did** tricks and **were**
            rewarded with fish.

10i. A *compound sentence* is a sentence that has two or more simple sentences, usually joined by a connecting word.

Two or more simple sentences can be joined to make a *compound sentence.* The words *and, but, or, nor, for,* or *yet* connect the simple sentences. In a compound sentence, each simple sentence is called an *independent clause.*

EXAMPLES   I forgot my lunch, **but** Dad ran to the bus with it.
She likes carrots, **yet** she seldom buys them.
Martina presided **and** Steve called the roll.

As you will see from the second example above, a sentence is regarded as compound if the subject is repeated.

☞ NOTE   A very short compound sentence is sometimes written without a comma, as in the third example above.

EXERCISE 16. Identifying Simple Sentences and Compound Sentences.   Number your paper 1–10. If a sentence is simple, write *S* after the number. If it is compound, write *C.*

EXAMPLE   1. That story is good, and you should read it.
1. *C*

1. Dad and I like clams, but my mother prefers oysters.
2. Some trees and shrubs live thousands of years.
3. It rained, but we marched in the parade anyway.
4. Mr. Edwards will lead the singing, for Ms. Ludlow is ill.
5. My cousins and their parents visited us last summer.
6. I had worked hard, yet I had not finished the job.
7. Abe peeled the onions, carrots, and potatoes and dumped them into a huge pot.
8. We made a shelter for our dog, but he will not use it.
9. Plants and pets should be protected from the cold.
10. All ravens are crows, but not all crows are ravens.

Diagraming Compound Sentences

In diagraming a compound sentence, you put together the diagrams of two or more simple sentences. First, find the subject and verb in each of the simple sentences. Then diagram each simple sentence. Connect the two diagrams as shown below.

EXAMPLE   Ostriches seem clumsy, but they can run fast.

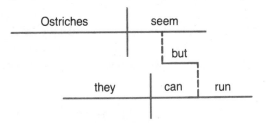

EXERCISE 17. Diagraming Subjects and Verbs in Compound Sentences.   Diagram the subjects and verbs in the following compound sentences.

1. People rushed to Alaska for gold, and many settled there.
2. Cactuses are desert plants, yet some grow in Florida.
3. We went for a walk, for it was a beautiful evening.
4. My first name is Charles, but everyone calls me Skipper.
5. The movie begins at one, but the doors open at noon.

REVIEW EXERCISE B. Identifying Simple Sentences and Compound Sentences.   Number your paper 1–10. If a sentence is simple, write *S*. If a sentence is compound, write *C*.

EXAMPLE   1. I would like to go, but I have homework.
          1. *C*

1. My brother is eight, and he collects postcards.
2. We find cards with pictures of bridges, for he prefers them.
3. He has several cards with pictures of stone bridges.
4. Stone bridges are strong, but they are costly.
5. Many bridges are beautiful, but they must also be sturdy.
6. Someone sent my brother a rare stamp on a postcard.

7. Suspension bridges look dangerous, yet they are safe.
8. Three different bridges connect Manhattan and Brooklyn.
9. Bridges must be inspected regularly.
10. My brother collects pictures of bridges, and I paint them.

CLASSIFYING SENTENCES BY PURPOSE

10j. Sentences may be classified, or grouped, by purpose.

(1) A *declarative sentence* **makes a statement. It is always followed by a period.**

EXAMPLES   Our media center has several computers.
            Patrick Henry lived in Virginia.

(2) An *imperative sentence* **gives a command or makes a request. It may be followed by a period or by an exclamation point.**

EXAMPLES   Stop shouting!
            Please pass the potatoes.

☞ **NOTE**   The subject of a command or a request is the word *you*. Often *you* is not expressed. In such sentences, the subject is understood to be *you*.

---

(3) An *interrogative sentence* **asks a question. It is followed by a question mark.**

EXAMPLE   When did *Apollo* land on the moon?

(4) An *exclamatory sentence* **expresses strong feeling. It is followed by an exclamation point.**

EXAMPLES   What an assignment that was!
            Imagine how hungry I was!

EXERCISE 18. Classifying Sentences by Purpose. Write the following sentences. Add the appropriate mark of punctuation to the end of the sentence. Label each sentence as *declarative, imperative, interrogative,* or *exclamatory.*

EXAMPLE   1. Did you travel this summer
              1. *Did you travel this summer?* —*interrogative*

1. My family traveled west
2. Have you seen the Grand Canyon
3. Our vacation took a week
4. You cannot imagine how pretty the sunsets were
5. The national park was very quiet
6. Do you think we needed air-conditioning
7. How cool it was at night
8. What a great movie we saw about the canyon
9. Did you take the short hike or the long one
10. Picture me on a donkey

Diagraming Interrogative Sentences and Imperative Sentences

To diagram the subject and the verb in an interrogative sentence, you must first find the verb. One way to find the verb is to change the question into a statement.

EXAMPLE   Can insects fly? (question)
              Insects can fly. (statement)

In the diagram, the subject comes first, followed by the verb or verb phrase.

EXAMPLE   Can insects fly?

insects	Can fly

Notice that *Can* is capitalized, as it is in the sentence.

In an imperative sentence, the subject is understood to be

you. Diagram the subject of an imperative sentence by writing *you* in parentheses.

EXAMPLE   Go home.

(you)	Go

Notice that *Go* is capitalized, as it is in the sentence.

EXERCISE 19. Diagraming Interrogative and Imperative Sentences.   Diagram the subjects and verbs in the following sentences.

1. Eat all your red beans and rice.
2. Have you written to your grandparents?
3. Where is the driver going?
4. Help me with these cartons.
5. Why are they wearing raincoats?

REVIEW EXERCISE C. Classifying Sentences by Purpose.
Write each of the following sentences and the punctuation mark that should follow it. Label the sentence *declarative, interrogative, imperative,* or *exclamatory.*

EXAMPLE   1. What a funny show that was
          1. *What a funny show that was!—exclamatory*

1. Please help me find my umbrella
2. How happy I am
3. Have you been to a video store
4. Go east for three blocks and look for a mailbox
5. My father and I are cleaning the attic
6. What a delicious ham this is
7. We toured the garment district
8. Do you like charcoal-grilled hamburgers
9. My surprise visit pleased my grandmother
10. When is your next piano lesson

CHAPTER 10 REVIEW: POSTTEST 1

A. Identifying Sentences. If a group of words is a sentence, write it, beginning with a capital letter and ending with a punctuation mark. Write *NS* if a group of words is not a sentence.

EXAMPLE 1. followed the trail on the map
         1. *NS*

1. we put up posters in the gym
2. our neighborhood has a homework hotline
3. mailed the invitations yesterday
4. finish my homework before dinner
5. the Washington Monument

B. Identifying Simple Subjects and Verbs. Write each sentence. Underline each simple subject once and each verb twice.

EXAMPLE 1. Every day my sister practices the piano.
         1. *Every day my <u>sister</u> <u>practices</u> the piano.*

6. Saturday we and our parents drove to the lake and swam.
7. My grandmother plays *Monopoly* with my friends and me.
8. They have plowed the fields and will plant potatoes.
9. At night you can rent roller skates at that rink.
10. On the sand lay a sick whale.

C. Identifying Simple Sentences and Compound Sentences. Number your paper 11–15. If a sentence is simple, write *S* after its number. If a sentence is compound, write *C*.

EXAMPLE 1. Mom is late, but she will be here soon.
         1. *C*

11. The stranger turned and disappeared among the trees.
12. The class has chosen a theme and will decorate the gym.
13. The bus stopped suddenly, but no one was hurt.
14. Raccoons and opossums steal our garbage.
15. The batter stepped up to the plate, and the crowd roared.

D. Classifying and Punctuating Sentences by Purpose.
Number your paper 16–20. For each sentence, write the last word and the appropriate punctuation mark. Then label each sentence *declarative, interrogative, imperative,* or *exclamatory.*

EXAMPLE   1. Have you heard from your friend
            1. *friend?—interrogative*

16. Answer the phone before the fourth ring
17. What fun the party was
18. Who cleaned up the mess
19. We sat on a bench and played checkers
20. Whose book is this

CHAPTER 10 REVIEW: POSTTEST 2

Writing Sentences.   Identify each sentence part as a subject or a predicate. For each subject, make a complete sentence by adding a predicate. For each predicate, make a complete sentence by adding a subject.

EXAMPLE   1. will drive us home
            1. *predicate—Will your mother drive us home?*

1. my favorite book
2. watched a good mystery
3. our class play
4. the oldest house in town
5. can swim under water

The Parts of Speech

NOUN, PRONOUN, ADJECTIVE

When you were quite young, you very likely built things with blocks. In much the same way, you now build sentences with the "building blocks of language"—words. There are eight kinds of words, called the *parts of speech*. In this chapter, you will learn about three of them: nouns, pronouns, and adjectives.

DIAGNOSTIC TEST

Identifying Nouns, Pronouns, and Adjectives. Number your paper 1–10. After each number, write the lettered, italicized words in the sentence. Then, next to each word, write the part of speech it is in the sentence.

EXAMPLE 1. (a) *Dad* tinkered with the (b) *rusty* key.
       1. *(a) Dad—noun; (b) rusty—adjective*

1. My (a) *best* friend plays (b) *soccer.*
2. (a) *We* went to (b) *Boston* last summer.
3. Help (a) *yourself* to some (b) *Chinese* food.
4. Martha invited (a) *us* to (b) *her* party.
5. What a (a) *beautiful* (b) *garden* you have!

6. (a) *My* directions were (b) *accurate.*
7. The jacket on the (a) *chair* is (b) *yours.*
8. A (a) *sharp* pencil is (b) *necessary* for this assignment.
9. (a) *She* takes private (b) *lessons.*
10. This story, short and (a) *funny,* is my (b) *favorite.*

THE NOUN

If someone asked you what you were wearing, your answer would probably include naming words called *nouns;* for example, *shirt, sweater,* or *shoes.* You can see or touch the items that these nouns stand for. You also use nouns to name things you cannot see or touch: *fashion, interest, style.* You use nouns to name things you may or may not be able to see or touch.

11a. A *noun* is a word that names a person, place, thing, or idea.

Persons	Mother, Scott, Tina, teacher, brother, Mayor Koch
Places	White House, state, Miami, school
Things	rocket, desk, hamster, computer
Ideas	anger, freedom, kindness, fear

> ☞ NOTE   Nouns of more than one word, like *John Smith, Empire State Building,* and *family room,* are counted as one noun.

EXERCISE 1. Identifying Nouns. There are twenty nouns in the following paragraph. Make a list of them on your paper. Before each noun, write the number of the sentence.

EXAMPLE   1. Clara had two brothers and two sisters.
1. *Clara*
1. *brothers*
1. *sisters*

1. Clara Barton was born in Massachusetts. **2.** She was educated in a rural school and grew up with a love of books. **3.** She began her career as a teacher. **4.** During the Civil War, however, she distributed medicine and other supplies. **5.** Later she helped find soldiers who were missing in action. **6.** She organized the American Red Cross and was its president for many years. **7.** She begged for money for the organization and worked with victims of floods and other disasters.

Proper Nouns and Common Nouns

A *proper noun* names a particular person, place, or thing and begins with a capital letter.

Persons Ms. Kahn, Maria, Aunt Josie, Alan B. Shepard, Jr.
Places Columbus, Maryland, Scotland, Asia
Things Big Ben, Mount Rushmore, *Little Women*

A *common noun* does not name a particular person, place, or thing and does not begin with a capital letter.

Persons uncle, doctor, teacher, child
Places school, park, church, store
Things computer, glue, baseball, pencil
Ideas sadness, health, ache, joy

Study the following lists of common and proper nouns. The proper nouns are capitalized because they name *particular* persons, places, or things. Make sure you understand the difference between these two kinds of nouns.

COMMON NOUNS	PROPER NOUNS
explorer	Henry Hudson
team	New York Yankees
country	Mexico
park	Yellowstone National Park

EXERCISE 2. Identifying Common and Proper Nouns.
There are twenty nouns in the following sentences. Number your paper 1–8. After each number, write the noun or nouns that

you find in that sentence. After each noun, write *C* if it is a common noun or *P* if it is a proper noun.

EXAMPLE   1. Which state is known as the Bluegrass State?
          1. *state—C*
             Bluegrass State—P

1. Many people think that Daniel Boone founded Kentucky.
2. This famous pioneer entered the territory through the Cumberland Gap.
3. He built a fort called Fort Boonesborough.
4. James Harrod started the first permanent settlement, however.
5. After the Revolutionary War, new settlers flowed in.
6. Later, railroads opened up the coalfields in the Appalachian Mountains.
7. Frankfort is the capital of the state.
8. A popular American song is "My Old Kentucky Home."

EXERCISE 3. Substituting Proper Nouns for Common Nouns.   Number your paper 1–10. In the following sentences, substitute a proper noun for each italicized common noun. You may need to leave out some of the words that come before a common noun.

EXAMPLE   1. The *principal* sent for the *student*.
          1. *Mrs. McGee sent for Paula Perez.*

1. The *student* is from a big *city*.
2. Usually, my *uncle* reads the *newspaper* after dinner.
3. The *child* watched a *movie*.
4. A *teacher* asked a *student* to read.
5. My *cousin* read that *book*.
6. Surrounded by reporters, the *mayor* entered the *building*.
7. Does the *girl* go to this *school*?
8. That famous, blind *singer* wrote the *song*.
9. My *neighbor* bought a *car*.
10. As a college student, the *coach* played for that *team*.

REVIEW EXERCISE A. Identifying and Classifying Nouns.
The following sentences contain twenty nouns, some common and some proper. Write the nouns on your paper after the appropriate sentence number. Capitalize all proper nouns.

EXAMPLE 1. The pilots studied at wright field in dayton, ohio.
          1. *pilots, Wright Field, Dayton, Ohio*

1. Many people think that general chuck yeager is the greatest pilot in america.
2. During world war II, he was shot down by the enemy.
3. He hiked through the pyrenees with the help of the french.
4. He returned to his base in england and was recommended for the silver star, a decoration awarded by the united states.
5. On a historic day two years after the war, he became the first pilot to fly faster than the speed of sound.

WRITING APPLICATION A:
Using Proper Nouns to Make Writing Exact

Proper nouns give exact information. When you use proper nouns in your writing, you are being more precise.

EXAMPLE That **man** lives in that **area.** [The nouns *man* and *area* are common nouns.]

        Diego Martinez lives in **Boulder, Colorado.** [The proper nouns *Diego Martinez, Boulder,* and *Colorado* give exact information.]

Writing Assignment

Suppose a visitor from outer space who has just become your friend says to you, "I do not understand the word *school.*" Explain what a school is by writing about your school. Use proper nouns when you can. For example, give the exact name of your school. As you tell about some school activities, give the names of some of the clubs and organizations. Underline each proper noun you use.

THE PRONOUN

Read the following sentences:

> When Cindy came to the bus stop, Cindy was wearing a cast.
> Cindy had broken Cindy's foot. Cindy's friend Kevin decided
> to help Cindy carry Cindy's books. Cindy thanked Kevin for
> Kevin's help.

In these sentences words like *she, he, her,* and *his* should replace
some of the nouns. These words are called *pronouns*.

> When Cindy came to the bus stop, **she** was wearing a cast. **She**
> had broken **her** foot. Cindy's friend Kevin decided to help **her**
> carry **her** books. Cindy thanked **him** for **his** help.

The pronouns in boldfaced type replace the nouns *Cindy* and
Kevin. A pronoun is used for, or in place of, a noun.

11b. A *pronoun* **is a word used in place of one or more than one
noun. It may stand for a person, place, thing, or idea.**

In the examples below, the pronouns are in boldfaced type. Can
you tell which noun or nouns each pronoun replaces?

Person Judy is late. Where is **she**?
 Place This stable is large. **It** has stalls for thirty horses.
 Thing Several swings are broken. **They** should be replaced.
  Idea Americans love freedom. **It** is very precious.

The noun that a pronoun stands for is called the *antecedent.* The
pronoun must agree in number with its antecedent.

EXAMPLES My **Aunt Merideth** sold **her** car. [The pronoun *her*
stands for the noun *Aunt Merideth. Aunt* is the
antecedent of *her.* Both are singular in number.]

Anthony, call **your** mother. [The pronoun *your*
stands for the noun *Anthony. Anthony* is the antecedent of *your.*]

Call **your** mother. [The antecedent of the pronoun
your is not stated.]

Personal Pronouns

There are several kinds of pronouns. Those you will study in this chapter are called *personal pronouns*. Here is a complete list of the personal pronouns. Study it carefully.

Personal Pronouns

I, me, my, mine   we, us, our, ours
you, your, yours   they, them, their, theirs
he, him, his
she, her, hers
it, its

Some personal pronouns can be combined with *-self* or *-selves:*

EXAMPLES   Janet helped **herself**.
                    Infants cannot take care of **themselves**.

Pronouns with *-self* are called *reflexive pronouns*. There are other kinds of pronouns besides personal pronouns and reflexive pronouns. You will study them later.

EXERCISE 4. **Identifying Pronouns.** Number your paper 1–10. After each number, write the pronouns in the sentence.

EXAMPLE   1. I loaned her my camera.
                    1. *I, her, my*

1. The dentist washed her hands before examining my mouth.
2. Dad told the mechanics to call him to let him know how much his bill would be.
3. Our aunt and uncle have decided that they will visit Greece this summer.
4. I asked myself how I could have been so careless.
5. He washed the mats and put them in the sun to dry.
6. Here is a postcard for you and me.
7. We helped ourselves to fruit and ice-cold milk.
8. You gave us your support when we needed it.
9. She did her math homework before playing soccer with us.
10. I found the weak battery and replaced it.

EXERCISE 5. Identifying Pronouns and Antecedents. In each of the following sentences, underline the pronoun and circle its antecedent. Write the complete sentence.

EXAMPLE   1. Viviana set up her game on the table.
           1. (Viviana) set up _her_ game on the table.

1. The passengers waved to their friends on shore.
2. The test was so long that John didn't finish it.
3. Rachel's neighbors asked her to baby-sit.
4. Carlos said he had already cleaned the kitchen.
5. The directions were long, but they were clear.

Possessive Pronouns

The personal pronouns listed below are called _possessive pronouns_. These pronouns are used to show ownership.

Possessive Pronouns

my, mine	his	its	their, theirs
your, yours	her, hers	our, ours	

The words in boldfaced type in the following sentences are possessive pronouns.

> Nina stored **her** suitcase under **her** bed.
> He has misplaced **his** library card.
> Is that paper **yours** or **mine**?

☞ NOTE   The possessive form of the pronoun _it_ is _its_. The word _it's_ is a contraction that stands for _it is_ or _it has_.

EXERCISE 6. Identifying Personal Pronouns.   Number your paper 1–10. After each number, write the personal pronoun or pronouns in the sentence. Do not overlook the possessive pronouns.

EXAMPLE 1. Their car is newer than ours.
1. *Their, ours*

1. Is your dog losing its hair?
2. This jacket is mine; that one must be yours.
3. My sister and I put up shelves in our bedroom.
4. Before the game, the coach convinced us that we could outscore them.
5. His report is good, but hers is better.
6. My locker is next to hers.
7. The books are theirs.
8. They treated themselves to a bucket of popcorn.
9. Are you riding your bike or walking?
10. She cataloged her stamp collection and then helped me with mine.

REVIEW EXERCISE B. Identifying Personal Pronouns.
Number your paper 1–10. After each number, write the personal pronoun or pronouns in the sentence.

EXAMPLE 1. Shall I send the invitation to him or to her?
1. *I, him, her*

1. For their anniversary, we are giving my grandparents a picture of our family.
2. I put your books in her car.
3. Let me help you with your packages.
4. We peeled the potatoes but forgot to add them to the stew, so it wasn't as good as usual.
5. He carefully wrapped the package and mailed it at the post office this morning.
6. Did they send it to you or to your parents?
7. Why did she call him last night?
8. Are we using her stereo or ours?
9. The brand-new car is theirs; it has many desirable features, such as automatic overdrive and a rear-window defroster.
10. They drove us to the bus stop.

GRAMMAR

WRITING APPLICATION B:
Using Pronouns to Make Your Writing Clear

When did you last organize the clutter in your closet? If a closet is in order, it is easy to find things in it. The message in your writing should also be easy to find. One way to make your writing easier to read is to use pronouns in place of nouns whenever possible.

EXAMPLE   Janet, Kim, and Edward planned a Halloween party. They talked it over with **Janet, Kim,** and **Edward's** parents. [The repeated nouns in bold-faced type should be replaced with a pronoun.]

Janet, Kim, and Edward planned a Halloween party. They talked it over with **their** parents. [The revision is less cluttered.]

Writing Assignment

You are in charge of a party for your homeroom. It is your job to organize the food, the games, and the decorations. Explain how you would assign the jobs. Use at least five pronouns correctly. Underline the pronouns you use.

THE ADJECTIVE

Read the following sentences. Which one gives you more precise information?

EXAMPLES The smell of apples filled the air.
           The **spicy** smell of *warm* apples filled the air.

The second sentence has two added words that help create a clear picture. The words *spicy* and *warm* describe the nouns *smell* and *apples*. Words that describe, or modify, nouns or pronouns are called *adjectives*. Adjectives make your writing clearer and more interesting.

11c. An *adjective* is a word that modifies a noun or a pronoun.

Most nouns, such as *color, state,* and *man,* have a very broad meaning because they name a whole class of people or things. When you add adjectives, you pinpoint the meaning of a noun so that it is more specific. For example, you might say *a bright color, a large state,* or *an elderly man.*

Adjectives answer the questions *What kind? Which one? How many?* or *How much?* The adjectives below are in boldfaced type.

What kind?	**gentle** dog
	foggy day
Which one? or *Which ones?*	**sixth** grade
	these books
How many? or *How much?*	**two** tickets
	full pitcher

Adjectives do not always come before the word they modify. Sometimes they follow it.

EXAMPLES   The dog is **gentle**. [The adjective *gentle* modifies *dog*.]

The tent, **warm** and **dry**, was under the tree. [The adjectives *warm* and *dry* modify *tent*.]

Study the adjectives in the following sentences. An arrow points to the word each adjective modifies.

That poster was chosen the winner. [*That* tells *which one* was chosen.]

We stayed at the Grand Canyon for **several** days. [*Several* tells *how many* days.]

The berries are **ripe**. [*Ripe* tells *what kind* of berries.]

Kitty Hawk is a **famous** city in North Carolina. [*Famous* tells *what kind* of city.]

> ☞ **NOTE** You use the adjectives *a, an,* and *the* almost every time you write a sentence. These words are called *articles.* In this chapter you do not have to identify the articles as adjectives except in the diagraming exercises.

EXERCISE 7. Identifying Adjectives. Number your paper 1–10. After each number, write the adjective or adjectives in the sentence. Do not write *a, an,* or *the.*

EXAMPLE   1. The sky was clear, and the night was cold.
　　　　　1. *clear, cold*

1. A bright moon rode down the western sky.
2. It shed a pale light on the quiet countryside.
3. Long meadows spread out to two hills in the distance.
4. The smell of the wild grass was strong.
5. The only sound was the sharp crackle of the fire.
6. Suddenly, several stars came out.
7. I was sleepy, and I longed for my comfortable bed.
8. I watched until the sky was bright with twinkling stars.
9. I was sad and happy at the same time.
10. Soon I went indoors and fell into a deep sleep.

EXERCISE 8. Writing Adjectives for a Story. The following story is about a haunted house. Complete the story by using appropriate adjectives. Underline the adjectives.

EXAMPLE   An __1__ dog lay in the middle of the __2__ garden.
　　　　　An old dog lay in the middle of the weedy garden.

　　　We walked up the __1__ steps of the __2__ house. A __3__ light could be seen under the __4__ door. I peered through the __5__ window and saw two __6__ figures. Suddenly, we heard some __7__ sounds. My friend gave me a __8__ look. We were about to run away when we heard __9__ voices. Our __10__ friends had been trying to scare us. They had succeeded!

Proper Adjectives

You recall that a proper noun names a particular person, place, or thing. A *proper adjective* is formed from a proper noun.

PROPER NOUNS	PROPER ADJECTIVES
Canada	Canadian police
Japan	Japanese islands
Australia	Australian sheep

Always begin a proper adjective with a capital letter.

EXERCISE 9. Finding Common and Proper Adjectives. Number your paper 1–10. After each number, write the adjectives—common or proper—that appear in the sentence. You should find twenty adjectives. Do not count the articles.

EXAMPLE 1. The Indian weaver made a blanket on a wooden loom.
1. *Indian, wooden*

1. Music can express sad or happy feelings.
2. The quartet sang several Irish songs.
3. The gold watch was made by a Swiss watchmaker.
4. She is a fine Spanish dancer.
5. On vacation, Mother enjoys long, quiet breakfasts.
6. Many Australian people are of British origin.
7. The Egyptian mummies are on display on the first floor.
8. We should be proud of our heritage.
9. The movie is based on a popular Russian novel.
10. In Canadian football there are twelve players on a team.

EXERCISE 10. Changing Proper Nouns into Proper Adjectives. Change the following proper nouns into proper adjectives. Write an appropriate noun after each proper adjective.

EXAMPLE 1. Alaska
1. *Alaskan husky*

1. Spain	5. Germany	8. Orient
2. South America	6. England	9. Africa
3. India	7. Russia	10. Rome
4. Ireland		

Diagraming Adjectives

You have already learned how to diagram subjects and verbs. Now you are ready to diagram adjectives. As you might expect, most adjectives are placed near the nouns they modify. Look at the patterns and the examples that follow.

PATTERNS

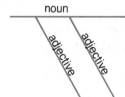

EXAMPLES   blue lake   a hard, steady rain

To diagram adjectives, write them on slanting lines below the nouns they modify. Use the same order in which the adjectives appear in the sentence. Since articles are adjectives, they are included in the diagram.

EXERCISE 11.Diagraming Nouns and Adjectives. Diagram the following nouns and adjectives. Do not forget to include the articles. Use the patterns shown above.

1. a dark night
2. a shuttered window
3. cold milk
4. a fluffy, warm quilt
5. a cool, refreshing swim

EXERCISE 12. Diagraming Sentences. Diagram the following sentences:

1. The little parakeet chirped.
2. A large box arrived.
3. The angry dog snarled.
4. Two astronauts floated.
5. The funny little robot beeped.

REVIEW EXERCISE C. Identifying Adjectives. Number your paper 1–10. After each number, write the adjectives that appear in the sentence. Do not include the articles.

1. Museums can be interesting.
2. In large cities, there are different kinds of museums.
3. Most museums have sculpture and paintings.
4. Some museums have one special kind of art.
5. It might be Oriental art or Indian art.
6. Some museums feature birds and prehistoric animals.
7. A curator holds an important job in a museum.
8. A curator knows numerous facts about a certain subject.
9. Some of the valuable objects require special temperature and humidity control.
10. A famous French museum is called the Louvre.

REVIEW EXERCISE D. Identifying Nouns, Pronouns, and Adjectives. Number your paper 1–10. After each number, write all the nouns, pronouns, and adjectives in the sentence. Label them as noun (*n.*), pronoun (*pron.*), or adjective (*adj.*). Do not list the articles *a, an,* and *the.*

EXAMPLE   1. Models make a great hobby.
           1. *Models, n.; great, adj.; hobby, n.*

1. Do you have a favorite hobby?
2. Models are enjoyable and educational.
3. They require little space.
4. I keep mine on my bookshelf my dad built in my room.
5. Models are packaged in kits.
6. My favorite models are historic ships and planes.
7. On my last birthday, I received two kits of submarines.
8. They came in boxes with directions in several languages.
9. The tiny parts are designed for an exact fit.
10. Bright decals add a realistic look.

WRITING APPLICATION C:
Using Adjectives to Make Your Writing Colorful

Adjectives help make your writing colorful. They give a special meaning to nouns and pronouns. In the example below, taken from a novel, a girl discovers a strange window.

> It was a funny kind of window, very tall and narrow, with two sets of curtains: straight-hanging white lace framed by drawn-back red velvet. It was open . . .
>
> —EDWARD ORMONDROYD

Notice the adjectives *funny, tall, narrow, straight-hanging, white, drawn-back, red,* and *open*. They help the reader see more clearly the window being described.

Writing Assignment

Describe a magical, make-believe world that only you can enter. Use and underline at least ten colorful adjectives. Here are some ideas:

Climbing through a picture on the wall
Walking through a TV screen
Entering a magic cave

CHAPTER 11 REVIEW: POSTTEST 1

Identifying Nouns, Pronouns, and Adjectives. Number your paper 1–10. After each number, write the lettered, italicized words in the sentence. Then, next to each word, write the part of speech it is in the sentence.

EXAMPLE   1. (a) *Her* brother has an (b) *important* exam on Saturday.
   1. (a) *Her—pronoun;* (b) *important—adjective*

1. The volcano, (a) *inactive* for years, is still a tourist (b) *attraction.*
2. Last summer we visited (a) *Alaska,* (b) *our* largest state —wasn't that exciting?
3. Put (a) *yourself* in (b) *my* position.
4. The (a) *Hawaiian* dancers wore (b) *colorful* costumes.
5. According to the accounts we have, several of the (a) *Roman* emperors could be (b) *cruel* at times.
6. (a) *We* watched the sun set behind the (b) *mountains.*
7. Our (a) *new* teacher is very (b) *friendly.*
8. (a) *They* made the winning touchdown just before the final (b) *whistle.*
9. Is (a) *Berlin* still a divided (b) *city?*
10. The pen with the (a) *blue* ink is (b) *mine.*

CHAPTER 11 REVIEW: POSTTEST 2

Writing Sentences Using Nouns, Pronouns, and Adjectives.
Write five original sentences in which you use the parts of speech given below. In each sentence, underline the word that is the listed part of speech.

EXAMPLE   1. An adjective that comes after the noun it describes
   1. *Our guide was very <u>helpful</u>.*

1. A proper noun
2. A possessive pronoun
3. An adjective that tells *how many*
4. A reflexive pronoun
5. A proper adjective

GRAMMAR

CHAPTER 12

The Parts of Speech

VERB, ADVERB, PREPOSITION, CONJUNCTION, INTERJECTION

In Chapter 11, you learned about three parts of speech: nouns, pronouns, and adjectives. There are five more parts of speech: verbs, adverbs, prepositions, conjunctions, and interjections. You will study them in this chapter.

DIAGNOSTIC TEST

Identifying Verbs, Adverbs, Prepositions, Conjunctions, and Interjections. Number your paper 1–10. After each number, write the lettered, italicized words in the sentence. Next to each word, write the part of speech it is in the sentence: *verb, adverb, preposition, conjunction,* or *interjection.*

EXAMPLE 1. We (a) *visited* a water park (b) *on* Saturday.
        1. *(a) visited—verb; (b) on—preposition*

1. A water park (a) *can be* (b) *really* great fun.
2. You (a) *should go* (b) *early* if you can.
3. If you don't, it (a) *may be* (b) *uncomfortably* crowded.

4. You (a) *can slide* (b) *down* a water slide.
5. (a) *Wow!* What a (b) *tremendously* exciting experience that is.
6. People land in the water (a) *and* splash everyone (b) *around* them.
7. Some parks (a) *rent* inner tubes (b) *inexpensively.*
8. You climb (a) *in* and (b) *whirl* around in the water.
9. You (a) *may get* tired, (b) *but* you won't be bored.
10. People (a) *of* all ages (b) *enjoy* water parks.

THE VERB

Every sentence must have a verb. The verb says something about the subject. Notice the verbs in these sentences.

EXAMPLES We **lived** in Boston for three years.
They **took** their dog to the vet.
Is a firefly a beetle?

12a. A *verb* **is a word that expresses action or otherwise helps make a statement.**

Action Verbs

An action verb is easy to recognize. It expresses physical or mental action. Here are some action verbs: *run, yell, paint, skate, think, fear, like,* and *learn.* Which four verbs express physical action? Which four verbs express mental action?

(1) An *action verb* **is a verb that expresses physical or mental action.**

EXAMPLES I **used** a computer in math class.
Fran **baby-sat** for her neighbor.
Todd **understands** the science assignment.
I **jogged** a mile today.

GRAMMAR

EXERCISE 1. **Identifying Action Verbs.** Number your paper 1–10. Write each action verb after the number of the sentence in which it is used.

EXAMPLE   1. The Maricopa Indians live in Arizona.
          1. *live*

   1. They make unusual pottery.   **2.** They need two kinds of clay for this pottery.   **3.** One kind forms the vessel.   **4.** The other colors it.   **5.** The potters mold the clay by hand.   **6.** They make useful bowls and vases.   **7.** The Indians paint designs on the pottery.   **8.** They sometimes use a toothpick.   **9.** The designs vary from family to family.   **10.** The Maricopa Indians teach their children this craft.

Linking Verbs

Not all verbs express mental or physical action. Instead they help make a statement by connecting the subject with a word in the predicate. The word in the predicate describes or explains the subject. Verbs that make a statement in this way are called *linking verbs*. The most common linking verb is *be*. The following list includes some forms of the linking verb *be*.

am	has been	may be
is	have been	can be
are	had been	should be
was	will be	would have been
were	shall be	

A verb phrase that ends in *be* or *been* is a form of the linking verb *be*. Notice the linking verbs in these sentences:

EXAMPLES   He **is** the shortstop.
          I **will be** there.
          I **might be** late this afternoon.
          They **have** never **been** happier

There are other linking verbs besides *be*. Notice how the linking verbs in the following sentences link the subject with a word in the predicate. The linking verbs are in boldfaced type. The words that are linked are in italic type.

EXAMPLES   *Rachel* **stayed** *calm* during the storm.
The *firefighters* **appeared** *tired.*
The bubbling *sauce* **smells** *good.*

(2) A *linking verb* is a verb that does not show action. It connects the subject with a word in the predicate.

Besides *be,* the verbs in the following list are often used as linking verbs:

appear	grow	seem	stay
become	look	smell	taste
feel	remain	sound	

Some verbs may be either action verbs or linking verbs. The meaning of the sentence tells you whether a verb is an action verb or a linking verb.

ACTION   They **sounded** the bell for a fire drill.
LINKING   Mom **sounded** happy about the new job.

ACTION   The judge **looked** at my science project.
LINKING   Sandra **looked** scary in her costume.

EXERCISE 2. Identifying Linking Verbs.   Number your paper 1–10. Write the linking verb from each sentence beside the number.

EXAMPLE   1. The cheerleaders sound hoarse.
1. *sound*

1. Track is my favorite sport.
2. Athletes are ready for different events.
3. A fast start is important in a sprint.
4. The long-distance race looks hard.
5. A hurdler must be fast and skillful.
6. The high jump is fun.

7. In the shot put, the ball is heavy.
8. The discus throw looks easy.
9. The pole vault might be harder.
10. My favorite event is the relay.

WRITING APPLICATION A:
Using Linking Verbs to Describe Yourself

Who are you? You might answer by telling your name, telling what you do, or telling about your personality. Linking verbs will help you to describe yourself. Here is an example. The linking verbs are in boldfaced type.

EXAMPLE   I **am** usually funny. Most of the time, I **can be** good company for my friends. Sometimes, though, I **become** moody. Then I **feel** lonely and not very funny.

Writing Assignment

Write a description of yourself. Try to describe your personality. Use at least five linking verbs. Underline these verbs.

EXERCISE 3. Identifying Action Verbs and Linking Verbs.
Number your paper 1–10. After each number, write the verb in the sentence. If the verb is an action verb, write *AV* after it. If it is a linking verb, write *LV* after it.

EXAMPLE   1. We studied knights yesterday.
　　　　　　1. *studied—AV*

1. Only a boy could be a knight.
2. At age seven he left his home.
3. At first he was a page.
4. Ladies taught him good manners.
5. At age fourteen the page became a squire.

6. His duties grew more difficult.
7. He rode into battle with his knight.
8. At age twenty-one the squire usually appeared ready for knighthood.
9. This birthday might be the most important day in his life.
10. The evening before, he kept a long vigil.

Helping Verbs

In Chapter 10, you learned that a verb may be made up of more than one word. This kind of verb is called a *verb phrase.* A verb phrase has two parts: a *main verb* and one or more *helping verbs.* Study the following sentences. The verb phrases are underlined. The helping verbs are in boldfaced type.

EXAMPLES   Many students **can** speak Spanish.
   I **will** learn all the capitals tonight.
   The dog **should have been** fed by now.

(3) A *helping verb* helps the main verb to express action or make a statement.

Here is a list of commonly used helping verbs. The helping verbs in italic type are forms of the verb *be.*

am	does
is	did
are	may
was	might
were	must
be	can
been	could
has	shall
have	should
had	will
do	would

Sometimes a verb phrase is interrupted by another part of speech. Two common interrupters are the words *not* and *always.* In a question, the verb phrase is often interrupted by the subject.

Read the following examples. You will notice that each verb phrase is interrupted. The interrupter is in italic type.

EXAMPLES   Suzanne **should** *not* **call** so late.
           I **have** *always* **liked** apples and cheese.
           Did *you* **watch** the half-time show?

EXERCISE 4. Identifying Verb Phrases and Helping Verbs.
Number your paper 1–10. After each number, write the verb phrase in the sentence. Then underline the helping verb or verbs.

EXAMPLE   1. We are going to Arizona this summer.
            1. *are going*

1. The Petrified Forest has always attracted many tourists.
2. Their imaginations have been captured by its beauty.
3. Visitors to the forest can see the Painted Desert at the same time.
4. The colors of the desert do not remain the same for long.
5. Specimens of petrified wood are exhibited at the Visitors' Center.
6. Have you ever seen a piece of petrified wood?
7. A guide will gladly explain the process to you.
8. Visitors can purchase the wood as a souvenir.
9. The Petrified Forest is not recommended for amateur hikers.
10. Hikes must be arranged with park rangers.

EXERCISE 5. Using Helping Verbs in Original Sentences.
Use each of the following word groups as the subject of a sentence. Add a verb phrase. Make some of your sentences questions. Underline the helping verb.

EXAMPLES   1. the pictures of Boulder Dam
            1. *The pictures of Boulder Dam <u>were</u> developed.*
            2. the new computer
            2. *<u>Was</u> the new computer delivered this morning?*

1. my bicycle   3. a tiny kitten
2. the astronauts   4. the hard assignment

5. a famous singer
6. some strange footprints
7. my grandmother

8. the subway
9. a funny costume
10. the refreshments

REVIEW EXERCISE A. Identifying Verbs. There are twenty verbs in the following paragraph. List them in order on your paper. Write the number of the sentence before each verb. Be sure to include helping verbs.

EXAMPLE   1. Fairy tales are often called "folk tales."
             1. *are called*

1. Long ago, many people could not read.   **2.** They would memorize stories.   **3.** Then they would tell them to their children.   **4.** Two brothers especially liked these stories. **5.** They wrote the stories down.   **6.** The stories were printed in German.   **7.** They were translated into other languages. **8.** Do you know some of the characters in these stories? **9.** You may have heard of Sleeping Beauty.   **10.** Hansel and Gretel are loved by many children.   **11.** Another popular character is Tom Thumb.   **12.** How many times have you heard the story of Cinderella?   **13.** You may also recall Snow White and the seven dwarfs.   **14.** Do you remember Rumpelstiltskin? **15.** All of these stories have been preserved by the brothers Grimm.   **16.** You can find them in your library.   **17.** Some people see them on film.   **18.** They may rent videocassettes. **19.** How many of the stories do you recognize?   **20.** Will future generations still enjoy them?

THE ADVERB

You have learned that an adjective modifies a noun or a pronoun. A modifier makes a word more exact. An *adverb* is also a modifier. It modifies a verb, an adjective, or another adverb.

12b. An *adverb* is a word that modifies a verb, an adjective, or another adverb.

EXAMPLES   Reporters **quickly** gather the news. [The adverb *quickly* modifies the verb *gather*.]

The route is **too** long. [The adverb *too* modifies the adjective *long*.]

Our paper boy delivers the paper **very** early.[The adverb *very* modifies another adverb, *early*. The adverb *early* modifies the verb *delivers*.]

Adjectives answer certain questions: for example, *What kind?* or *Which one?* Adverbs also answer certain questions: *Where? When? How? How often?* and *To what extent?* Read the following examples:

EXAMPLES   My dog ran **away.** [The adverb *away* tells *where.*]

I will call you **later.** [The adverb *later* tells *when.*]

I **softly** shut my door. [The adverb *softly* tells *how.*]

She **always** reads horse books. [The adverb *always* tells *how often.*]

He was **too** tired to watch TV. [The adverb *too* tells *to what extent.*]

☞ NOTE   The word *not* is an adverb. When *not* is part of a contraction like *hadn't,* the *n't* is an adverb.

The following words are often used as adverbs:

Where?	here	there	away	up
When?	now	then	later	soon
How?	clearly	easily	quietly	slowly
How often?	never	always	often	seldom
To what extent?	very	too	almost	so	really

The Position of Adverbs

An adverb may come before or after the word it modifies. Sometimes an adverb comes in the middle of a verb phrase.

Sometimes it comes first or last in a sentence. Read the following examples. The adverbs are in boldfaced type. The words the adverbs modify are in italic type.

EXAMPLES   I **seldom** *finish* my homework in class. [The adverb *seldom* comes before *finish*, the word it modifies.]

She *tiptoed* **quietly** from the room. [The adverb *quietly* comes after *tiptoed*, the word it modifies.]

He *has* **always** *enjoyed* reading. [The adverb *always* interrupts the verb phrase *has enjoyed.*]

Suddenly, he *heard* a sonic boom. [The adverb *suddenly* comes at the beginning of the sentence.]

He *worked* the math problem **easily**. [The adverb *easily* comes at the end of the sentence.]

EXERCISE 6. Identifying Adverbs and the Words They Modify.   Each of the following sentences contains at least one adverb. After the number of the sentence, write the adverb or adverbs. Then write the word each adverb modifies.

EXAMPLE   1. I very quickly ran the laps.
        1. *very—quickly*
          quickly—ran

1. Pegasus was a most unusual large winged horse of Greek mythology.
2. Pegasus flew easily into the sky.
3. He never grew weary.
4. The hero Bellerophon wanted Pegasus very badly, because he wanted to reach Mount Olympus.
5. Athena, the goddess of wisdom, quietly advised him how to catch the horse.
6. She quickly gave him a magic golden bridle.
7. With this, he could now charm Pegasus.
8. Bellerophon excitedly hurried to the fields to find the magic horse, Pegasus.
9. Pegasus was drinking slowly from a spring.
10. Bellerophon very gently bridled the magic horse.

WRITING APPLICATION B:
Sharpening Your Focus Through the Use of Adverbs

When you look through binoculars, you sharpen the focus in order to make the image clear. Adverbs can help make your writing clear by sharpening the focus. The first one uses very few adverbs. The adverbs that have been added in the second version are in boldfaced type.

EXAMPLES   The dog was creeping toward me. He was alone. He looked hungry, and his coat was matted and dirty. The dog looked up at me. I couldn't resist petting him. He wagged his tail. I knew we had each found a friend.

The dog was **gradually** creeping toward me. He was **completely** alone. He **also** looked hungry, and his coat was matted and **extremely** dirty. **Eagerly** the dog looked up at me. I couldn't resist petting him **gently.** He wagged his tail. I knew we had each found a friend.

Writing Assignment

Write about an incident, using at least five adverbs to help make the paragraph interesting. Underline each adverb. Arrange your ideas in the order in which the events happened. Here are some suggested topics:

Getting a New Pet   Planning a Trip
Planning a Party   Getting Ready for a Test

REVIEW EXERCISE B. Finding Adverbs in a Paragraph.
There are ten adverbs in the following paragraph. Write each of the adverbs in order, and write the number of the sentence before each adverb.

EXAMPLE   1. Williamsburg is a very interesting place.
          1. *very*

1. Visitors to Williamsburg can actually experience some aspects of everyday Colonial life. **2.** There is a wigmaker who still makes old-fashioned powdered wigs. **3.** Surprisingly, more men than women wore wigs in Colonial days. **4.** A silversmith carefully works on silver objects and jewelry. **5.** The bookbinder skillfully makes book covers out of leather. **6.** Certainly the blacksmith is necessary. **7.** The weaver always uses attractive traditional patterns. **8.** The bootmaker seldom has any complaints, for he is an able worker. **9.** Another very popular craftsman makes musical instruments. **10.** You would truly enjoy the crafts at Williamsburg.

EXERCISE 7. Writing Appropriate Adverbs. Write the following sentences. Fill each blank with an appropriate adverb.

EXAMPLE   1. —— I learned some Spanish words.
　　　　　　1. *Quickly I learned some Spanish words.*

1. I —— watch TV after school.
2. You will —— bait a hook yourself.
3. My little sister crept down the stairs —— .
4. You will —— find the answer to the problem.
5. She is —— eager for lunch.

Diagraming Adverbs

You have already learned how to diagram adjectives. Adverbs are diagramed in a similar way. Study the following patterns:

1. An adverb modifying a verb:

PATTERN

EXAMPLES   laughs loudly   went there early

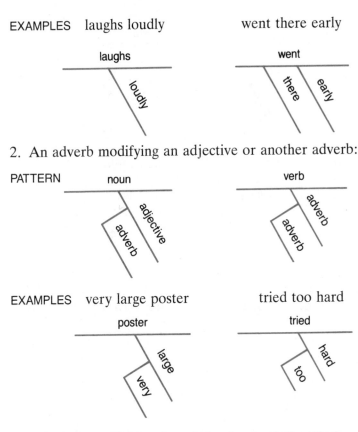

2. An adverb modifying an adjective or another adverb:

EXERCISE 8. **Diagraming Adverbs and the Verbs, Adjectives, and Other Adverbs They Modify.** Diagram the following groups of words. Use the patterns in the examples on pages 236–37.

1. badly skinned knee
2. highly trained gymnast
3. almost never finish
4. have not been studying hard
5. very carefully proofread

Diagraming Sentences with Adverbs

You have already diagramed sentences that contain subjects, verbs, and adjectives. Now you are ready to add adverbs to your diagrams. Study the following pattern:

PATTERN

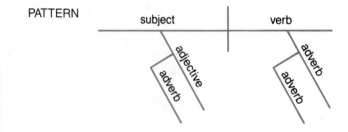

EXAMPLES   Several pictures will be taken soon.

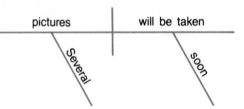

The deer and her fawn darted away very swiftly.

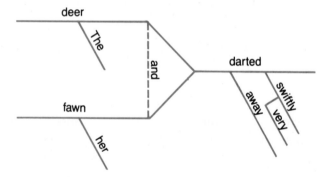

EXERCISE 9. **Diagraming Sentences with Adjective and Adverb Modifiers.**   Diagram the following sentences. Remember that the articles *a, an,* and *the* are diagramed as adjectives.

1. My best friend lives nearby.
2. The flight was postponed indefinitely.
3. Suddenly, a violent storm came up.
4. The mare and her colt grazed quietly.
5. The final speaker rose and spoke very quickly.

THE PREPOSITION

The preposition is an important word. It is used to show the relationship between words in the sentence. In the following sentences, the prepositions are in boldfaced type. How does the use of different prepositions give different meanings to the two sentences?

EXAMPLES   I hit the ball **over** the net.
            I hit the ball **into** the net.

12c. A *preposition* is a word that shows the relationship between a noun or a pronoun and some other word in the sentence.

The following words are often used as prepositions.

Commonly Used Prepositions

aboard	at	down	off	under
about	before	during	on	underneath
above	behind	except	over	until
across	below	for	past	up
after	beneath	from	since	upon
against	beside	in	through	with
along	between	into	throughout	within
among	beyond	like	to	without
around	by	of	toward	

Notice the prepositions in the following sentences. They are in boldfaced type.

EXAMPLES   Your math book is **underneath** your coat. [The preposition shows the relationship of *book* to *coat*.]

            The driver **behind** us honked his horn. [The preposition shows the relationship of *driver* to *us*.]

EXERCISE 10. Writing Appropriate Prepositions. Number your paper 1–5. Write two appropriate prepositions for each blank in the following sentences.

EXAMPLE   1. I saw her —— the mirror.
            1. *in, beside*

1. We drove —— the football stadium.
2. The poster was —— my bed.
3. She walked —— the used-book sale.
4. A bird flew —— the kitchen window.
5. We went —— the hill to the picnic grounds.

The Prepositional Phrase

A preposition is always used with a noun or a pronoun. This noun or pronoun is called the *object* of the preposition. Sometimes the object has words that modify or describe it.

EXAMPLES   He poured sauce **over the pizza.** [The preposition *over* relates its object *pizza* to *poured.*]

She dumped more leaves **on the huge pile.** [The object of the preposition, *pile,* is modified by the adjective *huge.*]

A preposition may have more than one object.

EXAMPLE   The flea collar is **for cats and dogs.** [The preposition *for* has the two objects *cats* and *dogs.*]

The preposition, its object or objects, and any modifiers of the object make up a prepositional phrase.

EXERCISE 11. Identifying Prepositions and Their Objects.
Number your paper 1–10. After each number, write the prepositional phrase in the sentence. Underline the preposition and circle its object. There may be more than one object.

EXAMPLE   1. Otters are related to weasels and minks.
    1. *to* (weasels) *and* (minks)

1. We planted a sapling behind the garage.
2. I bought a pattern for a sari.
3. They live near the airport.
4. My brother wants a guitar for his birthday.
5. The pictures won't be developed until Friday or Saturday.

6. I received a letter from my aunt and uncle.
7. The arctic falcon is the largest of all falcons.
8. Do you have the answer to the third question?
9. There are many uses for peanuts.
10. You might need a calculator for that problem.

Words as Different Parts of Speech

You cannot tell what part of speech a word is until you see it in a sentence. For example, some words may be used as nouns or adjectives. Study the following sentences.

EXAMPLES   *Noun*   **History** is my best subject.
           Adjective   I lost my **history** book.

Other words may be used as prepositions or as adverbs.

EXAMPLES   I came **aboard** the skiff. [*Aboard* is used as a preposition. Its object is *skiff*.]

           I came **aboard**. [*Aboard* is used as an adverb. It has no object. It tells *where*.]

           He swam **underneath** the dock. [*Underneath* is used as a preposition. Its object is *dock*.]

           He swam **underneath**. [*Underneath* is used as an adverb. It has no object.]

☞ NOTE   A preposition always has an object. An adverb never has an object. To determine whether a word is being used as an adverb or a preposition, look for an object.

EXERCISE 12. **Writing Sentences with Prepositions and Adverbs.** Write two sentences using each of the following words. In your first sentence, use the word as a preposition. Circle its object. In your second sentence, use the word as an adverb. Underline the adverb.

EXAMPLE   1. along
             1. *We walked along the* (pier.)
                 My little brother came along.

1. down   2. above   3. on   4. out   5. around

THE CONJUNCTION

When you want to join parts of sentences or whole sentences, you use the part of speech called a *conjunction*.

12d. A *conjunction* **is a word that joins words or groups of words.**

The conjunction *and* is frequently used to join words and groups of words. In the following sentences, the conjunctions are in boldfaced type.

EXAMPLES   Mother **and** I are Yankees fans. [The conjunction joins two subjects.]

              The car swerved **and** ran off the road. [The conjunction joins two verbs.]

              We drove through New York **and** Pennsylvania. [The conjunction joins the two objects of the preposition *through.*

Two other conjunctions that are often used to join parts of a sentence are *but* and *or.*

EXAMPLES   We tried **but** failed. [two verbs]
              Sue **or** I will make the salad. [two subjects]

The conjunctions *and, but,* and *or* can join whole sentences.

EXAMPLES   The wind blew, **and** the windows rattled.
              You should leave now, **or** you will miss the bus.

EXERCISE 13. Identifying Conjunctions. Number your paper 1–10. After each number, write the conjunction in the sentence.

EXAMPLE   1. Lena or I will pitch for batting practice.
            1. *or*

1. Julio and Roger made the soccer team.
2. Vera was deaf, but she could read lips.
3. I have enough money for popcorn or juice.
4. You rake the leaves, and I will sweep the path.
5. Did Nancy finish her report, or is she still working on it?
6. He dove for the ball but missed it.
7. For breakfast, I like toast or a bran muffin.
8. The choir sang for the parents and teachers.
9. I addressed the envelope but have not mailed it.
10. The coach blew the whistle, and the runners began the race.

THE INTERJECTION

One part of speech expresses strong feeling. It is called an *interjection*. An interjection is usually followed by an exclamation point.

12e. An *interjection* **is a word that expresses strong feeling.**

EXAMPLES   **Aha!** I knew you were hiding there.
          Oops! I punched in the wrong numbers.

The following words are often used as interjections.

alas	ouch
goodness	whew
hooray	wow
oh	yippee

PARTS OF SPEECH REVIEW

In Chapters 11 and 12, you have studied the eight parts of speech. It is time to review what you have learned about them. Remember that seeing how a word is used in a sentence is important. Only then can you identify the part of speech.

EXAMPLES   I will hang up in a **second.** [*Second* is a noun in this sentence.]

This is our **second** chorus concert. [*Second* is an adjective in this sentence.]

Can you **test** the switch? [*Test* is a verb here.]
Mr. Sanchez assigned a **test** for tomorrow. [*Test* is a noun here.]

The cat climbed **up.** [*Up* is an adverb here.]
The cat climbed **up** the tree. [*Up* is a preposition in this sentence.]

REVIEW EXERCISE C. Identifying Parts of Speech. Number your paper 1–10. After the proper number, write the italicized word and its part of speech. Be prepared to give reasons for your answers.

EXAMPLE   1. Some scientists *study* bones.
               2. *study*—verb

1. We saw several small animals *outside* the cabin.
2. My mother *drives* to work.
3. Those *plants* grow best in sandy soil.
4. Rhea bought *paper* cups for the party.
5. *Their* parents own a card store.
6. The coats in that shop are lovely, *but* the prices are high.
7. *Oops!* I dropped my books.
8. We play *outdoors* every day until dinnertime.
9. This assignment looks *difficult.*
10. You don't sound *too* happy.

CHAPTER 12 REVIEW: POSTTEST 1

Identifying Verbs, Adverbs, Prepositions, Conjunctions, and Interjections. Number your paper 1–10. After each number, write the lettered, italicized words and the part of speech for each: *verb, adverb, preposition, conjunction,* or *interjection.*

EXAMPLE   1. A tornado (a) *is* a terrible (b) *and* violent storm.
 1. *(a) is—verb; (b) and—conjunction*

1. The tornado (a) *came* (b) *without* warning.
2. (a) *Unfortunately,* we do (b) *not* have a basement.
3. I grabbed the dog (a) *and* ran (b) *into* the bathroom.
4. I crouched (a) *shakily* (b) *between* the sink and the tub.
5. The house (a) *was shaking,* and the air (b) *became* cold.
6. (a) *Suddenly* the roof blew (b) *off.*
7. The air (a) *was filled* (b) *with* loose boards.
8. Then everything (a) *grew* (b) *very* calm.
9. I (a) *was* frightened, (b) *but* my dog and I were not hurt.
10. (a) *Goodness!* Let's build a basement (b) *immediately.*

CHAPTER 12 REVIEW: POSTTEST 2

Writing Sentences Using Words as Different Parts of Speech. Write ten sentences using each of the following words first as an adverb and then as a preposition. Underline the word and give its part of speech after the sentence.

EXAMPLE   1. down
 1. *We looked* <u>down</u>. *—adverb*
 We looked <u>down</u> *the hole. —preposition*

1. over 2. near 3. through 4. up 5. underneath

SUMMARY OF PARTS OF SPEECH			
Rule	*Part of Speech*	*Use*	*Example*
11a	noun	names	His **report** is about **freedom**.
11b	pronoun	takes the place of a noun	I read **it** after **you** did.

11c	adjective	modifies a noun or pronoun	We have **Siamese** kittens that are **playful**.
12a	verb	shows action or makes a statement	She **was** ill and **missed** the test.
12b	adverb	modifies a verb, an adjective, or another adverb	He was **very** tired, but he practiced **really hard**.
12c	preposition	relates a noun or pronoun to another word	The students **in** the play went **to** the auditorium.
12d	conjunction	joins words or groups of words	Tina **and** Shannon are invited, **but** they can't go.
12e	interjection	shows strong feeling	**Wow!** What great fireworks!

CHAPTER 13

The Prepositional Phrase

ADJECTIVE AND ADVERB USES

The way a word is used in a sentence tells you what part of speech that word is. A group of words may also be used in a sentence as a single part of speech. One word group used in this way is called a *phrase*. In Chapter 12, you worked briefly with the prepositional phrase. In this chapter, you will see how a prepositional phrase can be used as an adjective or an adverb.

DIAGNOSTIC TEST

A. Identifying Prepositional Phrases. After the proper number, write (a) the prepositional phrase used in each sentence and (b) the word or words that the phrase modifies. Tell how the phrase is used by writing *adjective* for an adjective phrase or *adverb* for an adverb phrase.

EXAMPLE   1. We hiked through the woods.
            1. *(a) through the woods—hiked; (b) adverb*

1. The crowd waved banners during the game.
2. That book about comets has several diagrams.

3. Have you seen the pictures of their new house?
4. We always visit my grandparents in July or August.
5. Uncle Ed carefully knocked the snow off his boots.
6. Someone left a package on the front porch.
7. A party for the teachers is long overdue.
8. A clown handed balloons to the children.
9. The grass in the park is too high.
10. Help yourself to some pizza.

13a. A *phrase* is a group of words that is used as a part of speech. A phrase does not contain a subject and verb.

It is important to remember that phrases cannot stand alone. They must be used with other words as part of a sentence.

PHRASE **in the box** [The phrase does not have a subject or a predicate. It cannot stand alone as a sentence.]

SENTENCE We put the puppy **in the box.** [The phrase is part of a sentence in which the subject is *We* and the predicate is *put*.]

PREPOSITIONAL PHRASES

13b. A *prepositional phrase* is a phrase that begins with a preposition and ends with a noun or pronoun. A prepositional phrase may be used as an adjective or as an adverb.

Prepositions—words such as *at, by, of,* and *with*—show the relation of a noun or pronoun to another word in the sentence. The noun or pronoun that follows a preposition is called the *object* of the preposition. A preposition, its object, and any modifiers of the object are all part of the prepositional phrase.

In the following sentences, the groups of words in boldfaced type are prepositional phrases.

GRAMMAR

EXAMPLES   I met them **at the bus stop.** [The prepositional phrase
is part of a sentence. The subject is *I* and the verb is
met.]
The students **in our school** did well **on the test.**

☞ **NOTE**   In order to identify a prepositional phrase, you
must first find the preposition. Before you begin Exercise 1,
take time to review the list of prepositions on page 239.

EXERCISE 1. Identifying Prepositional Phrases. Number
your paper 1–10. After each number, write the prepositional
phrase in the sentence. Underline each preposition and circle its
object. Sometimes a preposition has more than one object.

EXAMPLE   1. The package was for my brother and me.
1. *for my* (*brother*) *and* (*me*)

1. Ana plays flute in the band.
2. We waited until lunchtime.
3. The house across the street has green shutters.
4. Do not make repairs on the brakes yourself.
5. The word *dinosaur* comes from two Greek words.
6. May I sit between you and him?
7. The woman in the blue uniform is my aunt.
8. The hikers walked through a cornfield.
9. He is saving money for a stereo and a guitar.
10. The messenger slipped the note under the door.

EXERCISE 2. Writing Appropriate Prepositional Phrases.
Write the following sentences, filling in each blank with an
appropriate prepositional phrase.

1. My favorite comic will appear —— .
2. That woman always sits —— .
3. The fans —— cheered every pitch.

4. The children ran —— .
5. The light —— is broken.

ADJECTIVE PHRASES

In Chapter 11, you learned that an adjective modifies a noun or a pronoun. A prepositional phrase can also be used to modify a noun or a pronoun. Such a prepositional phrase is called an *adjective phrase.*

ADJECTIVE   **Icy** chunks fell from the skyscraper.

ADJECTIVE PHRASE   Chunks **of ice** fell from the skyscraper.

13c. An adjective phrase modifies a noun or a pronoun.

You may remember that an adjective answers certain questions: *What kind? Which one? How many?* or *How much?* An adjective phrase answers the same questions. In the following examples, the adjective phrases are in boldfaced type and the words they modify are in italic type.

EXAMPLES   He ordered a *dinner* **of boiled shrimp.** [The adjective phrase modifies the noun *dinner.*]

She likes the *skirt* **with the big pockets.** [The adjective phrase modifies the noun *skirt.*]

These *tapes* **for two dollars** are a bargain. [The prepositional phrase modifies the noun *tapes.*]

EXERCISE 3. **Identifying Adjective Phrases.** After the proper number, write the adjective phrase used in the sentence. Then write the word or words the phrase modifies.

EXAMPLE   1. Philadelphia is called the City of Independence.
        1. *of Independence—City*

1. The first Independence Day celebration was a time for bonfires and noise.
2. Ships along the shore fired thirteen-gun salutes.

3. Every house and shop in Philadelphia was decorated and illuminated.
4. People of all ages enjoyed the brilliant fireworks.
5. One homeowner made a complaint about the festivities.
6. The roof of his house had caught fire!
7. Later, the use of fireworks was carefully controlled.
8. John Adams recorded the first foreign observance of American freedom.
9. A centennial exposition at Carpenter's Hall involved other countries.
10. It included exhibits by thirty-five nations.

An adjective phrase often follows another adjective. Sometimes both adjective phrases modify the same noun or pronoun.

EXAMPLE   That picture **of a farm couple** *by Grant Wood* is famous. [The two adjective phrases, *of a farm couple* and *by Grant Wood,* both modify the noun *picture.*]

Sometimes an adjective phrase modifies a noun or a pronoun in another adjective phrase.

EXAMPLE   A number **of paintings by that artist** show farm scenes. [The adjective phrase *of paintings* modifies the noun *number.* The adjective phrase *by that artist* modifies the noun *paintings,* the object of the preposition in the first phrase.]

EXERCISE 4. Identifying Adjective Phrases.   The following sentences contain adjective phrases. Write the phrases in order on your paper. Put the number of the sentence before each phrase. After each phrase, write the noun or pronoun it modifies. Some sentences contain more than one adjective phrase.

EXAMPLE   1. This book about birds of North America has won many awards for photography.
    1. *about birds—book*
    1. *of North America—birds*
    1. *for photography—awards*

1. This book about birds by a famous zoologist is called *Bird Behavior.*
2. It explains the importance of flight in the survival of the bird population.
3. The key to successful flight is the structure of the feather.
4. Birds with forked tails have built-in rudders.
5. Many birds of the North migrate to warm winter quarters.
6. Birds must make careful decisions about their nests.
7. Cliffs become the nests of immense throngs of sea birds.
8. A nest on a narrow ledge can be a problem.
9. A baby bird's demand for food is constant.
10. Food with high protein content is necessary.

WRITING APPLICATION A:
Using Adjective Phrases in a Description

A good description makes the reader see what you are describing. Adjective phrases are useful in a description. They can help communicate important ideas to your reader by explaining *what kind, which one, how many,* or *how much.* In the following description the adjective phrases are in boldfaced type.

EXAMPLE   It was a tree **of great beauty.** The needles **on each branch** were long and firm. Clusters **of pine cones** showed through the boughs. The branch **at the top** reached to the stars.

Writing Assignment

Write a description that makes your reader see what you see. In your description, use at least four adjective phrases. Underline them. Here are some suggested topics:

Your room   A secret place
Your friend   A park
A grandparent   Your pet

EXERCISE 5. Writing Adjective Phrases. Fill in the blank in each of the following sentences with an appropriate adjective phrase. Write the complete sentence.

EXAMPLE   1. That storm —— might be dangerous.
           1. *That storm from the east might be dangerous.*

1. The shelf —— is too high to reach.
2. My costume —— should win a prize.
3. The girl —— is one of my best friends.
4. The argument —— really wasn't very important.
5. The gift —— is from my aunt and uncle.

ADVERB PHRASES

A prepositional phrase that modifies a verb, an adjective, or an adverb is called an *adverb phrase.* An adverb phrase usually modifies the verb in the sentence.

ADVERB   We walk **there** every Saturday.

ADVERB PHRASE   We walk **along the lake** every Saturday.

Like adverbs, adverb phrases answer the questions *Where? When? How? How often?* and *To what extent?*

13d. An *adverb phrase* modifies a verb, an adjective, or an adverb.

EXAMPLES   *Where?*   We sang **at the local hospital.** [The adverb phrase modifies the verb *sang.* It tells *where.*]

           When?   We sang **on Friday.** [The adverb phrase modifies the verb *sang.* It tells *when.*]

           How?   We went **by bus.** [The adverb phrase modifies the verb *went.* It tells *how.*]

EXERCISE 6. Identifying Adverb Phrases. After the proper number, write the adverb phrase used in the sentence. Then write the word or words the phrase modifies.

EXAMPLE   1. My hamster disappeared for three days.
     1. *for three days—disappeared*

1. Dad hung a mirror in the front hall.
2. The cat is always jumping onto the table.
3. The acrobat plunged into the net but did not hurt herself.
4. Felice tiptoed down the stairs.
5. Mother discovered several field mice in the basement.
6. The napkins belong in the top drawer.
7. I will put a big red bow on the package.
8. We have planted day lilies along the fence.
9. We could see a valley beyond the mountains.
10. Every morning she jogs around the reservoir.

Two or more adverb phrases may follow one another.

EXAMPLE   I will go **to the library in the morning.** [Both adverb
     phrases, *to the library* and *in the morning,* modify the
     verb phrase *will go.*]

An adverb phrase may be followed by an adjective phrase that
modifies the object of the preposition in the adverb phrase.

EXAMPLE   We went **to an exhibit of rare coins.** [The adverb
     phrase *to an exhibit* modifies the verb *went.* The
     adjective phrase *of rare coins* modifies *exhibit,* the
     object of the preposition in the adverb phrase.]

EXERCISE 7. **Identifying Adverb Phrases.** Number your
paper 1–10. After each number, write the adverb phrase or
phrases used in the following sentences. After each phrase, write
the word or words the phrase modifies.

EXAMPLE   1. On Thanksgiving morning we watch the parade.
     1. *On Thanksgiving morning—watch*

1. On Thanksgiving we go to my grandparents' house.
2. They always invite us for dinner.
3. We usually leave in the morning.
4. About four o'clock, we sit down at the table.

5. Tall candles tower over the centerpiece.
6. A small cardboard pilgrim stands beside each plate.
7. The roast turkey sits on a huge platter.
8. Vegetables are arranged around it.
9. Beside the turkey is Grandmother's cranberry salad.
10. I will remember these wonderful Thanksgivings at my grand-parents' house for a long time.

WRITING APPLICATION B:
Using Variety in Placing Adverb Phrases

If you eat cereal for breakfast, you probably don't eat the same kind every day: most people like variety. One way to put variety into your writing is to be aware of, and make use of, the several possible positions for the adverb phrase. Notice where the adverb phrases are placed in these examples.

EXAMPLES **In the morning** we take a crafts class. [The adverb phrase comes first in the sentence.]

Then **at noon,** we eat lunch. [The adverb phrase comes in the middle of the sentence.]

We go to swimming class **in the afternoon.** [The adverb phrase comes last.]

Writing Assignment

Step into a time machine and begin your journey into the past or the future. Describe an adventure you have. Use at least five adverb phrases and try to vary their position in the sentences. Underline these phrases. A portion of a sample description is shown.

EXAMPLE   I stepped out of the time machine. Around me crowded a group of friendly people. They held in their hands beautiful baskets of strange fruits and pretty flowers.

EXERCISE 8. Writing Sentences with Adverb Phrases. Write five sentences using the following word groups as adverb phrases. Underline each phrase. Then draw an arrow from the phrase to the word or words it modifies.

EXAMPLE   1. for the airport

1. *They left for the airport.*

1. down the hall
2. by the door
3. in the cafeteria
4. under the car
5. on the diving board

REVIEW EXERCISE A. Identifying Adjective and Adverb Phrases. Number your paper 1–10. Each of the following sentences contains a prepositional phrase. After the number, write the phrase. After each phrase, write *adjective* for an adjective phrase, or *adverb* for an adverb phrase.

EXAMPLE   1. Abraham Lincoln lived in Springfield.
            1. *in Springfield—adverb*

1. Abraham Lincoln bought the Springfield house in 1844.
2. He bought it from a clergyman.
3. The cost of the house was $1,500.
4. It was the family home until 1861.
5. Mrs. Lincoln decided on the decorations and furnishings.
6. Records from some shops showed Mrs. Lincoln's purchases.
7. A description of each item is recorded.
8. Historians are restoring the house of this famous family.
9. Lincoln and his family soon moved to the White House.
10. The White House was designed by James Hoban.

Diagraming Adjective and Adverb Phrases

To diagram a prepositional phrase, adjective or adverb, place the preposition on a slanting line just below the word that the preposition modifies. The object of the preposition is on a horizontal line connected to the slanting line. The slanting line extends slightly beyond the horizontal line, as shown in the following pattern:

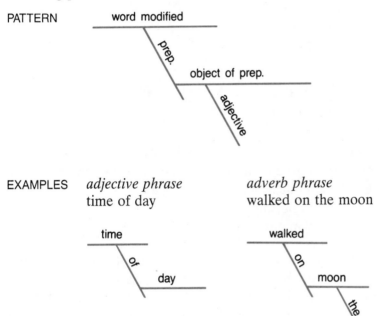

PATTERN

EXAMPLES   *adjective phrase*   *adverb phrase*
           time of day   walked on the moon

EXERCISE 9. Diagraming Adjective and Adverb Phrases.

Using the patterns shown, diagram the following words:

1. sang on the radio
2. went to the supermarket
3. film about astronauts
4. flew over the nest
5. closet for supplies
6. jogged before breakfast
7. friends of my parents
8. paddled down the rapids
9. bowl of fruit
10. forecast of snow

Now you are ready to diagram complete sentences containing prepositional phrases. Remember that prepositional phrases are used as adjectives or adverbs. Therefore, they are diagramed as modifiers. The following sentence contains both an adjective and an adverb phrase.

EXAMPLE   My friend from Australia lives in Adelaide.

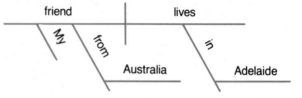

EXERCISE 10. Diagraming Sentences.   Diagram the following sentences. Each sentence contains an adjective phrase or an adverb phrase or both.

1. The freighter slowed for the first lock.
2. The film from our vacation was developed in one hour.
3. The cars in our lane stopped for the bus.
4. The roof on our building leaks.
5. The library in our school opens before first period.

REVIEW EXERCISE B. Identifying Adjective and Adverb Phrases.   Number your paper 1–10. Each of the following sentences contains one or more prepositional phrases. After each number, write the phrase or phrases used in the sentence. After each phrase, write *adjective* for an adjective phrase and *adverb* for an adverb phrase.

EXAMPLE   1. In China, farmers are considered the backbone of the country.
　　　　　1. *In China—adverb*
　　　　　of the country—adjective

1. Most people in China are farmers.
2. Many Chinese farmers work without the help of large machines.
3. Their farming is still done by hand.
4. Every piece of land in China is carefully prepared, planted, and weeded.
5. The crop is then harvested with careful attention to detail.
6. In the hills, the Chinese make flat terraces.

7. Irrigation channels direct the water from high terraces to lower terraces.
8. Farmers flood the terraces and build ridges around the rice paddies.
9. In flat sections, water is pumped from the ground.
10. The Chinese have been farming the same land for centuries.

REVIEW EXERCISE C. **Writing Sentences with Adjective and Adverb Phrases.** Use each of the following phrases in two separate sentences. In the first sentence, use the phrase as an adjective. In the second sentence, use the phrase as an adverb.

EXAMPLE   1. in that state
            1. *The people in that state are called "Hoosiers."*
              We once lived in that state.

1. from California
2. in my class
3. along the path
4. under the bridge
5. behind the desk

CHAPTER 13 REVIEW: POSTTEST 1

Identifying Adjective and Adverb Phrases. Number your paper 1–20. After the proper number, write the prepositional phrase used in the sentence. Then write the word or words that the phrase modifies. Tell how the phrase is used by writing *adjective* for an adjective phrase or *adverb* for an adverb phrase.

EXAMPLE   1. This newspaper article on weather patterns is interesting.
            1. *on weather patterns—article—adjective*

1. The hikers headed toward the mountains.
2. Yesterday we rode our bikes through the park.
3. I always wear heavy socks under my boots.
4. We had a party after the game.
5. Most children like books with colorful illustrations.

6. Students from many different countries attended the meet.
7. Dogs from that kennel always win prizes.
8. Several handicapped persons will run in the marathon.
9. The telephone in the kitchen isn't working.
10. The road to the village is flooded.
11. A camel is a common beast of burden.
12. I will rake the leaves after lunch.
13. The plant in the kitchen window is a begonia.
14. We always camp near a lake.
15. Have you read the book about the teen-age werewolf?
16. She rowed the boat across the lake.
17. Grandma Moses began to paint in her late seventies.
18. We covered the hot ashes with sand and rocks.
19. The students quietly took their places on the stage.
20. The groceries in that bag are yours.

CHAPTER 13 REVIEW: POSTTEST 2

Writing Sentences with Prepositional Phrases. Use each of the following prepositional phrases in a sentence. After each sentence, write the word that the prepositional phrase modifies.

EXAMPLE 1. across the street
1. *They live across the street.* —*live*

1. among the papers
2. about computers
3. under the surface
4. in the afternoon
5. for hours
6. through the puddles
7. over the treetops
8. before dinner
9. along the fence
10. toward us

CHAPTER 14

Complements

DIRECT AND INDIRECT OBJECTS, SUBJECT COMPLEMENTS

In Chapter 10, you learned that every sentence has a subject and a predicate. Some sentences contain another important part —one that completes the meaning begun by the subject and verb. This part is called a *complement*.

DIAGNOSTIC TEST

Identifying Complements. Number your paper 1–10. After each number, write the complement or complements in that sentence. Next to each one, write the kind of complement it is. Use these abbreviations:

> *d.o.* direct object   *p.n.* predicate nominative
> *i.o.* indirect object   *p.a.* predicate adjective

EXAMPLE   1. My grandparents sent me some old coins.
            1. *me—i.o.*
               coins—d.o.

1. A park ranger told us the history of Forest Park.
2. Tuesday is the last day for soccer tryouts.

3. She made her father a wallet for his birthday.
4. These peaches taste sweet and juicy.
5. The crossing guard helped the boys and girls.
6. Someone handed Sondra and me an ad for the concert.
7. Two common desert creatures are the lizard and the snake.
8. She has become an excellent speaker.
9. Tropical forests have given us many helpful plants.
10. The soil in that pot feels dry to me.

COMPLEMENTS WITH ACTION VERBS

Some verbs express action by themselves. In the following sentences, the verb is in boldfaced type.

EXAMPLES   The bell **rang.**
Our school day **had started.**

Many verbs, however, need a complement to complete the meaning begun by the subject and the verb.

EXAMPLE   The dog chased. [The dog chased *what?* The meaning begun by the subject and the verb is not complete.]

The dog chased the **car.** [The complement *car* completes the meaning by indicating the receiver of the action.]

A complement that indicates the direct or indirect receiver of an action is called the *object of the verb.* There are two kinds of objects: *direct objects* and *indirect objects.*

The Direct Object

In the following sentences, the complements are direct objects of the verb. Notice that they are nouns or pronouns.

EXAMPLES   Carrie helped *us.*
We cleaned *closets.*

14a. The *direct object* receives the action of the verb or shows the result of that action. It answers the question *What*? or *Whom*? after an action verb.

EXAMPLES   He enjoys his **hobby**. [Enjoys *what?* Enjoys hobby. *Hobby* receives the action of the verb *enjoys*.]

He builds **models**. [Builds what? Builds models. *Models* is the result of the action of the verb *builds*.]

Linking verbs do not express action. Therefore they cannot be followed by a direct object.

EXAMPLE   Julia Morgan was an architect. [The verb *was* does not express action. Therefore, *architect* is not a direct object.]

Do not mistake the object of a preposition for a direct object.

EXAMPLE   She studied **architecture** in Paris. [Studied what? Studied architecture. *Architecture* is the direct object of the verb *studied*. *Paris* is the object of the preposition *in*.]

A verb may be followed by a compound direct object.

EXAMPLE   She needs **glue, paint,** and **decals** for her model. [The compound direct object of the verb *needs* is *glue, paint,* and *decals*.]

EXERCISE 1. Identifying Direct Objects.   Number your paper 1–10. Each of the following sentences contains a direct object. After each number, write the object in the sentence. Remember that a direct object may be compound.

EXAMPLE   1. Do you enjoy books and movies about horses?
            1. *books, movies*

1. I enjoyed Marguerite Henry's story.
2. She wrote *King of the Wind.*
3. It won a prize in 1949.
4. It tells the story of Agba and a horse.

5. Agba loved an Arabian horse.
6. He fed milk and honey to the newborn colt.
7. Sometimes the playful colt bit Agba's fingers.
8. Agba and the horse had several unhappy experiences.
9. The head of the stables mistreated Agba and the horse.
10. Some days Agba received bread and water for supper.

The Indirect Object

Some action verbs have two complements—a direct object and an *indirect object*. Like all complements, the indirect object helps complete the meaning begun by the subject of the verb.

You have learned that a direct object answers the question *What?* or *Whom?* after an action verb. An indirect object answers the question *To what?* or *To whom?* or *For what?* or *For whom?* after an action verb. The indirect object always comes before the direct object in the sentence. The indirect object is either a noun or a pronoun.

EXAMPLES   Dad bought **me** some peanuts. [*Me* is the indirect object of the verb *bought*. It answers the question, "*For whom* were the peanuts bought?"]

I gave that **problem** some thought. [*Problem* is the indirect object of the verb *gave*. It answers the question, "*To what* was some thought given?"]

14b. The *indirect object* of the verb comes before the direct object. It tells to whom or what, or for whom or what, the action of the verb is done.

Do not mistake the object of a preposition for an indirect object.

EXAMPLES   We sent the hat to her. [*Hat* is the direct object of the verb *sent*. *Her* is the object of the preposition *to*. This sentence does not contain an indirect object.]

We sent **her** the hat. [*Her* is the indirect object of the verb *sent*. It comes before the direct object, *hat*. It answers the question *To whom?*]

A verb may be followed by a compound indirect object.

EXAMPLE   She gave **Ed** and **me** the list of summer activities.
[*Ed* and *me* make up the compound indirect object of the verb *gave*. *Ed and me* answers the question *To whom*? The direct object is *list*.]

EXERCISE 2. Identifying Direct and Indirect Objects.
Number your paper 1–10. Write the direct and indirect objects after the number of the sentence. Underline each indirect object once and each direct object twice. Some sentences do not have indirect objects. Remember not to confuse objects of prepositions with direct and indirect objects.

EXAMPLE   1. I sent my friends cards from Washington.
1. *friends, cards*

1. In Seattle, we visited Pioneer Square and Waterfront Park.
2. The hotel manager gave my aunt and me directions.
3. A guide told us the history of Pioneer Square.
4. Fire destroyed the district in 1889.
5. He sold us tickets for a tour of the underground town.
6. Waterfront Park overlooks the sound.
7. A huge, domed tank surrounds visitors to the aquarium.
8. The aquarium houses snappers, catfish, and other fish.
9. An attendant was feeding some eels their lunch.
10. On the ferry my aunt handed me a tuna sandwich.

EXERCISE 3. Writing Sentences with Direct and Indirect Objects.
Write five sentences. In each, use a different one of the following verbs. Include a direct object and an indirect object in each sentence. Underline the indirect object once and the direct object twice.

EXAMPLE   1. told
1. *I told my little brother a story*.

1. bought   2. owed   3. wrote   4. asked   5. drew

GRAMMAR

WRITING APPLICATION:
Using Direct and Indirect Objects to
Make Your Writing Clear and Complete

What is the difference in meaning between the two sentences that follow?

Mom taught.
Mom taught me a useful skill.

The first sentence is incomplete. In the second sentence, the direct object tells *what* Mom taught, and the indirect object *to whom* she taught it. In writing sentences, include a direct object when the action verb calls for a receiver of the action. Use an indirect object to make clear to what or to whom the action is done. In the following paragraph, pay special attention to the objects in boldface type. How do they help make the paragraph clear and complete?

EXAMPLE   Mom gave **me** a cooking **lesson.** First, she handed **me** the **recipe** for scrambled eggs. We read **it** carefully. Then we gathered the **ingredients.** We needed **eggs, milk,** and **butter.** Each serving required two **eggs** and two **teaspoons** of milk. We beat the **eggs** and **milk** with a fork. Then we poured the **mixture** into a hot, buttered skillet. The recipe gave **us** clear **directions** about stirring the eggs gently.

Writing Assignment

Write an explanation of how to do something. Be sure that you include all the information your reader will need. Use direct and indirect objects to make your explanation clear. Here are some suggested topics:

How to ride a horse
How to take care of a pet
How to learn to shoot in basketball

GRAMMAR

SUBJECT COMPLEMENTS

As you have learned, two kinds of complements may follow an action verb: the direct object and the indirect object. Another kind of complement—called a *subject complement*—follows a linking verb. There are two kinds of subject complements: the *predicate nominative* and the *predicate adjective*. These complements are called subject complements because they explain or describe the subject.

EXAMPLES   Mrs. Gomez is a helpful **neighbor.** [The subject complement *neighbor* explains the subject *Mrs. Gomez.*]

The airport in Atlanta is very **busy.** [The subject complement *busy* describes the subject *airport.*]

14c. A *subject complement* is a complement that explains or describes the subject.

Subject complements always follow linking verbs, not action verbs. In order to recognize subject complements, review the following linking verbs:

Common Linking Verbs

appear	grow	smell
be (all forms)	look	sound
become	remain	stay
feel	seem	taste

The Predicate Nominative

In the following sentences, the words in boldfaced type are predicate nominatives.

EXAMPLES   *The Nutcracker* is a beautiful **ballet.**
My sister has become a fine **swimmer.**

(1) A *predicate nominative* is one kind of subject complement. It is a noun or pronoun that explains or identifies the subject of the sentence. Predicate nominatives follow linking verbs.

EXAMPLES Seaweed is **algae**. [*Algae* is a predicate nominative following the linking verb *is*. It identifies the subject *seaweed*.]

My secret pal was really **you**! [*You* is a predicate nominative following the linking verb *was*. It identifies the subject *pal*.]

Do not mistake a direct object or the object of a preposition for a predicate nominative.

EXAMPLES She swam several laps. [*Laps* is the direct object of the action verb *swam*.]

She is the best **swimmer** on the team. [*Swimmer* is the predicate nominative after the linking verb *is*. It explains the subject *She*. *Team* is the object of the preposition *on*.]

A linking verb may be followed by a compound predicate nominative.

EXAMPLE Sir Walter Scott was a great **poet** and **storyteller**. [*Poet* and *storyteller* make up a compound predicate nominative. It identifies the subject and follows the linking verb *was*.]

EXERCISE 4. Identifying Predicate Nominatives. Number your paper 1–10. After the number of the sentence, write the predicate nominative from the sentence.

EXAMPLE 1. Mount Rushmore is a national memorial.
1. *memorial*

1. Two well-known poets are Dickinson and Frost.
2. Her mother will remain president of the P.T.A.
3. Athens has always been a center of art and drama.
4. The platypus and the anteater are mammals.
5. Atlanta is the seat of Fulton County.
6. The peace pipe was a symbol of honor and power.
7. Quebec is the largest province in Canada.
8. Hawaii became the fiftieth state of the United States.

9. That bird must be a tern.

10. The fourth planet from the sun is Mars.

The Predicate Adjective

Another kind of subject complement is the *predicate adjective*. It follows a linking verb and describes the subject. In the following examples, the predicate adjectives are in boldfaced type.

EXAMPLES   By 9:30 P.M., I was very **tired**. [*Tired* is a predicate adjective. It modifies the subject *I*.]

The baseball field looks too **wet**. [*Wet* is a predicate adjective. It modifies the subject *field*.]

This autumn scene is **sad** and **beautiful**. [*Sad* and *beautiful* make up a compound predicate adjective. It modifies the subject *scene*.]

(2) A *predicate adjective* is a subject complement. It is an adjective that modifies the subject of the sentence. A predicate adjective follows a linking verb.

EXERCISE 5. Identifying Predicate Adjectives. Number your paper 1–10. After the number of each sentence, write the predicate adjective used in that sentence.

EXAMPLE   1. The porpoise seemed restless.
    1. *restless*

    2. My father looks tired.
    2. *tired*

1. Everyone felt ready for the test.
2. That bowl of fruit looks delicious.
3. The front tire looks flat to me.
4. Everyone appeared interested in the debate.
5. That scratch may become worse.
6. She is talented in music.
7. During the TV show, I became tired and bored.
8. Van looks upset about his grades.

9. The queen is quite popular with her people.
10. The computer program does not seem difficult.

EXERCISE 6. Writing Predicate Adjectives. Complete each sentence with an appropriate predicate adjective.

EXAMPLE 1. That apple looks —— .
          1. *That apple looks juicy.*

1. The music sounds —— .
2. They became —— before the test.
3. The box feels —— .
4. My cousin is —— about my visit.
5. The concert was —— .
6. The small room smells —— .
7. I wonder if it tastes —— .
8. When she goes on stage, she does not want to appear —— .
9. From the looks of it, it should be —— .
10. My brother seems —— about the gift.

REVIEW EXERCISE A. Identifying Subject Complements. Number your paper 1–10. Write the subject complements in the following sentences. Then identify each complement as a predicate nominative (*p.n.*) or predicate adjective (*p.a.*). Remember that a subject complement may be compound.

EXAMPLES 1. Two nearby attractions are Mount Vernon and Arlington.
          1. *Mount Vernon, Arlington—p.n.*
          2. Mount Vernon is impressive.
          2. *impressive—p.a.*

1. Mount Vernon was the home of George and Martha Washington.
2. This famous estate also became their final resting place.
3. The plantation has remained interesting and beautiful.
4. The gardens and lawns are formal.
5. The setting seems perfect for the magnificent mansion.

6. The furnishings in the mansion are mostly reproductions.
7. In the master bedroom of the mansion, however, the furniture is original.
8. Washington was happy and busy at Mount Vernon.
9. He became President in 1789.
10. Martha Washington was the hostess of Mount Vernon.

REVIEW EXERCISE B. **Identifying Complements.** Number your paper 1–10. Write the complements in the following sentences. Then identify each complement as a direct object (*d.o.*), an indirect object (*i.o.*), a predicate nominative (*p.n.*), or a predicate adjective (*p.a.*).

EXAMPLE   1. My uncle gave me his collection of shells.
          1. *me, i.o.*
            collection, d.o.

1. Gerald Durrell is the author of thirty nature books.
2. In *The Amateur Naturalist,* he tells the reader interesting facts about mollusks.
3. Mollusks are the second largest group of animals.
4. They include slugs, snails, and bivalves.
5. Bivalves have two shells.
6. Both shells are usually identical in size and shape.
7. Mussels, oysters, and clams are bivalves.
8. Bivalves make burrows in the sand or mud.
9. Most slugs and snails have a single shell.
10. The shell can be very small or even absent.

DIAGRAMING COMPLEMENTS

The subject and verb form a sentence base. You already know how to diagram the subject and verb. Now you will learn how to diagram a sentence base that also contains a complement. As you have just learned, there are four kinds of complements: the direct object, the indirect object, the predicate nominative, and the predicate adjective.

Direct Objects

Write the direct object on the horizontal line right after the verb. Separate the direct object from the verb with a short vertical line. Study the pattern and the examples.

PATTERN

subject	action verb	direct object

EXAMPLES   We are expecting guests. [direct object]

We	are expecting	guests

Rachel enjoys soccer and tennis. [compound direct object]

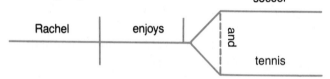

Notice that the vertical line before the direct object stops at the horizontal line.

Indirect Objects

Write an indirect object on a horizontal line below the verb. Connect the indirect object to the verb with a slanting line. Study the pattern and the examples that follow.

PATTERN

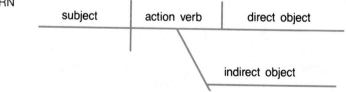

EXAMPLES   Ms. Carter taught us the metric system.

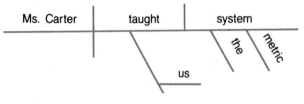

Dad fixed them some spaghetti.

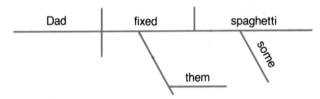

EXERCISE 7. Diagraming Direct and Indirect Objects.
Diagram these sentences.

1. He handed her the report.
2. Mark told me a joke.
3. The doctor wrote a prescription.
4. My grandmother sent me a letter.
5. Mom bought me some paper.

Predicate Nominatives and Predicate Adjectives

The diagram for a subject complement is similar to the diagram for a direct object. Instead of using a vertical line to separate the complement from the verb, use a diagonal line. Slant the diagonal line back toward the subject.

Study the pattern for diagraming subject complements below and the three examples that follow.

PATTERN

| subject | linking verb \ p.n. or p.a. |

EXAMPLES   My dog is a collie. [predicate nominative]

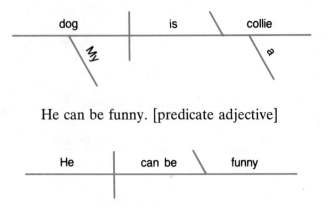

He can be funny. [predicate adjective]

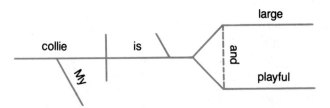

My collie is large and playful. [compound predicate adjective]

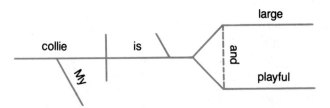

EXERCISE 8. **Diagraming Objects and Subject Complements.**   Diagram these sentences. Remember to slant the vertical line for a subject complement.

1. Prometheus gave mankind fire.
2. Eris was an evil goddess.
3. Paris gave a goddess the golden apple.
4. Helen was very beautiful.
5. The Greeks gave the Trojans a horse.
6. The wooden horse was huge and dangerous.
7. Aeneas was a famous hero.
8. The Cyclops was fierce and strong.
9. The gods could become very angry.
10. Penelope was sad and lonely.

REVIEW EXERCISE C. Identifying Complements. Number your paper 1–10. Write each complement after the number of the sentence. Then tell whether the complement is a direct object (*d.o.*), an indirect object (*i.o.*), a predicate nominative (*p.n.*), or a predicate adjective (*p.a.*).

EXAMPLE   1. Norman Rockwell was an American artist.
             1. *artist—p.n.*

1. Norman Rockwell drew more than three hundred magazine covers.
2. He usually gave his pictures some humor and fun.
3. In one picture, a doctor is examining a doll.
4. His picture of Thanksgiving dinner is popular.
5. His most famous work is *Four Freedoms*.
6. Rockwell gave details serious attention.
7. He chose real people for his models.
8. President Ford gave Rockwell an award.
9. He received the Medal of Freedom.
10. Many people recognize the pictures of Norman Rockwell.

REVIEW EXERCISE D. Writing Sentences with Complements. Write a sentence for each of the following kinds of complements. Underline the complement in each sentence.

EXAMPLE   1. A compound predicate nominative
             1. *My aunt is a swimmer and a jogger.*

1. A predicate adjective   4. A predicate nominative
2. An indirect object   5. A compound predicate adjective
3. A direct object

CHAPTER 14 REVIEW: POSTTEST 1

Identifying Complements. Number your paper 1–10. After each number, write the complement or complements in that sentence. Tell the kind of complement by using one of the abbreviations *d.o.* (direct object), *i.o.* (indirect object), *p.n.* (predicate nominative), or *p.a.* (predicate adjective).

EXAMPLE 1. Many forests are cold and snowy.
1. *cold—p.a.*
snowy—p.a.

1. The home of the former President is now a library and museum.
2. The sun disappeared, and the wind suddenly grew cold.
3. We made our parents a family tree for their anniversary.
4. The newspaper published a story and an editorial about the new buses.
5. My uncle gave my sister and me ice skates.
6. After the hike, everyone felt cold and sleepy.
7. A bird built its nest in the drainpipe.
8. I wrote my name and address in my book.
9. Your dog certainly appears healthy.
10. They always send us grapefruit and oranges from Florida.
11. Most stars in our galaxy are invisible to the unaided eye.
12. Workers captured an alligator in the sewer system.
13. A trip on the Staten Island ferry can be an adventure.
14. The air show featured balloons and parachutes.
15. The maples in the park are becoming gold and red.
16. My parents sang us their favorite song.
17. My aunt bought Ricardo and me tickets for the show.
18. The most popular sports are football and baseball.
19. The water in the pool looked clean and fresh.
20. Homemade bread tastes delicious.

CHAPTER 14 REVIEW: POSTTEST 2

Writing Sentences with Complements. Write four sentences. In each sentence, use a different kind of complement. Underline the complement in each sentence. In a sentence with an indirect object, underline only the indirect object. You may use compound complements. Next to the sentence, write the kind of complement that you have used.

EXAMPLE   1. *My goldfish is <u>unusual</u>.—predicate adjective*
             2. *He eats <u>oatmeal</u>.—direct object*

CHAPTER 15

Agreement

SUBJECT AND VERB

Writing a sentence is a little like sorting pairs of socks. To make a pair, the two socks must match. In a sentence, the two most important parts—the subject and the verb—must match, or *agree*. When someone says, "There's Harry and Jane" or "She don't," the subject and the verb do not agree. In this chapter, you will learn how to make subjects and verbs agree.

DIAGNOSTIC TEST

Choosing Verbs That Agree in Number with Their Subjects. Number your paper 1–10. After the proper number, write the subject of the sentence. Then, from the two verbs in parentheses, choose the one that agrees with the subject in number. Write the verb after the subject.

EXAMPLE 1. Here (are, is) the tickets for the game.
      1. *tickets, are*

1. The flowers in that garden (need, needs) water.
2. She and her cousin (play, plays) tennis every weekend.

3. Neither the tomatoes nor the peach (are, is) ripe.
4. There (was, were) several teachers at the game.
5. My brother and his dog (has, have) gone hunting.
6. (Was, Were) your friends at the concert last Saturday?
7. It (doesn't, don't) really matter to me.
8. My friends at school (doesn't, don't) live in our district.
9. (Was, Were) they invited to the party?
10. Here (come, comes) Elena and James.

NUMBER

All nouns and pronouns have number: either singular or plural. If a noun or pronoun stands for only one thing, it is singular in number. If it stands for more than one thing, it is plural in number.

15a. When a word stands for one person or thing, it is *singular* in number. When a word stands for more than one person or thing, it is *plural* in number.

EXAMPLES   car, I, baby, caterpillar [singular]
cars, we, babies, caterpillars [plural]

EXERCISE 1. **Identifying Singular and Plural Words.** Number your paper 1–10. If a word is singular, write *S* after its number. If it is plural, write *P*.

EXAMPLES   1. activities
1. *P*
2. lunch
2. *S*

1. peach   6. mice
2. libraries   7. we
3. highway   8. grades
4. knife   9. women
5. shelves   10. America

AGREEMENT OF SUBJECT AND VERB

Verbs have number, too. A subject and verb agree when they have the same number. If the subject is plural, the verb must be plural in order to agree. If the subject is singular, the verb must be singular.

15b. A verb agrees with its subject in number.

EXAMPLES   She sings. [singular subject and singular verb]
Birds sing. [plural subject and plural verb]

(1) Singular subjects take singular verbs.

EXAMPLES   The **ocean roars** in the distance. [The verb *roars* is singular to agree with the singular subject *ocean*.]
Marla plays the violin well. [The verb *plays* is singular to agree with the singular subject *Marla*.]

(2) Plural subjects take plural verbs.

EXAMPLES   **Squirrels eat** the seeds from the bird feeder. [The verb *eat* is plural to agree with the plural subject *squirrels*.]
The **dancers practice** after school. [The verb *practice* is plural to agree with the plural subject *dancers*.]

When a sentence has a verb phrase, the helping verb agrees with the subject.

EXAMPLES   The **movie is** starting.
The **movies are** starting.
The **girl has** been called.
The **girls have** been called.

> ☞ NOTE   An *-s* ending is often a sign of a plural noun. It is also the sign of a singular verb.

EXERCISE 2. Identifying the Number of Subjects and Verbs.
Number your paper 1–10. If the subject and verb are singular,
write *S* after the number. If the subject and verb are plural, write
P. All the subjects and verbs agree.

1. socks match
2. lightning crackles
3. leaves rustle
4. mosquitoes buzz
5. Lily baby-sits
6. bands march
7. boy jumps
8. they listen
9. singer practices
10. horses whinny

EXERCISE 3. Changing the Number of Subjects and Verbs.
Number your paper 1–10. All of the subjects and verbs in the
following sentences agree in number. Write each subject and verb
on your paper. Then change the subject and the verb to the
opposite number. If the verb is made up of more than one word,
write the whole verb phrase.

EXAMPLES
1. Thirty students are going on the field trip.
   1. *students are going*
      student is going
2. The trip is on Friday.
   2. *trip is*
      trips are

1. The museum is a favorite with our class.
2. Almost fifty exhibits are displayed there.
3. Visitors may touch many of the exhibits.
4. One exhibit provides an experience with complete darkness.
5. Visitors walk through a tunnel with no light at all.
6. Many different objects stick out from the wall.
7. Several visitors were frightened.
8. My classmates were puzzled by the texture of the objects.
9. Our teacher has gone through the tunnel many times.
10. The experience makes other senses as important as sight.

**EXERCISE 4. Choosing Verbs That Agree in Number with
Their Subjects.** Number your paper 1–10. In each sentence

USAGE

choose the verb in parentheses that agrees with the subject. Write the subject and verb after the proper number.

EXAMPLE 1. The calico kitten (pounces, pounce) on the ball.
 1. *kitten pounces*

1. Firefighters (risks, risk) their lives to save others.
2. The snowplow (clears, clear) the road quickly.
3. Old toys (is, are) gathering dust in the closet.
4. Many states (has, have) seat-belt laws.
5. Some students (chooses, choose) to play volleyball.
6. At the science fair, the winner (receives, receive) a plaque.
7. Strong winds (whistles, whistle) through the old house.
8. Club members (picks, pick) up the litter in the park.
9. The principal (makes, make) announcements each day.
10. Doctors (says, say) that loud music can harm the ears.

PROBLEMS IN AGREEMENT

When the verb comes immediately after the subject, you probably use a correct verb without even thinking. Sometimes, however, a phrase comes between the subject and the verb, and the agreement is not clear. In other cases, the subject may come after the verb; this may pose another problem in agreement. In such cases, you must think carefully about making the subject and the verb agree in number.

Phrases Between Subject and Verb

A prepositional phrase may come between the subject and the verb in a sentence. The object of the preposition is often different in number from the subject. You must be careful, therefore, to make the verb agree with the subject, not with the object of the preposition.

EXAMPLE Six **puppies** in the litter **have** been given away. [*Litter* is the object of the preposition *in,* not the subject of the verb.]

15c. The number of a subject is not changed by a phrase following the subject.

EXAMPLES   All **shades** of blue **are** my favorite colors.
              One of them **is** sitting on a broken chair.
              The **dancer** in these photos **has** performed well.

EXERCISE 5. Choosing Verbs That Agree in Number with Their Subjects.   Number your paper 1–10. Write the subject of each sentence after the corresponding number. After the subject, write the verb in parentheses that agrees with it.

EXAMPLE   1. Islands off the coast (has, have) a life of their own.
              1. *Islands, have*

1. The second largest island of the United States (is, are) located in the Gulf of Alaska.
2. The 13,000 citizens on Kodiak Island (is, are) of Eskimo, Russian, or Scandinavian descent.
3. Sacks of mail (is, are) flown to the island from the mainland.
4. The citizens of Kodiak (calls, call) Alaska the mainland.
5. Industries in the community (has, have) suffered in recent years.
6. One cannery on the island (cans, can) delicious salmon eggs, or roe.
7. The residents of the mainland (considers, consider) roe a delicacy.
8. The bears on the island (catch, catches) fresh salmon.
9. However, their search for leftovers (create, creates) problems for Kodiak.
10. The officials of one town (has, have) put a special fence around the garbage dump.

The Compound Subject

A compound subject is made up of two or more subjects that are connected by *and, or,* or *nor.* These connected subjects

USAGE

share the same verb. When two subjects are connected by *and,* the verb is plural, even if each subject is singular.

15d. Subjects joined by *and* take a plural verb.

Read the boldfaced examples of compound subjects, and notice that the verb, in italics, is plural.

EXAMPLES   **Red and blue** *are* the school's colors.
         Mr. Lewis and Mrs. Kirk *have* taken new jobs.
         New **uniforms and instruments** *were* ordered for the marching band.

EXERCISE 6. Choosing Verbs That Agree in Number with Their Subjects. Number your paper 1–10. Write the compound subject of each sentence after the proper number. Then choose the verb that agrees with the compound subject in number and write it after the subject.

EXAMPLE 1. Volcanoes and earthquakes (is, are) common in that area.
       1. *Volcanoes, earthquakes are*

1. A train and a truck (has, have) powerful engines.
2. Wind and rain (is, are) predicted for Thursday.
3. A desk and a bookcase (was, were) moved into my younger brother's bedroom.
4. Savannas and velds (is, are) two kinds of grasslands.
5. A car and a trailer (was, were) stalled on the highway.
6. A raccoon and a squirrel (raid, raids) our garden every night.
7. Ms. Wilson and her niece (goes, go) to class together.
8. Joan and Jarvis (was, were) asked to introduce the guest speaker.
9. Mosquitoes and earwigs (has, have) invaded our back yard.
10. Catsup and mustard (goes, go) well on hot dogs.

15e. Compound subjects joined by *or* or *nor* take a verb that agrees with the nearer subject.

EXAMPLES   A new **statue or** a **fountain** *has* been planned for the park. [The singular verb *has* agrees with the nearer subject *fountain*.]

Neither the **announcer nor** the **players** *were* happy with the decision. [The plural verb *were* agrees with the nearer subject *players*.]

Warm **booties or** a soft **blanket** *makes* a baby comfortable. [The singular verb *makes* agrees with the nearer subject *blanket*.]

EXERCISE 7. *Oral Drill*. Using Correct Verbs with Compound Subjects Joined by *Or* or *Nor*.   Read each of the following sentences aloud several times. Stress the words in italics each time you read.

1. Either a *desert* or a *jungle is* the setting for the play.
2. The *table* or the *bookshelves need* dusting first.
3. Neither the *bus* nor the *train stops* in our town.
4. Neither *jokes* nor funny *stories make* Gordon laugh.
5. *Flowers* or a colorful *picture makes* a room cheerful.

REVIEW EXERCISE A. Choosing Verbs That Agree in Number with Their Subjects.   Number your paper 1–10. Choose the correct verb for each sentence.

EXAMPLE   1. Tara and Chen (are, is) reading the same book.
            1. *are*

1. Some house plants (bloom, blooms) all winter.
2. His mother (teach, teaches) math.
3. The sailboats in the harbor (belong, belongs) to the village.
4. You and your cousins (are, is) invited to the party.
5. Either the clock or our watches (are, is) not accurate.
6. The magazines on the table (are, is) for the hospital.
7. A stretch of unpaved roads (lie, lies) ahead.
8. My brother and sister (deliver, delivers) newspapers.
9. Neither pencils nor an eraser (are, is) permitted.

10. The clowns and jugglers (has, have) always been my favorite circus performers.

REVIEW EXERCISE B. Choosing Verbs That Agree in Number with Their Subjects. Number your paper 1–10. Choose the correct verb for each sentence.

EXAMPLE   1. An exchange of ideas (are, is) necessary for world peace.
          1. *is*

1. Stories by that writer (has, have) unexpected endings.
2. Wind and rain (are, is) forecast for Thanksgiving.
3. Mrs. Shea or her father (sweep, sweeps) their front path every day.
4. My blouse and skirt (was, were) birthday gifts from my Dad.
5. Heavy rains in the spring (has, have) swollen the rivers.
6. The fate of the players (depend, depends) on the coach's instruction.
7. My sister or my parents (has, have) promised us a ride.
8. Neither the chief nor the deputies (need, needs) a new car.
9. Sherbet or fresh fruit (make, makes) a tasty dessert.
10. The windows in my room (are, is) stuck.

Subject After the Verb

In sentences that begin with *there* and *here* and in questions, the subject probably comes after the verb.

15f. When the subject follows the verb, find the subject. Then make sure that the verb agrees with it.

In each of the following sentences, find the verb. Then find the word about which the verb makes a statement.

EXAMPLES   There **are** fifty **runners** in the marathon race. [*Are* is the verb. What are? The plural subject is *runners*.]

Here **is** the overdue **book** about reptiles. [*Is* is the verb. What is? The *book* is. *Book* is the singular subject.]

Are the **birds** in the nest? [*Are* is the verb. What are? The *birds* are. *Birds* is the plural subject.]

> ☞ NOTE   When people are talking, they sometimes use the contractions *there's* and *here's* with a plural subject. These contractions are singular and can only be used with singular subjects. If the subject is plural, you must use *there are* or *here are*.

EXERCISE 8. Choosing Verbs That Agree in Number with Their Subjects.   Number your paper 1–10. Find the subject of each sentence and write it after the proper number. Then choose the correct verb in parentheses and write it after the subject.

1. There (is, are) three foreign exchange students at the high school.
2. (Was, Were) the fans cheering for the other team?
3. (Has, Have) the Washingtons moved into their new home?
4. Here (is, are) my copy of the words to the song.
5. (Has, Have) the bees left the hive?
6. (There's, There are) several answers to that question.
7. (Has, Have) the sixth-graders elected their officers?
8. (Here are, Here's) the shells from Driftwood Beach.
9. (There's, There are) a pint of strawberries in the kitchen.
10. There (is, are) Amy and Wanda in the doorway.

The Contractions *Don't* and *Doesn't*

The word *don't* is a contraction of *do not*. The word *doesn't* is a contraction of *does not*. When you use these contractions, make sure that they agree in number with their subjects.

USAGE

15g. The contraction *don't* is used with all plural subjects and with the pronouns *I* and *you.*

EXAMPLES **I don't** have it. **Dogs don't** meow.
You don't care. **They don't** know.
We don't agree. The **boots don't** fit.

15h. The contraction *doesn't* is used with all singular subjects except the pronouns *I* and *you.*

EXAMPLES **He doesn't** have it. **Don doesn't** like it.
She doesn't care. The **car doesn't** run.
It doesn't work.

☞ NOTE Careless errors in agreement are usually made with the pronouns *it, he,* and *she.* Remember that *doesn't* is used with these singular pronouns; *it doesn't; he doesn't; she doesn't.*

EXERCISE 9. *Oral Drill.* Using *Don't* and *Doesn't* Correctly.
Read the following sentences aloud several times. Stress the words in italics.

1. *He doesn't* want us to give him a party.
2. *Margo* and *Jim don't* have any money left.
3. *It doesn't* matter anyway.
4. The *bus doesn't* stop here.
5. *They don't* believe that old story.

EXERCISE 10. Writing *Don't* and *Doesn't* with Subjects.
Number your paper 1–10. Write the subject of the sentence and the correct contraction (*don't* or *doesn't*) after the number.

EXAMPLE 1. Our cats —— like catnip.
         1. *cats don't*

1. Those socks —— match.
2. It —— seem like a spring morning.
3. I —— have any homework for tonight.
4. Bill, of all people, —— know how to swim.
5. The cherries —— taste sweet.
6. She —— practice the piano enough.
7. This bedroom —— look very neat.
8. My boots —— fit me this year.
9. He —— like to play games.
10. They —— live on this street.

WRITING APPLICATION
Proofreading Your Writing
for Subject-Verb Agreement

When you write, you may sometimes try to put down your thoughts so quickly that it is easy to forget about subject-verb agreement. Always read what you have written very carefully. That is the best way to catch errors in agreement. Look at each verb and its subject to be sure that they agree in number.

Writing Assignment

Think about the most interesting thing you have ever seen at a fair or carnival. (You may substitute another crowded, busy place you have visited.) Describe it and tell what you thought was most interesting. Also mention how other people reacted to it. After you write your description, proofread it carefully. Make sure that each verb agrees with its subject.

REVIEW EXERCISE C. Choosing Verbs That Agree in Number with Their Subjects. Number your paper 1–10. Choose the correct verb in parentheses in each sentence and write it after the proper number.

1. Diego and Ralph (practices, practice) shooting baskets in the driveway.
2. There (is, are) at least two sides to every story.
3. Neither the teacher nor the students (knows, know) how to operate the film projector.
4. Neither Monica nor Courtney (wears, wear) jewelry.
5. (Doesn't, Don't) he like to eat Italian food?
6. Every afternoon, the band and the baton twirlers (marches, march) on the football field.
7. Either the dog or the cats (has, have) torn the carpet.
8. The peaches in that basket (are, is) from Georgia.
9. He (doesn't, don't) know the coach's name.
10. Your sneakers (doesn't, don't) look dirty to me.

CHAPTER 15 REVIEW: POSTTEST

Choosing Verbs That Agree in Number with Their Subjects.
Number your paper 1–20. After the proper number, write the subject of the sentence. Then, from the two verbs in parentheses, choose the one that agrees with the subject in number. Write the verb after the subject.

EXAMPLE   1. She and Brad (are, is) on the honor roll.
           1. *She, Brad, are*

1. Neither the passengers nor the pilot (was, were) injured.
2. There (are, is) two new rides at the amusement park.
3. The stuffed animals in my collection (sit, sits) on a shelf in my closet.
4. (Here are, Here's) some books about Hawaii.
5. Shel Silverstein and Ogden Nash (appeal, appeals) to children and grownups.
6. My neighbor and his son (is, are) building a log cabin.
7. (Was, Were) your parents happy with the results?
8. He (doesn't, don't) play chess anymore.
9. Why (doesn't, don't) she and Megan bring the lemonade?

10. Tickets for that concert (are, is) scarce.
11. The dishes on that shelf (look, looks) clean.
12. My mother and my brother (has, have) been in Florida since Sunday.
13. Either the cats or the dog (has, have) upset the plants.
14. Here (are, is) the instructions for the microwave.
15. There (go, goes) Jane and her brother.
16. I (am, is) crocheting an afghan.
17. Why (wasn't, weren't) you at the meeting yesterday?
18. She (doesn't, don't) like spectator sports.
19. Several paintings by that artist (are, is) on exhibit at the mall.
20. They (doesn't, don't) know the correct time.

CHAPTER 16

Using Verbs Correctly

PRINCIPAL PARTS, REGULAR AND IRREGULAR VERBS

You cannot speak or write sentences without using verbs. It is important then that you study verbs and verb forms carefully. The better you know them, the more easily you will be able to use verbs correctly in speaking and writing.

DIAGNOSTIC TEST

Writing the Correct Forms of Verbs. Number your paper 1–20. After each number, write the correct form of the verb given before the sentence.

EXAMPLE 1. *drive*   Our family has —— two hundred miles.
1. *driven*

1. *ride*   We had —— in the car for two hours.
2. *fall*   Six inches of snow —— last night.
3. *know*   I never —— snow was so beautiful.
4. *blow*   The wind had —— some of it into high drifts.
5. *go*   As we —— past them, they looked like white hills.

6. *bring* Joey —— some comics to read on the trip.
7. *choose* I —— to look at the scenery.
8. *break* Unfortunately, the car heater had —— .
9. *wear* We all —— our heavy coats and mittens.
10. *freeze* However, my ears almost —— .
11. *shrink* My favorite wool cap had —— to a tiny size.
12. *sing* During the long ride home, we —— some songs.
13. *eat* At noon, we —— lunch at a roadside cafeteria.
14. *begin* After lunch, Joey —— to feel sleepy.
15. *come* Why had he —— if he wanted to sleep?
16. *go* I had never —— so far on a trip before.
17. *drink* I should never have —— two cups of hot cocoa.
18. *run* When we stopped, Mom and I —— into the gas station.
19. *fall* Mom almost —— on a patch of ice.
20. *sink* All warmed up again, I —— into a deep sleep.

THE PRINCIPAL PARTS OF VERBS

The *principal parts* of verbs are the four basic forms. (*Principal* means "most important.") The principal parts are important because they are used in making all the different *tenses* of verbs. (Tenses are forms of verbs showing time.)

16a. The four principal parts of a verb are the *infinitive*, the *present participle*, the *past*, and the *past participle*.

The principal parts of the verb *wear*, for example, are

INFINITIVE	PRESENT PARTICIPLE	PAST	PAST PARTICIPLE
wear	wearing	wore	(have) worn

The first principal part of a verb is the *infinitive*. Another name for this principal part is the *present*.

tell   care   write   do

Two of the principal parts are called *participles*. The *present participle* of a verb always ends in *-ing*.

telling   caring   writing   doing

The *past participle* is the form that should be used with the helping verbs *have, has,* or *had.*

(have) cared   (has) written   (had) done

Notice that the present participle and the past participle are used with helping verbs—*am, is, are, has, have, had,* etc.

The *conjugation* of a verb is a list of its tenses, which are the forms showing time. You use all four principal parts when you conjugate a verb.

Principal Parts *of* Wear

INFINITIVE	PRESENT PARTICIPLE	PAST	PAST PARTICIPLE
wear	wearing	wore	(have) worn

Conjugation *of* Wear
Present Tense

Singular	*Plural*
I wear	we wear
you wear	you wear
he (she, it) wears	they wear

Past Tense

Singular	*Plural*
I wore	we wore
you wore	you wore
he (she, it) wore	they wore

Future Tense

Singular	*Plural*
I will (shall) wear	we will (shall) wear
you will wear	you will wear
he (she, it) will wear	they will wear

Present Perfect Tense

Singular	*Plural*
I have worn	we have worn
you have worn	you have worn
he (she, it) has worn	they have worn

Past Perfect Tense

Singular	*Plural*
I had worn	we had worn
you had worn	you had worn
he (she, it) had worn	they had worn

Future Perfect Tense

Singular	*Plural*
I will (shall) have worn	we will (shall) have worn
you will have worn	you will have worn
he (she, it) will have worn	they will have worn

USAGE

Regular Verbs

16b. A regular verb forms its past and past participle by adding *-ed* or *-d* to the infinitive form.

Regular verbs are called *regular* because the spelling of the main part of the verb does not change, except for the endings. Study the chart that follows.

INFINITIVE	PRESENT PARTICIPLE	PAST	PAST PARTICIPLE
wash	washing	washed	(have) washed
hop	hopping	hopped	(have) hopped
use	using	used	(have) used

Notice that regular verbs that end in *-e* drop the *-e* before adding *-ing* to form the present participle; for example, *use, using.* Sometimes the final consonant of a regular verb must be doubled before *-ing* or *-ed* is added; for example, *hop, hopped,* and *hopping.*

EXERCISE 1. **Forming the Past and Past Participles of Regular Verbs.** Number your paper 1–10. Write the past and past participle for each verb. Remember that some verbs double the final consonant before adding -ed.

EXAMPLE   1. work
            1. *worked, (have) worked*

1. skate	4. move	7. enjoy	9. laugh
2. pick	5. talk	8. rob	10. love
3. live	6. stun		

Irregular Verbs

A verb is called *irregular* when its past or past participle is not formed by adding *-ed* or *-d* to the infinitive. An irregular verb does not simply add endings to the infinitive to form the past and past participle. The best way to remember the principal parts of irregular verbs is to learn them by heart.

16c. An *irregular verb* is one that forms its past and past participle in some other way than a regular verb.

Irregular verbs form their past and past participles in a number of different ways.

by changing a vowel

sing	sang	(have) sung
drink	drank	(have) drunk
become	became	(have) become

by changing a vowel and consonants

go	went	(have) gone
do	did	(have) done
see	saw	(have) seen

by making no change

burst	burst	(have) burst
cut	cut	(have) cut
hurt	hurt	(have) hurt

USAGE

There is no easy way to remember all of the irregular verbs and their forms. You must use them often, both in speech and writing, so that they come to mind automatically.

By learning the forms of the irregular verbs, you can keep from using nonstandard forms. For example, you can avoid using *throwed* instead of *threw, bursted* instead of *burst,* or *brung* instead of *brought.* The following list contains the irregular verbs that you should know.

Common Irregular Verbs

INFINITIVE	PRESENT PARTICIPLE	PAST	PAST PARTICIPLE
begin	beginning	began	(have) begun
blow	blowing	blew	(have) blown
break	breaking	broke	(have) broken
bring	bringing	brought	(have) brought
burst	bursting	burst	(have) burst
choose	choosing	chose	(have) chosen
come	coming	came	(have) come
do	doing	did	(have) done
drink	drinking	drank	(have) drunk
drive	driving	drove	(have) driven
eat	eating	ate	(have) eaten
fall	falling	fell	(have) fallen
freeze	freezing	froze	(have) frozen
give	giving	gave	(have) given
go	going	went	(have) gone
know	knowing	knew	(have) known
ride	riding	rode	(have) ridden
ring	ringing	rang	(have) rung
run	running	ran	(have) run
see	seeing	saw	(have) seen
shrink	shrinking	shrank	(have) shrunk
sing	singing	sang	(have) sung
sink	sinking	sank	(have) sunk
speak	speaking	spoke	(have) spoken

steal	stealing	stole	(have) stolen
swim	swimming	swam	(have) swum
take	taking	took	(have) taken
throw	throwing	threw	(have) thrown
wear	wearing	wore	(have) worn
write	writing	wrote	(have) written

EXERCISE 2. Identifying the Correct Forms of Irregular Verbs. Number your paper 1–10. This exercise covers the first ten irregular verbs. Choose the correct one of the two verbs in parentheses, and write it after the proper number. If the correct verb is the past participle, write the helping verb in front of it. When your paper has been corrected, read each sentence aloud several times, stressing the correct verb.

EXAMPLES   1. I have (began, begun) to knit a scarf.
1. *have begun*
2. We (chose, chosen) to stay indoors.
2. *chose*

1. Earline has never (drank, drunk) buttermilk before.
2. We (did, done) our homework after dinner.
3. Anna and Dee have almost (broke, broken) the school record for the fifty-yard dash.
4. The wind has (blew, blown) fiercely for three days.
5. Last Saturday, Isaac and Charles (come, came) to my house for the afternoon.
6. The hot-water pipes in the laundry room have (bursted, burst) again.
7. We had (began, begun) our project when I got sick.
8. The Ruiz family has (drove, driven) across the country.
9. Has anyone (brung, brought) extra batteries for the radio?
10. I have finally (chose, chosen) the orange kitten.

EXERCISE 3. Identifying the Correct Forms of Irregular Verbs. This exercise covers the next ten irregular verbs in the list. Follow the instructions for Exercise 2.

USAGE

1. Before the lecture, I had never (knew, known) the difference between cricket and croquet.
2. The lake has finally (froze, frozen) hard enough for us to go skating on it.
3. My father has (gave, given) away all my comic books to the children's hospital.
4. The school bell (rang, rung) five minutes late every afternoon this week.
5. In New York, Julia (saw, seen) a musical about cats.
6. How many sixth-graders have never (rode, ridden) on the school bus?
7. It is amazing that no one has ever (fell, fallen) off the old ladder.
8. What is the longest distance you have ever (ran, run)?
9. Everyone has (went, gone) back to the classroom to watch the videotape of the spelling bee.
10. George (ran, run) to the corner to see the antique fire engine.

EXERCISE 4. Identifying the Correct Forms of Irregular Verbs. This exercise covers the last ten irregular verbs in the list. Follow the instructions for Exercise 2.

1. Who (swam, swum) faster, Jesse or Cindy?
2. That cute little puppy has (stole, stolen) our hearts.
3. The choir has never (sang, sung) beautifully.
4. Jimmy's toy boat (sank, sunk) to the bottom of the lake where we could not see it.
5. Have you (throwed, thrown) away yesterday's paper?
6. Maria had (wore, worn) her new outfit to the party.
7. Until yesterday, no one had ever (swam, swum) across Crystal Lake.
8. In *Alice's Adventures in Wonderland*, Alice (shrank, shrunk) to a very small size!
9. The students have (wrote, written) a letter to the mayor.
10. I have never (spoke, spoken) to a large group before.

USAGE

REVIEW EXERCISE A. Writing the Past and Past Participle Forms of Verbs. Number your paper 1–20. Write the correct form (past or past participle) of the verb given before each sentence.

EXAMPLE   1. *bake* We have —— two loaves of bread.
           1. *baked*

1. *do*   Has everyone —— the assignment for today?
2. *burst*   Suddenly, the door —— open.
3. *begin*   By two o'clock, the race had already —— .
4. *eat*   Have you —— lunch yet?
5. *bring*   Andy —— some records to the dance.
6. *blow*   She —— out the candles on the cake.
7. *fall*   One of the hikers had —— into the river.
8. *run*   We have —— ten laps of the track every day while in training for the meet.
9. *freeze*   The homemade ice cream finally —— .
10. *choose* Which play have they —— to perform?
11. *go*   On Sunday we —— to a family reunion.
12. *know*   Noriko —— the way to Lynn's house.
13. *write*   Ms. Brook has —— letters to all of us.
14. *shrink* Like magic, the box —— before my eyes!
15. *ring*   Who —— the doorbell a moment ago?
16. *drink*   The puppy has —— all the water in the dish.
17. *steal*   David —— third base in the ninth inning.
18. *swim*   Have you —— in the new pool at the park?
19. *see*   We had never —— a live koala before.
20. *come*   Jim —— early to help us with the decorations for the dance tonight.

REVIEW EXERCISE B. Revising Incorrect Verb Forms in Sentences. Number your paper 1–10. Read each sentence carefully. If the sentence is correct, write *C* after the number. If the form of a verb is wrong, write the correct form.

EXAMPLE   1. They done their best.
           1. *did*

1. Sailors have often saw dolphins in the ocean.
2. My wool slacks have shrank in the warm water.
3. The mad scientist drunk the secret potion.
4. Our assembly speaker has wrote many books for young adults and for children.
5. Tanya and Ruth swum from the raft to the shore.
6. Few divers have ever rode on the back of a whale.
7. Patricia has often wore her brother's college sweatshirt.
8. No one has yet spoken to the new student.
9. Ben and Cleon should have went straight home.
10. I have almost bursted the seams of my old jeans.

SIX CONFUSING VERBS

Three pairs of verbs in particular are often misused. People tend to get the meanings and spellings mixed up. Study the following explanations of how to use *sit* and *set*, *rise* and *raise*, and *lie* and *lay*.

Sit and *Set*

The verb *sit* means "to rest in a seated position" or "to take one's seat," as in a chair. The principal parts are *sit, sitting, sat,* and *(have) sat.*

EXAMPLES   Judy **sits** in the front row.
Two girls **sat** on the park bench.
They **have sat** there for an hour.

The verb *set* means "to place (something)" or "to put." The principal parts are *set, setting, set,* and *(have) set.*

EXAMPLES   Ellie **sets** the plates around the table.
They **set** the boxes by the door.
The workers **have set** their equipment asidè.

You will have almost no trouble if you think about the meaning of each verb. You should also remember that *set* usually

USAGE

takes a direct object. That is, a noun or pronoun usually receives the action of the verb *set*.

EXAMPLES   I will **sit** in the easy chair. [no direct object]
I will **set** the book on the counter. [direct object: *book*]

If you don't know whether to use *sit* or *set* in a sentence, try substituting *put*. If the sentence makes sense with *put*, use *set*.

EXERCISE 5. *Oral Drill*. Using the Forms of *Sit* and *Set* Correctly.   Read the following sentences aloud several times, stressing the words in italics. Think about the meaning of each verb as you read.

1. Josie *set* the mail on the kitchen table.
2. The clown *sat* on the broken chair.
3. Please *set* up the folding table.
4. Have you *set* the clock on the nightstand?
5. The Clarks' car has *sat* in the driveway for a week.
6. My little brother *sits* still for only a few seconds at a time.
7. The teacher *sets* the best projects in the display case.
8. They *set* the equipment on the ground.
9. I have *sat* here all afternoon.
10. No one ever *sits* by the bus driver.

EXERCISE 6. Writing the Forms of *Sit* and *Set*.   Number your paper 1–10. For each blank, write the correct form of *sit* or *set*.

1. At the party yesterday we —— the birthday presents on the coffee table.   **2.** Then we —— on the floor to play a game. **3.** Frank always —— next to Lisa.   **4.** The Johnson twins never —— together, even on their birthday.   **5.** Mrs. Johnson then —— a large cake on the dining-room table.   **6.** Mr. Johnson had already —— party hats and favors around the table. **7.** One of the twins —— on a hat by mistake.   **8.** Mr. Johnson —— out another party hat.   **9.** At every party everyone always —— quietly while the birthday person makes a wish. **10.** Yesterday we —— still twice as long for the Johnson twins!

Rise and *Raise*

The verb *rise* means "to go in an upward direction" or "to get up." The principal parts are *rise, rising, rose,* and *(have) risen.*

EXAMPLES   The sun **rises** in the east.
The dough **rose** in the hot oven.
We **had risen** from our seats.

The verb *raise* means "to lift up" or "to move (something) in an upward direction." Like the verb *set,* the verb *raise* usually has a direct object. The principal parts are *raise, raising, raised,* and *(have) raised.*

EXAMPLES   Please **raise** the window shade a little.
Beth **raised** her hand before answering.
The campers **have raised** the flag every morning.

Remember, *rise* does not take a direct object, but *raise* usually does.

EXAMPLES   The full moon **is rising.** [no direct object]
The kite **rose** quickly in the wind. [no direct object]
The winners **raised** the trophy for all to see. [direct object: *trophy*]
Will Congress **raise** taxes? [direct object: *taxes*]

EXERCISE 7. *Oral Drill.* **Using the Forms of *Rise* and *Raise* Correctly.**   Read the following sentences aloud. Think of the meaning of each verb as you stress the form in italics.

1. The audience had *risen* from their seats.
2. They *raised* the curtains for the play to start.
3. Never *raise* your arms while riding the roller coaster.
4. Dark clouds of smoke *rose* from the fire.
5. They always *rise* early on Saturday mornings.
6. The principal *raised* her eyebrows.
7. Has the sun *risen* yet?
8. The huge crane *raises* the steel beams off the ground.
9. Bread dough *rises* very slowly in a cold room.
10. We always *rise* at the sound of the last bell.

EXERCISE 8. Writing the Forms of *Rise* and *Raise*. Number your paper 1–10. Write the correct form of *rise* or *raise* for each blank.

1. Before each game we —— the flag.
2. The fans always —— for the national anthem.
3. Now the pitcher —— her arm to throw the ball.
4. However, the baseball has —— too far above the catcher's head.
5. Someone always —— in front of me to block my view.
6. I have —— my voice hundreds of times during one game.
7. When the sun —— too high, the players can't see the ball.
8. When someone hits a home run, the children —— their mitts to catch the baseball.
9. Yesterday no one —— when the other team hit a home run.
10. As soon as the ninth inning is over, we —— to leave.

Lie and *Lay*

The verb *lie* means "to recline," "to rest," or "to stay in a reclining position." The principal parts are *lie, lying, lay,* and *(have) lain.*

EXAMPLES　　My watch **is lying** on the dresser.
　　　　　　Mom always **lies** on the floor to do sit-ups.
　　　　　　Yesterday I **lay** down for a nap.
　　　　　　Those dirty clothes **have lain** in the corner of your room for days.

The verb *lay* means "to put down" or "to place (something)." The verb usually takes a direct object. The principal parts are *lay, laying, laid,* and *(have) laid.*

EXAMPLES　　The workers **are laying** the new carpet.
　　　　　　Aunt Esther **lays** her glasses on the chair.
　　　　　　Who **laid** those muddy shoes on the bed?
　　　　　　They **have laid** the beach blanket in a shady spot.

Remember that *lie* never has a direct object, but *lay* usually does.

EXAMPLES   The lioness **lay** in wait for her prey. [no direct object]
Aretha **laid** her clothes on the bed. [direct object: *clothes*]

EXERCISE 9. *Oral Drill.* Using the Forms of *Lie* and *Lay* Correctly.   Read the following sentences aloud and stress the words in italics. Think of the meaning of each verb.

1. The corrected test paper *lay* on the desk.
2. My teddy bear has *lain* under my bed for a long time.
3. Before the sale, the clerk *laid* samples on the counter.
4. Have they *lain* in the sun too long?
5. Yesterday, Kim *laid* the figurine on a velvet cushion.
6. Last week, I *lay* in bed with a cold.
7. The hero has *laid* a trap for the villain.
8. Finally, the baby is *lying* quietly in the crib.
9. Have you ever *lain* awake at night?
10. Allen *laid* his wet boots by the fireplace.

EXERCISE 10. Writing the Forms of *Lie* and *Lay*.   Complete each sentence by writing the correct form of *lie* or *lay*.

1. The television guide is —— under the chair.
2. How long has it —— there?
3. My brother Edgar probably —— it on the mantel last night when he came home.
4. He was —— on the floor to watch television.
5. My little sister always —— her toys right in front of the television set.
6. She cannot find all of the pieces because she has —— little parts from her games all over the house.
7. Whenever they find any of these parts, Mother and Father usually —— the little pieces on the bookcase.
8. Yesterday, Father —— down on some hard plastic pieces on the sofa.

USAGE

9. Now those pieces —— at the bottom of the wastebasket.
10. Today, every single toy —— safely in the toy chest, far away from Father.

WRITING APPLICATION:
Using Verb Forms Correctly
to Make Your Writing Clear

A verb is an essential part of a sentence. It is thus important that you write verbs correctly.

Writing Assignment

You have been living for a year on another planet and are now back on Earth. Write about your life on the other planet. Describe a typical day of activities there. Proofread your writing. Use a dictionary to check any verb forms you are not sure about.

REVIEW EXERCISE C. Identifying the Correct Forms of *Sit* and *Set*, *Rise* and *Raise*, and *Lie* and *Lay*. Number your paper 1–10. Choose the correct verb in parentheses for each sentence.

EXAMPLE   1. Five crows were (sitting, setting) on the fence.
    1. *sitting*

1. For many years, the trunk had (sat, set) in the attic.
2. Yesterday, Barbara (lay, laid) in bed until noon.
3. Never (sit, set) your roller skates on the stairs.
4. Marvel (sits, sets) in his favorite chair to watch hockey.
5. Where has Chester (lain, laid) the jigsaw puzzle?
6. The rocket is (rising, raising) into the sky.
7. Mom has (lain, laid) down for a nap.
8. The magician (rose, raised) the wand to make the dove disappear.

9. After the first jump, the official (rises, raises) the bar two inches higher.
10. Under the starry sky, the campers were (lying, laying) in their sleeping bags.

CHAPTER 16 REVIEW: POSTTEST

Revising Incorrect Verb Forms in Sentences.   Number your paper 1–20. In most of the following sentences, there is an error in the use of a verb. Read each sentence and write the correct verb after the corresponding number. If the sentence is correct, write *C*.

EXAMPLE   1. Last week I went to the movies.
    1. *C*
    2. The movie I seen was terrible.
    2. *saw*

1. My friends and I have set through many bad movies. **2.** Has anyone ever wrote a letter to the movie companies to complain about the movies?   **3.** My friends Skip and Lillian had went with me to see *The Unicorn Meets the Swamp Monster.* **4.** The creature seemed really scary.   **5.** First, it raised out of the swampy water.   **6.** Then it begun to walk slowly toward the unicorn.   **7.** The unicorn had been laying under a tree.   **8.** It hadn't seen the creature approaching.   **9.** I sunk deep into my seat, expecting the creature to pounce.   **10.** Then an announcement was made that the projector had broke.

11. It took a long time before the machine come back on.   **12.** Some kids throwed popcorn up in the air.   **13.** Others noisily drunk their refreshments through straws.   **14.** I had sat my popcorn on the floor, and someone kicked it over.

15. The theater manager choosed a cartoon to show us. **16.** The cartoon was about a penguin that had wore a fur coat. **17.** Because the water had froze, the penguin escaped from the angry polar bear. **18.** The bear was angry because the penguin had bursted into his house. **19.** The cartoon ended when the penguin swum all the way to Miami Beach. **20.** I wished I had brung a book to the movies.

CHAPTER 17

Using Pronouns Correctly

SUBJECT AND OBJECT FORMS

As you learned in Chapter 11, pronouns may be used in place of nouns. Like nouns, pronouns may be used as subjects and objects in sentences. Some pronouns change their forms according to how they are used.

You use pronouns every day in your speech and writing. Do you always know which form of the pronoun to use? In this chapter, you will learn about two forms: the subject form and the object form.

DIAGNOSTIC TEST

Identifying Correct Pronoun Forms. Number your paper 1–10. After each number, write the correct pronoun of the two in parentheses. Be able to give reasons for your answers.

EXAMPLE   1. Our parents and (they, them) play ball together.
           1. *they*

1. Could it be (she, her) at the bus stop?
2. The finalists were Melissa and (he, him).
3. Are you and (they, them) going to the basketball game?

4. You and (I, me) have been friends for a long time.
5. Our parents expect (we, us) four to study every night.
6. (We, Us) players surprised the coach by winning.
7. The teacher was really talking about you and (I, me).
8. Mom served my friend and (I, me) the leftover meatloaf.
9. Mr. Lee divided the money among the younger children and (they, them).
10. A neighbor drove Maria and (he, him) to the park.

THE FORMS OF PERSONAL PRONOUNS

Read the following sentences. Notice how the pronouns in boldfaced type are used differently in each sentence.

EXAMPLES **He** and **I** went to the post office.
The clerk gave a package to **him** and **me**.

Some pronouns change their forms according to how they are used. In the first sentence, *he* and *I* are subjects of the sentence. When you use pronouns as subjects and as predicate nominatives, use the subject form.

In the second sentence, the pronouns *him* and *me* follow the preposition *to*. When you use pronouns as objects of prepositions and as direct and indirect objects of verbs, use the object form.

There is a third form, called the *possessive form*. This form shows ownership (*my, your, his, her, our*). You may want to review possessive pronouns in Chapter 11.

In this chapter, you will learn about the subject and object forms. The following chart shows you the subject and object forms of the personal pronouns.

SUBJECT FORM		OBJECT FORM	
Singular	*Plural*	*Singular*	*Plural*
I	we	me	us
you	you	you	you
he, she, it	they	him, her, it	them

USAGE

☞ NOTE The pronouns *you* and *it* are easy to remember because they do not change.

EXERCISE 1. **Classifying Pronouns.** Number your paper 1–10. If the pronoun is always the subject form, write *S* after the number. If it is always the object form, write *O*. If the pronoun can be either the subject or the object form, write *S/O*.

EXAMPLE 1. they
         1. *S*

1. him   6. them
2. me   7. you
3. it   8. I
4. we   9. her
5. she   10. us

USAGE

THE SUBJECT FORM

When you use a pronoun as the subject of a sentence or as a predicate nominative after a linking verb, always use the subject form of the pronoun.

17a. Use the subject form for a pronoun that is the subject of a verb.

When a pronoun is used as a subject, it must always be one of these forms: *I, you, he, she, it, we, they.*

EXAMPLES **I** walked to school. [*I* is the subject of the verb *walked.*]

          He and **she** sat in the shade. [*He* and *she* are the subjects of the verb *sat.*]

EXERCISE 2. *Oral Drill.* **Using Pronouns as Subjects.** Read each sentence aloud several times. Stress the pronouns in italics.

1. *She* and Ahmed solve cryptograms.
2. *They* are very hard puzzles to solve.
3. Dad and *I* finished a jigsaw puzzle last night.
4. *We* worked for three hours!
5. Finally, *you* and *he* found the missing pieces.

People often misuse pronouns when they speak, especially when the pronoun is part of a compound subject. You have probably heard someone say, "Her and me went to the store." You know that you would not say, "Her went to the store" and "Me went to the store." You would say, "She went to the store" and "I went to the store." So, of course, you would say, "She and I went to the store." The easiest way to test if a pronoun is used correctly in a compound subject is to try each subject alone with the verb.

INCORRECT   You and him always win. [*You always win* is correct because *you* is the subject form. On the other hand, *him always wins* is incorrect.]

CORRECT   **You** and **he** always win. [Both pronouns are in the subject form.]

Remember to try each subject alone with the verb when you use a personal pronoun as part of a compound subject.

Sometimes a pronoun is followed by a noun—*we boys, us boys.* You can test for the correct pronoun by dropping the noun and trying the pronoun alone with the verb.

EXAMPLE   (We, Us) boys swam in the lake.
We swam in the lake. [not *Us swam in the lake.*]
We boys swam in the lake.

EXERCISE 3. Identifying the Correct Forms of Pronouns.
Number your paper 1–10. In the following sentences, choose the correct pronoun of the two in parentheses.

EXAMPLE   1. Brad and (me, I) wrote a skit based on the myth about Pygmalion.
     1. *I*

1. (Him, He) and I thought the myth was funny.

2. (We, Us) boys asked Angela to play a part in the skit.
3. Neither (she, her) nor Doreen wanted to play a statue that came to life.
4. Finally Brad and (me, I) convinced Doreen that it would be a funny version of the myth.
5. (Him, He) and I flipped a coin to see who would play the part of Pygmalion.
6. The next day (we, us) three were ready to perform.
7. Doreen and (me, I) giggled when Brad pretended to make the beautiful statue.
8. In the skit, when Pygmalion returned from the festival of Venus, (him, he) and the statue were supposed to hug.
9. Instead of hugging, (they, them) laughed so hard they could not say the lines correctly.
10. (Us, We) actors finally took a bow, and the class applauded.

17b. Use the subject form for a pronoun that is a predicate nominative.

A predicate nominative follows a linking verb. It explains or identifies the subject of the sentence. When a predicate nominative in a sentence is a pronoun, be careful to use the subject form of that pronoun: *I, he, she, we, they.*

EXAMPLES   The next singer is **she.**
The first speakers might be **he** and **I.**
On the team, the fastest runners are **we** three boys.

> ☞ NOTE   This rule is often ignored in the common statement *It is me* or *It's me.* Although *me* is the object form, it is considered acceptable as a predicate nominative in this particular usage. *It is her, him, us, them* are usually acceptable in spoken English, but not in writing. In doing the following exercises, use the correct pronoun forms of written English.

USAGE

EXERCISE 4. Writing Sentences with Pronouns Used as Predicate Nominatives. Complete the following sentences by adding pronouns as predicate nominatives. Write the whole sentence on your paper. Use a variety of pronouns, but do not use *you* or *it*. After your sentences have been corrected, read them aloud several times.

1. The person in the gorilla suit must be —— .
2. The next contestants will be —— and —— .
3. The winners should have been —— .
4. Can that singer be —— ?
5. It was —— sitting in the back row.

EXERCISE 5. Identifying Pronouns Used as Predicate Nominatives. Number your paper 1–10. Choose the correct pronoun in parentheses for each sentence.

1. Was that (he, him) at the door?
2. The winners are you and (me, I).
3. Mr. O'Connor said that the next ones are (them, they).
4. Could it have been (we, us)?
5. Every year the speaker has been (her, she).
6. That was Carl and (they, them) in the swimming pool.
7. The football fans in the family are Dad and (she, her).
8. Last on the program will be (us, we).
9. It might have been (he, him).
10. It was (he, him).

REVIEW EXERCISE A. Identifying the Correct Use of Pronouns. Number your paper 1–10. Write the correct pronoun or pronouns in parentheses after the corresponding number.

EXAMPLE   1. (Them, They) and (me, I) stood in line.
        1. *They, I*

1. Last night, Jennifer and (I, me) went to the library.
2. Mr. Kowalski and (he, him) were the judges.
3. Were (him, he) and (she, her) in the horse costume?

USAGE

4. That was (they, them) on television.
5. The candidates for club secretary were Aretha and (I, me).
6. At the party, were (she, her) and (they, them) singing songs?
7. This year (we, us) students can try out for the band.
8. Could the last runners be (they, them)?
9. It was not (we, us) players who started the argument.
10. It might have been (I, me) near the drinking fountain.

THE OBJECT FORM

When you use a pronoun as the object of a verb or as the object of a preposition, always use the object form of the pronoun.

17c. Use the object form for a pronoun that is the direct object of a verb.

A pronoun that is used as a direct object must always be one of these forms: *me, you, him, her, it, us, them.*

EXAMPLES   The teacher thanked **me** for the apple. [*Teacher* is the subject of the verb *thanked.* The teacher thanked *whom*? The direct object is *me.*]

The answer surprised **us**. [*Answer* is the subject of the verb *surprised.* The answer surprised *whom*? The direct object is *us.*]

Fred saw **them** and **me** last night.

When the direct object is compound, try each pronoun alone after the verb. "Fred saw they" and "Fred saw I" are not correct. The pronouns *they* and *I* are the subject forms. You would use the object forms *them* and *me* because these forms are used for the direct objects. The correct sentence is "Fred saw them and me last night."

The same rule applies to a pronoun followed by a noun. Try the sentence without the noun to see if the pronoun is in the correct form.

USAGE

EXAMPLE   Ms. Stone helped (we, us) students. [*Ms. Stone helped we* is not correct. The object form of the pronoun is *us. Ms. Stone helped us* is correct.]

Ms. Stone helped **us** students.

EXERCISE 6. *Oral Drill.* Using Pronouns as Direct Objects.
Read each sentence aloud, stressing the words in italics.

1. Kathy found *them* and *me* by the fountain.
2. Mr. Winters took *us* three to the Special Olympics.
3. Ten days ago, they beat *her* and *him* at croquet.
4. Tyrone frightened *us* with his rubber spider.
5. Ellis invited Luis, Jiro, and *me* to his party.

EXERCISE 7. Identifying Pronouns Used as Direct Objects.
Number your paper 1–10. Choose the correct pronoun of the two in each of the parentheses and write it after the number.

1. Ms. Jewel, our kindergarten teacher, recognized (we, us) girls at the shopping mall.
2. The spectators watched (we, us) and (they, them).
3. The shoes don't fit either (her, she) or (I, me).
4. Sean called Marco and (he, him) on the telephone.
5. Somebody asked (we, us) girls for the time.
6. The neighbors hired Tia and (us, we) to rake their yard.
7. The puppy followed Louis and (he, him) all the way home.
8. A magician visited (us, we) members of the Abracadabra Club.
9. Odessa thanked (her, she) and (me, I) for helping.
10. The usher showed Greg and (them, they) to their seats.

17d. Use the object form for a pronoun that is the indirect object of a verb.

The indirect object tells *to whom* or *for whom* something is done. Pronouns used as indirect objects must always be one of these forms: *me, you, him, her, it, us, them.*

EXAMPLES   Scott handed **me** a note. [*Scott* handed what? *Note* is the direct object. To whom? The indirect object is the pronoun *me*.]

Coley baked **them** some muffins. [*Coley* baked what? *Muffins* is the direct object. For whom? The indirect object is the pronoun *them*.]

Eliza sent **her** and **me** some oranges from Florida.

EXERCISE 8. *Oral Drill.* Using Pronouns as Indirect Objects.
Read each of the following sentences aloud. Stress the words in italics. They are pronouns used as indirect objects.

1. Mr. Krebs showed Bill and *them* the rock collection.
2. Paco told *me* the answer.
3. Ms. Edwards gave *us* students a surprise test.
4. We bought Mother and *him* an anniversary present.
5. The artists drew *us* and *them* some pictures.

EXERCISE 9. Identifying the Correct Forms of Pronouns Used as Indirect Objects.
Number your paper 1–10. Write the correct pronoun or pronouns after each number.

1. The store clerk gave (they, them) a discount.
2. We sewed (he, him) and (she, her) matching book bags.
3. Would someone please hand (me, I) a towel?
4. Those green apples gave Earl and (he, him) stomachaches.
5. The nice waiter brought (us, we) some ice water.
6. Why don't you sing (she, her) a lullaby?
7. Have they made (we, us) the costumes for the play?
8. An usher handed (me, I) a program of the recital.
9. The volunteers showed (we, us) and (they, them) a movie.
10. Please send (her, she) and (I, me) your new address.

REVIEW EXERCISE B. Revising Incorrect Pronoun Forms in Sentences.
Number your paper 1–20. In most of the following sentences, at least one pronoun has been used incorrectly. Write

USAGE

the correct pronoun after the proper number. If all of the pronouns in a sentence are correct, write *C*.

EXAMPLE 1. Ms. Fisher took we five to the museum.
          1. *us*

1. At the museum of natural history, Luisa and me wanted to see the Hopi Indian exhibit. **2.** The museum guide showed she and I the displays of pottery and baskets. **3.** She and I were very interested in the kachina dolls. **4.** After half an hour, Ms. Fisher found we two. **5.** Then Luisa, I, and her joined the rest of the group. **6.** A guide had been giving Ms. Fisher and them information about the Masai tribe in Africa. **7.** Them and us decided to see the ancient Egyptian exhibit next. **8.** A group of little children passed Ms. Fisher and we on the stairway, going to the exhibit.

9. It was them who reached the exhibit first. **10.** Jeff, the jokester, said that they wanted to find their "mummies." **11.** Ms. Fisher and us laughed at the terrible pun. **12.** She gave him and I a pat on the back. **13.** We asked her not to encourage him. **14.** The museum guide called the little children and we to the back of the room. **15.** There, he showed us and they a model of a pyramid. **16.** Then Ms. Fisher and him talked about how the Egyptians prepared mummies. **17.** It could have been her who talked about King Tutankhamen. **18.** As the groups were leaving, the guide gave the children and we some booklets about the ancient Egyptians. **19.** The ones he handed Luisa and I were about building the pyramids. **20.** All of the exhibits were interesting, but we visitors liked the mummies best.

17e. Use the object form for a pronoun that is the object of a preposition.

Prepositions show a relationship between words in a sentence. A prepositional phrase begins with a preposition and ends with an object. Use the object form for a pronoun that is the object of a preposition. Remember: the object forms are *me, you, him, her, it, us,* and *them.*

EXAMPLES   above **me**   beside **us**   to **her**
            for **him**   toward **you**   with **them**

When a preposition is followed by two or more pronouns, use the object form for each one. Try each pronoun alone with the preposition to be sure that you have used the correct form.

EXAMPLES   The puppy walked behind Tom and **me**. [*Tom* and *me* are the objects of the preposition *behind.*]

            Carrie divided the chores between **them** and **us**. [*Them* and *us* are the objects of the preposition *between.*]

EXERCISE 10. *Oral Drill.* **Using Pronouns as Objects of Prepositions.**   Read each of the following sentences, stressing the words in italics.

1. The lemonade stand was run *by* Chuck and *me.*
2. The younger children rode *in front of us* girls.
3. Just *between you* and *me,* that game wasn't much fun.
4. Everyone has gone *except* the Taylors and *them.*
5. Give the message *to him* or *her.*

EXERCISE 11. **Identifying the Correct Forms of Pronouns Used as Objects of Prepositions.**   Number your paper 1–10. Choose the correct pronoun of the two in parentheses and write it after the corresponding number.

1. Gene and Betty played against Mervin and (I, me).
2. If you have a complaint, tell it to Mr. Ramis or (she, her).
3. Peggy sent homemade cards to you and (them, they).
4. There is a bee flying around (he, him) and you.
5. I wanted to sit with Martha or (her, she) at the game.
6. The teacher divided the projects among (us, we) students.
7. This secret is strictly between you and (me, I).
8. The ball dropped in front of (we, us) players.
9. At first the principal was angry, but then she winked at (he, him) and (I, me).
10. One of the clowns threw confetti at us and (they, them).

USAGE

WRITING APPLICATION:
Using Correct Pronoun Forms
to Make Your Writing Clear

When you go to a party or a special event, you want to look your best. When you write a story or a report, you want your writing to be its best. Always take some time to read your sentences carefully. Using the correct pronoun forms shows your readers that you care about your work. It also shows that you want them to understand clearly what you are trying to say.

Writing Assignment

Write about a project you have done or have planned with other people. Your project might have been planning a surprise party, working on a report for school, running a lemonade stand, and so on. Describe what each person's task was and how you worked together as a group. Avoid repeating the names of people and tasks by using pronouns. Proofread your paper carefully for correct pronoun forms.

REVIEW EXERCISE C. Revising Incorrect Pronoun Forms in Sentences. Number your paper 1–20. If a pronoun is used incorrectly, write the correct pronoun after the corresponding number. If a sentence is correct, write *C*.

1. Lucy told Karen and I that space creatures had landed in a large spaceship.
2. She was certain it was them at the park.
3. Fortunately, they didn't see her.
4. Us girls laughed at the ridiculous story.
5. Lucy looked at we two with tears in her eyes.
6. So Karen and I agreed to go to the park to look around.
7. Lucy walked between Karen and me, showing the way.
8. In the dark, she and us hid behind some tall bushes.
9. Suddenly a strong wind almost blew we three down.

10. A green light shined on Karen and I, and a red one shined on Lucy.
11. Could it really be them?
12. One of the creatures spoke to us girls.
13. Very slowly, Karen, Lucy, and me stepped out from behind the bushes.
14. "You almost scared me and they silly!" shouted a male creature, pointing at the others.
15. Neither Karen nor her could speak, and I could make only a squeaking noise.
16. Then the man explained to we three girls that a movie company was filming in the park.
17. They and we could have been in an accident.
18. The fireworks hidden in the bushes might have hurt one of we girls.
19. Lucy told the director and he about being afraid of the space creatures in the park.
20. If you ever see the movie, the short purple creatures under the spaceship are us three girls.

USAGE

CHAPTER 17 REVIEW: POSTTEST

Revising Incorrect Pronoun Forms in Sentences. Number your paper 1–20. If a sentence is correct, write *C* after the number. If a pronoun is used incorrectly, write the correct form of the pronoun after the number.

EXAMPLE 1. The instructor complimented you and they on knowing the rules of safety.
　　　　　　1. *them*

1. The members of our bicycle club are Everett, Coral, Jackie, and me.
2. Us four call our club the Ramblers, named after a bicycle that was popular in the early 1900's.
3. Mrs. Wheeler gave her old three-speed bike to we four.

4. Everett and her taught Jackie how to ride it and shift gears.
5. Our cousins gave Coral and I two old ten-speed bikes.
6. Each of we Ramblers practices riding after school.
7. Sometimes we Ramblers ride with the members of the Derailers, a racing club.
8. On Saturday mornings, we and them meet at the school.
9. It was them who told us about the bike trail along the river.
10. Everett warned we three to be careful, because sometimes the Derailers are reckless.
11. He saw other riders and they at an intersection.
12. A car almost ran over two of them!
13. So when the Ramblers ride with the Derailers, it is us who obey all the safety rules.
14. Everett, Coral, Jackie, and I have entered a contest.
15. Other clubs and us are competing for a tandem bike.
16. Officials show we contestants a special safety course.
17. One by one, us riders go through the course.
18. Of all of we contestants, the most careless are the members of the Derailers.
19. Jackie and me are nervous as the judges make their decision.
20. Finally, the judges announce that the winners of the safety contest are us Ramblers.

CHAPTER 18

Using Modifiers Correctly

COMPARISON OF ADJECTIVES AND ADVERBS

You use modifiers to describe or explain the meaning of another word. An adjective modifier makes clear the meaning of a noun or a pronoun. An adverb modifier makes clear the meaning of a verb, an adjective, or another adverb. You can also use modifiers to show a comparison. "This wrestler is *strong*. That one is *stronger*. That large wrestler over there is the *strongest*." This chapter will help you to use modifiers correctly and effectively in your writing.

DIAGNOSTIC TEST

A. Identifying the Correct Forms of Modifiers. Number your paper 1–10. Choose the correct form of the modifier from the two in parentheses, and write it after the proper number.

EXAMPLE   1. We felt (sleepy, sleepily) after lunch.
        1. *sleepy*

1. Ice water tastes (good, well) on a hot day.
2. The wind howled (fierce, fiercely) last night.

3. Which one is (taller, tallest), Mark or Jim?
4. The canned goods make my backpack the (heavier, heaviest) of all the backpacks.
5. Sergio always plays (good, well) during an important game.
6. The basset hound is the (most sad-, saddest-) looking dog on the block.
7. They could see the eclipse (more clear, more clearly) than we could.
8. Which of the two coats will be (warmer, warmest)?
9. Of all the days in the week, Friday goes by (more slowly, most slowly).
10. Ernest didn't feel (good, well) about losing the game.
11. This is the (darker, darkest) of the three copies.
12. The (shorter, shortest) twin is the captain of the squad.
13. Mr. Smith advised me to be (more attentive, most attentive) than I had been in yesterday's rehearsal.
14. Joni's way of solving the math puzzle was (easier, more easier) than Phillip's.
15. Some people think that the flight of *Voyager* is the (most amazing, amazingest) of all the space flights.

B. Correcting Double Negatives.   Number your paper 16–20. Most of the following sentences contain an error in the use of negative words. If the sentence is incorrect, write it correctly after the proper number. If the sentence is correct, write *C*.

EXAMPLE   1. Mr. Knapp did not give us no homework.
          1. *Mr. Knapp did not give us any homework.*
                or
       Mr. Knapp gave us no homework.

16. No one of us knows nothing about Halley's Comet.
17. Willie has hardly said a single word all night.
18. Kristin hasn't never gone to the zoo.
19. We could not see no stars through our binoculars.
20. Whenever I want fruit, there is never none in the house.

COMPARISON OF ADJECTIVES AND ADVERBS

If you were telling a friend about three exercises that you had to complete in a fitness test in your gym class, you might say something like this: "The first exercise was *easy,* the second was even *easier,* and to my surprise, the third one was the *easiest* of all."

In describing the test exercises, you used different forms of the adjective *easy.* Each form expressed a slightly different meaning. The differences expressed by the different forms of adjectives and adverbs are called *comparisons.*

18a. The three degrees of comparison of modifiers are the *positive,* the *comparative,* and the *superlative.*

(1) The positive degree is used when only one thing is being described.

EXAMPLES   The announcer talks **fast.**
             This box is **heavy.**
             Western movies are **exciting.**
             I ran **quickly** to the door.

(2) The comparative degree is used when two things are being compared.

EXAMPLES   This announcer talks **faster.**
             The shopping basket is **heavier.**
             Spy movies are **more exciting** than westerns.
             He runs **more quickly** than I.

(3) The superlative degree is used when three or more things are being compared.

EXAMPLES   This announcer talks **fastest.**
             The brown carton is the **heaviest** of the three.
             Adventure movies are the **most exciting** of all.
             Chen runs **most quickly** of us six.

USAGE

Regular Comparison

There are two regular ways of forming the comparative and superlative degrees. One way is to add *-er* to the word for the comparative degree and *-est* for the superlative. Sometimes the ending of the word is changed before the *-er* or *-est* is added.

POSITIVE	COMPARATIVE	SUPERLATIVE
dark	dark**er**	dark**est**
sad	sadd**er**	sadd**est**
fancy	fanci**er**	fanci**est**
lonely	loneli**er**	loneli**est**

The other regular way is to use the word *more* for the comparative degree and the word *most* for the superlative.

POSITIVE	COMPARATIVE	SUPERLATIVE
difficult	**more** difficult	**most** difficult
cheerful	**more** cheerful	**most** cheerful
carefully	**more** carefully	**most** carefully
slowly	**more** slowly	**most** slowly

Do not be surprised if you find the rules for forming the comparative and superlative degrees a little confusing. Whenever you are not sure about which form to use, look up the word in a dictionary.

EXERCISE 1. Writing Comparative and Superlative Forms.
Number your paper 1–10. Write the comparative and superlative forms for each of the following modifiers. You may use a dictionary.

EXAMPLE   1. calm
          1. *calmer, calmest*

1. nervous
2. great
3. hot
4. funny
5. noisy
6. easily
7. poor
8. young
9. swiftly
10. intelligent

USAGE

EXERCISE 2. Using the Comparative and Superlative Forms Correctly in Sentences. Number your paper 1–10. After each number, write the form of the word in italics that will correctly fill the blank. You may use a dictionary.

EXAMPLE 1. *long* This has been the —— day of my life!
1. *longest*

1. *deep*   The ditch on the left is —— than the one on the right.
2. *cute*   The black puppy was the —— of the litter.
3. *lively*   You look —— than she does.
4. *carefully* After finding a jacket with a hole in the pocket, we examined the next one —— .
5. *wisely*   Of the five people on the panel, the judge answered the questions —— .
6. *close*   The bee is —— to you than to me.
7. *fast*   José has the —— bicycle of all the racers.
8. *frequently* It rains —— in March than in May.
9. *smart*   He must be the —— person alive.
10. *difficult* The test was —— than I expected.

USAGE

Irregular Comparison

Some adjectives and adverbs do not form the comparative and superlative degrees by adding *-er* and *-est* or by using *more* and *most*. These modifiers are compared *irregularly*. Study the following comparisons:

POSITIVE	COMPARATIVE	SUPERLATIVE
good	better	best
well	better	best
bad	worse	worst
many	more	most
much	more	most

Remember that you do not add anything to make irregular comparisons. For example, *worse,* all by itself, is the comparative form of *bad.* You do not say *worser* or *more worse.*

EXERCISE 3. Using the Irregular Comparative and Superlative Forms Correctly in Sentences. Number your paper 1–10. For each blank, write the correct form of the modifier given at the beginning of the sentence.

1. *bad*   Of all the excuses, this one is the ——— .
2. *much*   It certainly seems that we have ——— homework this year than last year.
3. *well*   Shawn feels ——— today than he did last night.
4. *good*   This melon has a ——— flavor than that one.
5. *bad*   Our team played the ——— game in history.
6. *bad*   This casserole tastes ——— on the second day.
7. *many*   Doreen has caught the ——— colds this winter of anyone in school.
8. *well*   The soloist plays the ——— of all the musicians in the orchestra.
9. *good*   Not one essay was ——— than another.
10. *much*   Of the five groups in the class, ours did the ——— work on the project.

18b. The modifiers *good* and *well* have different uses.

You use the modifiers *good* and *well* every day. It is important to learn all of the forms of these words and to use them correctly.

(1) Use *good* and its comparative and superlative forms to modify nouns or pronouns.

EXAMPLES   The farmers had a **good** crop this year. [The adjective *good* modifies the noun *crop*.]

The book was **better** than the movie. [The adjective *better* modifies the noun *book*.]

She is the **best** in school. [The adjective *best* modifies the pronoun *she*.]

(2) Use *well* and its comparative and superlative forms to modify verbs.

EXAMPLES   The day started **well**. [The adverb *well* modifies the verb *started*.]

The basketball team played **better** in the second half of the game. [The adverb *better* modifies the verb *played*.]

Carl ran **best** in the third race. [The adverb *best* modifies the verb *ran*.]

Exception: Well can also mean "in good health." When it has this meaning, it acts as an adjective.

EXAMPLE   Sherry is **well** today. [Here, *well* means "in good health" and modifies the noun *Sherry*.]

EXERCISE 4. Writing Sentences with the Correct Forms of *Good* and *Well*.

Write ten sentences using each of the following words at least once:

ADJECTIVE	good	better	best
ADVERB	well	better	best
ADJECTIVE	well	better	best

18c. **Use an adjective, not an adverb, after linking verbs.**

Linking verbs are often followed by predicate adjectives. These adjectives describe, or modify, the subject. Remember that linking verbs include forms of the verb *be* and verbs such as *feel, seem, appear, taste.*

EXAMPLES   The game **is new**. [The adjective *new* follows the linking verb *is*. It modifies the noun *game*.]

The fresh corn **tasted delicious**. [*Delicious* is a predicate adjective that modifies the noun *corn*.]

Some verbs, such as *look,* can be linking verbs or action verbs. *Look* as an action verb does not mean the same as *look* as a linking verb. As a linking verb it means something like *seem* or *appear* and is followed by a predicate adjective. As an action verb, *look* is followed by an adverb.

USAGE

EXAMPLES   The students **look restless.** [Here, *look* is a linking verb. It is followed by the predicate adjective *restless,* which modifies *students.* It means something close to "The students *seem* restless."]

The students **looked restlessly** at the clock. [Here, *looked* is an action verb. The adverb *restlessly* modifies *looked.* If you substitute *seemed* for *looked,* the sentence no longer makes sense.]

EXERCISE 5. Writing the Correct Modifiers After Linking Verbs and Action Verbs.   Number your paper 1–10. For each sentence, write the correct modifier of the two in parentheses.

1. The band seemed (nervous, nervously) before the show.
2. After taking the test, Ezra felt (calm, calmly).
3. We (eager, eagerly) tasted the potato pancakes.
4. Peg looked at her broken skate (anxious, anxiously).
5. The missing shoe appeared (sudden, suddenly) before me.
6. Sylvia looked (pretty, prettily) in her new outfit.
7. The plums tasted (sour, sourly).
8. Mr. Duncan was looking (close, closely) at the painting in the museum exhibit.
9. Erica was (happy, happily) to help us.
10. One by one, they felt the contents of the mystery bag (cautious, cautiously).

18d. Avoid double comparisons.

A double comparison is one that has an *-er* or *-est* form of a modifier and the word *more* or *most.* It can also be an irregular comparison with the word *more* or *most.* When you write or speak, you should always use a single form of comparison.

INCORRECT   I feel more better today.
  CORRECT   I feel **better** today.

INCORRECT   That was the most funniest joke we ever heard.
  CORRECT   That was the **funniest** joke we ever heard.

WRITING APPLICATION A:
Using Modifiers Correctly in Your Writing

It is important that you help your readers understand what your sentences mean. You can make your meaning clear by using modifiers correctly. If you compare two things, you should use the comparative form. If you compare more than two things, you should use the superlative form.

The gray cat has **softer** fur than the white cat.

This sentence shows an important difference between the two cats. It is easy to understand the meaning.

Writing Assignment

Write a comparison of at least two different things. For example, you might compare two or more sports teams, two or more animals, or two or more games. Read your writing to make sure that you have used the correct forms of the modifiers in your comparisons. Be sure to avoid double comparisons.

USAGE

REVIEW EXERCISE A. Writing Comparative and Superlative Forms in Sentences. Number your paper 1–10. For each blank, write the correct form of comparison for the word in italics.

EXAMPLE   1. *noisy*   This is the —— class in school.
         1. *noisiest*

1. *bad*   Yesterday was the —— day of my entire life.
2. *good*   Tomorrow should be —— than today was.
3. *old*   The —— Plains Indian tepee in the world is in the Smithsonian Institution.
4. *soon*   Your party ended —— than I would have liked.
5. *funny*   Of all the birds, the goony bird is the —— .
6. *rapidly*   Which can run —— , the cheetah or the lion?

7. *important*   Studying is —— than watching television.
8. *well*   The test had three sections, and I did —— on the essay questions.
9. *loudly*   Among the choir members, she sings the —— .
10. *strange*   This is the —— book I have ever read!

REVIEW EXERCISE B. Writing the Correct Modifiers After Linking Verbs and Action Verbs.   Number your paper 1–10. After the corresponding number, write the correct modifier of the two in parentheses.

EXAMPLE   1. Dinner tasted (good, well).
    1. *good*

1. I was feeling (happy, happily) until I lost my watch.
2. The family had been (safe, safely) in the storm shelter.
3. The motorist looked (angry, angrily) at the careless pedestrian.
4. The guests tasted all of the spicy dishes (glad, gladly).
5. The empty house looks (strange, strangely).
6. The flashlight works (good, well) with the new batteries.
7. We always feel (good, well) about helping other people.
8. Julius won the race (easy, easily).
9. Ernie looked (sleepy, sleepily) at the alarm clock.
10. Arlene finally feels (good, well) enough to come to school.

DOUBLE NEGATIVES

If you understand how negative words are used, you can avoid the mistake of using double negatives. Using double negatives means using two negative words instead of one. Negatives are words such as *no, not, none, never, no one, nothing,* and *hardly.*

EXAMPLES   We can count in Spanish.
    We can**not** count in Spanish.

    They ride their bikes on the highway.
    They **never** ride their bikes on the highway.

In the examples, the first sentence is positive. The second sentence contains a negative word. Notice how the negative word makes an important change in the meaning.

18e. Avoid the use of double negatives.

The use of two negative words when only one is needed to make the meaning clear is called a *double negative*. Use only one negative word in a sentence to express a negative meaning. Notice that the contraction *n't,* which stands for *not,* counts as a negative word.

DOUBLE NEGATIVE   Sheila didn't tell no one about her grade. [The two negative words are *n't* and *no.*]

CORRECT   Sheila did**n't** tell anyone about her grade.

CORRECT   Sheila told **no one** about her grade.

DOUBLE NEGATIVE   Rodney hardly said nothing. [The two negative words are *hardly* and *nothing.*]

CORRECT   Rodney **hardly** said anything.

CORRECT   Rodney said almost **nothing.**

EXERCISE 6. Revising Incorrect Use of Negative Words in Sentences. Each of the following sentences contains a double negative. Write each sentence, using only one negative word to make the meaning clear.

EXAMPLE   1. Those books don't have no pictures.
        1. *Those books don't have any pictures.*
                 or
        Those books have no pictures.

1. Harold was not allowed to go to no one's house.
2. Ms. Wooster never tries nothing new to eat.
3. No movie stars from Hollywood never visit our town.
4. We do not have nothing left over.
5. Ian used to have six mice, but now he doesn't have none.
6. I'm so excited I can't hardly sit still.
7. No one brought nothing to eat on the hike.

USAGE

8. Ronnie hasn't never won a race.
9. There isn't no more pudding in the bowl.
10. The music was so loud that we weren't hardly able to hear ourselves think.

WRITING APPLICATION B:
Using Words Correctly to Make Your Meaning Clear

If you are writing a sentence with a negative meaning, you need to use only one negative word. A double negative will make your reader wonder what you really mean.

I don't have none left.

This sentence actually says that you have some left.

I have none left. *or* I don't have any left.

Using one negative word makes your sentence accurate.

Writing Assignment

Everyone has a bad day now and then. Write about a day in which everything goes wrong. You can write about a real or an imaginary day. Use your imagination to describe the events of this day. Proofread your writing carefully to make sure that there are no double negatives.

REVIEW EXERCISE C. Revising Sentences by Correcting Modifiers and Double Negatives. Some of the following sentences are correct. Others contain double negatives or errors in the use of adjectives or adverbs. If a sentence is correct, write C after its number on your paper. If a sentence contains an error, rewrite it correctly.

EXAMPLE 1. Is hockey more popular than soccer?
1. C

1. Mark Twain's book *Life on the Mississippi* is the interestingest book I have ever read.

2. Mark Twain probably wouldn't care nothing about riding in cars and buses.
3. No one works as a steamboat pilot no more.
4. That pilot's hat looks nicely on you.
5. Our ideas change quick about what we want to be when we grow up.
6. Holly, the most smartest girl in our class, wants to become a scientist.
7. Being President could hardly be an easy job.
8. A person would have to be very brave and smart to do the job good.
9. I feel gladly that I don't have to decide right now.
10. Maybe in five years I will have a more better idea of what I want to become.

CHAPTER 18 REVIEW: POSTTEST

Revising Incorrect Use of Modifiers and Negative Words in Sentences. Most of these sentences contain an error in the use of a modifier or a negative word. Find the error and rewrite the sentence correctly. If a sentence is correct, write *C*.

EXAMPLE   1. Your bruise looks more worse today.
　　　　　　 1. *Your bruise looks worse today.*

1. Of all the students in class, Odelle writes better.
2. She thinks writing is the most enjoyable pastime of all.
3. Odelle writes more oftener in her diary than I do.
4. She hasn't never let a day go by without writing something.
5. Throughout history, many people have written regular in their diaries.
6. One of the famousest is the Englishman Samuel Pepys.
7. He recorded the most important events of the 1600's and the most small events of his daily life.
8. In the United States, Henry David Thoreau looked close at the world around him.

9. He wrote frequent about nature in his diaries.
10. Odelle is one of the most persistent people I know.
11. She writes even when she feels sadly.
12. When I don't feel good, I usually skip writing in my diary.
13. Of course, diaries are good practice for learning how to write well.
14. I'm not sure which I like best, writing in a diary or writing stories.
15. I let Odelle look at some of my bestest stories.
16. However, she hasn't let me read none of her diaries.
17. She says she doesn't never show her diary to anyone.
18. A nice thing about a diary is that you don't have to write nothing special.
19. You can skip a day occasionally.
20. To Odelle, skipping a day seems worser than having the measles.

CHAPTER 19

Capital Letters

RULES FOR CAPITALIZATION

You already know many of the rules for the use of capital letters. For example, you know that you always begin each sentence with a capital letter. You know that you should capitalize proper nouns and proper adjectives. In this chapter, you will review those rules and learn other rules for using capitals.

DIAGNOSTIC TEST

Recognizing the Correct Use of Capital Letters. Number your paper 1–20. One sentence in each of the following pairs of sentences uses capital letters correctly. After the proper number on your paper, write the letter of the correct sentence (*a* or *b*).

EXAMPLE   1. a. The Gettysburg Address was delivered by President Lincoln.
　　　　 b. The Gettysburg Address was delivered by president Lincoln.

　　　1. *a*

1. a. Peter's dog Buddy is a german shepherd.
　 b. Peter's dog Buddy is a German shepherd.

MECHANICS

2. a. Our Spring break begins on March 26.

   b. Our spring break begins on March 26.

3. a. Write to me at 439 Walnut Street.

   b. Write to me at 439 Walnut street.

4. a. Have you heard the story of the sinking of the *titanic*?

   b. Have you heard the story of the sinking of the *Titanic*?

5. a. In 1979 the Nobel Prize for Peace was given to Mother Teresa.

   b. In 1979 the Nobel prize for Peace was given to Mother Teresa.

6. a. As soon as I finish my English homework, I can go.

   b. As soon as I finish my english homework, I can go.

7. a. I would like to go to college after I finish high school.

   b. I would like to go to College after I finish high school.

8. a. We watched a scene from *Romeo and Juliet*.

   b. We watched a scene from *Romeo And Juliet*.

9. a. Eric's physical therapist is dr. Chun.

   b. Eric's physical therapist is Dr. Chun.

10. a. On Saturday my dad is taking us to Jones Beach.

   b. On saturday my dad is taking us to Jones Beach.

11. a. Dad used the General Electric waffle iron for making brunch.

   b. Dad used the general Electric waffle iron for making brunch.

12. a. do you like warm applesauce on your waffles?

   b. Do you like warm applesauce on your waffles?

13. a. The Peace Corps volunteers helped build a bridge.

   b. The Peace corps volunteers helped build a bridge.

14. a. The United Nations High Commissioner for Refugees operates camps in Tanzania.

   b. The united Nations High Commissioner for Refugees operates camps in Tanzania.

15. a. The Age of Reason brought many changes to society.

   b. The age of Reason brought many changes to society.

16. a. The *Viking* space probe was sent on a long journey through the universe.
    b. The *viking* space probe was sent on a long journey through the universe.
17. a. The last day of school is June 5.
    b. The last day of school is june 5.
18. a. The storm is coming from the West.
    b. The storm is coming from the west.
19. a. Are you going to sign up for art next session?
    b. Are you going to sign up for Art next session?
20. a. The Gulf of Mexico is usually a calm body of water.
    b. The gulf of Mexico is usually a calm body of water.

19a. Capitalize the first word in every sentence.

INCORRECT   tonight I have science, social studies, and math homework. i also have soccer practice.

CORRECT   Tonight I have science, social studies, and math homework. I also have soccer practice.

The first word of a direct quotation should begin with a capital whether or not it starts the sentence. For more on writing quotations, see Chapter 21.

Usually, the first word of every line of poetry begins with a capital letter.

EXAMPLE   There was an old man from Peru
Who dreamed he was eating his shoe.

Not all poets follow this style. If you are copying a poem, use capital letters exactly as they are used in the poem.

19b. Capitalize the pronoun *I*.

EXAMPLE   When **I** returned home last night, **I** was so tired that **I** went right to bed.

MECHANICS

EXERCISE 1. Proofreading Sentences for Correct Capitalization. Number your paper 1–5. If a sentence is correct, write *C* after the proper number. If it has an error in capitalization, write correctly the word or words that require capitals.

EXAMPLE 1. What time should i call?
           1. *I*

1. The library report is due at the end of the term.
2. My sister memorized the limerick that begins, "a tutor who tooted a flute."
3. Aren't you glad tomorrow is a holiday?
4. We need to buy some more shampoo.
5. My parents let me watch television only if i have finished all my chores.

19c. Capitalize proper nouns and abbreviations.

A proper noun, as you learned on page 209, names a particular person, place, or thing. Such a word is always capitalized. A common noun names a kind or type of person, place, or thing. A common noun is not capitalized unless it begins a sentence or is part of a title.

PROPER NOUNS	COMMON NOUNS	ABBREVIATIONS
November	month	Dr. (Doctor)
Winnie Matthews	woman	Nov. (November)
Red Sox	team	N.Y. (New York)
Kenya	country	S. (South)

(1) Capitalize the names of persons.

EXAMPLES Samuel Jackson, Sherry Evans, Martin Gomez

(2) Capitalize geographical names.

Cities, Towns:	Sarasota, Grand Rapids, Cheyenne
States:	Nevada, Idaho, Maine
Sections of the country:	the South, the Northwest

MECHANICS

Countries:	Denmark, Peru, Greece
Continents:	South America, Europe, Asia
Islands:	Sandwich Islands, Bermuda
Mountains:	Smoky Mountains, Mount Shasta
Bodies of Water:	Lake Erie, the Red Sea
Parks:	Zion National Park, Central Park
Streets, Highways:	Megins Road, Highway 59

☞ **NOTE** The words *north, west, southeast,* etc., are not capitalized when they indicate direction. They are only capitalized when they mean an area of the country.

EXAMPLES   Turn south when you get off the interstate.
I love to travel in the South.

EXERCISE 2. Writing Proper Nouns. Number your paper 1–10. In this exercise you are given a list of ten common nouns. For each common noun, write two proper nouns. You may use a dictionary and an atlas if necessary. Remember to use capitals.

EXAMPLE   1. lake
1. *Lake Louise, Lake George*

1. river	4. park	7. school	9. country
2. street	5. friend	8. store	10. beach
3. artist	6. singer		

EXERCISE 3. Recognizing the Correct Use of Capital Letters. Number your paper 1–10. If a sentence is correct, write *C* after the proper number. If it has an error in capitalization, write correctly the word or words that require capitals.

1. Maria Ayala and eileen Barnes are going to Chicago.
2. Our neighbor Ken Oshige has moved to canada.
3. Midway Island is in the Pacific.
4. We could see mount Hood from the airplane window.
5. It will take years for Africa to recover from the drought.

MECHANICS

6. Our kitchen window faces West.
7. The youth group will go canoeing on blue River.
8. My closest friend just moved to ohio.
9. Volcanoes National park is on the island of Hawaii.
10. The store is located on Maple Street.

(3) Capitalize names of organizations, business firms, institutions, and government bodies.

Organizations:	Boy Scouts, Friends of the Library
Business firms:	Westinghouse, Ralston-Purina
Institutions:	St. Mary's Hospital, Paine College
Government bodies:	Parliament, House of Representatives

> ☞ NOTE Do *not* capitalize words such as *hotel, theater,* or *high school* unless they are part of the name of a particular building or institution.

EXAMPLES	Outrigger Hotel	a hotel on the beach
	Beacham Theater	a theater in town
	Oak Ridge High School	my high school

(4) Capitalize the names of special events, holidays, and other calendar items.

Special events:	Super Bowl, Thanksgiving Parade
Holidays:	Christmas, Passover
Calendar items:	April, Sunday, Father's Day

> ☞ NOTE Do not capitalize the name of a season unless it is part of the name of a special event.

EXAMPLES Fall Festival, Winter Carnival

MECHANICS

(5) Capitalize the names of historical events and periods.

Historical events: **B**oston **T**ea **P**arty, **B**attle of **H**astings
Historical periods: **B**ronze **A**ge, **I**ndustrial **R**evolution

---

WRITING APPLICATION:
Using Capital Letters Correctly
to Make Your Writing Clear

The correct use of capital letters helps your readers understand your meaning. For example, if you write *Boats crowded little Lake Conway* instead of *Boats crowded Little Lake Conway*, readers may not understand that *Little* is part of the lake's name. Instead, they may wonder why all the boats crowded an unusually small lake. Be sure to use capital letters correctly.

Writing Assignment

Write a paragraph about a holiday celebration your family is having. Many friends and relatives will come. Some of them are from cities nearby, but a few will be coming from other states. Tell what the holiday is, whom you are expecting, and where those people live. Give their names and hometowns. Use capitalization where needed.

EXERCISE 4. Recognizing the Correct Use of Capital Letters. Number your paper 1–10. In each sentence below, find the word or words that should be capitalized but are not. After the proper number, write the word or words correctly.

EXAMPLE   1. Hart middle school is having a book fair.
    2. *Middle School*

1. Would you like to go to the theater on friday?
2. The special Olympics will be held in our town this year.
3. What plans have you made for mother's Day?
4. Our baby brother was born at memorial Hospital.

MECHANICS

5. The Rotary club donated equipment for our school's new gymnasium.
6. Do you know anything about the golden Age?
7. I am doing a project on the great leaders of the crusades.
8. My father works at Beattie brothers, incorporated.
9. Congress is composed of the senate and the house of representatives.
10. Will you see any fireworks on the fourth of July?

(6) Capitalize the names of nationalities, tribes, races, and religions.

Nationalities:	**P**uerto **R**ican, **F**rench, **C**hinese
Tribes:	**O**sage, **C**herokee, **I**roquois
Races:	**I**ndian, **C**aucasian, **O**riental
Religions:	**B**uddhist, **P**resbyterian, **M**oslem

(7) Capitalize the brand names of business products.

EXAMPLES **M**ichelin, **W**hirlpool, **F**ord

> ☞ NOTE Do not capitalize the noun that often follows a brand name.

EXAMPLE **W**hirlpool dishwasher

(8) Capitalize the names of ships, aircraft, planets, monuments, awards, and any other particular places, things, or events.

Ships, Trains:	the *Santa Maria,* the *Orient Express*
Aircraft, Spacecraft:	*Concorde, Columbia*
Planets, Stars:	Pluto, Mercury, the North Star
Monuments, Buildings:	Lincoln Memorial, Eiffel Tower
Awards:	Jefferson Award, Purple Heart

MECHANICS

> ☞ NOTE Planets, constellations, asteroids, stars, and groups of stars are capitalized. However, unless they are listed with other heavenly bodies, *sun, moon,* and *earth* are not capitalized.

EXERCISE 5. Recognizing the Correct Use of Capital Letters. Number your paper 1–10. After the proper number, write the letter of the sentence that uses capital letters correctly (*a* or *b*).

1. a. The speaker is methodist.
   b. The speaker is Methodist.
2. a. Bob has a Chevrolet truck.
   b. Bob has a Chevrolet Truck.
3. a. On a clear night, you can see venus.
   b. On a clear night, you can see Venus.
4. a. My parents will take a cruise on the *song of Norway*.
   b. My parents will take a cruise on the *Song of Norway*.
5. a. Meet me in front of the Woolworth Building.
   b. Meet me in front of the Woolworth building.
6. a. Donna received the Junior Achievement award.
   b. Donna received the Junior Achievement Award.
7. a. Keith made a model of *Gemini* for his science project.
   b. Keith made a model of *gemini* for his science project.
8. a. Helga Zimmerman is german.
   b. Helga Zimmerman is German.
9. a. Some Arapaho Indians lived near the Platte River.
   b. Some arapaho Indians lived near the Platte River.
10. a. Who were the first Europeans to settle in Mexico?
    b. Who were the first europeans to settle in Mexico?

EXERCISE 6. Writing Sentences Using Capital Letters Correctly. Write ten sentences of your own using each of the following words correctly, once as a common noun and once as part of a proper noun.

MECHANICS

1. ocean
2. day
3. east
4. war
5. club

19d. Capitalize proper adjectives.

PROPER NOUNS	PROPER ADJECTIVES
Mexico	Mexican border
Scandinavia	Scandinavian customs

19e. Do not capitalize names of school subjects, except for languages and for course names followed by numbers.

EXAMPLES   social studies, science, Spanish, English, art, Woodworking II, Family Life I, algebra, health

19f. Capitalize titles.

(1) Capitalize the title of a person when it comes before a name.

EXAMPLES   Judge O'Connor   Principal Walsh
Mayor Santos   Mrs. Marilyn Nakamura
Dr. Topping   Professor Vickers

(2) Capitalize a title used alone or following a person's name if it refers to a high official.

EXAMPLES   The President did not comment on the report.
Judy Taylor, president of the Art Club, asked for help with the mural.
Several of those senators will be retiring.
The Princess of Wales christened the ship.

☞ NOTE   When a title is used alone in direct address, it is usually capitalized.

EXAMPLES   What are his chances of recovery, **D**octor?

Your vote for this bill will be appreciated, **S**enator.

(3) Capitalize words showing family relationship when used with a person's name.

EXAMPLES   **U**ncle George, **A**unt Mary, **G**randpa Wilson

(4) Capitalize words referring to the Deity.

EXAMPLES   **G**od, **H**is blessing, **L**ord

☞ **NOTE**   The word *god* is not capitalized when it refers to the gods of ancient mythology.

EXAMPLE   Ra was the Egyptian god of the sun.

EXERCISE 7. **Correcting Words by Capitalizing Them.**
Number your paper 1–10. For each of the following sentences, find the one word that should be capitalized but isn't, and write it correctly on your paper.

EXAMPLE   1. I love french bread with onion soup.

       1. *I love French bread with onion soup.*

1. Valerie is taking biology 100.
2. Have you been to the new swiss restaurant?
3. The vikings had many different gods.
4. I asked doctor Rodriguez to renew the prescription for my allergy medication.
5. This hymn compares god to a strong fortress.
6. The recipe calls for a few slices of canadian bacon.
7. Danish, Yiddish, Icelandic, and Flemish are all germanic languages.
8. On Saturday, aunt Lisa will arrive from Savannah.
9. Was professor Jones your American history professor?
10. I learned to water-ski on grandpa Brown's lake.

MECHANICS

REVIEW EXERCISE A. Recognizing the Correct Use of Capital Letters. Number your paper 1–10. In each of the following sentences, find the word or words that should be capitalized but are not. After the proper number, write the word or words correctly.

1. There is a fountain in the middle of lake Eola in the heart of the city.
2. Denise attends York high school.
3. Some of these folk songs are hispanic.
4. During the class trip, I walked all the way up the Washington monument.
5. Someday I would like to ride my bicycle through europe with some of my friends.
6. all of our clothes and our travel gear would have to fit on the bicycles.
7. Eventually, i would like to bicycle along the coast from Maine to Florida.
8. The class wrote letters to nancy reagan and received a reply within a month.
9. There is a detour on highway 50.
10. Our first camping trip is planned for october, when the weather is brisk.

(5) Capitalize the first and last words and all important words in titles of books, periodicals, poems, stories, movies, television programs, paintings, and other works of art.

Unimportant words in a title are *a, an, the,* short prepositions (fewer than five letters), and coordinating conjunctions. If the last word in the title is a short preposition, however, it is capitalized. The words *a, an,* and *the* written before a title are capitalized only when they are part of the title.

Book:	*Tom Sawyer*
Periodical:	*National Geographic*
Poem:	"Casey at the Bat"
Story:	"Ghost of the Lagoon"

Movie, Television program:	*The Wizard of Oz, Star Trek*
Play:	*The Matchmaker*
Painting, Sculpture:	*Mona Lisa, David*
Musical composition:	"The Star-Spangled Banner"

EXERCISE 8. Correcting the Capitalization of Titles. Each of the following sentences has one mistake in capitalization. Write each sentence correctly.

1. "Heart And Soul" is the only piano duet my sister and I can play.
2. Do you have a subscription to *World* Magazine?
3. My little sister loves *the Cat in the Hat*.
4. I checked out *Around the World In Eighty Days* from the public library.
5. Did you watch *The Cosby show* last night?

REVIEW EXERCISE B. Using Capitalization Correctly in Sentences. Number your paper 1–10. If the sentence is correct, write *C* after the proper number. If there is an error in the use of capital letters, write the word or words correctly on your paper. Insert capitals where needed and eliminate unnecessary capital letters.

1. My aunt, Mrs. Willis, is the secretary of her community service club.
2. Additional tests were ordered by dr. Stonerock.
3. At the graduation exercises, judge Tucker congratulated the graduates and their parents.
4. Lancelot was king Arthur's closest friend.
5. Last winter, grandma White taught me to ice-fish.
6. Some of the South's Governors serve on that committee.
7. The magna Charta is being shown at various art museums in this state.
8. Watching "Living wild" helped me write my report.
9. My brother and I plan to see *Return of The Jedi* for the third time.
10. Someday I want to read *Treasure island*.

MECHANICS

CHAPTER 19 REVIEW: POSTTEST

Correcting Sentences by Capitalizing Words. Number your paper 1–20. Copy those words that should be capitalized but are not onto your paper, inserting the capital letters.

EXAMPLE   1. Our guest speaker will be mayor Masella.
               1. *Mayor*

1. I have finally learned to play "danny boy," my father's favorite song.
2. "hansel and gretel" is a well-known story for children.
3. The third annual walk for hunger will be on october 19.
4. A highway in hawaii is named for admiral nimitz.
5. All bills and receipts must be given directly to the treasurer, ms. lee.
6. The trip to spain during spring vacation will be coordinated by professor martinez.
7. Will a student from mr. Mallen's class come to the principal's office?
8. There are several statues of greek gods in the museum.
9. Write to senator smith about the new issues.
10. All members of congress need to know your opinions.
11. Our class pictures will be taken on tuesday.
12. Do you like Mary cassatt's paintings?
13. Would you like to see the mummies in the british museum?
14. A venezuelan exchange student will live with our family for eight months.
15. The graduation exercises at Newberry college were held last week.
16. When is easter this year?
17. Grandma asked me what i want for my birthday.
18. I would like a book about World war II.
19. Next spring Grandpa Williams is going to take me on a hiking trip to mount Elbert.
20. I would love to go on a raft trip down the Colorado river.

SUMMARY STYLE SHEET

Names of Persons

Marie Anderson	my aunt
Ellen Goodman	a writer
Dale Louis	our teacher

Geographical Names

Gainesville	a college town
Brevard County	a county on the coast
Hawaiian Islands	islands in the Pacific
Norway	a country
Mount Washington	a mountain
Rhine River	a river in Germany
Colonial Drive	a busy street
Mount Rainier National Park	a park in Washington

Organizations, Business Firms, Institutions, Government Bodies

the Rotary Club	a service club
General Mills	a food-processing company
Largo High School	my dad's high school
First Baptist Church	a downtown church
Department of Agriculture	a department of the government

Historical Events and Periods, Special Events, Calendar Items

the Revolutionary War	a lengthy war
Independence Day	a national holiday
the Super Bowl	a football game
February, March, April	a month
Tuesday, Wednesday, Saturday	a weekday, the weekend

Nationalities, Tribes, Races, Religions

Irish	a nationality
Mohawk	an American Indian tribe
Oriental	a race
Greek Orthodox	a religion
God and His creation	gods of ancient cultures

MECHANICS

Brand Names

Cheerios	a breakfast cereal
Schwinn	a ten-speed bicycle

Other Particular Places, Things, Events, Awards

the *Queen Mary*	a ship
the *Apollo*	a spacecraft
Nobel Prize	a prize
Ceres	an asteroid
Jupiter	a planet
Washington Monument	a monument in Washington, D.C.

Specific Courses, Languages

Art I	a ceramics class
Spanish	a foreign language
World History II	a history course

Titles

Judge Blum	a judge
Hello, Judge.	
the President of the United States	the president of the drama club
the Queen of England	a queen's order
Aunt Barbara	my favorite aunt
Julie of the Wolves	a novel
Time	a weekly magazine

Punctuation

END MARKS, COMMAS, SEMICOLONS, COLONS

Have you ever tried to read a paragraph that was not punctuated? It was confusing, wasn't it? When you speak, your voice indicates stops and pauses that make your meaning clear. When you write, however, you must use punctuation to show those stops and pauses. In this chapter and in Chapter 21, you will learn punctuation rules to help you make your writing easier to understand.

DIAGNOSTIC TEST

Using End Marks, Commas, Semicolons, and Colons Correctly to Punctuate Sentences. Number your paper 1–20. The following sentences lack necessary end marks, commas, semicolons, or colons. After the proper number, write the word before each missing punctuation mark and the mark itself.

EXAMPLE   1. I read my library book studied my spelling words
               and finished my math homework.
            1. *book, words,*

MECHANICS

1. Flora please pass the mustard.
2. Do you think it looks like rain
3. We are learning about meteorology the study of weather.
4. The shirts on sale come in the following solid colors blue, green, brown, and red.
5. Stacey ordered three shirts I chose only two.
6. Watch out
7. Courtney is going to camp in Virginia but I will stay at home to help take care of my brother.
8. She said she will swim ride horseback and play tennis.
9. Maybe I can teach my brother Zachary how to swim
10. Well I think we will have fun anyway.
11. My youngest sister was born on April 12 1986.
12. She is a lively talkative child.
13. Courtney's address at summer camp is Riverhead Lodge Stonehill VA 12345
14. I have been making baskets and Jenny has been learning to water-ski.
15. We are planning to visit friends in Lakewood California.
16. Mrs Sanchez will be our substitute teacher while Mr. Arico is on jury duty.
17. Connie Chung a national newscaster has a busy schedule.
18. She has to get up at 300 A.M. on workdays.
19. Yes newscasting can be exciting work.
20. The second annual meeting will be held Wednesday, February 28 at 2:00 P.M.

END MARKS

The term *end marks* means punctuation used at the ends of sentences. Periods, question marks, and exclamation points are used as end marks.

20a. A statement is followed by a period.

EXAMPLES   The letter carrier is across the street.
            I hope he'll bring me a letter.

20b. A question is followed by a question mark.

EXAMPLES   Will he have anything for me?
            Will he bring a letter or magazine?

20c. An exclamation is followed by an exclamation point.

EXAMPLES   Here he comes!
            It's a letter from Grandma and Grandpa!

20d. A request or an order is followed by either a period or an exclamation point.

EXAMPLES   Please set the table. [a request—no strong feeling is
            expressed]
            Don't touch that pan! [The exclamation point shows
            strong feeling.]

To determine which end mark to use, consider whether the sentence expresses excitement or strong feeling. If it does express strong feeling, use an exclamation point; it it does not, use a period.

EXERCISE 1. Correcting Sentences by Adding End Marks.
Number your paper 1–5. After the proper number, write the last word of the sentence followed by a period, a question mark, or an exclamation point.

EXAMPLE   1. What time is it
            1. *it?*

1. When does the bus come
2. It's late
3. Do you think it will ever get here
4. We were sent to the principal's office
5. I don't understand the assignment

MECHANICS

EXERCISE 2. Correcting a Paragraph by Adding Capital Letters and End Marks. Decide where the sentences in the following paragraph begin and end. Rewrite the paragraph, providing the needed capital letters and end marks.

Have you ever been to Hawaii do you know what the people on the islands wear in the nineteenth century, island people wore clothes made of plants the leaves were soaked in sea water for a week and then dried in the sun rough edges of the leaves were cut off, and the leaves were woven together today people see these original types of clothing only in museums one modern style of clothing is called aloha clothes on the islands, every Friday is observed as Aloha Friday on that day people wear some type of Hawaiian clothing and garlands of live flowers wouldn't it be fun if everyone in our town would wear Hawaiian prints and live flowers once a week

20e. An abbreviation is followed by a period.

EXAMPLES   Dr. [Doctor *or* Drive]   Feb. [February]
           A.M. [*ante meridiem*]   lb. [pound]
           C. S. Lewis [Clive Staples Lewis]

Make it a practice to check abbreviations in a dictionary.

EXERCISE 3. Correcting Sentences by Adding Punctuation. Write the following sentences, inserting end marks or periods for abbreviations where needed.

EXAMPLE   1. The caterpillar was four inches long
           1. *The caterpillar was four inches long.*

1. Mrs Hunter was my first-grade teacher.
2. Just after 3:00 PM the sun came out.
3. The letter was postmarked May 7, but it arrived in June
4. What traffic there was on First Avenue
5. Will Mr Daly be teaching the science course?

MECHANICS

WRITING APPLICATION A:
Using End Marks Correctly
to Make Your Purpose Clear

End marks show your readers your purpose. They signal whether you are stating a fact, asking a question, or expressing a strong feeling.

EXAMPLES   My science grade is A+. [a statement of fact]
My science grade is A+? [a question]
My science grade is A+! [an exclamation]

Writing Assignment

You have just won $500 in a local sweepstakes. You have decided to put $200 into your savings account and to give $50 to a charity. What will you do with the remaining $250?

In a paragraph, tell how you reacted when you first got the news and how you plan to spend the remaining money. Remember to use punctuation correctly. Try to include at least one exclamation and one question.

COMMAS

An end mark brings a complete thought to a full stop. A comma indicates a pause, since the idea is not yet completed. Without commas, writing would be difficult to understand.

20f. Use commas to separate items in a series.

A series is three or more items written one after the other. The items may be single words or groups of words.

EXAMPLES   The Alps are in France, Italy, Switzerland, Austria, and Yugoslavia. [single words in a series]

All Saturday morning I dusted, vacuumed, and polished. [single words in a series]

MECHANICS

We swam in the ocean, built castles in the sand, and played volleyball on the beach. [groups of words in a series]

I searched for the lost contact lens on the counter, on the floor, and in the sink. [groups of words in a series]

When the last two items in a series are joined by *and,* you may omit the comma before the *and* if the comma is not necessary to make the meaning clear.

Study the following examples:

EXAMPLES   Grandma, Mom, and Dad came to the game.
Grandma, Mom and Dad came to the game.

The first sentence tells the reader that three particular people came to the game. The second sentence tells Grandma that Mom and Dad came to the game.

☞ NOTE   Some words are used in pairs and may be set off as one item in a series.

EXAMPLE   pork and beans, ham and eggs

Always be sure that there are at least three items in the series before you insert commas. Two items do not need and should not have a comma between them.

INCORRECT   Today is sunny, and warm.
  CORRECT   Today is sunny and warm.
  CORRECT   Today is sunny, warm, and breezy.

If all items in a series are joined by *and* or *or,* do not use commas to separate them.

EXAMPLES   You see snakes and lizards and toads in the desert.
This morning, campers can choose tennis or swimming or archery.

EXERCISE 4. Proofreading Sentences for the Correct Use of Commas.   Number your paper 1–5. If a sentence needs commas to separate items in a series, write the word before each required comma and write the comma after it. If a sentence is correct, write *C* after the proper number.

EXAMPLE   1. Lauren Jack and Mark entered the essay contest.
    1. *Lauren,   Jack,*

1. I finished my dinner brushed my teeth and ran out the door.
2. The nurse checked his pulse took his temperature and gave him a glass of water.
3. For lunch we had milk an egg sandwich a dill pickle and a pear.
4. Caroline Mikkelsen her daughter and two female friends were the first women to visit Antarctica.
5. Arthur plays the piano and the guitar and the accordion.

20g. Use commas to separate two or more adjectives preceding a noun.

EXAMPLE   The carp is a large, drab relative of the goldfish.
    The chairperson gave a dynamic, moving speech.

Do not place a comma between an adjective and the noun immediately following it.

INCORRECT   My transportation is a rusty, ancient, bicycle. [The last comma is incorrect.]

    CORRECT   My transportation is a rusty, ancient bicycle.

☞ ·NOTE Some adjectives are so closely connected in meaning to the nouns they modify that no comma is needed to separate them from another adjective.

EXAMPLES   The stately pine tree shook in the wind. [not *stately, pine tree*]

MECHANICS

> Where is the erasable typing paper? [not *erasable, typing paper*]

You can test to see whether a comma is needed by inserting an *and* between the adjectives (*stately and pine,* for example). If the group of words sounds awkward, the comma is unnecessary.

EXERCISE 5. Proofreading Sentences for the Correct Use of Commas. If a sentence needs a comma, write the word that comes before the needed comma and write the comma after it. If the sentence is correct, write *C*.

EXAMPLE 1. It was a well-written interesting history book.
　　　　　 1. *well-written,*

1. His sunburned wrinkled face told a story.
2. The chef cut off the tough thick ends of the asparagus stalks.
3. The lively silver bass swam in the shallows.
4. There was a sleek shiny bicycle in the store window.
5. The sound of the soft constant rain put me to sleep.
6. The tart lemon juice was sprinkled on the salad.
7. May I have some more of those delicious fluffy pecan pancakes?
8. The old diary had ragged yellowed pages.
9. After our hike I washed in the cold clear spring water.
10. The crowded dining room is filled with people celebrating my parents' anniversary.

20h. Use a comma before *and, but, or, nor, for,* or *yet* when one of these words joins the parts of a compound sentence.

If you are not sure that you can recognize a compound sentence, you should review pages 200–201.

EXAMPLES Derek will bring the potato salad to the sixth-grade picnic, and Sarah will bring the apple juice.

I wanted to bring a green salad, but I was asked to bring apples.

A very short compound sentence does not need a comma.

EXAMPLE   I'm wet and I'm cold.

> ☞ **NOTE**   Do not confuse a compound sentence and a compound verb; do not place a comma between the parts of a compound verb.

COMPOUND SENTENCE   We ran relay races first, and then we ate our meal.

COMPOUND VERB   We **ran** relay races first and then **ate** our meal.

Note that repeating the subject makes a sentence compound.

EXERCISE 6. Proofreading Sentences for the Correct Use of Commas.
If a sentence needs a comma, copy the word that comes before the needed comma and write the comma after it. If a sentence is correct, write *C*.

EXAMPLE   1. The tropical storm brought a lot of rain but the tornado did the most damage.
    1. *rain,*

1. Laura sang and Linda danced.
2. The sailboat was hidden by the fog yet we strained to see some sign of it.
3. We visited my sister at boarding school and then we took her to a restaurant for dinner.
4. Would you like to go to the movies or should we do the yardwork first?
5. I need to telephone my friends and tell them to get ready.
6. I practiced my piano piece for hours but my nervousness caused me to make mistakes during the recital.
7. Forrest knew the rules yet he chose to disobey them.
8. Neither the sixth-graders nor the science teachers could make the experiment work.

MECHANICS

9. The large oak tree provided shade for the house but it blocked out too much sunlight for the grass to grow.
10. The lake contained large fish but it also was home to several alligators.

WRITING APPLICATION B:
Using Commas to Make Your Meaning Clear

Commas help to make your meaning clear to your readers. An omitted comma can make a difference in your meaning. Compare these examples.

EXAMPLES   My sister is pretty tall, and thin.
            My sister is pretty, tall, and thin.

Writing Assignment

Write a description of a family. It may be your own, one you have read about, one you have seen on television, or one that you invent. Use at least three adjectives to describe each member of the family. Use commas correctly.

Expressions That Interrupt

20i. Use commas to set off expressions that interrupt the sentence.

Two commas are needed if the expression to be set off comes in the middle of the sentence. One comma is needed if the expression comes first or last.

EXAMPLES   Our English teacher, Mrs. Shakespeare, has written a play about us.

            What do you think, Kami, of the karate demonstration?

Yes, I will call back this afternoon.

There are several kinds of expressions that interrupt a sentence. Each kind requires the use of a comma or commas.

(1) Appositives and appositive phrases are usually set off by commas.

An appositive is a word that identifies or explains the word it follows. An appositive phrase is an appositive with its modifiers.

EXAMPLES Mrs. Shaw, a gymnast, will coach us.
[*Gymnast* is an appositive identifying Mrs. Shaw.]

We found books on geology, the science of the earth and its rocks. [*The science of the earth and its rocks* is an appositive phrase explaining geology.]

When the appositive is a word or two closely related to the preceding word, the comma is not needed.

EXAMPLES my friend Robert
Alexander the Great
we students

EXERCISE 7. Writing Sentences with Appositives. Use each of the following groups of words as an appositive in a sentence of your own. Insert commas wherever needed.

EXAMPLE 1. the principal
1. *Mrs. Rivers, the principal, announced the winners.*

1. Sherri and Kerri
2. my favorite television show
3. the man on the bicycle
4. my cousin
5. my favorite holiday

(2) Words used in direct address are set off by commas.

We often address by name the person to whom we are speaking. This is called *direct address*. In written conversation, a name used in direct address is set off by commas.

MECHANICS

EXAMPLES   Terry, please clean your room before dinner.
What do you want for dinner tonight, Ann?
If you ask me, Heidi, that peach is spoiled.

(3) Use a comma after such words as *well, yes, no,* and *why* when they begin a sentence.

EXAMPLES   Well, I guess I could finish this job for you.
Yes, the dishes have been cleared off the table.
Why, it's sunny outside!

EXERCISE 8. Correcting Sentences by Adding Commas.
Number your paper 1–10. After the proper number, write the word or words that should be followed by a comma, and write the comma.

EXAMPLE   1. Jay Arn my father's brother will meet us at the park.
1. *Arn,   brother,*

1. Wood Buffalo National Park the world's largest national park is located in Canada.
2. The park was named for the wood buffalo a species slightly smaller than the plains buffalo.
3. Inez when did Lewis and Clark reach Washington?
4. Why you and I were in the same kindergarten class!
5. If you mow the lawn Kelly I'll rake the clippings.
6. I read about whooping cranes in *Natural History* a magazine about nature.
7. Did you bring the tickets Jorge?
8. No but it won't take me long to go back and get them.
9. Well just don't forget.
10. My cousin Bea my favorite relative wants to come along.

20j. Use a comma in certain conventional situations.

(1) Use commas to separate items in dates and addresses.

EXAMPLES   Theodore Roosevelt was born on October 27, 1858, in New York, New York.
Saturday, May 3, is the county soccer playoff.
My aunt lives in Northfield, Minnesota.

☞ NOTE   The Postal Service expects you to give the ZIP code number on every envelope you address. No punctuation is required between the state and ZIP code.

EXAMPLE   Cerritos, CA 90701

(2) Use a comma after the salutation of a friendly letter and after the closing of any letter.

EXAMPLES   Dear Grandma and Grandpa,   Dear Bruce,
Love,   Sincerely,

EXERCISE 9. Using Commas Correctly in Dates, Addresses, and Salutations. Write the following items and sentences, inserting commas where needed.

1. Yours truly
2. Shirley Chisholm was born on November 30 1924.
3. The first white female Indian chief was Harriet Maxwell Converse, who was born in Elmira New York.
4. After August, write to me at 327 Adams Way, Darrouzett TX 79024.
5. The Halloween Carnival is on Friday October 30 1987.

REVIEW EXERCISE A. Proofreading Sentences for the Correct Use of Commas. Number your paper 1–10. After the proper number, write each word that should be followed by a comma. Write the comma after each word.

1. I plan to spend a week with my uncle in Savannah Georgia.
2. He's a kind intelligent man.

3. He has invited me to come on Saturday April 3 in the evening.
4. Uncle Henry an engineer at Grumman Corporation will meet me at the train station.
5. We plan to visit the Riverfront a group of stores and museums lining the river.
6. We will shop for baskets visit the maritime museum and eat some fish.
7. The fish should be fresh of course.
8. I hope we'll have time to explore the old fort and then we could go to the nearby beach.
9. Well here comes the train now.
10. Uncle Henry here I am!

SEMICOLONS

The semicolon signals to the reader to pause a little longer than for a comma but not as long as for a period. Semicolons are frequently used in compound sentences. The semicolon is an effective mark of punctuation if not used too often.

20k. Use a semicolon between parts of a compound sentence if they are not joined by *and, but, or, nor, for,* or *yet.*

EXAMPLES   Todd's report is on Arizona **;** mine is on Utah.
The rain clouds are moving in quickly **;** I will cancel my tennis date.

Sometimes, instead of using a semicolon, it is better to separate a compound sentence into two sentences.

ACCEPTABLE   Amazon parrots make interesting pets; some can learn to repeat whole sentences or whistle tunes.
BETTER   Amazon parrots make interesting pets. Some can learn to repeat whole sentences or whistle tunes.

EXERCISE 10. Proofreading Sentences for the Correct Use of Semicolons. Number your paper 1–5. If the sentence needs

a semicolon, write the words before and after the semicolon and insert the punctuation mark. If the sentence does not require a semicolon, write *C*.

EXAMPLE   1. The guests served themselves, they had rice, shrimp curry, and many side dishes.
           1. *themselves; they*

1. The snow has been falling for hours, it already covers the ground-floor window.
2. My younger brother is getting ready for the Little League tryouts, he wants to be a shortstop on the team.
3. I ordered spinach salad, but I was told there was none left.
4. We washed and waxed the family car until it glowed, unfortunately, the rain quickly ruined our work.
5. My parents are very pleased with me today, I was one of the first to volunteer for the tutoring program.

COLONS

A colon usually signals that additional information is to follow.

20l. Use a colon before a list of items, especially after such expressions as *as follows* and *the following*.

EXAMPLES   This is the list of those absent today: Carmen Santiago, Justin Douglass, and Steven Byrd.

               Pack the following items for your overnight trip: a toothbrush, toothpaste, and your hairbrush.

The colon is never used directly after a verb or preposition. Omit the colon or reword the sentence.

INCORRECT   My report includes: a table of contents, three chapters, illustrations, and a list of sources.

CORRECT   My report includes the following parts: a table of contents, three chapters with illustrations, and a list of sources.

MECHANICS

CORRECT   My report includes a table of contents, three chapters, illustrations, and a list of sources.

20m. Use a colon between the hour and the minute when you write the time.

EXAMPLES 8**:**55 A.M., 9**:**15 P.M., 6**:**22 this morning

20n. Use a colon after the salutation of a business letter.

EXAMPLES   Dear Sir**:**   Dear Mrs. Jordan**:**
               Gentlemen**:**   To Whom It May Concern**:**

EXERCISE 11. Correcting Sentences by Adding Colons.
Number your paper 1–10. If a sentence does not need a colon, write *C* after the number. If a colon is required, copy the word the colon should follow and write a colon after it. If a colon is needed to divide numbers, write the numbers and the colon.

EXAMPLE 1. Bring the following to class each day your notebook, a pencil, an eraser, and your textbook.
         1. *day:*

1. We will tour the following cities Paris, Rome, and London.
2. A good baby sitter must be the following prompt, interested in the children, and careful.
3. To lessen your chances of getting some kinds of cancers, you should not smoke or chew tobacco.
4. Add these items to your shopping list tissues, toothpaste, and shampoo.
5. A good friend must be loving, loyal, and honest.
6. The first bell rings at 810 A.M.
7. Your homework includes studying your spelling words, working on your composition, and reading one chapter.
8. The recipe for Brunswick stew called for the following ingredients lamb, carrots, potatoes, and onions.
9. The next show begins at 600 P.M.

10. Dear Sir

I am quite displeased with your product.

REVIEW EXERCISE B. Proofreading Sentences for the Correct Use of End Marks, Commas, Semicolons, and Colons.
Rewrite each of the following items, inserting the necessary end marks, commas, semicolons, and colons.

1. Before you go to the movies, you must do the following chores feed the cat, take out the garbage, and dust.
2. The class begins at 835 P.M.
3. Kirk have you seen the movie at the Mall Theater?
4. Mrs Marshall wrote a letter thanking us for the flowers.
5. The tulips looked gorgeous, the lilies of the valley smelled heavenly.
6. The letter was mailed to Safety Harbor FL 33572.
7. We mailed the letter on Saturday March 21.
8. I was awarded a scholarship to music camp this summer
9. Why I never believed I would be that lucky.
10. Yours truly

Stephanie McDonald

CHAPTER 20 REVIEW: POSTTEST

Using End Marks, Commas, Semicolons, and Colons Correctly. Number your paper 1–20. After the proper number, write the word or words that should be followed by a mark of punctuation. Write the punctuation mark after those words.

EXAMPLE   1. Mr. Cotton my next-door neighbor asked me to pick up his mail while he is away.

1. *Cotton,   neighbor,*

1. The peaches and plums and strawberries will soon be ripe enough to pick.
2. Mrs. Keyes gave us a long difficult test on verb usage.

MECHANICS

3. Ray Charles an accomplished musician was blinded by glaucoma at the age of seven.
4. I have registered for ceramics photography and weaving classes.
5. When will dinner be ready
6. Ted offered to mow the lawn clean the garage and paint the shed while we're on vacation
7. Here comes the tornado
8. Cheryl will take gymnastics Eddie will take piano lessons.
9. Would 630 P.M. be too early for a meeting?
10. This jelly was made in Portsmouth New Hampshire.
11. The letter is finished now I must proofread it before I can mail it
12. Sincerely
    the Staff at Earl's Jewelers
13. We will read some books on court procedures and then we will go on a field trip to the county courthouse.
14. Richard Ginny and Manuel finished their science projects yesterday.
15. Quick, get me some ice
16. Yes I did clean up my room.
17. When you go cross-country skiing, bring the following items skis, boots, poles, ski wax, and a snack.
18. Shall we start around 9:00 AM?
19. Jim when is Thanksgiving this year?
20. The Scouts' Annual Dinner was held February 18 1987.

MECHANICS

SUMMARY OF USES OF THE COMMA

20f. Use commas to separate items in a series.

20g. Use commas to separate two or more adjectives preceding a noun.

20h. Use a comma before *and, but, or, nor, for,* and *yet* when they join the parts of a compound sentence.

20i. Use commas to set off expressions that interrupt the sentence.
    (1) Appositives and appositive phrases are usually set off by commas.
    (2) Words used in direct address are set off by commas.
    (3) Use a comma after such words as *well, yes, no,* and *why* when they begin a sentence.

20j. Use a comma in certain conventional situations.
    (1) Use commas to separate items in dates and addresses.
    (2) Use a comma after the salutation of a friendly letter and after the closing of any letter.

MECHANICS

CHAPTER 21

Punctuation

ITALICS, QUOTATION MARKS,
APOSTROPHES, HYPHENS

In this chapter you will learn about four more marks of punctuation: italics, quotation marks, apostrophes, and hyphens. These, together with those you studied in Chapter 20, are the chief marks of punctuation that you will need in your writing.

DIAGNOSTIC TEST

Proofreading Sentences for the Correct Use of Underlining (Italics), Quotation Marks, Apostrophes, and Hyphens. Each of the following sentences contains an error in the use of underlining (italics), quotation marks, apostrophes, or hyphens. Write the sentences correctly; number each sentence.

EXAMPLE   1. "Its important for everyone to vote," Jesse Jackson said.
　　　　　　1. *"It's important for everyone to vote," Jesse Jackson said.*

1. I like to sing This Land Is My Land.
2. Washingtons largest city is named for Chief Seattle.

MECHANICS

3. Chapter 2 is called The Siamese Cat.
4. I haven't read the book Treasure Island yet.
5. "I remember making a barometer in fourth grade. "I had to start over five times before it worked," commented Betsy.
6. "Can Lois help me make a weather vane"? asked Todd.
7. "It took me only forty five minutes to make a sundial," Carlos remarked.
8. Ted designed a new paper airplane, but the model crashed on its test flight.
9. All student's projects are due next Friday.
10. "Whose going to be finished first?" Mrs. Tolliver asked.

UNDERLINING (ITALICS)

In printed material, italics are letters that lean to the right—*like this*. When you write, you underline a word to show that it should be italicized in a publication. For example, your composition would read

My brother just finished reading The Horse and His Boy.

In a publication, it would look like this:

My brother just finished reading *The Horse and His Boy*.

21a. Use underlining (italics) for titles of books, periodicals, works of art, ships, films, television programs, and so on.[1]

EXAMPLES   The *Island Princess* is a cruise ship.
I saw some good articles in *Time* and *Newsweek*.

EXERCISE 1. Using Underlining (Italics) Correctly. Number your paper 1–5. After the proper number, write the word or words that should be printed in italics and underline them.

MECHANICS

---

[1] For titles that are not italicized but are enclosed in quotation marks, see rule 21j on page 378.

EXAMPLE   1. We saw Rodin's famous work, The Thinker.
          1. *The Thinker*

1. The monthly magazine Popular Science reports new scientific discoveries.
2. I have seen Walt Disney's movie Fantasia three times.
3. One mission of the space shuttle Discovery was to repair a satellite.
4. Did you get the tickets for the play The Mousetrap?
5. Do you like the fashions in this issue of Seventeen?

WRITING QUOTATIONS

When you write, you will sometimes use the exact words that were spoken or written by someone else. These exact words are called *quotations*. This section will help you to punctuate quotations correctly.

21b. Use quotation marks to enclose a direct quotation—a person's exact words.

EXAMPLES   "When you've finished your homework," my mom said, "let's go out for a two-mile run."
          "Let's go home," Jeanne suggested.

If a person's words are not quoted exactly, no quotation marks are needed. This is called an indirect quotation.

INDIRECT QUOTATION   He said that the flight is canceled. [not his exact words; no quotation marks needed]
DIRECT QUOTATION   He said, "The flight is canceled." [his exact words; quotation marks needed]

21c. A direct quotation begins with a capital letter.

EXAMPLES   Mrs. Talbott said, "Please get a pencil."
          Kristina asked, "Is it my turn?"

21d. When a quoted sentence is divided into two parts by an interrupting expression such as *she said* or *Paul answered,* the second part begins with a small letter.

EXAMPLE   "Could you take care of my lawn," asked Mr. Franklin, "while I'm on vacation next month?"

If the second part of a broken quotation is a new sentence, then it is capitalized.

EXAMPLE   "I don't know," I said. "My mother wants me to practice the piano more."

21e. A direct quotation is set off from the rest of the sentence by commas.

To set off means to separate. If a quotation comes at the beginning of a sentence, a comma follows it. If a quotation comes at the end of a sentence, a comma comes before it. If a quoted sentence is interrupted, a comma follows the first part and comes before the second part.

EXAMPLES   "I think," remarked the speech teacher, "you put a lot of time and effort into your presentation." [quotation interrupted, with a comma after the first part and before the second part]

I replied, "Yes, I did." [quotation at end, with a comma before it]

"Your work deserves an A+," stated Mrs. Hailey. [quotation first, followed by a comma]

☞ NOTE   No comma is needed if an end mark is used instead.

EXAMPLES   "I received an A+?" I asked.
"You certainly did!" answered Mrs. Hailey.

MECHANICS

EXERCISE 2. Punctuating and Capitalizing Quotations.
Some of the following sentences contain an error or errors in
punctuation. If a sentence is correct, write *C* on your paper next
to the sentence number. If a sentence is incorrect, rewrite it
correctly, inserting commas, quotation marks, and capital letters
where needed.

EXAMPLE 1. We're going tubing next Saturday said Charles.
　　　　　 1. *"We're going tubing next Saturday," said Charles.*

1. I'd like to go with you I replied.
2. So would we responded Barbara and Jim.
3. Barbara said I'll bring enough tubes for everyone.
4. Jim said I'll bring the sandwiches and grape juice.
5. I offered to bring raw vegetables and baked beans.
6. My dad will drive Charles said he has a van.
7. The river is fed by a glacier Jim stated.
8. That means Barbara added that the water will be cold.
9. It should feel good I said if Saturday is as hot as today is.
10. Charles asked us to meet him at 8:30 A.M. in front of the
    school auditorium.

21f. A period or comma following a quotation should be placed
inside the closing quotation marks.

EXAMPLES "I can't wait to go tubing," I said excitedly.
　　　　　 Jim added, "It should be lots of fun."

21g. A question mark or an exclamation point should be placed
inside the closing quotation marks if the quotation is a question or
an exclamation. Otherwise, it should be placed outside.

EXAMPLES "Are we almost there, Dad?" asked Charles. [The
　　　　　 question mark is inside the closing quotation marks
　　　　　 because the quotation itself is a question.]

　　　　　 Barbara screamed, "This water is freezing!" [The
　　　　　 exclamation point is inside the closing quotation
　　　　　 marks because the quotation itself is an exclama-
　　　　　 tion.]

Who said, "Let's go tubing on Saturday"? [The question mark is outside the closing quotation marks because the quotation is not a question, but the sentence as a whole is a question.]

Stop calling me a "little girl"! [The exclamation point is outside the closing quotation marks because the quotation itself is not an exclamation, but the sentence as a whole is an exclamation.]

EXERCISE 3. Punctuating and Capitalizing Quotations. Rewrite each of the following sentences correctly, inserting punctuation and adding capitalization where needed.

EXAMPLE 1. Let us continue with our study of France said Mr. Harris.

1. *"Let us continue with our study of France," said Mr. Harris.*

1. Rita remarked I really enjoyed learning about France.
2. I impressed my parents by counting and singing in French said Pete.
3. I thought it might be fun to talk about French food today Mr. Harris continued.
4. Oh, no moaned Billy not right before lunch.
5. Can you think of any foods or dishes that you consider French asked Mr. Harris.
6. Lyle answered how about French bread?
7. Yes said Mr. Harris.
8. I think that omelets are French replied Mimi.
9. Who first said you can't make an omelet without breaking eggs?
10. It's a proverb answered Mr. Harris tomorrow we will learn some French sayings.

EXERCISE 4. Revising Indirect Quotations to Create Direct Quotations. Revise each of the following five sentences by changing the indirect quotation to a direct quotation. Be sure to use capital letters and punctuation correctly.

EXAMPLE   1. I asked the cashier for change for a dollar.

          1. *"May I please have change for a dollar?" I asked the cashier.* (or *I asked the cashier, "Would you please give me change for a dollar?"*)

1. The cashier replied that she wasn't allowed to make change unless a purchase was made.
2. I said that I needed a new pen.
3. The cashier told me that it cost forty-nine cents.
4. I said that I would give her $1.49.
5. She told me that I would then get a dollar in change.

21h. When you write dialogue (conversation), begin a new paragraph every time the speaker changes.

EXAMPLE   "What are we going to do at the next club meeting?" Eddie asked.

         Aaron thought for a moment. "We're supposed to plan the presentation for the school program."

         "I can help with the scenery," Eddie offered.

21i. When a quotation consists of several sentences, put quotation marks only at the beginning and the end of the whole quotation. Do not put them around each sentence in the quotation.

INCORRECT   "That would be great if you could work on the scenery." "Zachary and Judy offered to make costumes," Aaron answered.

CORRECT   **"**That would be great if you could work on the scenery. Zachary and Judy offered to make costumes, **"** Aaron answered.

21j. Use quotation marks to enclose the titles of short works such as articles, short stories, poems, songs, and individual episodes of television programs; and of chapters and other parts of books.

EXAMPLES   Can you reach all the high notes in "The Star-Spangled Banner"?

Jennifer recited Joyce Kilmer's poem "Trees."

An article called "A Short History of Hairstyles" was published in Thursday's newspaper.

21k. Use single quotation marks to enclose a quotation within a quotation.

EXAMPLES   "Tonight you must read the chapter 'Comets and Asteroids,'" stated Mr. Mendoza.

"Mrs. Engle distinctly said, 'Your book reports are due Thursday,'" Krista told me.

EXERCISE 5. Using Quotation Marks.   Write each sentence, inserting single or double quotation marks where needed.

EXAMPLE   1. I have just finished reading The Circulatory System in our health book, Dell told me.
    1. *"I have just finished reading 'The Circulatory System' in our health book," Dell told me.*

1. Diane is trying to learn Tarantella for the piano recital.
2. Eddie, can we meet after school tomorrow? We need to practice our presentation, Aaron mentioned.
3. I'm sure I heard Mrs. Garcia say, School is being closed because of the storm, I told Kenneth.
4. I can pronounce all the words in the poem Jabberwocky Zona told Lou.
5. Ted said my dad will pick us up on Saturday at 7:30 A.M. After the race, he is taking us to Molly's for brunch.

REVIEW EXERCISE A. Punctuating Dialogue.   Copy the following dialogue, using quotation marks and other marks of punctuation wherever necessary. Remember to begin a new paragraph each time the speaker changes. The punctuation marks that are already included in the exercise are correct.

Mom, I'm so hungry I complained that I could eat a whole chicken, four ears of corn, and two bowls of salad. Goodness, it sounds as if you're ready for dinner. How did you know what we're having tonight? Mom responded. Just wishful thinking, I guess I answered. May I have some now? Mom answered Dinner's not even started yet. How about having some celery with cream cheese? That sounds good I commented but I'm too weak to clean the celery. Mom smiled and said I have to take your brother to his piano lesson now. See you later. What? You're going to desert me now? I'm sorry Mom replied. I have to leave now or we'll be late. Why don't you just take a pear?

WRITING APPLICATION A:
Using Dialogue in Narration

Dialogue not only helps to show action in a story but also reveals parts of your characters' personalities better than descriptions can. When writing dialogue, use quotation marks and paragraphing carefully so that your readers will understand which character is speaking.

Writing Assignment

Write a one-page narration in which some friends discuss their plans for giving a going-away party next week for a classmate who is moving to another state. After you have revised your work, proofread it carefully for correct use of quotation marks and paragraphing. Then write a final copy of your narration.

APOSTROPHES

The apostrophe is used (1) to show ownership or relationship, (2) to show where letters have been omitted in a contraction, and (3) to form the plural of numbers, letters, or signs.

MECHANICS

The Possessive Case

The possessive case of a word shows ownership or relationship.

EXAMPLES   Mrs. Long's diamond
            its walls

Personal pronouns in the possessive case (*hers, his, its, ours, yours, theirs*) do not require an apostrophe.

21l. To form the possessive case of a singular noun, add an apostrophe and an *s*.

EXAMPLES   the child's toy
            Tanaka's store
            Tess's painting

EXERCISE 6. Writing Sentences with Singular Possessives.

Write one sentence for each of the given words, using each in the possessive case.

EXAMPLE   1. baby
            1. *The baby's rattle was in the crib.*

1. truck   4. tree
2. aunt   5. radio
3. he

21m. To form the possessive case of a plural noun ending in *s*, add only the apostrophe.

EXAMPLES   highways' intersection
            the beetles' legs

21n. To form the possessive case of a plural noun not ending in *s*, add an apostrophe and an *s*.

EXAMPLES   men's clothing
            children's section

EXERCISE 7. Writing Sentences with Plural Possessives.
Write the plural form of each of the following words. After each plural form, write a sentence using it as a possessive.

EXAMPLE   1. plant
          1. *plants—The plants' leaves were all brown.*

1. pen   2. photograph   3. woman   4. dentist   5. reporter

EXERCISE 8. Writing Possessives. Number your paper 1–10. Rewrite each of the following expressions using the possessive case. Insert an apostrophe in the right place.

EXAMPLE   1. the speeches of the politicians
          1. *the politicians' speeches*

1. the basketball of Elisabeth
2. the books of the children
3. the office of the principal
4. the bed of the kittens
5. the prize of the winner
6. the dog of Grant
7. the pen of my aunt
8. the sword of the knight
9. the prizes of the winners
10. the animals of the farm

Contractions

A *contraction* is a word made by combining two words and leaving out some letters. An apostrophe takes the place of the missing letters.

EXAMPLE   He will turn his paper in tomorrow.
          He'll turn his paper in tomorrow.

21o. Use an apostrophe to show where letters have been left out in a contraction.

The most common contraction is made by shortening *not* to *n't* and combining it with a verb. The spelling of the verb is usually unchanged.

EXAMPLES   is not   isn't   has not   hasn't
           are not   aren't   have not   haven't

does not	doesn't	had not	hadn't
do not	don't	could not	couldn't

However, with some verbs, the spelling does change.

EXAMPLE   will not   won't

Contractions may also be formed by joining nouns or pronouns with verbs.

EXAMPLES	I am	I'm	they would	they'd
	let us	let's	Beth is late.	Beth's late.
	you are	you're		

Its and It's

Its is a pronoun in the possessive case. It does not have an apostrophe. *It's* means *it is* or *it has*. It is a contraction and requires an apostrophe.

EXAMPLES   *Its* brakes are noisy. [*Its* is a possessive pronoun. No apostrophe is needed.]

It's been warm today. [*It's* means *it has*. It is a contraction and requires an apostrophe.]

Whose and Who's

Whose is a pronoun in the possessive case. It does not have an apostrophe. *Who's* means *who is* or *who has*. It is a contraction and requires an apostrophe.

EXAMPLES   Whose paper is finished? [*Whose* is a possessive pronoun.]
Who's at the door? [*Who's* means *who is*.]

MECHANICS

EXERCISE 9. Writing Contractions Correctly.   Number your paper 1–10. Write correctly any word requiring an apostrophe. If the sentence is correct, write *C*.

EXAMPLE   1. Well be leaving soon.
          1. *We'll*

1. Youve broken the antique glass pitcher.
2. Its about time you handed in that paper.
3. Whose umbrella is this?
4. Were going to hold a surprise party for our teacher.
5. I cant ask my grandmother about it.
6. He wouldnt be in the hospital now if he had worn his seat belt.
7. Lets go to the library.
8. Youd think she was an expert.
9. Its too bad I missed the circus.
10. Ill wash the car after breakfast tomorrow.

21p. Use an apostrophe and *s* to form the plural of letters, numbers, and signs, and of words referred to as words.

EXAMPLES   You wrote +'s instead of x's on all these problems.
Try not to use so many *and*'s in your speech.

WRITING APPLICATION B:
Using Apostrophes to Make Your Writing Clear

Using an apostrophe can change the meaning of a word or change it to the possessive. Compare the following examples:

EXAMPLES   The shell was on the sand.
She'll walk on the sand.

The boys sang well.
Four boys' jackets were left in the auditorium.

Writing Assignment

Write a story using all of the following words: *we'll, well, book's, books, who's, whose, it's, its, bird's,* and *birds.* You may use more than one of the words in a sentence. Underline the words. Check your work for correct usage.

MECHANICS

HYPHENS

The hyphen is used (1) to indicate that a word has been broken at the end of a line or (2) to show that two or more words are being used together as one.

21q. Use a hyphen to divide a word at the end of a line.

If you find that there is not enough room on a line for a whole word, you may divide it by using a hyphen. Always use the dictionary to find the right way to divide a word.

(1) Words must be divided so that each syllable can be pronounced as it is pronounced in a complete word.

UNACCEPTABLE Uncle Steve, Aunt Sue, and Kendra will journey eighty miles to join us.
ACCEPTABLE Uncle Steve, Aunt Sue, and Kendra will journey eighty miles to join us.

(2) Words of one syllable may not be divided.

UNACCEPTABLE They are bringing salad, ham, and rye bread.
ACCEPTABLE They are bringing salad, ham, and rye
bread.

(3) Words may not be divided so that one part is a single letter.

UNACCEPTABLE I understand that the family car is parked a-
cross the street.
ACCEPTABLE I understand that the family car is parked
across the street.

21r. Use a hyphen with compound numbers from twenty-one to ninety-nine.

EXAMPLE We have forty-eight photographs on our walls.

MECHANICS

REVIEW EXERCISE B. Using Apostrophes and Hyphens Correctly. Number your paper 1–10. After the proper number, write correctly the word that needs an apostrophe or a hyphen.

EXAMPLE 1. Wheres my history book?
1. *Where's*

1. Do you know where the world atlases and the diction aries are?
2. There are two *rs* in *tomorrow*.
3. He cant tie a square knot.
4. All the elephants toenails were trimmed by the zookeeper.
5. Issaye Miyakes designs are unusual.
6. I have a collection of Tina Turners albums.
7. Forty nine students signed the card.
8. The mens chorus gave a beautiful performance last night.
9. Whos going to the fair this weekend?
10. Its almost time to leave.

CHAPTER 21 REVIEW: POSTTEST

Proofreading Sentences for the Correct Use of Underlining (Italics), Quotation Marks, Apostrophes, and Hyphens. Each of the following sentences contains at least one error in the capitalization or punctuation of a quotation or in the use of underlining (italics), quotation marks, apostrophes, or hyphens. After the proper number, write the sentence correctly.

EXAMPLE 1. We havent finished our dinner yet.
1. *We haven't finished our dinner yet.*

1. I built a model of the Santa Maria for extra credit in social studies.
2. My teachers house is being painted.
3. Each classroom has twenty four desks.
4. This recipe calls for lentils, grated cheese, garlic, and oni ons.
5. The pots boiling over!

6. Whos going to sample this dish?
7. Dont forget the soy sauce.
8. The three chefs recipes were prepared by the chefs themselves on television.
9. Richard's last name has two *l*s.
10. Have you read any of Sir Walter Scotts works?
11. We could hear the flapping of the geeses wings.
12. Jamie said that she had read the poem The Unicorn.
13. "Wasnt that a song?" asked Carrie.
14. "I think a folk singer wrote it" answered Tony.
15. Jane said "she would hum a few lines of it."
16. Brad commented, "I think my parents have a copy of it".
17. "Would they let you bring it to class"? Elena asked.
18. "Who said, Time is money"? Gerald asked.
19. "Benjamin Franklin wrote it," answered Carlotta, "in a book called Advice to a Young Tradesman."
20. "I think," commented Theo, "That I understand it."

CHAPTER 22

Spelling

IMPROVING YOUR SPELLING

Mistakes in spelling make the writer's meaning unclear and confuse the reader. For instance, if you read the sentence *That durt road is closed in the winter,* you can figure out what is intended. However, the writer's mistake in spelling may have slowed you down. In written communication, good spelling skills are valuable.

Spelling may be difficult for you. Fortunately, you can improve this skill. With the help of some useful spelling rules and procedures, and with some effort, you can become a better speller.

GOOD SPELLING HABITS

1. *Keep a list of your own errors.* Each person may have difficulty with different words. Words that are spelling "demons" to you may be easy for someone else. For this reason, it is best to make your own personal spelling list. In your list write the words that you often misspell, and review them often in order to master them. When you study the spelling of these and other words, follow these steps.

MECHANICS

a. Look carefully at the word correctly spelled. Make note of each letter, especially any letters you missed.

b. Say the word carefully. Make sure that your pronunciation is correct and that you say each syllable.

c. Write the word correctly. As you write it on your spelling list, divide it into syllables and put in the main accent mark. Then practice writing the word from memory. Check your spelling to see if it is correct.

2. *Use the dictionary as a spelling aid.* When you are not sure how to spell a word, look it up in a dictionary. Guesses are often wrong.

3. *Spell by syllables.* A syllable is a part of a word that can be pronounced by itself. *Necessity* has four syllables: *ne-ces-si-ty.* Breaking a long word into its syllables gives you shorter units to learn. It is much easier to learn two or three letters at a time than many all at once.

4. *Avoid mispronunciations that lead to spelling errors.* Some spelling errors are the result of poor pronunciation. A student who says *liberry* instead of *library* is likely to misspell the word. As you study a word, be sure you are pronouncing each syllable distinctly.

5. *Proofread to avoid careless spelling errors.* You might make spelling errors when you write a first draft because you are trying to write your sentences quickly. Careful proofreading of your written work will enable you to correct many of these errors. Be particularly careful to check the words that you have listed in your own spelling list.

SPELLING RULES

The spelling rules that follow will help you with many words that you use frequently. Learn and use these rules, and you will become a better speller. However, there are exceptions to each rule that must simply be memorized. Add them to your spelling list and practice them.

MECHANICS

ie and *ei*

22a. Write *ie* when the sound is long *e*, except after *c*.

  EXAMPLES   chief, believe, brief, receive, ceiling
EXCEPTIONS   leisure, neither, weird, seize

    Write *ei* when the sound is not long *e*, especially when the sound is long *a*.

  EXAMPLES   neighbor, weigh, reindeer, height
EXCEPTIONS   friend, fierce

This verse can help you to remember the *ie* rule. In the verse, the *i* before the *e* refers to words with the long *e* sound.

    I before *e*
    Except after *c*,
    Or when sounded like *a*,
    As in *neighbor* and *weigh*.

EXERCISE 1. Writing Words with *ie* and *ei*.   Write the following words correctly by supplying the missing letters (*e* and *i*).

EXAMPLE   1. bel . . . ve
            1. *believe*

1. p . . . ce   5. f . . . ld   8. n . . . ce
2. gr . . . f   6. v . . . n   9. ach . . . ve
3. fr . . . nd   7. . . . ghth 10. sl . . . gh
4. s . . . ze

PREFIXES AND SUFFIXES

22b. When a prefix is added to a word, the spelling of the word itself remains the same.

A *prefix* is a letter or a group of letters added to the beginning of a word to change its meaning.

EXAMPLES

dis + satisfy = dissatisfy   mis + lead = mislead
fore + sight = foresight   over + due = overdue
im + possible = impossible   pre + cook = precook

EXERCISE 2. Writing Words with Prefixes. Number your paper 1–10. Then write these words in order, spelled correctly.

EXAMPLE   1. mis + place
               1. *misplace*

1. fore + father   5. un + common   9. dis + loyal
2. un + fair   6. im + patient   10. over + coat
3. in + dependent   7. pre + historic
4. mis + use   8. mis + spell

22c. When the suffixes *-ness* and *-ly* are added to a word, the spelling of the word itself is not changed.

A *suffix* is a letter or letters added at the end of a word to change its meaning.

EXAMPLES   stubborn + ness = stubbornness
              beautiful + ly = beautifully

EXCEPTIONS   Most words ending in *y* do not follow this rule. Instead, the *y* is changed to *i*.

EXAMPLES   friendly + ness = friendliness
              happy + ly = happily

22d. Drop the final *e* before a suffix beginning with a vowel.

EXAMPLES   cause + ing = causing
              reverse + ible = reversible

EXCEPTIONS   Words ending in *-ce* and *-ge* usually keep the silent *e* when the suffix begins with *a* or *o*.

EXAMPLES   charge + able = chargeable
              courage + ous = courageous

MECHANICS

22e. Keep the final *e* before a suffix beginning with a consonant.

EXAMPLES   spine + less = spineless
excite + ment = excitement
force + ful = forceful

EXCEPTIONS   argue + ment = argument
true + ly = truly

EXERCISE 3. Writing Words with Suffixes.

Number your paper 1–10. Write correctly the words formed as follows:

EXAMPLE   1. sudden + ness
         1. *suddenness*

1. active + ity
2. careful + ly
3. suspense + ful
4. decorate + ed
5. divide + ing
6. outrage + ous
7. state + ment
8. evaporate + ing
9. locate + ion
10. breathe + ing

22f. Change *y* to *i* before adding a suffix to a word that ends with a consonant followed by *y*.

EXAMPLES   creamy + ness = creaminess
pretty + er = prettier
lonely + est = loneliest

The *y* remains unchanged if the suffix added begins with an *i*.

EXAMPLE   carry + ing = carrying

The *y* remains unchanged if the suffix is added to a word ending with a vowel followed by *y*.

EXAMPLES   bay + ed = bayed
key + ed = keyed

22g. When adding a suffix to a one-syllable word ending in a single consonant, double the consonant if a single vowel comes before it.

EXAMPLES   beg + ing = begging
               sad + er = sadder
               quiz + ed = quizzed

However, if the one-syllable word ends in two vowels followed by a single consonant, do not double the consonant before adding the ending.

EXAMPLES   sleep + ing = sleeping
               pain + ed = pained

EXERCISE 4. Writing Words with Suffixes. Number your paper 1–10. Write correctly the words formed as follows:

1. say + ing
2. slim + er
3. squeak + ing
4. rainy + est
5. steady + ness
6. beat + ing
7. rely + ing
8. easy + ly
9. chop + ed
10. step + ing

THE PLURALS OF NOUNS

There are several helpful rules for the formation of plurals. Most nouns follow these rules, but there are exceptions. In addition, some nouns form irregular plurals. To most words you can simply add -s or -es to form the plural, but the plural of *foot* is *feet,* and the plural of *sheep* is *sheep*.

22h. Observe the rules for spelling the plurals of nouns.

(1) The regular way to form the plural of a noun is to add an -s.

EXAMPLES   snack, snacks   oven, ovens

(2) The plurals of nouns ending in s, x, z, ch, or sh is formed by adding -es.

These words end with sibilant, or hissing, sounds. The *e* adds an extra syllable and makes the plural pronounceable.

MECHANICS

EXAMPLES   mass, masses   batch, batches
                suffix, suffixes   dash, dashes
                buzz, buzzes

EXERCISE 5. Writing the Plurals of Nouns. Number your paper 1–10. Write the plural of each of the following nouns after the proper number.

EXAMPLE   1. box
             1. *boxes*

1. tax	4. lens	7. loss	9. waltz
2. dish	5. prefix	8. peach	10. radish
3. address	6. branch		

(3) Nouns that end with a consonant followed by *y* form the plural by changing the *y* to *i* and adding *-es*.

EXAMPLES   nursery, nurseries   puppy, puppies

(4) Nouns ending with a vowel followed by *y* form the plural by adding *-s*.

EXAMPLES   boy, boys   turkey, turkeys

(5) Nouns that end with a vowel followed by *o* form the plural by adding *-s*.

EXAMPLES   rodeo, rodeos   patio, patios

(6) Nouns ending with a consonant followed by *o* form the plural by adding *-es*.

EXAMPLES   tomato, tomatoes   echo, echoes

EXCEPTIONS   auto, autos   Eskimo, Eskimos

A number of nouns that are connected with music end in *o*. Most of these form the plural simply by adding *-s*. The rules given above are not always true for these words.

EXAMPLES   piano, pianos   trio, trios
soprano, sopranos   stereo, stereos

EXERCISE 6. Writing the Plurals of Nouns. Number your paper 1–10. Write the plural of each of the following nouns.

1. cargo	4. laundry	7. emergency	9. radio
2. apology	5. piano	8. chimney	10. studio
3. valley	6. potato		

(7) The plurals of a few nouns are formed in irregular ways.

EXAMPLES   woman, women   goose, geese
mouse, mice

(8) Some nouns are the same in both the singular and the plural.

EXAMPLES   salmon, Sioux, deer, fowl

EXERCISE 7. Writing the Plurals of Nouns. Number your paper 1–10. Using a dictionary, find the plural of each of the following nouns. Write each plural after the proper number.

1. moose	4. sheep	7. tooth	9. trout
2. ox	5. radius	8. child	10. gentleman
3. mouse	6. Sioux		

WORDS OFTEN CONFUSED

A number of sets of English words sound alike or similar, yet are spelled differently. For example, *coarse* and *course* have quite different meanings, yet they sound the same. (They are homonyms.) Other pairs of words, such as *quiet* and *quite,* can be confused if they are not pronounced carefully. Study the sets of words that follow, being sure to connect each word with its correct meaning, spelling, and pronunciation.

MECHANICS

already	*at an earlier time* The show had *already* begun.
all ready	*all prepared* The floats were *all ready* for the parade.
altar	*a table or stand used for religious ceremonies* On the *altar* stood a beautifully carved cross.
alter	*to change* You need to *alter* the length of the skirt.
altogether	*entirely* There is *altogether* too much chatting in this study hall.
all together	*everyone in the same place* The family is *all together* at the table.
brake	*a device to stop a machine* The right *brake* on the Dodge is squeaking.
break	*to fracture; to shatter* The whistle from the factory would *break* the stillness every day at noon.

EXERCISE 8. Choosing Spelling Words to Complete Sentences Correctly. Number your paper 1–5. Write the word from the pair in parentheses that will make the sentence correct.

EXAMPLE 1. The architect agreed to (altar, alter) the design.
1. *alter*

1. You didn't (brake, break) the platter, did you?
2. There were huge bouquets on either side of the (altar, alter).
3. Christmas decorations are (all ready, already) up downtown.
4. The family will be (all together, altogether) on the holiday.
5. Don't forget to release the emergency (brake, break).

capital	*a city, the location of a government* Isn't Juneau the *capital* of Alaska?
capitol	*the building in which a legislative body meets* (capitalized when referring to official building of U.S. Congress) Our class trip included a tour of the state *capitol* during a legislative meeting.
cloths	*pieces of cloth* Old flannel shirts make good *cloths* for dusting.
clothes	*wearing apparel* Denise wears *clothes* that are brightly colored.
coarse	*rough, crude, not fine or smooth* The *coarse* salt can be used to help melt snow on the roadways.
course	*path of action; series of studies;* also used in the expression *of course* The counselor suggested several *courses* for us to take. I cannot, *of course*, speak for anyone but myself. The doctors simply had to let the disease run its *course*.
desert [des′ert]	*a dry, sandy region; a wilderness* Plants and animals that live in the *desert* can survive on little water.
desert [de·sert′]	*to abandon, to leave without permission* Although the ship was sinking, the loyal crew would not *desert* the captain.
dessert [des·sert′]	*the final course of a meal* *Dessert* was his favorite part of the meal.

MECHANICS

EXERCISE 9. Choosing Spelling Words to Complete Sentences Correctly. Number your paper 1–5. Write the word from the pair in parentheses that will make the sentence correct.

1. The (desert, dessert) begins to grow cold before the sun sets.
2. His (clothes, cloths) had been neatly folded and packed in his suitcase.
3. The sailor set a (coarse, course) for the port of Pango Pango.
4. When was the (capital, Capitol) built, and how long has Congress been meeting there?
5. To lose weight, you might try skipping (desert, dessert) for a month.

hear	*to receive sound through the ears* If you want your audience to *hear* you, you must speak louder.
here	*in this place* I have the answer right *here* in this sealed envelope.
its	*a personal pronoun showing possession* It has often been said that you cannot judge a book by *its* cover.
it's	*contraction of it is or it has* *It's* beautiful out today! *It's* never been proven.
lead [lēd]	[present tense] *to go first, to be a leader* They let the Indian guide *lead* them through the twisting, dark paths in the forest.
led	[past tense of *lead*] *went first* The guide *led* them for the entire week.
lead [lĕd]	*a heavy metal* *Lead* is no longer used in household paints.

loose	*to free; free; not tight* Someone had turned the big cats *loose*. A *loose* wheel on a bike is dangerous.
lose	*to suffer loss* The loud noise from the hallway made me *lose* my concentration.

EXERCISE 10. Choosing Spelling Words to Complete Sentences. Number your paper 1–5. Write the word (or words) in parentheses that will make the sentence correct.

1. We could (hear, here) the clank-clanking of the heavy (lead, led) chains.
2. Charlie turned the mustang (loose, lose) because he felt it should run free.
3. (Its, It's) a fine night for sleeping!
4. (Hear, Here) is the spot where we lost their trail.
5. The dog will surely (loose, lose) (its, it's) way on the long journey.

passed	*[past tense of pass] went by* Finally we *passed* the truck that was poking along the highway.
past	*that which has gone by; beyond; by* We can learn from what has happened in the *past*. The band marched *past* the school.
peace	*a condition of quiet, calm order; freedom from violence* Having done what she set out to do, Nel felt at *peace* with herself.

MECHANICS

piece   *a part of something*
What a satisfaction there is in fitting in that last *piece* of a jigsaw puzzle!

---

plain   *simple, uncomplicated; not decorated; a flat area of land*
The directions that came with the invitation were *plain* and clear.
The wheat fields stretched across the *plain* as far as the eye could see.

plane   *a tool; an airplane; a flat surface*
Wood shavings curled from the *plane* to the workshop floor.
The *plane's* motor droned overhead.
You will learn a great deal about triangles when you study *plane* geometry.

---

principal   *the head of a school; main or most important*
The middle-school *principal* visited the high school.
The committee's *principal* task is preserving the park.

principle   *a rule of conduct; a general truth or rule*
Freedom of speech is one of the *principles* upon which democracy is founded.

EXERCISE 11. Choosing Spelling Words to Complete Sentences. Number your paper 1–5. Write the word of the two in parentheses that will make the sentence correct.

1. The (plain, plane) coat appeals to me more than the fancy one.
2. The golden rule is a good (principal, principle) to live by.
3. The (passed, past) two weeks have seemed like a dream.
4. One puzzle (peace, piece) was missing.

5. She used a (plain, plane) to smooth the rough edge of the door.

---

stationary   *in a fixed position; not movable*
The posts to hold the volleyball net had been made *stationary* with concrete.

stationery   *paper for writing letters*
The *stationery* he ordered had a design of shooting stars across the top border.

---

their   possessive form of *they*
The natives stood motionless; *their* intentions were not obvious.

there   *a place;* also used to begin a sentence
I'm sure I put the hamper down *there;* someone must have moved it.
There are more than a million volumes in that library.

they're   contraction of *they are*
They're right behind you.

---

threw   [past tense of *throw*]
Zeke *threw* the ball to the first baseman.

through   a preposition
You must step *through* the metal detector before boarding your plane.

EXERCISE 12. Using Spelling Words to Complete Sentences Correctly.   Number your paper 1–5. Write the word (or words) from the parentheses that will make the sentence correct.

1. The final event, the 100-yard dash, will begin over (their, there, they're).

2. The girls (threw, through) everything into (their, there, they're) lockers and hurried to class.
3. Earth was once thought to be (stationary, stationery) in space.
4. (Threw, Through) one of the doors would bound a fierce tiger; (threw, through) the other would emerge a beautiful woman.
5. Do you think (their, there, they're) not coming?

to	a preposition; also sometimes used to introduce a verb We are going *to* Utah *to* visit relatives.
too	*also; more than enough* Am I invited *too*? You are *too* kind!
two	a number There are *two* apples left in the refrigerator.
weak	*feeble; not strong* Gordon began to walk several miles each day in order to strengthen his *weak* heart muscles.
week	*seven days* The club holds meetings once a *week*.
who's	contraction of *who is* or *who has* *Who's* wearing a watch?
whose	possessive form of *who* I know *whose* backpack that is.
your	possessive form of *you* Rest *your* eyes occasionally when reading at night.
you're	contraction of *you are* *You're* a talented person.

EXERCISE 13. Choosing Spelling Words to Complete Sentences Correctly. Number your paper 1–5. Write the word (or words) from the parentheses that will make the sentence correct.

1. (Who's, Whose) books and papers are those on the dining room table?
2. Walking (to, too, two) the store, he began to feel (weak, week).
3. (Your, You're) Dad is attending the concert (to, too, two), isn't he?
4. It took over a (weak, week) to complete the project in health class.
5. If (your, you're) not making that noise, (who's, whose) doing it?

REVIEW EXERCISE. Choosing Spelling Words to Complete Sentences Correctly. Number your paper 1–10. After each number, write the word (or words) from the parentheses that will make each sentence correct.

1. Which of these (to, too, two) boxes of (stationary, stationery) do you like better?
2. Every street in the (capital, capitol) was crowded with cheering, dancing people after the announcement of the (peace, piece) treaty.
3. The (principal, principle) raised his arms for silence, and the students grew quiet to (hear, here) what he would say.
4. It will be difficult to (altar, alter) that burlap curtain because the fabric is so (coarse, course).
5. Mom said (its, it's) (all together, altogether) too quiet with the boys gone away to camp.
6. The man who'd been hired to (lead, led) the wagon train planned to rob its people and (desert, dessert) them.
7. Riding in a red and gold 1904 Oldsmobile, the mayor (lead, led) the parade.
8. The coach did not need to give a pep talk; the players were (all ready, already) for the big game.

MECHANICS

9. (Your, You're) dusting (clothes, cloths) are on the counter.
10. The (to, too, two) friends (passed, past) the time pleasantly reading (there, their, they're) books under a shade tree.

COMMONLY MISSPELLED WORDS

Some words that cause spelling problems need to be memorized. The list of fifty "demons" below contains words that you should be able to spell automatically, without pause. Note the letters that are underlined. These letters are the ones that students most often miss when attempting to spell each word correctly.

Fifty Spelling Demons

ache	cough	guess	ready	though
again	could	half	said	through
always	country	hour	says	tired
answer	doctor	instead	seems	tonight
blue	does	knew	shoes	trouble
built	don't	know	since	wear
busy	early	laid	straight	where
buy	easy	minute	sugar	women
can't	every	often	sure	won't
color	friend	once	tear	write

One Hundred Spelling Words

The list that follows includes words that sixth-graders should know. They are grouped by tens so that you may study them group by group. Again, the underlining points out places in the words that give students the most trouble.

absence	apology	ballad
achieve	arithmetic	benefit
adjective	assignment	brief
advertisement		brilliant
against	autobiography	career
aisles	average	careless
angle	bacteria	ceased

MECHANICS

century
choice
communicate
conservation
constitution
courteous
criticism
curiosity
decimal
delicate

disguise
divide
early
ecology
eighth
environment
equipment
exact
excellent
experience

explanation
fantasy
faucet
fiction
fourth
gasoline
gene

genuine
grammar
height

heir
humorous
imitation
interview
legislature
liter
magazine
medicine
message
musician

myth
nuclear
occurrence
ounce
passage
pesticide
physical
pieces
poisonous
popularity

population
practice
preferred

prejudice
pyramid
recipe
remainder
rescue
resources
review

rumor
safe
seize
separate
similar
solar
solemn
species
surface
temporary

theme
tragedy
treasure
trial
tropical
vegetable
veil
weapon
wonder
wrestle

MECHANICS

PART FOUR

RESOURCES FOR WRITING AND STUDYING

CHAPTER 23

Using the Library

A GUIDE TO RESOURCES IN A LIBRARY

The library, or media center, is a rich collection of human knowledge. It stores much information and offers many services to help you learn about many subjects. If you know how to use it, the library can be a source of pleasure—in reading and in learning—throughout your life.

CONTENTS OF THE LIBRARY

The stories, facts, and ideas you can find in the library are stored in many forms: books, magazines, newspapers, pamphlets, tapes, records, films, and computers. Deciding which of these library resources to use will depend on the kind of information you are looking for.

Books

23a. Books are divided into two general categories: fiction and nonfiction.

A fiction book tells one long story (a novel) or several shorter stories (a collection of short stories). Each story is drawn from the author's imagination. Some stories may be based on a real event or on the life of a real person, but they are still fiction. That is, the author has invented part of the action—or a character or two—to make a good story. You will find fiction books placed together in their own special section of the library.

On the main bookshelves of the library are many books of nonfiction. Nonfiction books contain factual information about real people, events, and things. They also may include an author's opinion about something that happened or about the way people think and feel.

All of the books in the library's *reference section*, for example, are nonfiction books. They include general works of factual information such as encyclopedias, atlases, and almanacs. This reference section will also have books that lead you to other forms of information, such as the *Readers' Guide to Periodical Literature*.

Another special section of the library contains the nonfiction books called *biographies*. These books describe the life of one real person (individual biography) or the lives of several persons (collective biography). If the author is writing about his or her own life, the book is an *autobiography*.

Magazines, Newspapers, and Pamphlets

23b. Magazines, newspapers, and pamphlets contain information on recent events, discoveries, and inventions.

Magazines and newspapers are called *periodicals* because they are published at regular periods, or certain times, during each year. The issues may appear every day, once a week, once a month, four times a year, or at other regular periods. Each issue presents new information about recent events. It may also present new ideas about people, places, and things of the past.

Some magazines are general works: each issue covers many different subjects. Other magazines deal with just one subject, such as antiques, cooking, or photography. Newspapers give you the latest information on events in your community and state, as well as in the nation and the world.

Because pamphlets are not published at regular times, they are not periodicals. However, they are published frequently. The United States government alone publishes hundreds of pamphlets every year. Your local government, many national associations, businesses, and colleges also publish pamphlets. These brief pieces of printed material can give you up-to-date information on a wide variety of subjects, from growing tomatoes to planning a career in dentistry.

Each of these three kinds of printed materials—magazines, newspapers, and pamphlets—is kept in its own special section of the library.

Tapes, Records, and Films

Many libraries also store certain *nonprint* materials. These may include audiotapes, videotapes, record albums, film slides, and filmstrips (with and without sound tracks). Nonprint materials may contain stories, favorite music, or factual information on certain subjects. They, too, are placed in special sections of the library.

EXERCISE 1. Distinguishing Kinds of Library Information.
Number your paper 1–10. After the numbers, write whether each of the following items is a *fiction book,* a *nonfiction book,* a *periodical,* a *pamphlet,* or *nonprint* material.

EXAMPLE 1. A brief description of basic facts about domes, published by an architects' association
　　　　　1. *pamphlet*

1. An encyclopedia of science
2. A collection of stories by Edgar Allan Poe
3. Your local newspaper
4. An atlas of North America
5. *Newsweek*

6. The novel *Charlotte's Web*
7. A biography of Theodore Roosevelt
8. A list of courses in electronics, printed by a college
9. The *World Almanac and Book of Facts*
10. Songs sung by Marian Anderson

HELP FROM THE LIBRARIAN

When you need to find information, do not be afraid to ask the librarian for help. The librarian can help you locate the circulation desk, the card catalog, the reference section, and other sections of the library.

Remember that there is more than one library you can use. Besides your school library, you can use the library in your community. This library is likely to be larger than your school library. You will be able to find materials there that are not available at school.

USING THE CARD CATALOG

The easiest way to find specific books in the library is to look them up first in the card catalog. The card catalog is a cabinet of small drawers. The drawers hold file cards for every book in the library.

Cards in the catalog drawers are arranged alphabetically according to the words in the top line of information in the center of each card. Labels on the drawers show what part of the alphabet they cover. The first drawer may cover A—AN, the second AO—AZ, the third B—BIO, and so on. (For a review of alphabetical order, see pages 430–31.)

The Kinds of Catalog Cards

23c. The card catalog lists books by title, author, and subject.

The card catalog contains more than one card for every book. For each fiction book it has at least two cards: a *title card* and an *author card*. For each nonfiction book it has at least three cards: a title card, an author card, and a *subject card*. You may find several subject cards for one book. If a book has more than one author, you will find a separate author card for each one of the authors.

The Title Card

If you know a book's title, look for its title card. The top line of information on this card will be the exact title of the book. The card will be placed alphabetically in the drawers according to the first word of the title, unless the first word is *a, an,* or *the.* In that case it will be filed according to the title's second word. For example, *The Swiss Family Robinson* will be listed under *S.*

The Author Card

If you want to find a book by a particular author, look for the author card. On this card the top line of information will be the author's name, with the last name first. For example, Louisa May Alcott will be placed alphabetically under "Alcott, Louisa May." A book that has two or more authors will have an author card for each author.

The Subject Card

Sometimes you may not have a particular book or author in mind. Instead, you may want to find all the books you can on a certain subject. The subject cards in the card catalog can be very helpful on these occasions.

Every nonfiction book in the library has at least one subject card. The subject heading is the first line of information on this card. It will be placed alphabetically according to the heading's first word. Below the subject heading you will find the author's name and the title of a particular book on that subject.

Under one subject heading you are likely to see subject cards for several books. You also may find that a very general subject, such as geography, is further divided with cards for smaller subject categories. Geography, for example, may be divided into "Geography—Asia," "Geography—Europe," "Geography —U.S.," and so on.

---

j612.399
Asi

How did we find out about vitamins?

Asimov, Isaac
How did we find out about vitamins? Illustrated by David Wool; Walker & Co., 1974.
64p.

Title Card

---

j612.399
Asi

Asimov, Isaac
How did we find out about vitamins? Illustrated by David Wool; Walker & Co., 1974.
64p.

1. Vitamins   2. Deficiency Diseases
1. Wool, David, illus.   II. Title

Author Card

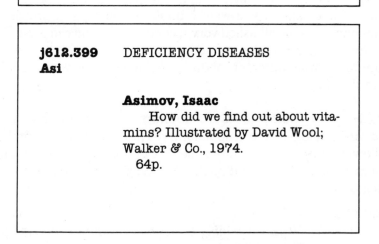

j612.399
Asi   VITAMINS

Asimov, Isaac
How did we find out about vitamins? Illustrated by David Wool;
Walker & Co., 1974.
64p.

j612.399
Asi   DEFICIENCY DISEASES

Asimov, Isaac
How did we find out about vitamins? Illustrated by David Wool;
Walker & Co., 1974.
64p.

Subject Cards

The Call Number

Perhaps the most important information on a nonfiction book's
catalog cards is the *call number*. It is typed or written in the *upper
left corner* of each card for a nonfiction book. This number tells
you exactly where the book is located—in a special section or on
the library's main shelves. A letter with a call number, such as
J523, usually means the book is in a special section. (*J* usually
stands for "juvenile".)

Be sure to write down the call number when you find cards for a nonfiction book that interests you. You will find the same number marked on the spine of the book.

Other Card Information

On every book's catalog cards you will find more information than just the title, the author, and—for a nonfiction book—the call number and subject heading. The cards also tell you the publisher, the year the book was published, how many pages it has, and whether or not it is illustrated.

Depending on your interest in the book, all of this information can be important. If you want a book on robots, you probably want one that was published very recently. Then you can expect it to have the latest information on these modern machines. If you want to see what different robots look like, then you want a book with illustrations.

EXERCISE 2. **Using the Card Catalog.** For this exercise, use the card catalog in your school library. Find a card on each of the following subjects. Then, after the proper number, write the call number, title, author, and publication year of the book listed on each card.

EXAMPLE   1. Swimming
            1. *797.2, Swimming Basics by C. Rob Orr and Jane B. Tyler, 1980*

1. Bicycles
2. Shirley Chisholm
3. The moon
4. Cartooning
5. Whales
6. Greek mythology
7. Humorous poetry
8. Pocahontas
9. Personality
10. Citizenship

The Dewey Decimal System

23d. The Dewey decimal system gives nonfiction books their call numbers.

The numbering system used for nonfiction books is named after Melvil Dewey, the American librarian who developed it. The Dewey decimal system assigns call numbers to nonfiction books according to their subjects. Thus, you will find books with factual information on similar subjects placed near each other on the library shelves.

The first step in assigning numbers to books is to place a book in one of ten major subject categories. Each of the ten categories has its own range of numbers as follows:

000–099   General Works (encyclopedias and other reference materials) [*Some libraries use an* **R** *with the call number on a reference book.*]
100–199   Philosophy (ideas about the meaning of life, psychology)
200–299   Religion (world religions, mythology)
300–399   Social Sciences (government, law, business, education)
400–499   Language (dictionaries, grammar books)
500–599   Science (mathematics, chemistry, plants, animals)
600–699   Technology (how-to books, applied sciences such as engineering and aviation)
700–799   Arts and Recreation (music, art, sports, hobbies)
800–899   Literature (poems, plays, essays)
900–999   History (includes geography, travel, and biography)

All of the books placed in one of these ten categories will be in the same section of the library. For instance, among books whose call numbers are in the range of 600–699, you may find *Wildland Fire Fighting* by Margaret Poynter.

The number range for each of the major subjects is further divided into tens and then ones. *Wildland Fire Fighting*, for example, is in the smaller subject category and number range of 630–639, agriculture. Those books with the number 634 have to do with orchards, fruits, nuts, or forestry. By using decimals, the numbers make even smaller subject categories. The exact call number for Margaret Poynter's book is 634.9, under forestry.

Most libraries place biographies in a separate section of the library. The call numbers of these books begin with a *B* or the number *92.* Under the *B* or *92,* you will see the initial of the last name of the person being written about. (In some libraries the last name is spelled out.) For example, the call number of *Walt Disney: Master of Make-Believe* by Elizabeth Rider Montgomery will be listed in this way:

B (or **92**)
D (or **Disney**)

Biographies are placed on the shelves alphabetically according to the last name of the person written about (*Disney*, for instance). If you see more than one book about the same person, then look for the author's name in alphabetical order.

EXERCISE 3. Classifying Nonfiction Books. Write the titles and call numbers of the books you found for Exercise 2. Then for each one, write the name of the major subject category of the Dewey decimal system the book was placed in according to its call number. Use the chart on page 417.

EXAMPLE   1. *Swimming Basics*, 797.2
             Arts and recreation

The Fiction Section

23e. Fiction books are placed in alphabetical order according to the author's last name.

If you look up a fiction book in the card catalog, you will see that in place of a call number there is just the letter *F* or nothing at all. Fiction books are not arranged by subject. Instead, they are arranged alphabetically by the author's last name. If the library has several books by the same author, those are further arranged alphabetically by the first word of the title (not counting *a, an,* or *the*).

For example, suppose you want to find *Sing Down the Moon* by Scott O'Dell. First locate the fiction section of the library. Then look for the shelf that holds fiction books by authors whose last names begin with *O*. You will soon find O'Dell. If you see more than one book by the author, then look at the titles. Before coming to *Sing Down the Moon,* you may find *The Black Pearl* (placed under *B,* not *T*), *The Feathered Serpent* (placed under *F,* not *T*), *Island of the Blue Dolphins*, and *Sara Bishop*.

☞ NOTE   Books by authors whose last names begin with *Mc* are alphabetized as though the name were spelled *Mac*. A last name that begins with *St.* is alphabetized as though it were spelled out, *Saint*.

EXERCISE 4. **Arranging Books of Fiction.**   Number your paper 1–10. After the numbers, write the authors and titles of the following books in the order in which you would find them on the fiction shelves. Remember that the alphabetical order is first for authors' names. The first answer is given as an example.

EXAMPLE   1. *Lewis Carroll, Through the Looking Glass*

Boy with a Pack by Stephen W. Meader
A Wrinkle in Time by Madeleine L'Engle
Mara, Daughter of the Nile by Eloise Jarvis McGraw
Through the Looking Glass by Lewis Carroll
Shadow of a Bull by Maia Wojciechowska
Robinson Crusoe by Daniel Defoe
Horsecatcher by Mari Sandoz
Twenty Thousand Leagues Under the Sea by Jules Verne
The Ghost Belonged to Me by Richard Peck
A Wind in the Door by Madeleine L'Engle

USING REFERENCE WORKS

Reference works include books, magazines, newspapers, pamphlets, and other forms of information on a wide variety of subjects. Since these materials contain much helpful information, they need to be available to library users at all times. For that reason you may use them only while you are in the library.

Encyclopedias

23f. An encyclopedia is a collection of articles on many different subjects.

Encyclopedias contain articles written by experts that cover almost every subject. An article may also refer you to other articles and to other nonfiction books that deal with the subject.

You may find more than one encyclopedia in the library's reference section. The following four are well known and are available in many libraries.

Britannica Junior Encyclopedia
Collier's Encyclopedia
Compton's Encyclopedia
World Book Encyclopedia

Like most encyclopedias, each of these consists of many volumes. The articles in them are arranged alphabetically by subject title.

To find information on a particular subject, first locate the correct volume of the encyclopedia. On the spine of every volume will be printed the letter or letters of the alphabet covered in that book. The subject of *meteors,* for instance, would be found in a volume marked *M.*

When looking in a specific volume, use the *guide words* at the top of the pages to follow the alphabetical order. You use them as you use the guide words in a dictionary (see page 431). An article on meteors, for example, might be found between *medicine* and *Minnesota.*

If you do not find articles on your subject right away, think about similar subject titles you might look up. Also think about a larger subject that includes the one you are interested in. For example, information on making a *videotape* recording might be found in an article on *tape recorders.*

Use an encyclopedia's index to make sure that you have found all the information the encyclopedia has on your subject. The index may be the encyclopedia's first volume (as in *Britannica Junior*). It may be the last volume (as in *World Book*), or it may be at the end of each volume (as in *Compton's*). Every encyclopedia also has an explanation of how to use its index. This section usually appears at the beginning of the index. Subject titles in the index are listed alphabetically. For each subject the index will tell you the volume and page number of related articles and illustrations.

EXERCISE 5. Using Encyclopedias.   Use an encyclopedia to look up four of the following topics. On your paper, write the name of the encyclopedia you are using. Then write the volume number (or letter) and the number of the page on which you found the information. Take brief notes on two of the four topics. Be prepared to report on these two in class.

EXAMPLE   1. The first ballet
  1. *World Book Encyclopedia, volume 2, page 36h*
     Performed in 1581 for French Queen Catherine and guests at a royal wedding. Told myth of Circe in a spectacular $5\frac{1}{2}$-hour "entertainment" of music and dance.

1. The gold rush
2. Where ozone is found
3. What plastics are made of
4. The origin of the boomerang
5. Why we dream when we sleep
6. Who invented the microscope
7. The multiple careers of Clara Barton
8. When and where cats were first pets

Atlases

Atlases are reference books that contain detailed maps of the world, its countries, and its large cities. Most atlases also give you information about the climate, soils, industries, and natural resources of the world and individual nations. You can also learn the location of cities and towns, lakes, mountains, and so on. The following atlases are found in many libraries.

Goode's World Atlas
Hammond Ambassador World Atlas
National Geographic Atlas of the World
New York Times Atlas of the World

Become familiar with at least one atlas. It will be a valuable reference for you in studying history and geography.

Almanacs

An almanac is a reference book that contains many lists of facts. Some examples are a list of minerals mined last year in the United States, a list of current and past winners of the Olympic Games, and lists of noted authors, scientists, and political leaders. Because almanacs are published every year, they contain up-to-date information. They also present many historical facts. For example, an almanac may show you the current flags of nations and tell you about the history of the United States flag as well.

Two almanacs you are likely to find are the *Information Please Almanac* and the *World Almanac and Book of Facts*. The best way to find information in an almanac is to use its index. Look for it at the front of the *World Almanac* and at the back of *Information Please*.

Biographical Dictionaries

A biographical dictionary gives you important facts about the lives of famous persons. Some reference books in this category are *Twentieth Century Authors, Webster's Biographical Dictionary, Who's Who,* and *Who's Who in America.*

EXERCISE 6. Using Atlases, Almanacs, and Biographical Dictionaries. Number your paper 1–10. After the numbers, write down where you would look first—in an *atlas,* an *almanac,* or a *biographical dictionary*—for information on the following items.

EXAMPLE   1. The names of countries bordering Turkey
          1. *atlas*

1. The place and date of birth of airplane pilot Amelia Earhart
2. The amount of U.S. silver mined in 1915
3. The continent on which Khartoum is located
4. The 1984 National Spelling Bee champion
5. The flow of winds across the Pacific Ocean
6. The books written by James Thurber
7. The average television viewing time in the U.S.
8. The location of the desert in Chile
9. The school where George Washington Carver taught
10. The winner of the Nobel Prize for Peace in 1979

The *Readers' Guide*

23g. The subjects and authors of magazine articles are listed in the *Readers' Guide to Periodical Literature.*

To find magazine articles on a certain subject, look in the library's reference section for the *Readers' Guide to Periodical Literature.* It lists the articles you can find in each issue of more than one hundred magazines. You will see that the *Readers' Guide* consists of several volumes. The paperbacks cover the most recent magazine articles. Each large hardcover volume contains all the paperbound books published in a year's time (or in two years' time for articles appearing before 1965).

In all volumes of the *Readers' Guide,* the magazine articles are arranged alphabetically by subject and by author. Each subject or author entry gives the complete title of the magazine article and information about where to find it. Sometimes a brief note about the article is added after the title.

The following sample from the *Readers' Guide* shows the arrangement of information in more detail. Suppose you are writing a report on icebergs and want to find recent articles on the subject. An entry in the sample below will lead you to an article called "Iceberg Patrol" in the magazine *National Geographic World*. It appears in volume 102 on pages 20–23 ("102:20–3") of an issue published for February 1984 ("F '84"). The entry also tells you the article is illustrated ("il").

subject entry ——— | Ice on rivers, lakes, etc. |
Going with the floe [towboats and barges trapped by
author of article ——— ice on the Mississippi] S. Tifft. il *Time* 123:19 Ja
division of main
subject
23 '84
| Control |
In Buffalo, trying to bust the boom [dealing with Lake
magazine's name ——— Erie ice] *Sci News* 125:73 F 4 '84
Ice palaces
article title ——— | Gone with the thaw. | il *House Gard* 156:100-3 Ja '84
Ice removal *See* Snow and ice removal
Ice skating *See* Skating
Ice skating rinks *See* Skating rinks
Icebergs
page numbers and ——— Iceberg Patrol. il *Natl Geogr World* 102:20-3 F '84
issue date
Icebreakers *See* Ice breaking vessels
Iceland
| See also |
cross reference ——— Law—Iceland
ICI *See* Imperial Chemical Industries plc
author entry ——— | Icke, Vincent |
A numerical astrophysical observatory. *Phys Today* 37:9
F '84

The *Readers' Guide* uses many abbreviations to save space. If you do not recognize the shortened name of a magazine, find the list of abbreviations for magazines at the front of the book. Also at the front of the book will be the list of other abbreviations used. The following abbreviations are examples:

ann	annual	**por**	portrait
ed	edition or editor	**rev**	revised
jt auth	joint author	**w**	weekly

EXERCISE 7. Using the *Readers' Guide*. Choose five of the following subjects. Find a *Readers' Guide* entry for one magazine article on each of the five subjects. Write the entry on your paper. Then briefly explain the information given in that entry.

EXAMPLE   1. Elephants
              1. *Around the Mall and beyond [baby elephant Jayathu at the National Zoo]. E. Park. il* Smithsonian *15:22+ S '84.*
               "Around the Mall and Beyond" is about a baby elephant. It is written by E. Park and appears in the September 1984 issue of Smithsonian *(volume 15). The article begins on page 22 and continues on later pages of the issue ["+"].*

1. Skyscrapers
2. Home repair
3. X-rays
4. Lightning
5. Puerto Rico
6. Telephones
7. Sports safety
8. Children's plays
9. U.S. Senators
10. The sun

The Vertical File

The vertical file provides up-to-the-minute information. It is a special filing cabinet in the library that contains hundreds of file folders. The folders hold pamphlets, booklets, and sometimes newspaper clippings. Each folder contains information about a particular subject. It is placed alphabetically according to the subject title.

Microfilm and Microfiche

A library's collection of magazines, newspapers, and government documents may be much too large to store on regular library shelves. For this reason, many libraries use special reducing photography to copy these materials. Hundreds of pages can then fit on a small roll of film—*microfilm*—or a small film sheet —*microfiche.*

Rolls of microfilm are stored in small, labeled boxes. The microfiche are placed in labeled paper covers.

When the pages of books and periodicals are photographically reduced on microfilm or microfiche, they are, of course, too tiny to read just by looking at them. However, a library that uses this storage method will also have microfilm or microfiche *projectors.*

These machines enlarge the page images back to a readable size. You can read as many pages as you need to by moving the film roll up and down or the film sheet from side to side.

Computers

A number of libraries now keep the card catalog and lists of periodicals on a computer. When using a computerized system, you simply type into the computer what information you need. If you are interested in fossils, for example, you might type "subject: fossils." The computer will search its records for the titles and locations of books and periodicals on your subject. It will then display what it finds on the computer screen.

In some libraries you may be able to get a printed copy (called a printout) of the displayed information. If not, you can take notes from what appears on the screen. Your librarian can tell you what is stored on the computer and how to use it.

REVIEW EXERCISE. Using the Library.   Answer the following questions. If you need to, you may refer to information in this chapter.

EXAMPLE   1. What kind of reference book would you use to find the names of winners of the Academy Awards in 1983?
         1. *almanac*

1. Where can you quickly find the call number of a book?
2. In which Dewey subject category would you find a book about raising vegetables? (Refer to page 417.)
3. What are the three kinds of catalog cards for a nonfiction book?
4. What is nonfiction?
5. Which of these three fiction books would come first on the library shelves?
    a. *The Borrowers* by Mary Norton
    b. *M. C. Higgins, the Great* by Virginia Hamilton
    c. *The Magicians of Caprona* by Diana Wynne Jones

6. What are the two kinds of catalog cards for a fiction book?
7. What kind of reference book would you go to first for an overview of a new subject you are studying?
8. What kind of nonfiction book would be marked with a *B* on its spine?
9. What are two kinds of reference books you could use to find the birthplace of Elizabeth Blackwell, the first woman doctor?
10. What are two kinds of reference books you could use to locate the mountains of New York?
11. What are two more examples (besides Academy Award winners) of the kinds of information you can find in an almanac?
12. If you did not find a separate article in the encyclopedia on the World Series, what larger subject could you look up?
13. What part of an encyclopedia can help you find all the articles related to a particular subject?
14. In which reference book would you find the following entry?

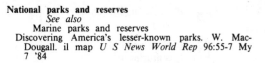

15. What do the numbers "96:55–7" in the above entry tell you?
16. What does the abbreviation *il* stand for in the above entry?
17. What is kept in the library's vertical file?
18. What kinds of information are stored on microfilm or microfiche?
19. Why do libraries use microfilm or microfiche?
20. What kind of information can you get by using a library's computer?

CHAPTER 24

Using the Dictionary

A GUIDE TO INFORMATION
IN A DICTIONARY

Hh	⊟	Early Phoenician (late 2nd millenium B.C.)	⊟ Early Latin (7th century B.C.)

A dictionary is a treasury of words and information about words. You will find in it the meanings of a word and more. A dictionary will show you how to say a word, how to spell it, and how to use it in speaking and writing.

This chapter is a general guide to using any dictionary. Also read the instructions at the front of your own dictionary. The following sample is a section of a dictionary page. The notes in red tell you the kinds of information you will find in all dictionaries. Refer to this example often as you work through the chapter.

guide word ——————

chilly

spelling of
adjective forms ——————

chill·y [chil′ē] *adj.* **chill·i·er, chill·i·est** 1 Causing coldness or chill: a *chilly* rain. 2 Feeling cold: I am *chilly*. 3 Not friendly or warm: a *chilly* greet-

related word ——————
entry word ——————

ing. —**chill′i·ness** *n.*

chi·mae·ra [kə·mir′ə *or* kī·mir′ə] *n.* Another spell-ing of CHIMERA.

spelling of
verb forms ——————

chime [chīm] *n., v.* **chimed, chim·ing** 1 *n.* (*often pl.*) A set of bells each of which has a different pitch. 2 *n.* The sounds or music produced by chimes. 3 *v.* To sound or ring: The bells *chimed* all over

example of
meaning ——————

town. 4 *v.* To indicate (the time of day) by chim-ing: The clock *chimed* three. 5 *n.* A metal tube or set of tubes making bell-like sounds when struck. —**chime in** 1 To interrupt. 2 To agree or be in harmony.

pronunciation ——————

chi·me·ra [kə·mir′ə *or* kī·mir′ə] *n.* 1 (*written* **Chi-mera**) In Greek myths, a fire-breathing monster, part lion, part goat, and part serpent. 2 Any hor-rible idea or fancy. 3 An absurd, impractical, or

part of speech ——————

impossible idea.

chi·mer·i·cal [kə·mer′i·kəl *or* kī·mer′i·kəl] *adj.* 1 Fantastic; imaginary. 2 Wildly impossible.

spelling of
plural ——————

chim·ney [chim′nē] *n., pl.* **chim·neys** 1 A tall, hol-low structure that carries away smoke or fumes, as from fireplaces, stoves, or furnaces. 2 A glass tube for enclosing the flame of a lamp.

two-word entry ——————

chimney sweep A person who makes a living by cleaning away the soot from inside chimneys.

chimney swift A bird that looks like a swallow and often builds its nest in an unused chimney.

note about use
of word ——————

chimp [chimp] *n. informal* A chimpanzee.

chim·pan·zee [chim′pan·zē′ *or* chim·pan′zē] *n.* An ape of Africa

illustration ——————

that lives in trees, has large ears and dark brown hair, and is smaller and more intelligent than the gorilla. ✦ *Chimpan-zee* comes from a native African name.

chin [chin] *n., v.* **chinned, chin-**

numbered
definitions ——————

ning 1 *n.* The part of the face just below the mouth. 2 *v.* To hang by the hands and lift (one-self) until the chin is level with or above the hands.

Chimpanzee

ARRANGEMENT OF A DICTIONARY

The word entries in a dictionary are listed in *alphabetical order*. Each page has *guide words* to help you follow the alphabetical order.

Alphabetical Order

24a. Use the alphabet to find words.

When you use a dictionary, it may help you to think of the alphabet in three parts:

abcde   fghijklmnop   qrstuvwxyz

You can see that these parts do not contain an equal number of letters. However, words beginning with *a* through *e* take up just about the first third of any dictionary. Words that start with *f* through *p* take up the middle third, and *q* through *z* the last third.

If you want to look up the meaning of *feat*, for example, you turn to the middle third of your dictionary. Then look for the section of words that begin with *f*.

At that point you are not through with using the alphabet. All the words beginning with *f* are in alphabetical order according to the second letter of each word, then the third letter, the fourth letter, and so on.

EXERCISE 1. Writing Words in Alphabetical Order.   Number your paper 1–20. After the numbers, write the following words in alphabetical order.

starfish	analyze	conceal	grateful
abundant	volume	lagoon	top
easy	dome	conduct	
ray	bump	note	
gratitude	scheme	inhale	
energy	hearty	lunar	

Phrases

Sometimes two or more words have their own special meaning when they are used together. A few examples are *funny bone, base line,* and *high school.* Such phrases will be listed in alphabetical order as though they were spelled as one word. Words with hyphens in them are also placed alphabetically as though the letters were not separated.

Abbreviations

Dictionaries give the meanings of abbreviations as well as of words and phrases. Many list abbreviations right along with words in the main part of the book. Some place them together in a special section at the back of the book. If the main part of your dictionary includes abbreviations, they are placed alphabetically just as they are spelled. For example, the abbreviation for miles per gallon, *mpg,* follows *movie* because *p* comes after *o.*

EXERCISE 2. Writing Entries in Alphabetical Order. Number your paper 1–10. After the numbers, write the following items in alphabetical order.

Sat.	Sr.
self-respect	safety pin
self-rising flour	safe-deposit box
saddle soap	sec.
St. (for Street)	self-confidence

Guide Words

24b. Use guide words to find the right page.

At the top of each page, in most dictionaries, you will see two words, often in darker type. These words are *guide words.* The one at the left is the same as the first entry that begins on that page. The guide word at the right tells you the last word defined on that page. If the word you want to find comes alphabetically between these two words, you will have the right page.

EXERCISE 3. Using Guide Words. Number your paper 1–5. Look up the following words in your dictionary. For each word, write the guide words from the dictionary page on which you found the word. Also write the number of that page.

EXAMPLE 1. career
      1. *carbon paper, caret, 116*

1. wardrobe   3. legend   5. obvious
2. earnest   4. qualify

INFORMATION IN A DICTIONARY

Whenever you look up a word in a dictionary, you will find a wealth of information to help you understand how the word is used in the English language.

Word Meanings

24c. Find the exact meaning you want.

When disturbed by wind or speeding boats, water moves in *waves*. Does the word mean the same when we coax a baby to *wave* goodbye? What do we mean by a *heat wave*? Like many English words, *wave* has several different meanings. The example shows how one dictionary defines *wave*.

wave [wāv] *v.* **waved, wav·ing,** *n.* **1** *v.* To move or cause to move back and forth or with a fluttering motion. **2** *v.* To wave something, especially the hand, as in giving a signal. **3** *n.* The act of waving. **4** *n.* A disturbance consisting of a peak followed by a dip that travels across the surface of a liquid. **5** *n.* Any energy, as light or sound, that exists in the form of pulses or alternations of one kind or another. **6** *n.* A single such pulse or alternation. **7** *n.* Something that seems to travel or pass like a wave: a *wave* of protest; a tropical heat *wave*. **8** *v.* To form into a series of ridges and dips: to *wave* one's hair. **9** *n.* One of a series of wide curves or ridges in the hair.

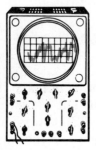

Sound wave from an oboe shown on an oscilloscope

Notice that the different meanings are numbered. Read all of these numbered definitions before deciding which one fits a sentence you have in mind. You might try replacing the word in the sentence with words from the definitions. If the sentence still makes sense, you have found the right meaning. For example, study these sentences:

The sailor *waved* a flag.
The sailor *moved a flag back and forth with a fluttering motion* [from definition 1 in the dictionary sample].

To help you understand different meanings, dictionaries often include a sample phrase or sentence after a numbered definition. The examples given in the following entry show you how you might use the word *creak*.

> **creak** (krēk) *v.i.* **1.** to make a sharp, grating, or squeaking sound: *My new shoes creak when I walk.* **2.** to move with such a sound: *The gate creaked open.* —*v.t.* to cause to creak. —*n.* sharp, grating, or squeaking sound. [Imitative.]

EXERCISE 4. **Finding Word Meanings.** Number your paper 1–10. Each of the following sentences has one word in italics. Look up these words in your dictionary. Write the meaning of the word that best fits the sentence.

EXAMPLE   1. *Lap* this bandage around your leg.
            1. *wrap or wind*

1. We went to the city *park* yesterday.
2. We had to *park* six blocks away.
3. The huge animal reached for a peanut with its *trunk*.
4. Lightning split the *trunk* of that oak.
5. There is poison ivy in the *brush* near the pond.
6. Please clean this *brush* before the paint dries.
7. Dena enjoys reading books about *space* travel.
8. To play this computer game, you use the *space* bar.
9. This *plant* does not require direct sunlight.
10. Computer parts are manufactured in that *plant*.

Synonyms and Antonyms

Words that have almost the same meaning are *synonyms.* Words with opposite meanings are *antonyms.*

You are likely to find synonyms in the numbered definitions for a word. For instance, the words *wet* and *damp* may be used in defining the word *moist*. Many dictionaries also list synonyms for a word separately, at the end of the entry. A short paragraph about the differences among the synonyms may be included. These small sections usually begin with the abbreviation *Syn.* The following example tells you about synonyms for the word *wave*.

> *SYN.*—**wave** is the general word for a curving ridge or swell in the surface of the ocean or other body of water; **ripple** is used of the smallest kind of wave, such as that caused by a breeze ruffling the surface of water; **roller** is applied to any of the large, heavy, swelling waves that roll in to the shore, as during a storm; **breaker** is applied to such a wave when it breaks, or is about to break, into foam upon the shore or upon rocks; **billow** is a somewhat poetic or rhetorical term for a great, heaving ocean wave

An antonym for a word, such as *light* for the word *heavy,* usually follows the abbreviation *Ant.* at the end of the entry. A note after *Ant.* or *Syn.* may also refer you to another entry.

EXERCISE 5. Finding Synonyms. Number your paper 1–5. After the numbers, write the following words. Then write at least one synonym for each word. Use your dictionary.

EXAMPLE 1. boast
           1. *brag*

1. collide   3. hazard   5. throw
2. hardy   4. lovely

Part of Speech

Some words may be used as more than one part of speech. The word *tax*, for instance, is a noun here: The *tax* is 5 percent. It is a verb here: The city will *tax* you for that item. For each meaning of a word, the dictionary will tell you the word's part of speech. The following abbreviations are used:

adj.	adjective	*n.*	noun
adv.	adverb	*prep.*	preposition
conj.	conjunction	*pron.*	pronoun
interj.	interjection	*v.*	verb

Related Forms of a Word

At the end of many dictionary entries, you will find words that are closely related to the entry word. For instance, the adverb *sincerely* might be found at the end of the entry for the adjective *sincere*. Once you know the meaning of the main word, you can easily understand the meaning of the related form.

Spelling

24d. Use your dictionary to check spelling.

A dictionary is the place to check for the correct spelling of a word. You can find the word even if you are not sure how to spell it. For instance, you may have looked for the word *schedule* under *skedule* and had no success. What other letters could make the same sound as *k*? You know from words such as *choir* and *chemistry* that *ch* can have the sound of *k*. Look under *sch* instead of *sk*. You will find *schedule*.

Variant Spellings

Sometimes the dictionary will give you two spellings for a word. You may find, for example, both *adviser, advisor* and *coconut, cocoanut*. The spelling used most often is listed first in the entry. Some dictionaries list the less common spelling at the end of the entry.

Unusual Plurals

For most nouns you form the plural by simply adding *-s* or *-es* to the end of the word. However, some nouns are different. The plural of *tooth,* for example, is *teeth*. When the plural spelling of a word is unusual, the dictionary will list it. For instance, *galaxies* will be listed for *galaxy* because you must change the *y* to *i* before adding *-es*. The abbreviation *pl.* will come just before the plural spelling.

Forms of Verbs

The *past tense* of a verb is usually formed by adding *-d* or *-ed* to the word. When the past tense is formed in another way, the dictionary will spell it for you. Three examples are the words *sing* (*sang*), *read* (*read*), and *study* (*studied*).

The *-ing* form of a verb will also appear sometimes in dictionary entries. Usually this form, called the *present participle,* is made by simply adding *-ing* to the word. It is not so simple for some verbs. For example, the word *smile* becomes *smiling.* The final *e* is dropped before you add *-ing.* Other verbs ending in a consonant may double it before adding *-ing,* such as *begin, beginning* and *put, putting.* The dictionary will show you how to spell the form when it is unusual.

Comparatives and Superlatives

You add *-er* to many adjectives to show that one thing is being compared with another (*tall, taller*). You add *-est* to show that one thing is being compared to two or more other things (*tall, tallest*). If the adjective's spelling is changed in any way before *-er* or *-est* is added, the dictionary will list the spelling.

EXERCISE 6. Using the Dictionary for Spelling. Number your paper 1–5. After the proper number, write the correctly spelled form asked for in the following items. Use your dictionary to check the spelling.

EXAMPLE   1. *-est* form of *happy*
           1. *happiest*

1. *-ing* form of *ride*   4. *-er* form of *hot*
2. plural of *lily*   5. *-est* form of *sleepy*
3. past tense of *eat*

Capitalization

Most dictionaries show that proper nouns begin with a capital letter. Some adjectives also must begin with a capital letter, such as *Alaskan* and *Swedish.*

A few of these words may be capitalized or not, depending on the meaning you use. For instance, a *democrat* is any person who believes in the form of government called a democracy. A *Democrat* is a member of the political group called the Democratic Party. Any time you are not sure of capitalization for a word, you can look in the dictionary.

EXERCISE 7. Checking for Capitalization. Find each of the following words in a dictionary. Be ready to tell when each word should or should not be capitalized.

EXAMPLE   1. arctic
          1. *arctic: extremely cold*
             Arctic: region near North Pole

1. father   3. republican   5. god
2. west   4. union

Syllables

All of the words listed in the dictionary will be divided into syllables. Some dictionaries leave a space between the syllables: au to ma tion. Others show a dot or a hyphen between them: char·ac·ter·is·tic or mer-chan-dise.

EXERCISE 8. Dividing Words into Syllables. Number your paper 1–10. After the proper numbers, write the following words, separating the words into syllables. Leave spaces between syllables. Look up the words in a dictionary to be sure you are dividing them correctly.

EXAMPLE   1. mammoth
          1. *mam moth*

1. measure   6. apologize
2. geology   7. barrier
3. rocket   8. respectable
4. entertain   9. temporary
5. satellite   10. simplify

Pronunciation

24e. Use your dictionary to learn pronunciation.

If you are not sure how to pronounce a word, you can look it up in the dictionary. Dictionaries give the pronunciation in brackets or between bars right after the entry word.

When you look up a word's pronunciation, you will notice the word spelled again in brackets. This spelling uses symbols. The symbols help you to pronounce the word correctly. For example, the pronunciation given for the word *sight* is "sit." This spelling means that only the sounds of *s, i,* and *t* are used to say the word. The letters *g* and *h* in *sight* are silent. To check for correct spelling, you look at the entry word itself, not its pronunciation.

The Accent Mark

If a word has two or more syllables, one of the syllables will be stressed, or accented. When you accent a syllable, you say it with more force than the other syllables. The word *orbit,* for example, is accented on the first syllable; the word *volcano,* on the second syllable. The dictionary shows you which syllable to accent by placing an accent mark next to it. The mark may come after it (or'bit) or before it ('or bit).

Sometimes changing the accented syllable changes the meaning of the word. Say the word *conduct,* for instance. If you accent the first syllable (con'duct), you are using the noun for "the way that one behaves" (your *conduct* at lunch). If you accent the second syllable, you are using the verb for "to lead" (if you *conduct* the band). Notice the position of the accent whenever you look up a pronunciation.

EXERCISE 9. Marking the Accent on Words. Number your paper 1–10. Write each of the following words, leaving spaces between syllables. Then use an accent mark to show which syllable is stressed. Use your dictionary to be sure the words are correctly divided and accented.

EXAMPLE   1. occasion
                  1. *oc ca' sion*

1. hockey   3. citizen   5. disgust
2. consider   4. oxygen

Longer words with three or more syllables are sometimes pronounced with two accented syllables. The syllable said with the
most stress has the *primary accent.* Among the other syllables is
another that also is stressed, but not quite as much. It has the
secondary accent. For example, say the word *encyclopedia* (en cy
clo pe di a). The syllable said with the most force is *pe.* It has the
primary accent. You may also notice that you stress the syllable *cy*
more than *en, clo, di,* or *a.* That syllable has the secondary
accent.

Dictionaries will show the primary and secondary accents in
various ways. Many print the primary accent darker than the
secondary accent (en cy' clo pe⁗ di a). Others use a double mark
for the secondary accent (en'' cy clo pe' di a). Read the
introduction to your dictionary to understand the accent marks
used in it.

EXERCISE 10. Marking the Primary and Secondary Accents.
Number your paper 1–5. Look up each of the following words in
your dictionary. After the number for each one, write the word
correctly divided. Then place the accent marks where they
belong. Use the same kind of accent marks you find in your
dictionary. Practice pronouncing the words.

EXAMPLE   1. scholarship
                  1. *schol⁗ ar ship'*

1. determination   4. quarantine
2. appreciate   5. unexpectedly
3. ornamental

Symbols for Sounds

The dictionary maker must show in writing how a word sounds
when it is spoken. The English alphabet has twenty-six letters for

a spoken language that has more than one hundred sounds. The dictionary must have a way to show, for instance, that the *ou* sound in *rough* is different from the *ou* sound in *though* and *cough*. It must also be able to show that the *oo* sound in *too* is the same as the vowel sound in *crew, shoe, two,* and *glue.* To help solve these problems, the dictionary maker uses special symbols as well as alphabet letters to show pronunciations.

Many of these symbols are special marks placed above the letters in pronunciation spellings. They are *diacritical marks.* The system of diacritical marks used in one dictionary may differ from the system used in another. To learn the marks used in your dictionary, study the *pronunciation key,* usually found at the front of the book. The key may also appear at the bottom of every page in the main part of the book.

A few diacritical marks are the same in many dictionaries. Two common ones are the long, straight mark for a *long vowel* and the curved mark for a *short vowel.*

The sound of a long vowel is the sound of the letter's own name.

EXAMPLES   place   (plās)   side   (sīd)   use   (ūs)
          beat   (bēt)   bone   (bōn)

The long, straight diacritical mark for a long vowel is called a *macron* (pronounced mā′ kron).

Vowels that are called "short" do not say their own names. The sounds of short vowels are given in these examples.

         a as in mat   **o** as in hop
         e as in set   **oo** as in good
         i as in kick   **u** as in cut

To show the short-vowel sounds, some dictionaries use the curved diacritical mark called a *breve* (pronounced brĕv or brēv). Other dictionaries show short vowels by leaving them unmarked. You may find yet another method for showing short vowels in your own dictionary. Remember to study the pronunciation key.

EXERCISE 11. Recognizing Diacritical Marks. Number your paper 1–10. Look up the following words in a dictionary. After the number for each word, write the pronunciation given for it. Mark long vowels with a macron. Mark short vowels with a breve if your dictionary uses that mark. Practice pronouncing the words.

EXAMPLE   1. shiny
            1. *shī′ nē*

1. migrate	4. uppity	7. refuse	9. satisfy
2. beauty	5. toll	8. offspring	10. gauge
3. bracket	6. gleam		

Another special symbol for a sound is the *schwa*. It looks like an upside-down *e* (ə). A schwa stands for a certain weak vowel sound that is usually heard in unaccented syllables. This unclear, blurred sound might be spelled "uh." For example, the pronunciation of *alone* is ə lon′. Notice also the use of the schwa in pronunciations for *chimera* and *chimerical* in the sample dictionary section on page 429. Many words that end in *-er* also have the schwa sound in the last syllable because it is not stressed. The words *litter* (lit′ ər) and *driver* (dri′ vər) are examples.

EXERCISE 12. Recognizing the Schwa.

Number your paper 1–5. Look up the following words in your dictionary. After the number for each one, write the pronunciation given in the dictionary. Practice pronouncing the words.

EXAMPLE   1. tragedy
            1. *traj′ə de*

1. imposter	3. navigator	5. tradition
2. luxurious	4. benefit	

REVIEW EXERCISE. Using the Dictionary.

Number your paper 1–20. Answer the following questions. You will need to refer to your dictionary or to earlier pages in this chapter.

1. In which third of the dictionary would you find words that begin with *n*?
2–3. What are two synonyms of the word *applaud*?

4. What is an antonym of the word *commotion*?

5–6. What are two other kinds of dictionary entries besides single words?

7. Of the following three words, which would be shown in the dictionary with a macron over a vowel: *rattle, heard, mean*?

8. What is a guide word? (Use complete sentences in your answer.)

9–11. If the words *multiply* and *musician* are in large type at the top of a dictionary page, would the words *muscle, multiplication, mumps* be defined on that page? (Write the word and then answer *yes* or *no*.)

12–14. What are three reasons for looking up a word in the dictionary? (Use complete sentences in your answers.)

15. Would the word *basin* come before or after the word *basic* in the dictionary?

16. What is one way to find the exact word meaning you want in the dictionary?

17. As what parts of speech can you use the word *distress*?

18–20. How is the pronunciation written for the words *anthem, eliminate, severe*?

CHAPTER 25

Vocabulary

LEARNING AND
USING NEW WORDS

You meet new words every day. Some you meet by hearing—in conversations, at movies, on TV, on radio. Others you meet by seeing—in books, magazines, papers. This chapter will show you some ways to learn and use the new words you hear and see. Before studying these ways of building your vocabulary, see how many of the following sixth-grade vocabulary words you already know.

DIAGNOSTIC TEST

Selecting the Closest Meaning. Number your paper 1–10. Each numbered word is followed by four words. Next to the proper number on your paper, write the letter of the word or phrase that is closest in meaning to the numbered word.

EXAMPLE   1. foe   a. deer   c. enemy
                          b. cousin   d. warrior

          1. *c*

1. appropriate   a. proper   c. powerful
                      b. weak   d. interesting

2. caution   a. disturbance   c. fuel
              b. warning   d. ornament
3. declare   a. lock   c. give up
              b. whisper   d. announce
4. fragrant   a. difficult   c. rusty
              b. sweet-smelling   d. fast
5. interrupt   a. ask   c. break in
              b. view   d. consider
6. maximum   a. main reason   c. lowest
              b. greatest amount   d. nearest
7. ordinarily   a. quickly   c. never
              b. usually   d. eagerly
8. reliable   a. hurried   c. frightening
              b. dependable   d. perfect
9. severe   a. happy   c. strict
              b. several   d. sad
10. thorough   a. complete   c. even
              b. nasty   d. divided

A VOCABULARY NOTEBOOK

25a. Keep a list of new words and their meanings in your notebook.

A good way to learn new words is to keep a personal vocabulary list in your notebook. When you read or hear an unfamiliar word, write it on your list. Then look it up in the dictionary to be sure you know the correct meaning. Remember that some words may have more than one meaning. Write the definition or definitions in your notebook. Then write one or two sentences to show how you might use the word.

You may add a word or even several words daily. Review your list occasionally and try to use the new words as often as you can. You will be amazed at how your vocabulary grows along with your list.

MEANING FROM CONTEXT

Of all the words that you use daily, how many have you actually looked up in a dictionary? Probably you have learned few in this manner. More often, you have guessed the meanings of words from the situations in which they were used. That is, you have guessed the word's meaning from the context.

25b. Learn new words from context.

The *context* of a word means all the other words and sentences that surround it. From studying the context, you can sometimes understand the meaning of an unfamiliar word. For example, if you did not know the definition of the word *destination*, you could probably guess what it means from the rest of this sentence:

> Everyone in the family was happy when they reached their *destination* and could finally get out of the car.

The context hints strongly that *destination* means "the place towards which someone or something travels." If you check the word's meaning in the dictionary, you will find this guess is correct.

Since you will often find unfamiliar words in your reading, your ability to figure out their meanings from context is an important skill. Look at another example. You are assigned to read a story about Eleanor Roosevelt. In one scene she is giving her first public speech. The description of Mrs. Roosevelt includes these two sentences:

> Eleanor appeared calm and sure as she stood behind the microphone. She looked directly at her audience. Only the slight tremor in her voice revealed her nervousness.

You may not know the word *tremor*. However, if you consider it in context, you can guess its meaning. If she looked calm, but something in her voice sounded nervous, *tremor* must mean a "shakiness" in her voice. In the dictionary *tremor* is defined as a "shaking" or "quivering."

EXERCISE 1. Using Context to Select Word Meanings.
Number your paper 1–10. Read the following paragraph about an
Indian legend. Look for context clues to the meanings of the
numbered words. Then, from the list of words and phrases,
choose the one that is closest in meaning to each numbered word.
Write it next to the proper number on your paper. After you have
finished, check your answers with the dictionary. You will not
need all of the words on the list. The first answer is given as an
example.

EXAMPLE   1. g   *old story*

a. ages
b. convinced
c. formal act
d. pretended
e. winning
f. tricked
g. old story

h. something that stands for
   something else
i. a person killed or injured
j. sorrow
k. a killing or slaughter
l. arrangement

There is an Indian (1) *legend* that explains why Spanish moss
hangs from trees in the South. A brave chief fell in love with a
maiden from another tribe. Although the tribes had been enemies for (2) *generations,* he (3) *persuaded* the other leaders that
his marriage to the maiden could end the fighting. When the
brave chief and his men arrived for the wedding (4) *ceremony,*
they were (5) *betrayed.* The visiting Indians were attacked, and
one (6) *victim* was the peaceful chief. While the (7) *victorious*
warriors celebrated the (8) *massacre,* the young maiden buried
the chief beneath a giant oak tree. To show her (9) *mourning,* she
cut her long hair and hung it on the branches as a (10) *symbol* of
her love.

EXERCISE 2. Using Context to Select Word Meanings.
Number your paper 1–10. Next to each number, copy the word or
phrase from column B that is closest in meaning to the italicized
word in each sentence in column A. You will not use all the words
in column B.

	A		B
1.	The choir sang an *anthem*.		attack
2.	The soldiers fought off the *assault* on the fort.		contest
			earlier
3.	The tree fell across the road, creating a *barrier* to traffic.		life's work
			song of praise
4.	Jennifer has decided on a *career*.		specific area
5.	Reed won the piano *competition*.		a blocking
6.	We arrived just in time for the plane's *departure*.		leaving
			canvas bag
7.	The bicycle rodeo was open to everyone in our school *district*.		easily broken
			arrival
8.	Ms. Pamonicutt warned us to be careful with the *fragile* vase.		
9.	The scout carried his supplies in his *knapsack*.		
10.	We learned that rule in a *previous* lesson.		

Sometimes writers give extra help with a word's meaning by defining the word for the reader in the same sentence. Notice in the following sentences how the words in boldfaced type have been explained by the writer.

The university was known for its outstanding department of **geology,** the science of studying the history of the earth as recorded in rocks.

Marcus hopes to become an **architect,** a person who designs buildings.

USING THE DICTIONARY

25c. Learn the meanings of new words by looking them up in the dictionary.

You may not always be able to figure out a word's meaning from the context. Many times you need to look up the word in a dictionary. Often several meanings are listed for one entry word.

You must read all the meanings to find the one that best fits the context of your sentence.

Notice how the context changes the meaning of the word *bureau* in the following sentences.

Dad and I painted the old *bureau* for my bedroom.

The local weather *bureau* makes use of advanced computer systems to study weather patterns.

If you check a dictionary, you will find that the word *bureau* can mean a chest of drawers, often with a mirror; a department or subdivision within a government or business; or an agency that provides information. Which meaning of *bureau* fits each of the two sentences above?

EXERCISE 3. Finding the Correct Meaning in the Dictionary. Number your paper 1–10. After the proper number, write the italicized word in the sentence and the correct meaning from the dictionary for the word.

1. *Foul* smells came from the deserted yard where people had thrown their garbage.
2. The referee blew her whistle when one of the players committed a *foul*.
3. If you misbehave in class, you will get a low grade in *conduct*.
4. Josh got a chance to *conduct* the sixth-grade chorus at rehearsal yesterday.
5. We had to *pry* open the crate with a screwdriver.
6. Don't *pry* into the personal business of others.
7. The bank president assured us that our money was safely locked in the *vault*.
8. At the sports festival, we enjoyed watching competitors in the pole *vault*.
9. I used that *term* correctly in my science report.
10. The math club will have a chess tournament next *term*.

EXERCISE 4. Learning New Words from the Dictionary. Number your paper 1–5. Next to the proper number, write the word from the following list that correctly answers the question. Use a dictionary if you do not know the meaning of the words on the list. You will not use all the words.

a. disguise   e. nephew
b. geology   f. self-confidence
c. journalism
d. majority

1. If you think that you would enjoy writing for newspapers or magazines, what should you study in college?
2. Who is your brother's son?
3. How many people must vote for a proposal in order for it to pass?
4. In order to really believe in yourself and your abilities, what do you need to develop?
5. What do you wear so that those who know you will not recognize you?

EXERCISE 5. Learning New Words from the Dictionary. Number your paper 1–10. Copy the words from column A. Next to each word, write the word or phrase from column B that is closest in meaning. Two definitions will not be used. Use a dictionary to look up words you do not know.

A	B
1. absorb	get rid of
2. abundant	known for certain
3. analyze	soak up
4. appreciate	safe
5. captivity	more than enough
6. definite	serving as a decoration
7. eliminate	set up
8. establish	examine critically
9. ornamental	be grateful
10. quantity	eating more than necessary
	state of being a prisoner
	amount

SYNONYMS AND ANTONYMS

Using the same words over and over makes your writing dull. The use of synonyms and antonyms will add interesting variety.

Synonyms

25d. Synonyms are words that have similar meanings.

Synonyms can help you to avoid using the same word several times in one sentence or in sentences that closely follow each other. Read the following examples to see the difference synonyms can make in writing.

> What a scene! While the TV blared, Dad *slept* in his chair, and my brother *slept* on the couch.

Can you think of other words that you could use instead of *slept* in picturing this scene? Here is just one possibility:

> What a scene! While the TV blared, Dad *napped* in his chair, and my brother *snoozed* on the couch.

In this example *napped* and *snoozed* are synonyms. They both clearly show that someone is sleeping, but they also tell you how that person is sleeping. The sentence is clearer and more interesting when the repetitions of *slept* are replaced.

You can find synonyms in a thesaurus. Some dictionaries list synonyms for entry words, too, after the definitions.

EXERCISE 6. **Finding Synonyms.** Number your paper 1–5. After the number, write the two words that are synonyms in the pairs of sentences.

EXAMPLE 1. The room was quiet during the test.
　　　　　　 She closed her eyes and made a silent wish.
　　　　 1. *quiet, silent*

1. Can the machine make a duplicate of this page?
   Is this an exact copy?

2. Did you have any errors on your paper?
   Yes, I found two mistakes.
3. The princess in the play wore a gorgeous gown of gold and silver.
   It was a beautiful autumn day.
4. The principal informed everyone that lunch would be late.
   The teacher told the class to finish the assignment.
5. The accident happened because of the reckless way he rode his bicycle.
   Please don't be careless with the new books.

EXERCISE 7. Choosing Synonyms. Number your paper 1–10. Next to the proper number, write the italicized word in each sentence. Then choose a synonym from the following list for the italicized word in each sentence, and write it beside its synonym. You may use a dictionary.

EXAMPLE   1. A clairvoyant is someone who *foretells* future events.
           1. *foretells, predicts*

offspring	pleaded	occasion	predicts
nominated	involve	particle	reaction
security	prohibits	respected	

1. The class *named* Allison to run for class president.
2. A concert at school is a special *event*.
3. Female animals are usually very protective of their *young*.
4. The game stopped when the player got a *piece* of dirt in his eye.
5. The class *begged* for more time to finish the project.
6. The object is to *include* the entire class in the fund-raiser.
7. The law *forbids* driving a car on the beach.
8. What was Sofia's *response* to your idea?
9. The graduation speaker was an *admired* person from the community.
10. As a *safety* measure, always lock your doors at night.

25e. Know the exact meanings of synonyms.

Although synonyms are similar in meaning, they cannot always be exchanged for each other in a sentence because of slight differences in meaning. Read the following sentences that use the synonyms *dainty* and *pretty*.

> Look at the *dainty* floral design on this box.
> The view from the cabin window was a *pretty* scene.

Each of these synonyms has its own special meaning. You could say "the *pretty* floral design," but you would not say "a *dainty* scene" because *dainty* means "delicately beautiful." It is not a word you would use to describe a wide view.

Consult a dictionary for exact meanings. The synonym you use must fit the context of the sentence.

EXERCISE 8. Choosing the Best Synonym. Number your paper 1–5. After the proper number, write the word in parentheses that best fits the context of the sentence. You may use a dictionary to find exact meanings.

1. In order to get a good night's sleep, Kelly put a Do Not (Disturb, Upset) sign on the door.
2. Mike certainly has a (sincere, hearty) appetite.
3. The police found a briefcase full of (counterfeit, copied) money in the car.
4. It is (doubtful, suspicious) that I will win the national spelling competition.
5. Those oily rags in the corner of the basement are a fire (risk, hazard).

Antonyms

25f. Antonyms are words that have opposite meanings.

Sometimes in your writing, you want to show how certain things are different or how they contrast. Words that have opposite meanings, called antonyms, can make these differences clear. Read the following sentences. The antonyms are italicized.

Lee's uncle is *stingy* with his money but *generous* with his time.

In driving class you learn to be a *careful* driver, not a *reckless* one.

Stingy is the opposite of *generous,* and *careful* is the opposite of *reckless.* These antonyms express contrasts clearly and make the sentences interesting.

Many thesauruses list antonyms for entry words after the synonyms. A few dictionaries list antonyms for some entries. If they are listed, the antonyms appear after the synonyms.

EXERCISE 9. **Using Antonyms.** Number your paper 1–10. Next to the proper number, write the antonym for the italicized word in each sentence.

1. Vince was *lazy,* but Robin was (ambitious, sleepy).
2. A child's first set of teeth is (temporary, important); the second set is *permanent.*
3. Does the cafeteria have *stiff* straws or (flexible, sturdy) ones?
4. Frightening the teacher with a rubber snake was not a *mature* act; it was a very (funny, juvenile) thing for an eighth-grader to do.
5. *Few* stayed for the meeting, even though (some, numerous) people had signed the attendance list.
6. In our national elections we don't vote *publicly;* we cast our ballots (privately, separately).
7. The boys weren't in a *little* hole; they were lost in a (dark, mammoth) cave.
8. Mavis and Nina hoped that their dresses would be *different,* but they were (identical, lovely).
9. Peter remained *calm* during the thunderstorm, but his little sister became (homesick, frantic).
10. The lion became a fierce *hunter;* a young antelope was her intended (partner, prey).

EXERCISE 10. Finding Antonyms. Number your paper 1–5. Next to the proper number, write the italicized word from each sentence. From the following list, find an antonym for the italicized word in each sentence and write it beside the appropriate word.

EXAMPLE   1. The young firefighter's *cowardly* act was written up in the newspaper.
          1. *cowardly, heroic*

> heroic
> amateur
> denied
> tragic
> dramatic
> lunar
> keen

1. Toshio's mother is a *professional* photographer.
2. The students' request for a candy machine in the cafeteria was *granted.*
3. The accident that destroyed the school's science lab was *fortunate.*
4. Billie Jo performed well in the play's *comic* scenes.
5. Hunting dogs must have a *weak* sense of smell.

PARTS OF A WORD

Some words in the English language can be divided into parts. Look at the word *review*. The root, sometimes called the base word, is *view*. You know that *view* means "to look at." *Re-* is a prefix that means "again or back." Therefore, *review* means "to look at again."

Look at the word *painless*. In this word, the root or base word is *pain,* which means "an ache or soreness." The suffix *-less* means "without." Therefore, *painless* means "without ache." You can learn a new word if you know the meaning of the main part of the word, or root, and the meaning of the prefix or suffix.

PREFIXES

25g. A prefix is a group of letters that is added to the beginning of a word.

Learning to recognize prefixes and their meanings can help you decide the meanings of new words that use these prefixes. The following list contains some common prefixes, their meanings, and examples of new words formed by the addition of a prefix to a root.

PREFIX	MEANING	ROOT	NEW WORD
extra-	beyond *or* more than	terrestrial	extraterrestrial
fore-	before	tell	foretell
im-	not	mature	immature
in-	not	direct	indirect
micro-	small	film	microfilm
pre-	before	cook	precook
re-	again	place	replace
un-	not	happy	unhappy

Notice that some prefixes have the same meaning. You may need to use a dictionary to see which prefix is the correct one to add to a particular word.

EXERCISE 11. Making New Words with Prefixes. Number your paper 1–10. For each word listed, there is a prefix meaning given in parentheses. Using the list of prefixes above, choose an appropriate prefix. Next to the proper number, write the new word that you have formed.

EXAMPLE   1. view (before)
              1. *preview*

1. historic (before)
2. fortunate (not)
3. computer (small)
4. expensive (not)
5. expectedly (not)
6. cast (before)
7. ordinary (more than)
8. organize (again)
9. patience (not)
10. accurate (not)

SUFFIXES

25h. **A suffix is a group of letters that is added to the end of a word.**

Learning to recognize and use suffixes will also help you with your vocabulary. Some suffixes, such as *-less*, change the meaning of the base word. Most suffixes, however, change only the form of the base word so that it may be used as a different part of speech. For example, if you want to describe a person you can depend on, it would be incorrect to use the following sentence:

He is a depend worker.

The verb *depend* does not work as a describing word, or adjective. You must add the suffix *-able* to make the correct word.

He is a dependable worker.

The suffix *-able* changes the verb *depend* to the adjective *dependable*.

If you want to use the adjective *active* as a noun, you add the suffix *-ity* to get *activity*. Sometimes there will be a spelling change when you add the suffix. With *active* you drop the *e* before adding *-ity* to make *activity*. You may need to consult a dictionary for spelling changes. When you learn to recognize suffixes, some unfamiliar words may turn out not to be new words at all.

A list of common suffixes and examples follows.

SUFFIX	ROOT	NEW WORD
-able	respect	respectable
-al	universe	universal
-ance	appear	appearance
-ence	differ	difference
-fy	note	notify
-ion	inspect	inspection
-ity	creative	creativity
-less	fear	fearless
-ment	manage	management
-ous	luxury	luxurious

EXERCISE 12. Making New Words with Suffixes. Number your paper 1–10. Write correctly the words formed by combining each base word and suffix. Use a dictionary to check spelling changes.

EXAMPLE   1. victory + ous
            1. *victorious*

1. guide + ance
2. survive + al
3. honor + able
4. hope + less
5. invest + ment
6. demonstrate + ion
7. public + ity
8. confer + ence
9. simple + fy
10. fury + ous

EXERCISE 13. Using Words with Suffixes. Number your paper 1–10. Use the ten new words you formed with suffixes in Exercise 12 to fill in the blanks in the following sentences.

1. Since the directions were hard to understand, we asked Mr. Rennaldo to —— them for us.
2. The senator, who spoke at graduation, was a well-respected, —— woman.
3. Catalina's parents had a —— with the math teacher.
4. Do you really think an underwater pen is a good —— ?
5. When Sara planned her schedule, she went to her teacher for —— .
6. Mr. Holbert was —— when he saw the broken windows and muddy floors.
7. The committee made colorful posters to get —— for the carnival.
8. All living things must have nourishment for —— .
9. In science, Lita gave a —— of her experiment.
10. When the car broke down, the situation looked —— .

REVIEW EXERCISE. Selecting the Closest Meaning. The following words are words you have studied in this chapter. Number your paper 1–10. Beside each number, write the letter of the word or words closest in meaning to the numbered word.

1. duplicate
   - a. file
   - b. copy
   - c. view
   - d. piece

2. security
   - a. safety
   - b. landscape
   - c. ability
   - d. body

3. plead
   - a. join
   - b. bèg
   - c. press down
   - d. sneak

4. prohibit
   - a. shake off
   - b. handle carefully
   - c. rush
   - d. forbid

5. keen
   - a. low
   - b. sharp
   - c. crazy
   - d. free

6. eliminate
   - a. lower
   - b. get rid of
   - c. introduce
   - d. nominate

7. inexpensive
   - a. common
   - b. powerful
   - c. cheap
   - d. cold

8. survival
   - a. cure
   - b. living
   - c. practice
   - d. revenge

9. publicity
   - a. housing
   - b. exercise
   - c. information for attention
   - d. free help

10. unexpected
    - a. not planned
    - b. without hope
    - c. not new
    - d. rapidly

Word List

The following list is made up of three hundred words that you may find in your reading this year. You should be familiar with some of the words because you have studied them in this chapter or elsewhere. Add the words you do not know to the vocabulary list you are keeping in your notebook. Remember to write a sentence illustrating how you might use the new word. Review this word list during the year and try to use these words in your writing and speech. This is a good opportunity to enlarge and improve your personal vocabulary.

abdomen	amateur	anthem
absorb	ambitious	apologize
abundant	analyze	applaud
adjust		

application
appreciate
appropriate
architect
assault
associate
assume
astonish
automation
aviation

ballad
ballot
barrier
benefit
betray
biography
boast
bombard
braille
bureau

campaign
candidate
captivity
career
caution
ceremony
characteristic
collapse
collide
commotion

competition
complaint
compliment
conceal
conduct

conference
congratulate
conscience
consent
contrast

contribute
cooperate
corporation
counterfeit
courteous
cultivate
dainty
debate
debt
declare

decrease
definite
demonstration
deny
departure
descendant
descriptive
desirable
desperate
destination

detect
determination
disadvantage
disastrous
discomfort
discourage
disguise
disgust
dissolve
district

disturb
document
doubtful
doubtless
dramatic
dread
duplicate
earnest
eavesdrop
eliminate

employer
engage
entertain
envy
error
escort
essential
establish
eternal
exception

exclaim
export
extraordinary
fatal
feat
flammable
flexible
foe
forefathers
foul

foundation
fragrant
frantic
furious
galaxy

gallant
gasp
generation
generous
genuine

geology
glimpse
gorgeous
gossip
gratitude
guidance
hazard
hearty
heir
heroic

hesitate
hibernate
hoist
honorable
identical
ignite
ignore
imitate
impatience
import

impostor
inaccurate
incident
inexpensive
inform
inhale
innumerable
inspiration
interrupt
interview

intrusion
investment
inviting
involve
irregular
issue
journalism
justify
juvenile
keen

knapsack
legend
leisure
license
lieutenant
linger
locally
lunar
luxurious
majority

mammoth
management
marvel
massacre
maximum
merchandise
migrate
miraculous
mischievous
mobile

mourning
navigator
nephew
nominate
notion

nuisance
numerous
oath
obvious
occasion

offense
offspring
omit
ordinarily
ornamental
paralysis
particle
persuade
pharmacy
pierce

plead
plot
portion
portrait
possess
precipitation
predict
prehistoric
previous
prey

privacy
profession
prohibit
promotion
protest
pry
publicity
qualify
quantity
quarantine

quote
ransom
reaction
realm
rebel
receipt
reckless
reduction
reference
regret

regulate
rehearsal
reign
relate
reliable
remedy
request
requirement
resemble
reservoir

resident
resign
respectable
responsibility
revolution
routine
sacrifice
satisfy
scheme
scholar

security
self-confidence
self-respect
separation
session
severe
simplify
solitary
specify
static

stray
suburbs
summarize
superior
surgery
survey
survival
suspicion
symbol
sympathy

temporary
tension
terminal
terrain
text
theme
thorough
threat
toll
tradition

tragedy
transparent
twilight
unexpectedly
unfortunate
unite
unmanned
urge
vacuum
vault

vicinity
victim
victorious
villain
visual
vivid
vocal
wardrobe
widespread
yacht

CHAPTER 26

Studying and Test Taking

SKILLS AND STRATEGIES

Each year in school, you are asked to do more studying on your own. You must complete class assignments, take notes, and prepare for tests. This chapter will teach you several strategies that can help you improve your studying and test-taking skills.

STUDY SKILLS

You study not only to gain information, but also to understand and use what you have learned. The following strategies can help you improve your studying.

Getting Ready to Study

26a. Plan your study time.

You will finish more homework, and finish on time, if you plan ahead. List your after-school chores and activities. Then set aside a regular time for study each day.

Next, list all your homework assignments and their deadlines. Note which ones you must do immediately and which ones are not due for some time. You can then decide exactly what to study on certain days of the week. Setting up a regular time for study and scheduling your assignments will help you keep up with homework.

26b. Plan your study space.

Where you study is as important as when you do it. You should work at a desk or table, in a place that is quiet and well lighted. Your best place to study may be at home or at the public library. Wherever you work, make sure that you have proper supplies —paper, pencils, pens, and a dictionary—and that your work area is neat and well organized.

Following the SQ3R Method

26c. Use the SQ3R Method.

One method for studying textbooks and other books is the *SQ3R Method,* which was developed by Francis Robinson, an educational psychologist. It has the following five steps:

1. *Survey.* Survey, or look over, the assigned reading by noting the title, all headings, words in **boldface** or in *italics,* and summaries or review questions. Also look at drawings and charts. Read the beginning and summary paragraphs for main ideas.

2. **Q**uestion. List the questions that you should be able to answer after reading the assignment. An easy way to do this is to turn each heading into a question. For example, if the heading in a science book is "Living Things in the Soil," you might write, "What living things are in the soil?" You may also be able to use questions that your teacher gives you or that are in the book.

3. **R**ead. Now read the material carefully to find answers to your questions. Look for main ideas and supporting details. Use

the glossary or a dictionary to look up words you do not know. Take notes.

4. R*ecite*. Read your questions again. Try to recite, or say, the answers in your own words to test your understanding. Now write your answers to the study questions.

5. R*eview*. Review by asking yourself the questions again. Answer them without looking at what you have written. Then check your answers against your notes and the book. Immediately after this check, review the assigned reading again.

EXERCISE 1. Using the SQ3R Method with a Homework Assignment.   Choose a chapter in your social studies or science textbook. Use the SQ3R Method to study it.

Using Books Effectively

26d. Survey the main parts of a book.

When you use any book as a study or reference tool, you will save time by familiarizing yourself with the parts of that book. Knowing the following parts of a book will enable you to use the book effectively.

1. The table of contents. A list at the beginning of the book that includes chapter titles and subdivisions and the page number where each begins.
2. Index. An alphabetical list at the end of the book that includes the specific topics treated in the book and the exact page or pages where the topic is treated.
3. Glossary. An alphabetical list of technical and difficult words and terms used in the book, with definitions and explanations for each.

Recognizing Main Ideas

26e. Find the main ideas of the material being studied.

In studying, it is important to find the main idea in a paragraph. The main idea is the most important point the writer is making.

(1) Main ideas may be stated.

The main idea of a paragraph is usually stated as a complete sentence. For example, the main idea of a paragraph about Halloween costumes might be *You can turn yourself into a Halloween vampire with a few yards of black cloth and some make-up.*

The topic of the following paragraph is the cordless telephone. The main idea is stated in the first sentence.

> People who depend on the telephone for business often use cordless phones. They can take them wherever they go. The phones have small antennas. They can receive calls from anywhere in the world. As these phones get smaller, easier to make, and cheaper to use, more and more people will carry them.
>
> CAROLYN JABS

The main idea may also be stated in the middle or at the end of a paragraph.

(2) Main ideas may be implied.

In some paragraphs, the main idea is not stated. It is implied, or suggested. You must read closely to find the details that lead you to a main idea.

The following paragraph describes a family pet. The main idea is implied, not stated.

> Sitka's roots went back to Alaska some two generations. A brute of an animal in size, weighing close to one hundred pounds, with the markings of a gray wolf, and stretching six feet from nose to tail, he made anyone who met him pause and catch his breath. Yet he was never known to growl or mutter at any person, young or old, even in trying circumstances that would have sent most dogs into fits of rage.
>
> JEROME HELLMUTH

This paragraph is about a dog, Sitka. The first sentence tells you that his ancestors lived in Alaska. The next sentence describes his wolflike appearance and large size. The last sentence tells you that Sitka is an unusually gentle dog. These details add up to the main idea of the paragraph: *Even though Sitka is a big dog who looks like a wolf, he is very gentle.*

EXERCISE 2. Finding the Main Idea.   Write the main idea for each of the following paragraphs. It may be stated or implied.

1

While her classmates shouted greetings, Laura Rivera sat silently. It wasn't that Laura, fourteen, from Miami, Florida, didn't want to join in. She simply couldn't. Laura can't walk or talk. She was born with cerebral palsy—a disorder of the nervous system. But today, Laura Rivera tells her family what she wants for supper, talks to friends, and answers teachers' questions at school. True, her "voice" comes from a machine and sounds deep. But that doesn't matter one bit. This computer-synthesized voice is hers, and Laura is thrilled.

R. A. DECKERT

2

Shopping early has many advantages. Last-minute shoppers often are in such a hurry they buy anything they can find. Sometimes they spend more than they have to. An early start gives you time to check around for the lowest price and the best quality. If you don't find what you want, you still have time to think of another gift, or to make something. As Amy Anhofshi of Sterling Heights, Michigan, said, "Take your time. Don't buy just anything."

EDITORS OF *PENNY POWER*

Finding Details That Support Main Ideas

26f. Find details that support main ideas.

When you study, you must find the details that give more information about the main ideas. Details may supply examples, reasons, facts, or descriptions—knowledge that is often tested.

In the following paragraph, the main idea is stated in the first sentence. The other sentences give supporting details.

> Cycling equipment is functional, lightweight, and most of all, colorful. From the bicycles to the jerseys, color is what strikes a spectator's eye the most. Traditionally, the shoes and shorts have been black, but now even these items are turning up in red, blue, white, and silver.
>
> BRUCE LEAF

The main idea of this paragraph is *Cycling equipment is colorful.* Notice that the first sentence also tells you that cycling equipment is functional and lightweight. The main idea is color, however, because the supporting sentences all give details about color: (1) The bicycles, jerseys, shoes, and shorts are all colorful; (2) black is the usual color for shoes and shorts; (3) shoes and shorts are now red, blue, white, or silver.

EXERCISE 3. Finding Supporting Details. Read the following paragraph. Find the main idea and the details that support it. Then complete the assignment.

> People have barely begun to explore the world of the sea. Divers seldom descend below fifty fathoms. Even then they only explore at that depth on the continental shelf near the coast. They can know only of part of the sea's fauna. Who can say what creatures live in those mysterious depths?
>
> BETTY SANDERS GARNER

Write two sentences explaining why we know about only a part of the sea's fauna (animal life). Use your own words.

Distinguishing Between Fact and Opinion

26g. Distinguish between fact and opinion.

Almost everything you read contains both facts and opinions. When you study, you must be able to tell the difference.

(1) A statement of fact contains information that can be proved true or false.

Statements of fact tell about things that have already happened or are happening now. The truth of the statements can be checked. For example, here are two statements of fact:

> Shirley Chisholm was the first black woman to be elected to the U.S. Congress.
> Light waves travel faster than sound waves.

(2) A statement of opinion is one that states personal belief or feeling. It contains information that cannot be proved true or false.

A prediction about the future is an opinion because it cannot be proved true or false in the present. Statements of likes or dislikes are opinions because they are personal and are not the same for all people. Here are three statements of opinion.

> Parrots are interesting pets.
> I will get up on time tomorrow.
> There must be advanced civilizations somewhere in space.

A statement of opinion may contain words such as *It's true that* or *Everyone agrees that,* but these statements are still opinions. Do not let misleading words trap you into accepting an opinion as a fact.

OPINION   It's a fact that girls are not as athletic as boys.

Opinions may be written to look like facts. You will be a better reader if you learn to tell the difference. To prove statements true or false, use reliable sources such as an encyclopedia, a dictionary, an almanac, an expert, or your own experience.

EXERCISE 4. Distinguishing Between Facts and Opinions. Number your paper 1–5. If the statement is an opinion, write *opinion* after the proper number. If the statement is a fact, write *fact* and give a source you could use to check it (encyclopedia, science textbook, almanac, etc.).

EXAMPLES   1. A kilometer is equal to one thousand meters.
             1. *fact—math textbook*
             2. UFO's (unidentified flying objects) from other solar systems have visited earth.
             2. *opinion*

1. It's true that learning a foreign language is difficult.
2. Legends are stories that have been handed down from one generation to another.
3. Thomas Jefferson signed the Declaration of Independence.
4. Everyone needs at least eight hours of sleep every night.
5. Most young people enjoy shopping for clothes.

Taking Notes

26h. Take effective study notes.

Taking notes while you read helps you in two ways. You remember information better when you write it down, and you can use notes to review information quickly when you prepare for a test. Here are some strategies for taking notes.

    1. Take notes on sheets of paper, not cards.
    2. Look for key phrases, or make up your own, to use as headings in your notes. If the book has headings, use those.
    3. Under the headings, write the main ideas and supporting details *in your own words*. Be brief, but write enough so that you will understand the notes later.
    4. Write your notes in an organized way. For example, you could put headings on the left, main ideas and details on the right. Using a system makes it easier to take notes and study them.

Now read this paragraph and the following sample notes.

    A volcano is an opening, or vent, in the crust of the earth. It is caused by high temperatures deep below the earth's surface. The temperatures are so high that rock melts miles below the ground. This melted rock is called magma. As the rock melts, a light gas is produced. The gas pushes the magma upward. Finally, the bubbling magma reaches the surface, or crust, of the earth. It bursts through in an explosion, making the vent called a volcano.

Study Notes: Volcanoes

cause—high temps. deep below earth, rock melts

magma—melted rock, made miles below ground, gas produced, pushes magma up

explosion—magma bursts through earth's surface

EXERCISE 5. Taking Study Notes. Choose a homework assignment in your science, social studies, or English textbook. Take study notes, using the strategies you have learned. Be ready to share your notes.

WRITING IN OTHER SCHOOL SUBJECTS

26i. Use writing to learn about ideas in history class.

Much of what you learn about a subject comes from your classroom lessons and from your studying. You can also learn about a subject, such as history, by completing different kinds of writing projects. You may already write library reports in your history class (see pages 113–23). You can also use other kinds of writing to learn about ideas in history class.

When you write in history class, use what you know about writing narration, description, and exposition (Chapters 2 and 5). Also use what you know about the writing process (Chapter 1) and about writing paragraphs and compositions (Chapters 3, 4, and 5).

Writing Book Reports in History

One kind of writing to use in history class is the book report. You may already write book reports for your language arts class (see pages 124–27). For history class, your book report should be on a book that tells about an idea, an event, or a period of time. For example, you might write about *"The Earth Is Flat"—And Other Great Mistakes* by Laurence Pringle, *Plants That Changed History* by Joan Elma Rahn, or *The Luttrell Village: Country Life in the Middle Ages* by Sheila Sancha.

Your book report can also be on a book that tells about someone's life, called a biography. For example, for history class you might report on *Seafaring Women* by Linda Grant De Pauw, *The Voyages of Captain Cook* by Dorothy Hoobler and Thomas Hoobler, or *The Walls of Windy Troy: A Biography of Heinrich Schliemann* by Marjorie Braymer.

Begin by reading your book carefully. Take notes about important ideas or details as you read. You might also read an encyclopedia article about the subject of the book. This will help you to understand more about the subject.

When you write your book report, tell what the book is about and what you think of it. Be careful, though, not to give so much detail about one part of the book that you neglect other parts. Give clear reasons for liking or not liking the book. You might also answer this question: How does this book help you to understand history? Then be sure to evaluate, revise, and proofread your book report (see pages 124–27).

Writing Dialogues and Stories

You can also write imaginary dialogues and stories in history class. These conversations and stories should be about people in history. For example, you might write a dialogue between Magellan and Columbus, in which they talk about exploring. Or, you might write an interview between Queen Elizabeth I of England and a television reporter. You might even want to put yourself in the dialogue, perhaps as an interviewer. (For more on writing dialogue, see pages 39–40.)

You might also write a story in which you are a person telling about an important event in history. For example, you might be Hannibal telling about crossing the Alps with elephants in 218 B.C. No matter whom you write about, follow the steps of the writing process to write your story (see pages 30–50).

Keeping a Writer's Notebook

You can also keep a writer's notebook in history class. In your notebook you can write about the ideas and people you are studying. In this way, your writer's notebook is like the one you may keep in your language arts class.

You can use your notebook in two ways. First, you can write down what you think about the material you are studying. This will help you find out what you understand. Second, you can write about questions or ideas your teacher gives you. For example, your history teacher might give you these items:

1. Explain why the land between the Tigris and the Euphrates was called the "fertile crescent."
2. Compare the role of the citizen in the Greek democracy and in the Roman republic.
3. Discuss three discoveries made by explorers after Columbus's first voyage to America.

Items like these will help you to understand the people, ideas, and events you are studying. When you write in your notebook, be sure to apply what you know about writing sentences and paragraphs.

EXERCISE 6. Writing in History Class. Use the writing process to do one of the following activities.

1. Write a book report on a book that tells about an event or person in history.
2. Write a dialogue or a story about a person you are studying.
3. In your writer's notebook, write what you think about an idea, a person, or an event you are studying now. Or, write about an item your teacher gives you.

TEST–TAKING SKILLS

You take several types of tests in school. Some test your recall of facts; others test your understanding of ideas. Some ask for short answers; others require a paragraph or more. You can learn skills that will help you prepare for and take different kinds of tests.

Objective Tests

26j. Prepare for objective tests by studying the specific information that will be included on the test.

Objective tests ask you to recall specific facts, such as dates, names, and events. You usually choose an answer or write a short one. The kinds of questions include multiple-choice, true-or-false, fill-in-the-blank, short-answer, and matching.

Follow these steps to prepare for objective tests.

1. Find out exactly what the test covers (for example, Chapter 5, "The Aztecs, Incas, and Mayas," pages 75–110).
2. Gather all your materials about the topic: notes, textbook, written assignments, special handouts.
3. Review the information. Pay special attention to names, dates, and definitions. If you do not understand your notes, reread the textbook or ask your teacher for help.
4. Make up and answer questions that might be on the test. Check your answers.
5. Study until you can answer all questions from memory.

Follow these steps to take objective tests.

1. First, read the directions closely. Do *exactly* as they say. For example, the directions may tell you to read all questions before you begin answering. If you do not understand the directions, ask questions before you begin.
2. Skim all the questions. Note how many there are, which ones seem easy, which ones are difficult, and how much time you have to complete the test. Plan how fast you must work. (Remember, you will spend less time on easy questions and more time on difficult ones.)
3. Answer the easy questions first and come back to the harder ones.

4. For a *multiple-choice* question (a question with three or four choices for the answer), read *all* choices *before* you answer. Decide which ones must be wrong. From the answers that are left, pick the one that makes the most sense.

5. For a *true-or-false* question, see if *any* part of the statement is false. If so, mark the statement false.

6. For a *fill-in-the-blank* or *short-answer* question, write a specific answer, using the words of the textbook.

7. For a *matching* question, be sure you understand how the groups of items are related before you begin.

EXERCISE 7. Using Test-Taking Skills. Write your answers.

1. List ten terms or items of information from this chapter that might be on an objective test.
2. Using the ten items on your list, write ten questions for a test. Include the following types of questions:
   a. multiple-choice   c. fill-in-the-blank
   b. true-or-false   d. short-answer

EXAMPLE   1. fact
            A statement that contains information that can be proved true or false is a ——— .

Essay Tests

26k. Plan your time and your answer for an essay question.

Essay questions test your understanding as well as your memory of what you have learned. On essay tests, you write a paragraph or more. There is no *one* right answer for an essay question, but your teacher will expect you to include specific ideas and details.

Follow these steps to prepare for essay tests.

1. Identify what topics or specific readings the test covers.
2. Review your notes and reread the textbook if necessary.
3. Memorize main ideas and supporting details.

4. Make up essay questions that will test your understanding of the information. Write your answers and check them.

Follow these steps to take essay tests.

1. Read the directions carefully. You may not have to answer all the questions. Often you have a choice.

2. Skim the questions. Note which ones will be easier or harder for you. If you have a choice of questions, decide which ones to answer.

3. Figure out how much time you can spend on each question. Remember to leave time for planning, writing, and revising.

4. Read the question very carefully to see exactly what *task* you are asked to do. The task is usually given in an important, or key, verb such as *describe* or *compare.* Some other key verbs are *contrast, list, outline, discuss, explain,* and *show.*

5. Go through the stages of the writing process.

    a. *Prewriting.* Gather ideas in a list or brief notes. Write a topic sentence that states your main point and contains key words from the question. Jot down some supporting details.

    b. *Writing.* Use your notes to write the answer. Write clear, complete sentences. If your answer has more than one paragraph, be sure each paragraph has a topic sentence and supporting details. Also, be sure the ideas are connected.

    c. *Revising.* Reread the question and your answer. Be sure that you have clearly and fully answered the question.

    d. *Proofreading.* Check your answer for errors in grammar, usage, spelling, and mechanics.

EXERCISE 8. Finding Key Verbs in Essay Questions. In any textbook, find five essay questions that use different key verbs to state the task. Write the questions and underline each key verb. If you cannot find five questions, write your own.

EXAMPLES   1. *Explain what causes an earthquake.*
                2. *For any two states in the West, compare the natural resources.*

PART FIVE

SPEAKING AND LISTENING

CHAPTER 27

Speaking

SKILLS FOR DIFFERENT SPEAKING SITUATIONS

As you grow older, you find yourself dealing with people in new ways. Often you are expected to take telephone messages or give directions. In school you may deliver an oral book report to your classmates or take part in group discussions.

Learning to speak in these new situations is not hard. A few rules, and some practice, will ease the way.

TELEPHONING

Nearly everyone has a chance to talk on the telephone at least once a day. It is important to use the telephone with efficiency and courtesy.

27a. Learn to use the telephone correctly.

When you speak with someone on the telephone, that person forms a mental picture of you. You will want to make that picture as favorable as possible. To do so, keep in mind the following tips for showing good manners on the telephone.

Making Calls

1. Be sure to dial the correct number. If you get a wrong number, tell the person who answers that you are sorry to disturb him or her.

2. Try not to call at inconvenient times such as mealtime or bedtime. Call at these times only in an emergency.

3. Say who you are as soon as the person answers. If the person you are calling is not there, leave your name and number and perhaps a short message.

4. Speak clearly. Do not shout or mumble into the receiver.

5. Keep pencil and paper by the phone. You may need to take notes on the conversation.

6. Do not stay on the telephone too long. Since you placed the call, it is your responsibility to end it.

Receiving Calls

1. Answer right away and say who you are.

2. Listen carefully and jot down any important information.

3. If the person has called at an inconvenient time, ask if you may return the call later.

4. Take a message if the call is for someone who is out. First write down the message. Then repeat it to make sure your notes are correct. Remember to check the spelling of names and addresses. Finally, leave the message where the person who was called will find it easily.

EXERCISE 1. Practicing a Telephone Dialogue. Prepare a correct telephone dialogue with a classmate. Choose one of the following suggestions for your dialogue.

1. A student is calling to ask for help with a class project.
2. A close friend of your parents has called. Since your parents cannot come to the phone, you take a message.
3. Telephone a classmate to ask about her swimming lessons. Your parents have asked you to check on the time, place, and cost. You want to know if the instructor is a good teacher.

GIVING DIRECTIONS AND EXPLANATIONS

Giving clear and complete directions is a useful skill for everyday living. You never know when you may be called on to help a person who is lost. Also, you may be asked to give a clear explanation of how to train a dog or play a game. Your directions and explanations should always be clear and complete.

27b. Give directions and explanations that are orderly, complete, and accurate.

(1) Arrange information in a clear and logical order.

Before you give information to anyone, think about what you plan to say. Make each step as simple and easy to understand as possible. Explain the steps in an order that makes sense.

UNCLEAR   "Take the road by the oak tree to the busy intersection. Then turn right, and after a while you will see the yellow building belonging to Poe's Hardware. If you miss it, retrace your steps."

CLEAR   "Drive north on Buttonwood Avenue to Main Highway. Turn right on Main, and after four blocks turn left on 27th Street. At this corner you'll see Poe's Hardware on your left."

(2) Give complete information.

When giving directions or explanations, remember to include each step. If you leave out even one step, your listener may become lost or confused.

(3) Use language to suit your purpose and audience.

Remember to avoid slang and words that are too difficult or too informal for your audience and purpose.

(4) Review the steps.

Remember that your purpose is to give directions someone else can follow. When you give directions, repeat them so that the other person can easily remember them. It might be helpful to ask the person to say the directions aloud. You can then check to see if your instructions have been understood.

EXERCISE 2. Giving Directions. Choose a landmark, park, or other place of interest. Think about the steps someone would need to take to reach this place from your school. Write a set of clear directions for making this trip. Your teacher may ask class members to read their directions aloud. The class can decide whose directions would be easiest for a stranger to understand.

EXERCISE 3. Giving Directions and Explanations. Prepare directions or an explanation for one of the following incidents.

1. Your parents plan to pick you up at a school function held in a downtown theater. They need to know when you should be picked up, and exactly where you will be waiting.
2. While your family is on vacation, a friend has volunteered to take care of Muffins, the family dog. Explain to your friend what Muffins will need while you are gone.
3. You have just given your younger brother a kite for his birthday. He needs to know how to assemble it.
4. A visitor to the school asks for directions to the principal's office.

PREPARING AND DELIVERING A BOOK REPORT

From time to time your teacher may ask you to give an oral book report. This assignment will be easier if you learn some basic tips for preparing and delivering a book report.

Preparing a Book Report

Preparing an oral book report is similar to planning a written one. When you plan a speech such as a book report, you can follow the same steps you would use in planning a written piece.

Take some time to review the discussion of prewriting on pages 5–19 of Chapter 1.

27c. Select a book on a suitable subject.

As you think about what book to choose for your report, keep in mind two points. First, select a book on a subject that is a part of your own interest or experience. You will then be able to speak with more enthusiasm about the book.

Second, select a book on a subject that will appeal to your audience. Thinking about the interests of your audience is just as important when you speak as when you write. For example, your classmates would probably be interested in hearing about an exciting mystery. They probably would not be interested in a book on selling vacuum cleaners.

EXERCISE 4. Selecting Books for Reports. Think about the kinds of books you have recently read or would like to read. These books could include adventure stories, mysteries, novels, or books that explain how to excel at something, such as dancing or horseback riding. List at least five kinds of books for your book report. Remember that a suitable subject fits your own interests and your audience's interests.

27d. Limit the focus of your book report.

Once you have chosen a book and read it, you will need to limit the focus of your book report. Obviously, you cannot discuss every detail about the book. This would take too long.

Suppose, for example, that you plan to give a book report on *A Christmas Carol* by Charles Dickens. This popular novel has many exciting details, but there will not be time to discuss them all. To limit the focus of your report, you could include details of the setting (time and place), give the names of the most important characters, and describe a few of the major events.

If you were planning a book report on a biography (the true story of someone's life), you could include the dates of the person's life, explain why he or she is important, and tell about some of the important events in that person's life.

Always keep your purpose in mind. Your purpose is to explain what the book is about and to interest your audience in reading it. Give enough details so that the audience knows why the book appeals to you. If your purpose is to persuade others to read the book, give at least three reasons for reading the book. However, do not give too many details or tell how the book ends. If you explain too much about the book, your audience will not need to read it.

EXERCISE 5. Limiting the Focus. Think of two or three books that have interested you and that would interest your audience. Is your purpose to give your audience information, or is it to convince them to read the book? After you have decided on your purpose, limit the focus of your report to the most important details or reasons. The details or reasons you choose should be suitable for a report of about five minutes.

27e. Select supporting details from the book.

Selecting details that will support what you have to say is like gathering information for writing. For instance, you might reread your book and make notes in a writer's journal about details that will interest your audience. This will help you to plan and organize your report.

EXERCISE 6. Selecting Supporting Details. Using any method for gathering information, select supporting details for a book report. You might choose one of the books you thought about for Exercise 5.

27f. Organize your material so that your audience can easily follow you.

The next step is to organize your report. At this point it is often helpful to make notes to look at while you speak. Write them on

3 × 5-inch cards so you can hold them easily in your hand. Remember, however, that you will want to speak—not read—to your audience. Your notes should contain just a few words or a sentence about each important point you plan to make.

An oral book report, like a piece of writing, can be divided into three sections: (1) the introduction, (2) the body, and (3) the conclusion.

The Introduction

Your first job is to attract your listeners' interest and attention. An opening remark like "This book is very interesting" will not make your audience sit up and take notice.

Instead, you might first say something about the main character or setting of the book.

EXAMPLE   *A Christmas Carol,* by Charles Dickens, is the story of Ebenezer Scrooge, who lives in nineteenth-century London and hates Christmas. How could anyone hate Christmas?

As you plan your introduction, keep in mind the purpose of your report. Begin with a remark that will make your audience want to know more about the book.

The Body

The body of your book report includes the main points you plan to make. It contains the supporting details that you selected from the book. Present these details in the clearest and most interesting way possible. If you plan to retell part of the plot, relate the events in the order in which they happened.

EXERCISE 7. **Preparing an Introduction and Body.**   Choose a book you have recently read that would be good for a book report. Think of an interesting way to begin your report. Next, select the details that support what you have to say. Remember to limit the focus of your report. On 3 × 5-inch cards, make notes about what points your introduction and body will cover.

The Conclusion

In the conclusion of your book report, sum up why the audience will enjoy reading the book. You might want to close with an especially exciting detail or a question. This final point should make your audience even more curious about the book's ending.

EXAMPLE *A Christmas Carol* will keep you guessing. Can a person like Scrooge ever learn the meaning of Christmas? And will Tiny Tim, who is very ill, die?

EXERCISE 8. Studying Conclusions. Look at the following concluding remarks. Which would be good endings for a book report? Be ready to explain your answers.

1. In conclusion, I want to thank you for listening to me ramble on about this book. Also, thank you for being patient, especially since I talked too long.
2. Anyone who wants to travel to Scotland should read this mystery about the Loch Ness monster. But sometimes the writer will bore you with too many details.
3. *Alice's Adventures in Wonderland* is funny and strange. You won't want to miss reading about the croquet game played with flamingos!
4. Well, I don't have much more to say, except that I liked this book a lot and am sure you will too.
5. *Charlotte's Web* is a touching story. Do you think Wilbur the pig will become country sausage in your grocer's freezer?

EXERCISE 9. Preparing a Conclusion. Prepare a suitable conclusion for the book report you began in Exercise 7. Remember to include this final point on your 3 × 5-inch cards.

Delivering a Book Report

As you take notes for a book report, you think about *what* to say to your audience. *How* you say something can often be just as important as what you say. Suppose you nervously shift your weight from one foot to the other or keep looking at the clock as you speak. These *nonverbal,* or unspoken, gestures will distract or even annoy your audience.

27g. Learn to deliver a book report effectively.

When speaking, look directly at your audience. Move your glance slowly from one side of the room to the other. Focus on the faces of your listeners and watch for their reactions. If their reactions tell you that you are speaking too softly or too quickly, change your volume and rate. The way you pronounce words is also important. Say each word carefully and clearly. Use a variety of words to express your ideas.

If you are holding note cards, glance—but do not stare—at them as you speak. Look at your audience, not at your notes.

When facing your audience, look confident. Stand firmly, but not stiffly. Keep your shoulders back and your head high. Smile at your audience now and then.

Gestures can make your book report more interesting. They should be natural and help emphasize what you are saying. Remember that any movement you make while speaking is a gesture. If you scratch your head, your audience may think you are not sure of what to say next. Use gestures that highlight what you have to say.

EXERCISE 10. Studying Gestures. Write down the following list of gestures and what you think each gesture means. Which gestures would be appropriate during a book report?

1. Pacing back and forth across the room
2. Staring at the floor
3. Keeping arms tightly folded across the chest
4. Cupping one ear with hand
5. Yawning

EXERCISE 11. **Delivering a Book Report.** Deliver the book report you have prepared in this part of the chapter. You may first want to practice your report in front of a parent or friend. Plan to use effective gestures and nonverbal signals.

PARTICIPATING IN GROUP DISCUSSIONS

You have often chatted with your family, friends, classmates, and teachers. These conversations usually travel from one topic to another. They are informal. No one has planned ahead of time what you will talk about. An informal conversation brings people together, but not always for a specific purpose.

Some conversations do have specific purposes. These conversations are known as *group discussions.* You have probably been a part of several conversations like these. Maybe you and your family have talked about where to spend your next summer vacation. At school your class may have discussed ways to raise money for a school outing. In each case, you and your friends, family, classmates, and teachers talked together for a specific purpose. The group probably reached an agreement or solved a problem.

A popular kind of group discussion in school is a *round-table discussion.* Everyone sits in a circle. This way, all members of the group can see and hear each other easily.

Sometimes a leader directs a round-table discussion. The leader makes sure the group keeps to the chosen topic and accomplishes what it set out to do. Now and then an audience may listen to the round-table discussion. However, members of the audience rarely participate.

Group discussions follow some general rules, unlike informal chats among friends and family. These rules help prevent the group from wasting time by straying from the subject.

27h. Learn how to participate in a group discussion.

When you join in a group discussion, you will want to remember several tips. Some of these tips are important ways to show courtesy and respect to other members of the group.

1. *Prepare carefully for a discussion.* Sometimes you will know ahead of time what your group will talk about. To make conversation easier, spend some time gathering information about the topic. You can read newspapers, magazines, or books. Talk to people who know about the topic.

2. *Give every member your full attention.* Listen to others with the attention you would like to receive when it is your turn to talk. A careful listener shows courtesy and respect. Do not interrupt a speaker or chat while someone is speaking. If you disagree with someone, work out your differences quietly. Shouting angrily will only lead the group away from the purpose of the discussion. Pay attention to the leader's directions.

3. *Participate fairly in the discussion.* There are times when one person may try to take over the conversation. This person may interrupt others or talk at every opportunity. Other people may not get an equal chance to express their ideas. Make sure that every member is allowed to participate fairly.

4. *Stay on the discussion topic.* When the conversation moves smoothly, it may be easy to wander away from the discussion topic. Do your best to stick to the chosen topic, so that your group can accomplish what it set out to do. If necessary, politely remind others to stay on course.

5. *Listen with an open mind.* One purpose of a group discussion is to let people exchange ideas in an orderly manner. Some ideas may sound strange to you, but always listen with an open mind. Be willing to learn from the other group members.

6. *Take care to speak correctly and distinctly.* The meaning of a word often varies with the way it is pronounced. If your words are mispronounced or if you mumble or run words together, group members may have difficulty following you.

7. *Work to improve your participation.* Practice being able to contribute effectively to a group discussion. This skill will help you throughout school and your adult life. Ask yourself the following questions to review your performance. Your goal is to answer "yes" to each question.

a. Did the group keep to the topic?

b. Did everyone prepare carefully for the discussion?

c. Did all group members receive an equal chance to participate?

d. Did group members ask questions when ideas were unclear?

e. Did group members qualify their statements? That is, were they careful to explain or give background information?

f. Did group members help to extend the discussion by adding more information or comments?

g. Did everyone show courtesy and respect for the other members of the group?

h. Did everyone help the group meet its purpose?

i. Did group members avoid slang and words that were too informal for the purpose of the discussion?

EXERCISE 12. Studying a Group Discussion. Some radio or TV talk shows feature group discussions about community issues. Listen to such a group discussion. Then apply the nine questions given above to the discussion on the talk show you have listened to or watched. Be ready to explain whether you think the group discussion was effective.

EXERCISE 13. Participating in a Group Discussion. With three to five classmates, form a discussion group. Choose one of the following topics or a topic provided by your teacher. Settle on a purpose for your discussion and try to accomplish it in the time your teacher allows. When the discussion is over, review your performance by asking the nine questions given above.

1. Ways to improve your school's playground or library
2. Why safety skills are important for bicyclists or swimmers
3. How to get along with your parents, teachers, or brothers and sisters
4. Ways to solve a problem in your community
5. The major differences between growing up in a city and growing up on a farm

CHAPTER 28

Listening

SKILLS FOR SUCCESSFUL LISTENING

Good listening habits will always help you to learn and get along with others. Being a good listener is part of being successful.

LISTENING CAREFULLY

To listen carefully, you must first keep your mind on what is being said. You also need to be sure you understand all the information that is being given.

Showing Courtesy

28a. Show good listening manners.

Like all good manners, courteous listening requires that you think about being the other person. If you were the speaker, how would you like your listeners to treat you? Study the following tips on courtesy.

1. *Look at the speaker.* Focus your eyes on the speaker. Doing so will help focus your mind on the ideas being expressed. At the

same time, your obvious attention shows the speaker that you are interested in what is being said.

2. *Do not interrupt the speaker.* Save your comments and questions until the speaker has finished. You may hear an answer to your question in the speaker's final comments. Waiting also allows the speaker to express completely all the thoughts planned for the talk.

3. *Do not doodle, read, whisper, or fidget.* Such activities force you to miss what is said, and they may embarrass the speaker. You may, however, take notes on ideas you want to remember.

EXERCISE 1. Observing Listening Manners. During the next week, notice how many times you are a member of an audience. You may be in class, at home, at a movie, at community events with your family, or in group discussions with friends. Think about each occasion. Did other listeners show good listening manners? Did some miss what was said because they were not looking at the speaker? Write down what you noticed. Be prepared to share your observations in class.

EXAMPLE   Tuesday: Family discussion about next summer
　　　　　　　1. Brother interrupted mother (he was too excit-
　　　　　　　　　ed)
　　　　　　　2. Sister had to ask mother to repeat something
　　　　　　　　　(she had been staring at telephone, expecting a
　　　　　　　　　call)

Listening for Main Ideas

28b. Listen for the speaker's purpose and main ideas.

The speaker often begins a talk by telling you its purpose. A speaker may intend to give you factual information or to explain how something is done. The talk may also be about opinions on a particular issue. The speaker may wish to persuade you to agree with an idea or to do something about it.

Finding the speaker's purpose will help you follow the main ideas of the talk. Keep the purpose in mind as you listen. Then separate the main ideas from the details and examples that support those ideas.

When a speaker is giving a prepared talk before a group, the ideas are usually presented in a very organized way. For instance, the opening remarks may include a statement such as "This play has three special qualities that make it a favorite of mine." Then you know that you should listen for three main ideas. Sometimes the speaker emphasizes each one by saying "first," "second," "third." A speaker may begin with a question, such as "What are the benefits to our community of building this museum?" You can expect to hear main ideas that describe different benefits. Near the end of a prepared speech the speaker often will summarize the main ideas. Listen for this helpful review.

Following the main ideas in an informal discussion may be harder. There may be several speakers and therefore less organization to the talk. Listen for ideas expressed by more than one speaker. Listen for ideas that are repeated often.

Whether a talk is informal or prepared, listen also for connections between the main ideas. Some speakers may pause before introducing each main idea. Other speakers may use *transitional* words to connect ideas, such as these:

| finally | however | so |
| furthermore | next | therefore |

To help you remember a speaker's main ideas, take brief notes. Use your own words and some of the speaker's words. Quickly write down each main idea and a few details about it. Use abbreviations and other shortcuts to jot down the ideas.

EXERCISE 2. **Listening for Main Ideas.**   Ask someone to read aloud to you three or four paragraphs in a science or social studies textbook. As you listen, take brief notes. Then compare your notes with what you find when you read the passage silently. Also compare your notes with the notes of others who listened to the passage. Did you find the main ideas? What were the supporting details?

Understanding Instructions

28c. Listen to each step given in instructions.

You may be listening to a class assignment or to an assignment for a job at home. At other times you may want to know how to find something, someone, or some place. All of these occasions require listening to instructions or directions.

When someone is giving you instructions or directions, listen to each step. If you can, jot down each step. Do not interrupt the speaker. If you do not understand a step, ask about it when the speaker has finished. Repeat the steps aloud to yourself if you need to. Make sure you know the right order of the steps.

EXERCISE 3. Following Instructions. Your teacher will read the following instructions to you. Have paper and pencil ready. There will be only brief pauses between each set of instructions. Now close your book, listen, and carry out the instructions.

1. If you were born in the first six months of the year, subtract 2 from your age; if you were born in the last six months of the year, multiply your age by 2.
2. If yesterday is not the day before tomorrow, write your name without capital letters.
3. Write *8,* no matter what the sum of 4 and 7 is.
4. If you think porpoises are mammals, write the word *yes.*
5. Write *no* if the following statement is correct: You are listening to these instructions in English.

EXERCISE 4. Following Directions. Ask a classmate to help you complete these activities. When you are the listener, use good listening techniques and manners. Remember to repeat the directions aloud, to take notes if necessary, and to ask questions if you do not understand.

EXAMPLE   1. Ask for directions to the school library.
(Notes)   1. *—off main hall, front of school*
—from front entrance, turn left

—*pass one hallway on right*
—*then second door on left*

1. You are a stranger visiting your school. You are looking for the music teacher. Ask your classmate for directions to the music teacher's office or classroom.
2. Ask for directions from school to your classmate's home.
3. Find out how to locate in the library a novel written by Mabel Louise Robinson.
4. Ask where you can buy postage stamps and how to get there.
5. Borrow a map of your state. Ask your classmate to use the map to give you road or highway directions. Ask for directions to a city that is at least one hundred miles from your home.

LISTENING CRITICALLY

Once you are listening carefully, you can also listen critically. You can make judgments about what you hear. Whenever you are listening, pay attention *and* think about what is being said. Listening critically is especially important when the speaker is trying to convince you to do something or to think a certain way. Ask yourself: Are the speaker's ideas based on facts or opinions? Are the opinions based on logical reasoning? Is there another motive, or purpose, behind what the speaker is saying? Does the speaker have a particular bias or point of view? The main purpose of listening attentively is to be able to *evaluate* a speaker's ideas.

Separating Fact from Opinion

28d. Separate fact from opinion.

Decide which of a speaker's remarks report facts and which express feelings or opinions. A statement of fact contains information that can be proved true or false.

EXAMPLES The only month with fewer than thirty days is February.
It rained on Mother's Day last year.

When you listen to statements of fact, ask yourself certain questions to help judge them.

Can I check this statement of fact myself to see if it's true?
Does the statement of fact make sense according to my own knowledge of the subject?
Is the information up-to-date?

Be alert for statements that are partly factual. They may be misleading. Careful speakers will use words such as *often, probably,* or *many* to show that a fact may not be true in every single case. They *qualify* their statements.

MISLEADING   **Everybody** is going to the July Fourth picnic.
QUALIFIED   **Many** people are going to the July Fourth picnic.

Careful speakers will also name their sources of information whenever possible. As you listen, ask yourself: Who says so?

VAGUE   **Experts say** we will have nice weather for the holiday.
CLEAR   **Weather forecasters on television channels 6 and 14 have predicted** fine weather for the holiday.

An opinion is being expressed when the speaker tells what someone thinks or believes. An opinion cannot be proved true or false. Ask yourself: Is the speaker expressing strong personal opinions? Do these opinions affect the conclusions made by the speaker? Listen for certain words, such as *surely, certainly, always, best,* and *worst.* These words usually let you know that the speaker is giving an opinion.

Study the following examples:

FACT   Fireworks are **often** a part of July Fourth celebrations.
OPINION   July Fourth is the **highlight** of the summer.

FACT   Spring is **a** colorful time of year in New England.
OPINION   Of the four seasons, fall is the **most** beautiful.

Notice that it is easy to agree with a statement that you know can be proved true. You may or may not agree with the two opinions given as examples. Do not accept a speaker's opinion without doing some thinking on your own.

EXERCISE 5. Recognizing Facts and Opinions. Number your paper 1–10. Ask someone to read aloud to you the following sentences. After listening to each statement, write after the number whether the statement is a *fact* or an *opinion*.

EXAMPLE   1. Thanksgiving Day is in November.
           1. *fact*

1. February is the shortest month of the year.
2. It will surely rain on Labor Day this year.
3. Leap Year brings good luck.
4. There are twelve months in a year.
5. These Mother's Day cards are the best money can buy.
6. Halloween falls on October 31 every year.
7. All months should have the same number of days.
8. December is the happiest month of the year.
9. A winter without snow will be disappointing.
10. May 12 is someone's birthday.

Identifying Logical Reasoning

28e. Listen for logical reasoning.

When you hear someone express an opinion, ask yourself if the reasons the speaker gives are logical. That is, do the reasons make sense and have facts to support them?

LOGICAL   You should take an umbrella. The sky is cloudy and the sidewalks are wet.

NOT LOGICAL   You should take an umbrella. Today is Tuesday, and last Tuesday it rained very hard.

Which of the reasons makes sense to you? Cloudy skies and wet sidewalks are current, provable facts. On the other hand, last Tuesday's weather probably has nothing to do with the weather today.

When a speaker's purpose is to persuade you to agree with an opinion or to do something, listen carefully for logical reasons and facts that support them.

EXERCISE 6. Evaluating Opinions. Number your paper 1–5. Ask someone to read aloud the following opinions. After listening to each opinion, write *yes* if it seems to be based on sound reasoning. Write *no* if it does not. Discuss your answers in class. You may want to discuss the example first.

EXAMPLE 1. "I think moviemakers are producing nothing but scary movies. They are the only kind I saw this summer."
1. *no*

1. "Vote for Gina for class president. She has the best grades in the class."
2. "I found in my experiments that geraniums need plenty of sunshine. Those that I kept in the shade part of the day or all day bloomed less often or not at all."
3. "Swimming is much easier in a lake than in the ocean. There are usually fewer waves."
4. "It's no wonder he plays the piano so well. His father is a pianist."
5. "My friend was injured while playing kickball, but I don't think kickball is a dangerous sport."

Evaluating Television

28f. Evaluate what you hear on television.

When you watch television, you are listening as well as seeing. The speakers on television programs and the commercials provide you with information. How much of it is based on fact? How much of it is fiction? How much of what you hear is someone's opinion? Always ask yourself these kinds of questions when you watch television.

Claims made in advertisements, for example, should never be accepted without question. You must learn to distinguish between fact and opinion. Evaluate the evidence given for the opinions expressed.

EXERCISE 7. Evaluating Television.   Study the week's television schedule. Pick one show you think the entire class should watch. Write down your reasons for this choice. Discuss your choice in class. When you listen to a classmate's choice and reasons, evaluate the evidence for the opinion.

EXERCISE 8. Evaluating Advertisements.   The next time you are watching television, take notes on one of the commercials. Jot down main ideas and some details. Then, from memory and from your notes, write answers to the following questions:

1. Does the advertisement offer facts or opinions about the product? Give examples.
2. Does the advertisement offer evidence for its claims about the product? Give an example.
3. Based on what the advertisement says, do you think the product is worthwhile? Why or why not?

REVIEW EXERCISE. Listening Carefully and Critically.   Number your paper 1–5. Your teacher will read aloud the following questions. Answer the questions as you listen. Study the example and then close your book.

EXAMPLE   1. When you listen to a speech, what do you listen for first?
          1. *The speaker's purpose*

1. What should you take notes on while listening to a speech?
2. When a speaker's main idea is an opinion, what do you listen for?
3. I am going to read three statements—a, b, and c. For each one, write whether it is a statement of fact or an opinion.
   a. Recess is the best part of the school day.
   b. The Grand Canyon is in Arizona.
   c. The Civil War was fought during Abraham Lincoln's term as President.
4. I will now read two more statements—a and b. Which of the two is a tip on good listening manners?

    a. Ask a question as soon as you think of it.

    b. Look at the speaker.

5. Listen to the following opinion: "If you buy this toothpaste, you will make more friends. It will give you clean teeth and fresh breath." Write *yes* if the opinion seems to be based on sound reasoning. Write *no* if it does not. Give a reason for your choice.

INDEX

INDEX

D

of topic sentence, 53–54, 63–64
transitions for, 68, 69
See also specific types of writing

Q

Question mark
as end mark, 202, 355
with quotation marks, 376–77
Questioning. *See 5 W-How?* questions
Questions, test, answering, 472–75
Quotation marks, 374–80
diagnostic test, 372–73
dialogue, paragraphing of, 378
for direct quotations, 374–79
for titles, 378–79
single, for quotation within quotation, 379

R

Raise, rise, 303
Rambling style, correcting, 174–75
Readers' Guide to Periodical Literature, 423–24
Reading skills
distinguishing between fact and opinion, 467–69
finding supporting details, 466–67
meaning from context, 445–47
recognizing antonyms, 433–34, 452–54
recognizing homonyms, 395–402
recognizing main ideas, 464–66
recognizing prefixes, suffixes, and roots, 454–58
recognizing synonyms, 433–34, 450–52
SQ3R Method, 463–64
See also Study skills
Reasoning, logical, listening for, 497
Reasons
in book report, 124
in composition of opinion, 127
Reference books, 419–24
almanacs, 422
atlases, 421–22
biographical dictionaries, 422
dictionaries, 428–42
encyclopedias, 420–21
Readers' Guide, 423–24
Reflexive pronouns, 213
Regular comparison, 326

Regular verbs, 295
Report. *See* Book report; Library report
Resolution, of story. *See* Outcome, of story
Review, book. *See* Book report
Revising
answer to essay-test question, 475
book report, 126
business letter, 144–46
combining sentences, 161–74
composition of opinion, 129
correcting a monotonous style, 176–77
correcting a rambling style, 174–75
defined, 4, 71
descriptive paragraph, 85–86
expository composition, 109–10
expository paragraph, 89–90
for content, organization, and style = general
general, 22–24
library report, 122
narrative paragraph, 81–82
paragraphs, general, 71–73
social letter, 139
story, 46–48
symbols for, 24
See also Techniques for Revising charts
Ride, principal parts of, 297
Ring, principal parts of, 297
Rise, raise, 303
Roman numerals, in outline, 104
Roots, as aids to work meaning, 454
Run, principal parts, 297
Run-on sentence, 157

S

Salutation
of business letter, 142, 368
of social letter, 135, 365
Schwa, 441
See, principal parts of, 297
Semicolon, 366
diagnostic test, 353–54
Sense details, in description, 83
Sentence
capitalization of, 339
classified by purpose, 202
classified by structure, 199–200
combining, 161–74

T

Supplement:
Glossary
and Guidelines

CONTENTS

Glossary

As you use this textbook, you might come across names and words that are unfamiliar to you. This Glossary provides pronunciations and definitions for such unfamiliar names and terms.

A

A·leu·tian Is·lands [ə lōō'shən] *n*. A chain of islands in the Pacific Ocean, extending southwest from Alaska.

al·gae [al'jē] *n.pl*. A large group of simple plants that live in water and do not have true roots, stems, or leaves.

al·ma·nac [ôl'mə nak'] *n*. A book published once a year, containing lists, charts, tables, calendars, and information about a variety of subjects in many fields.

Ap·pa·la·chi·an Moun·tains [ap'ə lā'chən] *n*. A mountain system in eastern North America that extends from southeast Canada to Alabama.

as·ter·oid [as'tə roid'] *n*. One of many very small, rock planets that orbit the sun, mainly between the orbits of Mars and Jupiter.—*pl*. **as·ter·oids**

B

blotch [bloch] *n*. A spot or mark.—*v*. **blotched**

brute [brōōt] *adj*. Savage.

C

cal·i·co [kal'i kō] *adj*. Spotted or streaked.

Cape Horn [kāp hôrn] *n*. The southernmost tip of South America.

chap·er·one [shap'ə rōn'] *v*. To accompany a group of young people on an outing or to a social gathering.

com·pu·ter–syn·the·sized [kəm pyōō' tər sin' thə sīzed'] *adj*. Produced or formed by a computer.

cres·cent [kres'ənt] *n*. Something that has the shape of the moon when only a thin, curved part of it can be seen.

Pronunciation Key

a and; hat / **ā** ate; stay / **â** care; air/ **ä** father; hot / **b** boy; cab / **ch** chew; such / **d** dog; lid / **e** end; yet / **ē** she; each / **f** fun; off / **g** give; big / **h** hold / **i** it; this / **ī** ice; my / **j** jet; gem; edge / **k** kind; cat; back / **l** let; ball / **m** make; time / **n** not; own / **ng** having / **ō** over; go / **ô** all; law / **oo** look; full / **ōō** pool; who / **oi** oil; boy / **ou** out; town / **p** put; hop / **r** run; car / **s** set; miss / **sh** show / **t** ten; date / **th** think / **t̲h̲** these / **u** cut; butter / **ur** turn; bird / **v** very; live / **w** win; away / **y** you / **z** zoo; cause / **zh** measure / **ə** ago; lemon

Abbreviation Key

adj. adjective; *adv*. adverb; *n*. noun; *v*. verb; *prep*. preposition; *pl*. plural

D

de·fi·cien·cy dis·ease
[di fish'ən sē di zēz'] *n.* A disease
caused by a lack or shortage of
particular vitamins or minerals in a
person's diet.
dip·lo·mat [dip'lə mat'] *n.* A person
who is good at dealing with other
people.

E

ear·wig [ir'wig'] *n.* An insect having
short, horny front wings and clawlike
extensions at the end of a stiff, slender
body.—*pl.* **ear·wigs**

F

fath·om [fath' əm] *n.* A unit of length,
usually of water depth, equal to six
feet.—*pl.* **fath·oms**
fau·na [fô' nə] *n.* Animal life.
fig·u·rine [fig'yə rēn'] *n.* A small
carved or molded statue.
frig·ate [frig'it] *n.* A fast,
medium-sized sailing warship, used in
the eighteenth and nineteenth
centuries.

G

Ge·ron·i·mo [jə rän'ə mō'] *n.* An
Apache Indian chief who lived from
1829 to 1909.

H

Hal·ley's com·et [hal'ēz kom'it] *n.* A
comet that reappears every 75 to 76
years, named after Edmund Halley, an
English astronomer, who predicted its
return after observing it in 1682.

Ho·pi In·di·an [hō'pē in'dē ən] *n.* A
member of a North American Indian
tribe living in northeast Arizona.
hu·man·i·tar·i·an [hyōō man'ə târ'ē ən]
n. A person devoted to improving
human welfare.

J

jer·sey [jur'zē] *n.* A knitted pullover
shirt or sweater, often worn as part of
a sports uniform.—*pl.* **jer·seys**

L

Lou·vre [lōō'vrə] *n.* A famous art
museum in Paris, France.

M

Mar·i·co·pa In·di·an
[ma ri cō'pä in'dē ən] *n.* A member of
a North American Indian tribe living
in the lower Colorado River area.
Ma·sai [mä sī'] *n.* A member of a
tribe of people living in areas of
eastern Africa.
Mi·ya·ke, Is·saye [mē yä'kā, ē'sā] *n.*
A contemporary Japanese fashion
designer.

O

o·boe [ō'bō] *n.* A woodwind
instrument that has a long tube for a
body and a double reed for a
mouthpiece.
om·e·let [äm'lit] *n.* A mixture of eggs
and milk beaten together that is
cooked and then folded over.—*pl.*
om·e·lets

pa·pier mâ·ché [pā′pər mə shā′] *n.* A mixture of shredded paper and glue, used to make dolls, models, and so on, that hardens when it dries.

pa·vil·ion [pə vil′yən] *n.* An open building with a pointed roof and a raised floor, often used for exhibits.

Pepys, Sam·u·el [pēps] *n.* An English government official who lived from 1633 to 1703, famous for the diary he kept.

pi·ña·ta [pēn yä′tə] *n.* A decorated, candy-filled container, hung from the ceiling at traditional Latin American celebrations.

plan·e·tar·i·um [plan′ə tar′ē əm] *n.* A building or room with a domed ceiling on which a device projects images of planets and stars in their courses.

pro·vince [präv′ins] *n.* A large division or part of a country, similar to a U.S. state, having its own government.

Pyr·e·nees [pir′ə nēz′] *n.* A mountain range along the border of Spain and France.

S

sa·ri [sä′rē] *n.* A long piece of cotton or silk cloth wrapped around the body and over the shoulder, traditionally worn by Hindu women.

skiff [skif] *n.* A small, light rowboat, sometimes having a sail and a centerboard.

Swa·hi·li [swä hē′lē] *n.* A language of East Africa, often used for trade and business transactions.

T

Tai·no In·di·an [tī′nō in′dē ən] *n.* A member of an extinct Indian tribe that lived in the West Indies.

Tut·ankh·a·men [tōōt′änk ä′mən] *n.* An Egyptian king of the fourteenth century B.C., famous for his richly decorated tomb that was discovered in 1922.

GUIDELINES FOR USING LANGUAGE

1. Avoid clichés and trite expressions in writing or speaking.

   Trite expressions, or **clichés** (klē shāz′), are words or expressions that are dull and overused. They are "tired" because they have been used so much and so often that they no longer create clear pictures in the reader's or listener's mind. Examples of clichés or trite expressions are *nice, great, busy as a bee, fat as a pig, dead as a doornail,* and *cool as a cucumber.*

2. Avoid slang in formal writing or speaking.

   Slang words are new words, or old words used in new ways. Slang words are colorful and interesting, but they are very informal and usually go out of style very quickly. For that reason, slang is not a part of formal English, the English you use in school or at work. Examples of slang words include *bug,* to bother; *cop out,* to give up; and *wicked,* good.

3. Avoid colloquialisms in formal writing.

   Colloquialisms are words sometimes found in spoken English but usually not in formal written English. They are more widely used than slang words. Some colloquialisms eventually become part of formal written English. Some examples of colloquialisms are "clue him in," "put our heads together," and "foot the bill."

4. Avoid jargon in formal writing or speaking.

   Jargon is words or phrases that people use when they are talking or writing about specific activities—a sport, a hobby, a job. For people who know about the activity, jargon can be a shortcut to meaning. However, for people who do not know about the activity, jargon can be confusing. Examples of jargon are *lead,* the beginning of a news story; *split,* a time interval in running; and *byte,* a unit of memory in computers.

GUIDELINES FOR NOTE TAKING

When You Are Listening
1. Ask yourself what you want to get out of the talk. Then listen and take notes.
2. Listen for the speaker's purpose and write it down.
3. Write down each main point and any important supporting ideas. Listen for words that signal important ideas, such as *first, next,* and *finally.* Remember that some speakers pause as they introduce each important idea.
4. Do not try to write down everything the speaker says.
5. Use whatever words come quickly and easily to you.
6. Do not worry about complete sentences; use abbreviations and leave out unimportant words. Remember that your purpose is to record the speaker's main ideas.
7. Sometimes the speaker's main ideas are spoken too quickly for you to note them. If so, ask the speaker for more information at the end of the talk.

When You Are Reading
1. Read the selection closely.
2. Use chapter titles and headings in the book or article to organize your notes. Leave room to write down main ideas and supporting details under the titles and headings.
3. As you read, look for transitional words and statements that point out important ideas—*first, next, therefore, three important reasons, the last point,* and so on.
4. Write main ideas and details under the chapter titles and headings.
5. Use your own words for most of your notes.
6. Do not worry about complete sentences; use abbreviations and leave out unimportant words.
7. Use quotation marks correctly. Note the page number if you decide that the writer's exact words are important.
8. Review your notes to see whether you have forgotten anything.

GUIDELINES FOR RECOGNIZING A SPEAKER'S MAIN IDEAS

1. Listen for a statement of the purpose or reason for the speech. Such a statement usually occurs in the introduction to the talk.
2. Listen for the speaker's main ideas. Sometimes they are stated directly and sometimes they are not. Think *as* you listen. Separate the main ideas from the supporting details.
3. Listen for the ideas and words that the speaker emphasizes with his or her voice. The speaker may emphasize by speaking more loudly or by changing tone of voice.
4. Listen for repeated words or phrases. A speaker often repeats, or restates in other words, ideas he or she wants to emphasize.
5. Listen for planned pauses. Good speakers may stop talking for a brief moment to add emphasis to what they will say next.
6. Listen for transitional words such as *first, now, next, the key point is,* and so on. Good speakers often include these clues to signal their main ideas.
7. Take notes on the important information. This will help you pay attention during the talk, as well as help you remember the main ideas after the talk.

GUIDELINES FOR RESPONDING TO A SPEAKER

1. Listen quietly while the person is speaking.
2. Look at the speaker. The look on your face and your posture show your interest and appreciation.
3. Take notes to record the speaker's main ideas and interesting points.
4. Be courteous. Do not doodle, read, whisper, or move around in a distracting way.
5. Make a note of any questions you have. Ask questions when they are invited, after the speaker finishes.
6. Laugh or applaud when appropriate—for example, after the speaker has told a humorous story or has ended the talk.

GUIDELINES FOR CONVERSATION

1. Read and listen for information and ideas to learn more about a variety of topics. You cannot take part in a conversation if you have nothing to talk about.
2. Listen when other people are talking and respond to what they have to say.
3. Ask questions to draw other people out and to make clear what they have said.
4. Repeat what the other person has said to check how well you understand the meaning.
5. Use nonverbal techniques—gestures, eye contact, facial expressions, posture—to show your interest in the other person's ideas.
6. Choose specific and concrete words to express your own thoughts.
7. Use nonverbal techniques—gestures, eye contact, facial expressions, posture—to help express your own ideas.

GUIDELINES FOR PARTICIPATING IN GROUP DISCUSSIONS

1. Be prepared with information about the topic. Gather information by reading books, magazines, newspapers, and encyclopedias. Talk with people who know about the topic.
2. Share information fairly and politely. Remember that your purpose is to work together as a group to exchange ideas about the topic.
3. Ask questions. Your group's work will go more smoothly if you ask for explanations of information and ideas that are not clear to you.
4. Try to help the group stay on the topic. Although it is tempting to discuss interesting ideas that may come up, stick to your specific topic and purpose.
5. Be considerate of the views of others. Remember that group discussions give you a chance to hear different ideas.
6. Speak loudly and clearly. Make it possible for all members of the group to hear and understand what you have to say.
7. If you are the discussion leader, act the part. Start the discussion, keep it moving and on the topic, settle any disagreements, and end the discussion.

GUIDELINES FOR PEER-EVALUATION OF A SPEECH

On a separate sheet of paper, write the speaker's name and the topic of the speech. Number your paper 1–10. Beside the appropriate number, answer the guideline question by writing *yes* or *no*.

Content
1. Was the introduction interesting?
2. Was the purpose or main idea clearly stated?
3. Were the ideas clearly organized and easy to follow?
4. Was the conclusion strong and interesting?
5. Were audiovisual aids used well?

Delivery
6. Did the speaker look at the audience?
7. Did the speaker talk loudly enough for the audience to hear and understand?
8. Were words pronounced clearly and correctly?
9. Were arm movements and facial expressions used to help the listener understand the speaker's ideas?
10. Did the speaker appear to be well-prepared and comfortable?

PEER-EVALUATION: GUIDELINES FOR WRITING THAT EXPLAINS OR EXPRESSES OPINIONS

On a separate sheet of paper, write the name of the writer, the title of the paper, and your name. Number your paper 1–10. Beside the number, write *poor, good,* or *very good* to indicate how well the writer meets each of the following guidelines. You may also include any other comments that may help the writer.

1. The topic or the main idea is clearly stated.
2. The other sentences help make the main idea clear.
3. The conclusion sums up the writer's main points.
4. Transitions, words like *first, next,* and *finally,* are used to connect ideas.
5. Words and phrases are specific, vivid, and interesting.
6. Clichés and trite expressions are avoided.
7. Each sentence is a complete sentence, not a fragment or a run-on.
8. Each sentence begins with a capital letter and ends with the correct punctuation mark.
9. Each paragraph is indented.
10. The paper is written neatly and legibly.

A WRITER'S CHECKLIST FOR SELF-EVALUATION: EXPOSITORY WRITING

To evaluate your own paper, number a sheet of paper from 1 to 10. Ask yourself each of the following questions and write *yes* or *no* beside the number.

1. Have I explained the purpose of my paper?
2. Is the introduction interesting?
3. Have I written at least one paragraph for each main idea?
4. Have I included enough details to support each main idea?
5. Have I presented my ideas in an easy-to-follow order?
6. Have I used connecting words such as *first, next,* and *finally* to make clear the order of ideas?
7. Does the conclusion call attention to my main idea or sum up my main points?
8. Have I used words and sentences that my readers will understand?
9. Have I checked my spelling? capitalization? punctuation?
10. Have I followed my teacher's directions or used correct form to make a neat final copy of my paper?

PROOFREADING CHECKLIST

On a separate sheet of paper, write the numbers 1–12. Then check your paper carefully against each of the following points. If an item is completed correctly, place a checkmark beside the number. After you finish the checklist, make any needed corrections on your paper.

1. The paper is neat.
2. Each sentence begins with a capital letter.
3. Each sentence ends with a period, question mark, or exclamation point.
4. Each sentence is complete. It has a subject and a predicate, and it expresses a complete thought.
5. A singular verb is used with each singular subject and a plural verb is used with each plural subject.
6. Singular pronouns are used to refer to singular nouns and plural pronouns are used to refer to plural nouns.
7. Each word is spelled correctly.
8. Double negatives are avoided.
9. All proper nouns and proper adjectives are capitalized.
10. No words have been accidentally left out.
11. No words have been accidentally written twice.
12. Apostrophes are used correctly with contractions and possessive nouns.

NOTES

NOTES

NOTES

NOTES

NOTES

NOTES